To Joyce,

Best Wishes

David Cronin

Michael Quinn (1846–1934)

It May Be Forever

An Irish Rebel
on the American Frontier

David M. Quinn

First published by AuthorHouse 09/23/05

ISBN: 1-4208-8091-8 (sc)
ISBN: 1-4208-8092-6 (dj)

Library of Congress Control Number: 2005907990

Printed in the United States of America
Bloomington, Indiana

This book is printed on acid-free paper.

Cover design: The Agrell Group, lagrell@commspeed.net

Cover Illustration: Lewis Agrell

Layout and design: The Agrell Group

Contents

To the Reader

Like most Americans, I grew up thinking of myself as just that, an American. The history and heritage of my ancestry had sunk to the bottom of the melting pot, out of sight and out of mind. It was my good fortune, therefore, to be introduced to things Irish during graduate studies at Fordham University in 1968. I lived in a rooming house on Bainbridge Avenue, in what was then one of the last Irish enclaves in the Bronx. The Irish Echo was on the newsstands. From the bars came the sounds of Irish brogue and jukebox tunes such as Black Velvet Band and The Wild Colonial Boy. Two classmates of fond memory, James Kiernan Costello and George Flanigan, introduced me to my first Saint Patrick's Day parade in Manhattan. I was hooked.

In time, I took up genealogy, first traveling to Ireland in 1982. On many subsequent visits, both personal and business, I spent hours hunched over microfilm readers and perusing antique documents crumbling with age. Climbing over stone walls, eluding the farmer's ornery bull, and peering at faded tombstones were also part of the search process. Similar efforts were later expended in England and in the U.S.

Friends and acquaintances in Ireland have expressed bemusement at the interest we Americans show in our Irish roots. And it must be admitted that some Yanks can carry their devotion to things Irish to maudlin extremes. But I wanted to discover and tell stories of where we came from, for indeed, it helps explain who we are. And there's something special about the Irish-American immigrant experience that began so low on the social ladder and culminated with the election of John Kennedy as President of the United States.

I have written of Michael Quinn, my great, great uncle. Selecting him as my protagonist was easy, by virtue of his interesting and adventurous life. More difficult was the decision to write his story as a historical novel rather than as a straight biography. But the novel affords creative freedom that biography denies. The inclusion of photos, exhibits, and a glossary may contrast with typical novel format, but I hope that the reader will appreciate the choices I have made.

There was a good deal of history uncovered during the two and a half years of research in Ireland, England, and America. I have tried to maintain a maximum degree of accuracy given the limitations of the records available to me. Nevertheless, it was necessary, indeed desirable, to invent some of the details of his story. I sincerely apologize to any and all characters, and their descendents, who may object to these elements of invention.

David M. Quinn
Prescott, Arizona
2005

Acknowledgments

I would like to recognize the insights of Mr. Anthony Towey of Castlerea, whose knowledge of local history is only matched by his kindness to inquiring visitors. Also notable for his courtesy and interest is Mr. Thomas Wills-Sandford, great grandson of William Roberts Wills-Sandford. He and his wife most generously opened their London home to us and shared freely of their family history.

Ms. Alice Lock and the staff at the Tameside Library in Ashton-under-Lyne have been most helpful. So too was the staff at Lawrence History Center in Lawrence, Massachusetts. The latter was a rich resource on Irish immigration and the history of textile manufacture in that region. Also deserving of my thanks are the librarians in Rapid City and Deadwood, South Dakota.

I would also highlight the materials and advice provided by Mr. David Burke of the Ancient Order of Hibernians in Lawrence. The assistance of the American-Irish Historical Society in New York City was invaluable. Mr. W. F. Duhamel of Duhamel Broadcasting Enterprises, and descendant of Pierre (Pete) Duhamel, has been most generous with elements of his family history. The kindness of his secretary, Ms. Sharon Beal, must also be noted.

Among those who provided inspiration for this book are Michael Shaara, late author of *The Killer Angels*, and his son Jeff Shaara, who has continued in his father's literary style. Peter Berresford Ellis, the noted Irish historian and author was of great influence with his novel, *The Rising of the Moon*. Two successful novelists of the American West were kind enough to read excerpts and provide critique, Mary Sojourner and Kate Horsley.

The Hassayampa Institute for Creative Writing and the Professional Writers of Prescott have both provided valuable input on the craft of writing. My editor, Kathryn Agrell, has been most supportive and insightful. Her suggestions were always valuable and candid. My failures are my own and in spite of her best efforts.

Finally, my special thanks go to my wife, Betsy, who has patiently followed me through countries, states, archives, libraries, private homes, and much of the landscape that once was the Wild West. Her encouragement, numerous readings, and critiques reflect her abiding love and her training in English Literature.

Dedication

To the People of Ireland, who for centuries would not rest till they had secured their liberty and were "a nation once again."

To the Lakota People, especially the students and faculty at Red Cloud Indian School in Pine Ridge, South Dakota, that they might seize their rightful place in American society, while preserving their proud heritage.

To my father, George Quinn, my role model and my link to our Irish past.

Kathleen Mavourneen

Kathleen, Mavourneen*, the grey dawn is breaking,
The horn of the hunter is heard on the hill;
The lark from her light wing the bright dew is shaking;
Kathleen, Mavourneen, What! slumbering still?
Oh! hast thou forgotten how soon we must sever?
Oh! hast thou forgotten, this day we must part;
It may be for years, and it may be forever?
Oh! why art thou silent, thou voice of my heart?
It may be for years, and it may be forever?
Oh! why art thou silent, Kathleen, Mavourneen?

Kathleen, Mavourneen, awake from thy slumbers,
The blue mountains glow in the sun's golden light;
Ah! where is the spell that once hung on my numbers,
Arise in thy beauty, thou star of my night,
Arise in thy beauty, thou star of my night
Mavourneen, Mavourneen, my sad tears are falling,
To think that from Erin and thee I must part,
It may be for years, and it may be forever?
Then why art thou silent, thou voice of my heart?
It may be for years, and it may be forever;
Then why art thou silent, Kathleen, Mavourneen?

Words by Louisa Macartney Crawford (1790–1858)
Music by F.W. Nicholls Crouch

* My darling one

Prologue

✠

A family lost, nearly frozen, pushed their way through the knee-high drifts that streaked the treeless plain. Falling snowflakes, nearly as big as poker chips, almost obscured them from view. They were Lakota—a man, his wife, and two young girls. When they saw the two white men, the daughters ran and hid behind their folks, sheltering under thin blankets. The family stood and stared at Mike Quinn and Rico Sandoval with suspicion. The angry guns of Wounded Knee had only been silent for a week. They appreciated that the snow-filled arroyo between them was a protective barrier.

"*Mire*, Señor Mike!"

Mike halted and peered into the flying snow in the direction Rico pointed. "Jaysus, what are those folks doin' so far from the agency? Afoot in this weather, with no supplies, must be crazy—or scared half to death."

The tall, lean, and goateed cattleman dismounted and handed frozen reins to the vaquero. He fantasied that the dull, gray sky might soon shatter like the patches of thin ice underfoot.

Rico hunkered under his dented, brown sombrero and wine-red serape, his back to the wind. "They look scared to me. After the trouble, they just run off, anywhere, to get away from the army, I think."

Mike stepped away from their mounts and the Winchesters sheathed beside their saddles. He removed his gloves and extended his open hands as a sign of peace. The freezing wind bit at the exposed flesh. "They've gotta know we mean 'em no harm. If we don't reach 'em, they'll likely be wolf-bait by mornin'."

The survivors turned away, unmoved by his gesture. Mike broke into a run along his side of the ravine. He waved his arms and shouted into the wind, "Hold up! We got food!"

The family halted and looked back. But he was too far away, too far to hear, too far to understand. They pressed on again, disappearing into the windblown snow.

Rico stared after them and silently made the sign of the cross. Mike drew to a halt, tore off his hat and slapped it against his thigh. "What the deuce!" he spat in disgust.

Chapter One

Cloonfower

✠

1846

Patrick Quinn picked his way carefully along a footpath not much wider than the fattest snake St. Patrick expelled from Ireland. As he traipsed, he rehearsed his frustrations like an old woman fingering the beads of her rosary. Since dawn he'd been seeking day wages at larger farms in the parish, but without success. It was well past suppertime as he hurried back to his family. *Cate will surely be weary of toil and toddlers. I mustn't add to her worries.*

Beside the path, drenched pastures of deep, thick grass smelled of earthworms. Further on, the lush, green meadows were replaced by a brown expanse of bog land, scarred black where the turf pits lay. A midsummer sun forced its way into the evening sky. Through the lingering rain clouds, shafts of gold created and interrupted the lengthening shadows.

He approached their mud-wall cabin, a drooping, gray structure that begged a coat of whitewash. Its roof of tattered thatch resembled an urchin in bad need of a haircut. Cate, nearly seven months pregnant, sat at the threshold and took no notice of Pat's arrival.

"Ah, Cate, have I missed the children then? I didn't mean to be so late."

She nodded and put a finger to her lips. "Please God, you're home. Did you find any work at all?"

"None for pay. Helped Flanagans birth a calf. No one has work but for his own." Pat grabbed at tense muscles at the back of his neck, but he managed to force a smile. "I fear I chased away a daydream or such just now. What were you thinkin'?"

Cate didn't look up. She stared at her dirty, bare feet. "Oh, I've been prayin' . . . beggin' God 'tis no mortal sin to have these feelin's which I do. Here you have six mouths to feed in hard times and I'm cursin' you with another."

He reached out and stroked her tear-stained cheek with the smooth back of his otherwise rough hand. "Ach! Are you now producin' babes all by yourself? Your mind is in a needless dither, woman. 'Tis all of Cloonfower which is misfortunate! You bring me no curse at all."

Cate smiled but her furrowed brow did not smooth. Pat sat down upon a large stone mottled with the orange-yellow acne of lichen and washed himself with water from a wooden bucket. He was a lean, wiry type, and not particularly handsome. But he had a marvelous smile and gentle ways that had easily captured Catherine Finan's heart almost twelve years before. His thirty-one years were beginning to show around his blue-gray eyes and his mouth. Smile lines he called them. Longish, dark brown hair, flecked with a few bits of gray, curled a bit at the back of his neck. He wore his faded shirt tucked into mud-spattered, black woolen trousers that ended in tatters between his knee and ankle.

Life was hard, but it was so for all the cottiers in Cloonfower. Still, things might have been worse if Pat had been one given to despair and bitterness. But he was wont to look away from the ugly face of poverty, happy to believe things would soon look up.

"I'll bring your supper out here," said Cate. "Nora brought a pot of flummery on her way to Shanbally and I've saved it warm for you."

Pat dried himself and made no comment. As Cate turned to go into the cabin, he eyed her. Seen in profile, her ponderous belly reminded him of her worry and want. Soon she'd be due with their fifth child. Increasingly, their efforts to put food on the table had to be supplemented by these gifts of oaten porridge from her older brother, Peter, and his wife, Nora. Pat's pride was wounded in the face of such charity. But neither of them could afford the luxury of resentment. It wasn't Peter's fault that he was a generous brother and better placed in life.

Cate returned with his supper and set the steaming bowl beside him. Three years younger than he, she had been only sixteen when they married. She still retained her handsome features—greenish, hazel eyes and long, auburn hair, which when pulled back, revealed a face and neckline of considerable beauty. Pat loved her dearly, but he was shamed by her worn, ragged clothes, by her long hours of work, and by the knowledge he was helpless to give her better.

Cate had been born into modest prosperity. The Finans had long been among the top tenants in Cloonfower, with more acreage and better ground than many. Despite her now reduced circumstances, Cate complained little. But feeding ten-year-old Margaret, eight-year-old James, six-year-old John, and two-year-old Roderick was a challenge each day. With another on the way, Pat knew she must feel that life was closing in on her.

It took but little time for Pat to consume the bowl of porridge. Setting the empty bowl aside, he took Cate's hand and pulled her to a seat beside him. The late sunset of the Irish summer had gilded in crimson the clouds hung low in the blue-gold sky. Though it was late, they sat and silently watched the glow gradually surrender to inexorable darkness.

As the chill came up, Pat wrapped his arms about his weary wife.

"It shan't be long now till the harvest. Things will be better then. You'll see."

Cate nodded without comment. "Let's be in then."

Pat picked up the water bucket and placed it at the threshold. He entered the single room whose darkness was relieved only by a faint glow of a dying turf fire.

Cate quickly washed her feet and left the bucket outside the door. It was now too dark for pitching muddy water into the yard. It might land on the fairies. She would take care of it in the morning.

The townland of Cloonfower, which means "meadow of the spring," sits on the western edge of Kilkeevin Parish, in the County of Roscommon. Blotched by bog land, the district produced more turf than crops. Where good land could be found, it was often devoted to grazing. Still, the potato was the staple for the Quinns, as it was for over three million peasants in Ireland. This was most unfortunate as the country was reeling from the partial failure of the previous potato harvest. Ireland's great hunger had begun, though it was not yet recognized as such. Its full horror had yet to fall upon the land.

Then in August of 1846, in the course of a few days, the new crop of potatoes turned. The plants blackened and collapsed, unleashing a sickening odor from lazybeds across the breadth of the country. Fully three quarters of the nation's crop was laid waste. Fear and confusion gripped families as the specter of famine crouched in the dark corners beside their hearths.

Centuries of confiscation and colonization had left most of the native Irish with no land of their own. In Roscommon, nearly all the land was owned by a handful of British proprietors. One of these was William Robert Wills of Willsgrove, landlord of Cloonfower and a good portion of Kilkeevin Parish. William, a tall, silver-haired gentleman in his late sixties, was the very image of an Anglo-Irish patrician.

Ten years younger than William, Mary Sandford Wills was a feisty, slightly sardonic spirit, despite the recurring bouts of asthma that had plagued her since childhood. She was the niece of the late Lord Henry Moore Mount Sandford, first Baron of Castlerea.

Recently, another uncle, George, the third Baron, had died in his dotage, without a male heir. The hereditary title was, therefore, extinguished. But the vast Sanford estate was intact, and it now devolved upon Mary and her husband. When she and William wed thirty years ago, it had been a love match and an alliance of fortunes. It was the joining of both estates and of the two family names that William had announced at the Relief Committee meeting that morning.

"You should have seen the blood drain from the face of that old fart, Lorton," William crowed to his wife as they lurched along in their black brougham carriage from Roscommon town to Castlerea. Their destination was Castlerea House, Mary's ancestral home and the seat of the Sandford estate.

Mary looked at her husband with a wry smile. "You use rather coarse terms for the Lord Lieutenant of the county."

William chuckled. "Well, he is an old fart! He's paid little courtesy to either of us in the past. But when I announced the union of our estates, his air turned around quicker than a London hackney. Now that I'm to be the largest landholder in the Parish, he is suddenly most solicitous of our good health and comfort."

Mary gazed absently out the side window at the flat, monotonous countryside. "I suppose this meeting was like all the others, much harrumphing but no great actions taken."

William grimaced with injured pride at this second rebuke. He turned and faced Mary to address an earnest self-defense. "What can we do? Both London and Dublin are happy to let us sink in this sea of declining rents and rising poor taxes. I reminded Lorton that starving bogtrotters pay no rent. But he, of course, complained that his hands are tied."

Never deferential to political authority, Mary waved her fine, embroidered handkerchief dismissively. "His hands may be tied, but what of London? Lord John Russell's hands are not tied!"

"We are told, my dear, that the Prime Minister feels it is down to Irish property to care for Irish poverty. Ireland is only deemed part of the kingdom when they want something from us. God knows if this famine had broken out in Berkshire or Kent, the government would be rushing forward with aid." William fiddled with his blue, silk cravat as he contemplated the abandonment felt by the Anglo-Irish propertied class.

"Surely they could, at least, open the workhouse in Castlerea," Mary said. "It is simply unconscionable that such a facility of relief is not yet available to the needy."

"Yes, yes, that was all agreed. Can you believe it? Some fool had its doors closed for lack of uniforms for the inmates!"

After a few minutes of naught but plodding hoofbeats and creaking carriage wheels, Mary turned and fingered the lapel of William's chesterfield. He knew a request was coming. "William, I do hope we can leave for France before winter sets in. The cold and the damp are bad enough, but now the ghostly faces of the poor fill the streets and shops of Castlerea. I can't be seen anywhere in public without attracting a mob of beggars. God save them!" She pulled her shawl close, as if the chill of winter had already arrived.

"God better save them," William replied. "No one else is going to do so."

Mary shrugged and repeated her request, "Can we leave soon, dear?"

"Don't worry, my love. We'll leave for France just as soon as the merger of the estates is settled. In the meantime, we must get used to our new appellation."

"Whatever you say, Mr. Wills-Sandford."

Cate Quinn delivered her baby, a boy named Michael. The birth of a male child was usually the cause of great pride and pleasure among the extended family, indeed the entire clachan. But their capacity for joy and satisfaction drained from them with the potato blight. Given the odds of infant mortality, Pat promptly arranged to have Michael christened. Along with a few relatives and friends from Cloonfower, the family walked the dirt lanes to the chapel of St. Joseph, on the west edge of Castlerea.

The parish priest was Father Keane. He was a large man in his early fifties. His prematurely snow-white hair was cropped short and always in disarray, as if he'd just got out of his bed. He had the hands of a farmer, and his piety was of an earthy character, rooted in the land and the everyday life of his people. He did not suffer fools gladly, and he spoke his mind freely.

After initiating young Michael with the Christian rite of baptism, Keane sent the family on their way with his good wishes and blessings. As he returned to the sacristy, he shook his head sadly. It might as well have been the last rites I was just performin'. Such is the chance that this wee one will survive the comin' year.

As the worried priest traveled his parish, he had seen much evidence of the growing hunger and homelessness. Whereas only a few families in the parish had been ruined last year, now virtually all were severely impoverished. Dressed in little more than rags, they

St. Joseph's Chapel, where Michael Quinn was baptized (Courtesy of the Castlerea Public Library)

8

scavenged the fields for charlock and nettles to make their meager soups. A realization of impending doom imprinted the faces of his parishioners like a brand.

As the christening party made its way back to Cloonfower, Pat walked and talked with his brother-in-law, Peter Finan, a tall, rough-hewn farmer in his early forties. His reddish brown hair and beard framed a face of strong features and kindly expression. He wore a rough woolen shirt, trousers, and brown leather boots, the last a sure sign of relative affluence.

A champion of the rights of the cottiers, Peter was busy decrying the rising evictions of tenants who had fallen behind in their rents. "None to report here, praise God! But in Ballintober, there's whole families sittin' by the side of the road with no place to go. Master Wills is keen to put more acres into grazin'."

Pat turned and, walking backwards, called to his daughter as she followed with Cate, Nora, and the other women. "Margaret, will you carry Michael for your Ma a spell, dearie? Here, I'll take Roderick with me." Pat lifted young Roderick onto his shoulders and resumed his pace along the puddled track. "Sorry, Peter, go on."

Recovering from the distraction, Peter winked at the toddler and returned to his rant. "You know, in the old days, the Ribbonmen would be settin' things to right. Why, back in 1820, me own father was one of them, and their numbers was so great, the Brits had to reinforce the garrison at Castlerea. Today, there's many a man who'd be takin' measures but for the grip of hunger."

Pat looked off at the cloudy sky that threatened rain before they would reach Cloonfower. But he wasn't thinking about the weather. "Sure, the Ribbonmen was always heroes in our house. When me brother, Martin, was denied his conacre, didn't the lads recover it for him? They was our only defenders against thievin' landlords."

Peter nodded in solidarity. "Why, 'twas only several months back, the lads in Aughrim took their spades on an evenin' and turned over the sod denied for praties."

"The landlord was makin' way for the grazin'?" Pat asked.

"Aye. There's the greater profit for the master. Of course, left turned, the ground would be no use for grazin' for the season."

"'Twould seem enough to get the tenants their conacre back," Pat concluded.

"Not right off, though. The bastard landlord vowed he'd hire day laborers to quickly turn the fields back. But, the next day, a mysterious notice appeared on the church door. 'Twas a warnin' signed 'Molly Maguire.' 'Whoever undertakes the turning back of sod shall have his tongue nailed to his forehead.'" Peter smiled sardonically at the grim, but effective, threat.

Pat gave a shudder. "I could never carry out such a sentence, nor rake a man's skin with the cardin' tool as they do. You'll recall when Father Keane gave us all 'who-began-it' one Sunday. Said Bishop Browne had decreed that any Catholic man who took part in such cruel justice would be excommunicated and damned to hell."

Peter spat in disgust. "Ah, there's the clergy for you! Why don't that feckin' bishop damn a landlord or two for bundlin' families into the road and pullin' down their cabins?"

Pat looked behind him to check the progress of the women and children. "Do you think, Peter, that we'll be evicted? Sure, most of Cloonfower is good for nothin' but cuttin' turf. What gain will Master Wills have for puttin' us off our leases? He'll just have to find someone else to cut his turf."

"We can't live on cuttin' turf, Pat! There's got to be a proper crop, fit for to feed our families. If not, they won't have to evict us. We'll be starved out."

A few weeks later, in a foggy pre-dawn, Pat slipped into the straw-stuffed bed he shared with Cate and the baby. His breathing was hard; his body steamed with perspiration. Cate knew he had been missing through much of the night, as she had been up nursing Michael. As she awakened, the memory of his absence jolted her into indignation. Her voice packed as much anger as a whisper could convey.

"Where have you been most the night? I'm here alone with the wee ones whilst you're out ramblin' about the countryside!" She felt his body tense; his labored breathing suddenly hushed. In the dark she couldn't make out his expression, but she faced him as she vented her fear-born anger. "I was worryin' where you was and what bad cess might be on you."

"That, Cate, is me own business entirely. You're to say nothin'." A rare flash of temper colored his voice. He brought his lips close to her ear and whispered, "When you rise, you'll find a haunch of mutton in the pot. Put on water and make your soup. And let none be the wiser!"

A sense of dread replaced her anger. "God save us, Patrick Quinn! Am I married to a sheep stealin' Ribbonman? What if the magistrate catches you out? 'Twill be the workhouse for us and a prison ship for you."

"Cate, I told you already, 'tis not for discussion! I'll hang before I watch me family starve. Now get ready to feed us. 'Twill be a spell 'fore we see meat again." With that, he pulled the thin coverlet over his shoulder and turned away.

The new year, 1847, brought on the worst stage of Ireland's famine. Starvation, sickness, and emigration were erasing whole communities. It was clear, even to desperate ones such as Pat Quinn, that sheep stealing was no strategy for long-term survival. An alternative of sorts emerged one Sunday when Father Keane took to the pulpit at St. Joseph's. His face was a mask of ill temper as he gave the announcements after the Mass.

"The District Relief Committee has requested that I tell you of a grand and generous public works project that should commence shortly."

An excited murmur swept through the modest whitewashed chapel. The miserable, and much reduced, congregation watched their priest struggle to contain his anger, which might go unleashed as it had in times past.

"A new road is to be constructed 'tween Castlerea and Swineford. Work is offered to those in need, for the bounteous sum of eight pence a day!"

Epithets never before uttered within the walls of this holy space erupted spontaneously from the faithful. Keane raised his hands to silence the impious outburst. "Now, now, we must all pray to our merciful Lord that you and your families may survive such generosity."

Pat fumed at Cate as they trudged home from the Mass. "Father Keane had it right! How can one feed a family on 8p a day?"

Cate shrugged. "I was thinkin' 8p might be better than nothin'. Besides, is there not a chance James could get a helper's position at half wage? We might have 12p between the both of you!"

"Why the lad is but nine years, Cate!" Pat paused to reconsider his opposition. "Still, it may be worth tryin' him to see if he can manage it."

One morning in late February, Pat and James left Cloonfower before dawn. Men and boys streamed out of each boreen, joining them in an hour's walk to the site of the roadworks near Cloonkeen. Bellies noisily protested their emptiness. None of the usual joking or gossip was bandied among them. This was a grim community of silence, each privately calculating his own chances of survival.

Days spent over picks and shovels, and pushing heavy wheelbarrows, were more than some could endure. Several times a day, a laborer would collapse and be carried off, not to be seen again. Young James struggled to play his manly role, but the foreman was unimpressed. The skinny, brown-haired lad would hoist his shovel, but in his malnourished state, he lost most of the dirt and gravel before he reached the barrow.

"You'll have to fill that barrow more quickly than that young man!"

Pat quickly inserted himself between the ham-handed taskmaster and the boy. "I'll mind that he does, sir. He's me boy and I'll be quick after him if he slacks at all, sir."

Reluctantly mollified, the foreman pulled his flat cap snug and grunted. "See to it then! No room 'ere for slackers."

It was a long wait till the noonday break, when meager portions of bread and thin soup were carefully measured out to these "fortunate" ones. Dropping to the ground beside their tools, the laborers gobbled their bits so quickly, it was more memory than meal. But their respite was all too brief.

Pat glared at the back of his nemesis as the foreman walked down the line, shouting and urging the workers back to their tasks. *A left-footer if I ever did see one.*

But he didn't have to worry about the foreman for long. It was only a few weeks later that the road project was abruptly cancelled. Now the British government in London was bent upon lowering the cost of Irish relief.

Expressing concern over the potential for abuses, they cancelled all funding for "make-work" projects. Rather it was determined that direct provision of food should replace public works. District Relief Committees were ordered to establish outdoor soup kitchens in the major towns to feed the hungry masses. Initially the promised food was not available due to delays in locating and securing the necessary staples. When food did finally arrive, the quantities were woefully inadequate. Food prices had been driven to treacherous heights as Irish traders insisted upon the freedom to ship their commodities to the highest bidder and opposed any importations that would collapse their heady profits. Absent leadership by the government, great quantities of Irish wheat, barley, and oats were exported to England, under armed guard, throughout the famine years.

The Quinns and their neighbors were beyond desperation. On a wintry evening, men from the clachans gathered by an open fire at the edge of the turf beds. A waning moon cast scant light. Only when they faced the fire were the participants' faces dimly recognizable. A strong west wind blew the flames sideways.

An old, gnarled farmer was the first to voice his worry and anger. "Me wife cannot make it to Castlerea for the soup."

Another cottier near the fire added his lament, barely able to restrain his sobs. "We go as often as we can, but the wait, 'tis beyond endurance. Me children are collapsin' 'fore their turn comes up."

A bitter voice from the back of the crowd answered him. "You were lucky to get soup at all! Last week, we waited in line for hours, only to be told the pot's gone empty."

After a spate of such grievances, Peter Finan stepped forward. Once a big man, with powerful shoulders and arms, his coat now hung on his frame like a draped curtain. His full and florid face had turned drawn and gray. But his neighbors still hushed to hear his views. He raised his arms high to quiet the jabbering assembly. "Enough! We've only one chance to feed our families. Master Wills must give us soup and bread! And we must have grain meal to carry home to those not fit to travel for their relief!"

Pat jumped in, hoping to support his brother-in-law's efforts to rouse some action. "How can we convince him, Peter?"

"We must speak and act as one! Everyone who is able must show himself, and his family with him, at Castlerea House tomorrow. We've no force but our numbers. God willin', we'll be heard."

Pat listened as the debate resumed. Some expressed skepticism, while others defended the wisdom of Peter's proposal. Gradually, murmurs of assent passed through the group. "Tomorrow then!" Having reached a consensus, they kicked out the fire and turned for home.

By early the next day, word of their decision had spread throughout the parish. Desperate peasants from the entire Wills-Sandford estate moved toward Castlerea. The journey was no more than a few miles for most, but it was nevertheless tortuous for the emaciated men, women, and children. Many could barely place one foot before another. Some had the distended belly of starvation.

It was midafternoon when the crowd of weary peasants had fully gathered before the gray stone walls at the gates of Castlerea House. The weakest among them simply sat in the middle of the street. There hadn't been such a crowd in Castlerea since the harvest markets of years ago. Nearly five hundred persons were massed in front of the great demesne this day.

Sporadic spits of rain marked the slate-skied March day. Constables from the garrison were scattered about the market, in passive observation. They were under the strict orders of Captain Kerr to avoid any provocation. In panic, the gatekeeper at Castlerea House securely bolted the gates against the crowd and rushed off to the estate office to alert the agent.

Owen Young came from a family of prominent businessmen in Harristown. He had previously been agent to the late Baron Mount Sanford. William Wills-Sandford had been happy to retain him for his business acumen, his connections to the other landowners, and his loyalty to the Sandford family. Now in his late forties, Young was a portly man with thinning red hair. He wore a heavy woolen suit and high brown boots. A flat cap protected his pate against the inclement weather. It was obvious that Owen Young was not among the hungry.

He was not a harsh man, but neither was he particularly solicitous of the tenants. Young was simply devoted to the protection and growth of his master's assets and incomes. He had seen the violence of Ribbonmen over the years, but he knew these enfeebled tenants posed no such threat. He strolled from the estate office into the market square, the callow gatekeeper fairly dancing at his side with anxiety. Owen pushed his way through the crowd. So as to be seen and heard, he climbed the stone wall next to the gatehouse. "What business brings all of you to the demesne today?" he asked.

Dominic Flanagan, a well-respected tenant, was the designated spokesman. "We wish to speak with Master Wills, sir." Like most all the tenants, he was not yet trained to the newly hyphenated name of his master, Wills-Sandford.

Young shook his head, his hands open and outstretched. "You've wasted your journey. The master and mistress have gone to France and shan't return until late in May."

The agent noticed the cottier trembling as he spoke. No peasant was accustomed to holding forth before such an audience. Still, Flanagan was emboldened by shouts of support from the crowd. "He must grant us some relief! We can't pay our rents and we've no food. You must get word to him! Is there nothing you can do, Mr. Young?"

Owen mopped the chilling rain from his clean-shaven cheeks and adopted a patient, patronizing tone. "I assure you, the master is keenly aware of your trouble. And he's entirely sympathetic. He's authorized me to grant temporary relief from rents, but only in worthy cases. As for food, you must look to the workhouse or the church. The estate has no supplies of its own for its many tenants."

A cottier challenged Young in a loud, surly voice. "Workhouse! More like hell it is!"

Young made no attempt to debate the virtues of the workhouse scheme. "The estate has nothing more to offer."

The crowd gave out a moan of despair. The agent climbed down from the wall and walked briskly back to his office. Pat and his family slowly pushed their way out of the market square and back toward the road to Cloonfower. Many others passed through the streets of Castlerea, accosting all they met and knocking on the doors of the shops to beg a few coins or a bite to eat.

For the next few weeks, the Quinns tottered on the brink of starvation. The English Parliament had decreed that no relief, whether open air or workhouse based, should be allowed to any person or family employing greater than one-quarter of an acre of land. The regulation forced many Irish to choose between their homes and food. Some peasants put their own cabins to the torch to qualify for the sparse relief being offered. It became increasingly evident that the propertied interests would see the land cleared of its surplus cottiers and way made for cattle and sheep.

Chapter Two

Guests of the Crown

✠

Cate arose first to rekindle the smoldering fire. Only a few bricks of peat remained in a jumble by the hearth. For months Pat had been quietly spiriting these from the landlord's turf pits. The children lay abed, clinging to the warmth of covers and kin. Everyone was still tired after being kept awake through much of the night. Michael had cried for hours with pangs of hunger. When she opened the door a splash of daylight invaded the still dark cabin. Pat shielded his eyes with the coverlet and groaned softly. "Damn, 'tis mornin' already?"

After a minute's debate with his conscience, he kicked back his blanket and pulled on his threadbare shirt and trousers. He crossed the room, approaching Cate from behind, and gave her a squeeze and a kiss on the back of her neck. She smiled and silently pulled his arms tight across her empty belly. Making as little noise as he was able, he retrieved the water bucket to fetch fresh water from the brook across the way. Cate stooped to blow on the dying embers and toppled over in front of the hearth.

Pat dropped the bucket and rushed to her side. "Cate! Oh, Jaysus!"

She was still conscious. More embarrassed than hurt, she looked up at him from the dirt floor. "Oh, I just went so dizzy." She raised herself up to a sitting position and he felt her forehead.

"You've given your portions of soup to the children! I knew it. Will you save them at the cost of their mother?"

The commotion stirred Margaret and she jumped up from her straw pallet. "Ma! Is she sick? What is it?"

Pat barred her way with his arm. "Hush, girl. 'Tis the hunger. You light the fire and we'll make soup. James! Get out of bed and go for water, lad."

By the time it was put together, the soup was more water and desperate hope than the usual charlock and bits of Finan barley. Cate sipped the thin broth while Pat shooed the children out of the cabin.

"We must go, Cate! There's nothin' left to eat, and Peter and Nora have little to share."

Cate covered her mouth with both hands and began to cry softly. But this time Pat was adamant and would not let the matter rest.

"We must get to the workhouse! And we have to leave 'fore we lose the strength of our legs."

Cate looked up at him and sneered. "What difference is it? 'Tis death, whether here or there!"

Pat lowered his fist with a crash upon the table. "There be food there, damn it! God may spare us the fever, but He shan't be bringin' bacon to the door!" He walked to the threshold and watched his listless children sitting in the yard. When he spoke again, it was as if to himself more than to her. "I swore me family will not starve. 'Tis the only way."

The workhouse at Castlerea had been built two years prior. It was designed to house nine hundred souls, giving temporary shelter, food, and labor to the indigent. But there had been no anticipation of famine with its numbers, sickness, and the inability of inmates to work. The workhouses of Ireland were administered under a punitive philosophy, aimed at discouraging malingerers and the undeserving. Families were separated

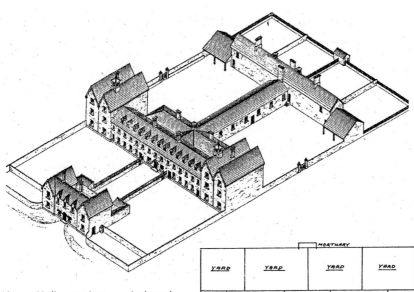

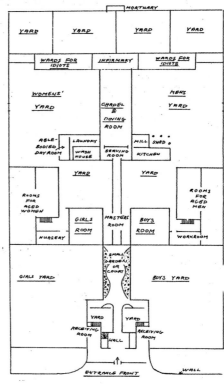

Above: Bird's eye view—typical work-house

Right: Workhouse Design for 800 persons similar to Roscommon (Co. Roscommon Remembers An Gorta Mór, 1999 Rev. Francis M. Beirne, Editor)

according to gender and age. Typhoid fever and dysentery made admission nearly a guarantee of contagion. Fully eight hundred thirty of the current nine hundred and ninety inhabitants were so stricken. The Master and Matron of the house had recently died of the fever. Its medical officer had left town in such a hurry that he neglected to collect his wage. Though Master Wills-Sanford had recently donated his former home at Willsgrove for use as an auxiliary workhouse, the facilities were still overcrowded. And the risk of disease was as high as ever.

It was a sunny April day when Pat, Cate and their children presented themselves at the front gate of the workhouse at Castlerea. The warm spring air belied the somber occasion. The workhouse complex was a massive cluster of gray stone buildings surrounded by a high stone wall. At the entrance, there was a two-story gabled cottage with a slate roof. It was here that admissions were considered.

With infant Michael in his arms, Pat walked up to the heavy wooden door and swung its large iron knocker. A thin, uniformed warder confronted them. His greasy, disheveled hair and dirty clothes betrayed any dignity of position. He offered few words and showed no interest whatsoever in their plight. He ushered them into a receiving room overheated by the fireplace at the rear. The Quinns stood in their weariness. It had been a long, difficult walk from Cloonfower. The baby wailed with hunger.

The new master of the workhouse entered the reception room. He was a short harried man of middle age, in shirtsleeves and waistcoat. His expression suggested that he felt the workhouse needed no more inmates presently and he questioned Pat closely. "You'll not be havin' any land or leasehold?"

"Me patch, small as it was, has been surrendered entirely, sir."

The master seemed disappointed at this reply. After a few minutes of paperwork, he stood and summoned the loitering warder. "Colin, take the females and the little ones to the nursery. I'll show the others where to go."

As they were about to leave, Margaret broke down. "Da, I don't want you to leave us!"

Pat placed his hands on her shoulders, looked into her eyes, and spoke gently. "Don't worry, dearie, everythin' will be all right. Now, be a brave girl for your Ma. She'll be needin' your help with the boys."

Cate handed the baby to Margaret and hugged Pat for a long time. Then she stooped and kissed James and John, whose blank expressions betrayed their lack of understanding as to what was about to happen. The warder, impatient at the delay, cleared his throat. Once Cate had gathered her brood, he led his charges out through the back door of the reception house and down a path between two walled yards. Sad, ragged figures populated these yards—females and the very young on the left, men and boys on the right. Most inmates, however, were not well enough to use the exercise yards, despite the clement weather. Those not down with fever were often too weak from the meager diet of bread and "stirabout."

A three-storied residence building ran nearly the width of the compound. On its ground floor were the day rooms where the few who were able were required to work. The upper floors served as great open dormitories. Behind the residence were the dining hall, the chapel, the laundry and the kitchen. At the very rear of the compound was an infirmary, a ward for those deemed idiots, a small mortuary, and the toilet block.

As Cate, Margaret, Roderick and Michael were escorted to the nursery, Margaret was still sobbing and complaining. She pressed her mother's patience. "I don't like this place! Why can't we go with Da? We must stay together, all of us!"

"Hush your gob, girl! We have no choice in it at all. Besides, Da and your brothers are nearby. They'll be safe now, as will we." Cate was as angry with herself as with her daughter. She knew she was offering assurances that she herself did not believe. Drawing upon her anger and resentments, she resolved to keep her children close to her at all times. She was anxious that they avoid all contact with diseased inmates. After the evening meal, Cate brushed and arranged, as best she could, the filthy bedding on which they were to sleep. A night of wrenching emotions followed for her. To her relief, Margaret and the little boys slept through the night.

Early the next morning, shouted commands awakened Pat, James, and John. "Arise! No malingerin' now. Let's be up wit' you."

A small nervous warder was in charge of the men and older boys of the workhouse. As he walked between the long rows of cots that lined the large dormitory, he maintained a safe distance from his potentially diseased charges. Ostentatiously brandishing a long blackthorn stick, he prodded inmates who didn't move quickly enough to suit.

The inmates stumbled down the staircase and out to the toilet block. Then they marched to the dining hall, a parade of the living dead. There was little talk among them, only the groans of misery voiced by some. They moved slowly, feebly, as if in a trance. Pat's boys stayed close. Six-year-old John was unwilling to release his clutching grip upon his father's hand.

They quickly consumed their thin porridge. Then a matron arrived to take charge of the youngest ones, prompting a loud protest from John. Pat could offer but few words to the boy as he and James were herded out the door with the others who were strong enough to work. They stood for some minutes, huddling against the cool of morning before their warder arrived to make assigments to the various work details. To the new arrivals, a routine speech was delivered. "All you who be able must work if you wish to eat. Sure, 'tis only right, your bein' guests of the Crown and all."

When most of the group had departed to their tasks, Pat and James were assigned to the cadre for the removal of corpses from the infirmary and the dormitories. Pat cursed the decision beneath his breath. *Ach, the divil has made the choice. 'Twill be the fever for us.*

It was a smelly, ghastly task. Pat kept the worst of it for himself and his fellows. He gave James work that involved little or no direct contact with the blackened, often-bloated bodies of the poor victims. For hours each day, they carried their morbid charges on litters to the mortuary. There the bodies were wrapped, each in sheets of cotton duck, and carted to a large pit that served as a mass grave. After pitching the burden of their barrows into the hellhole, they shoveled a layer of lime upon the wretched heap.

Cate caught only a glimpse of her husband and the boys most days, usually when passing between the residence and the dining hall. But occasionally, if the weather was fine, they would meet for a visit by the wall between the exercise yards. Miserable they might be, she thought, but they would not starve. Sickness was their chief enemy now. Months passed, often with some transitory illness afflicting one or another of them. Mostly, it was relapsing fever with its high temperatures, nausea, and nosebleeds. This was far less lethal than the typhoid and dysentery. But the odds were against them.

One winter morning, Pat grasped at Cate's sleeve as she entered the dining hall. His face was a map of tearful agitation. She sent Margaret and Roderick ahead to breakfast and turned back to her husband, her baby in her arms.

"Cate! James is off to infirmary. 'Tis the bloody flux is what I'm hearin'."

She closed her eyes and leaned on his shoulder. "Ah, Pat, no! I must go and see our boy."

He shook his head sadly. "I tried. The matron would have none of it. None may come to infirmary save the sick and them that tend them."

Pat had to leave, and Michael squirmed and cried to be fed. As Cate walked away she whispered, "Dear Mother of God, pray for us."

James had contracted dysentery, carried by the flies amid his daily activities among the corpses. For over a week he suffered with diarrhea, nausea, aches and shivers. Then one evening, the silver-haired matron summoned both Pat and Cate, "You must come at once. The boy is failin'."

A kindly but firm woman, she took Cate's hand and led them to the infirmary. Young James lay upon a dingy cot, his watery eyes shining from within a hollow shell of a body. At the sight of her son, Cate recognized immediately what was but moments away. Pat, however, blathered on, choking back tears. "James, me lad, you'll be right again soon. We'll pass the spring back in Cloonfower, all of us together again. You'll be glad of it then, eh?"

The boy languished in a silent sweat. Cate mopped his fevered forehead, and softly keened an ancient, wordless lament.

"Stop it, woman!" Pat barked. "The fever will pass! You'll see. We must have faith!"

She made no response, gave no sign of even hearing her husband's foolish outburst. She continued to softly wail and moan as she had learned from years of watching her mother and the other womenfolk. It was if she were taking the pain of her child into her own body. Cradling the boy's head, she rocked slightly, lost in the mournful reverie. Pat hid his face in his hands, and in so doing, missed the moment when his son let slip his grasp on this grievous existence.

James was now one more client for Pat's work detail. He carried his own son, an awfully light burden, from the infirmary to the mortuary. Father

Keane was notified, and the next morning he led a procession that had become too familiar to him. Throughout the famine and sickness, the faithful priest continued to bravely attend to his flock, even those within the workhouse.

As they walked, Pat complained bitterly to Keane. "'Tis a sacrilege, Father, me boy not havin' the Mass, not even a restin' place in the churchyard!"

The weary priest clapped a hand upon Pat's shoulder. "They're just after keepin' the sickness down, Pat. 'Tis no other way."

Intoning the Latin prayers for the dead, the priest and the family arrived at the edge of the lime pit. When the time came, James's slight, shrouded body was toppled down the embankment into the morass of whitened bundles. The stench was even more horrific than the sight.

In the days that followed, Pat was in shock, listless as he went mechanically through the motions of work. Grief drove out of him his inveterate optimism. In contrast, Cate's sorrow seemed restrained by the force of will and determination. "We must to save our strength for our other little ones," she said. "We'll not be surrenderin' another of them, please God!"

In August 1848 the Quinns received a message from Peter Finan. Father Keane delivered it to them personally. The somber cleric, gaunt from his own labors and deprivations, spoke to them in the master's office. "Cate, your brother wants that your family request release from the workhouse."

Pat, impatient at such nonsense, interrupted. "But how shall we be fed, and where—?"

Cate placed her hand gently upon her husband's arm. "Patrick, hush."

The plainspoken priest was not so restrained. His bushy eyebrows invaded his forehead and his face went from gray to red. "By the saints and the sinners, man! Will you let me say what I've come to say? Finan is offerin' his own roof over your heads! Your cabin, well, 'twas pulled down long ago. Peter has harvest in oats and barley. He says 'twill be sufficient for all. You may even recover your conacre, though such is not certain."

Duly chastised, Pat resigned himself to the proposal despite his doubts of its sustainability. Peter's generosity brought from Cate a rare smile of relief. She rushed to Father Keane and kissed his hands. "Please tell me brother that we pray for God's blessin' upon him and Nora. We'll be lookin' for the day when he may come fetch us."

It was a crisp, bright autumn day when Peter came to the workhouse to collect them. Pat and John were ushered into the reception house, where the family had been admitted eighteen months before. The curious boy hurried to the window and peered out, looking for any sign of his uncle's arrival. Pat slumped upon a stool before the admittance desk. Through the open door to an adjacent room, he stared at the workhouse master, who was sitting at his high clerk's desk, engrossed in his papers. He offered neither greeting nor wishes of good fortune to his charges. A half-hour of waiting ensued. Pat, dulled to the reunion about to take place, scarcely took notice when Cate entered with Margaret, Roderick and Michael. When their presence finally registered with him, tears washed over what had once been his smile lines. John rushed to embrace his mother. Then, bending to kiss her husband, Cate slipped her arm under his own and helped him to his feet. "Come, Pat, we'll be goin' now."

They led the children through the door into bright sunlight that briefly dazzled them. Pat could see Peter waiting in the street beside a donkey cart, appearing surprisingly aged and still thin from his own ordeal. At first, a look of pained recognition crossed Peter's face, then a welcoming smile. He strode to Cate and Patrick and threw his big arms around both of them. Tears flowed into tears, and the children pressed upon him. Young Roderick, with little memory of this giant of an uncle, nevertheless clutched at the leg of Peter's trousers.

For the next year-and-a-half, the Finans and the Quinns lived as one family, sharing the leasehold that Peter had bravely maintained through the worst. Hard times were not over, for the potato crop of 1848 was nearly one-third lost due to continuing blight. But between cutting turf and the various crops Peter had sown, he and Patrick were able to eke out subsistence for the lot of them. Pat and Cate had another child in June of 1849, a daughter named Mary Ann. Happy as they were, nothing could fill the void in their hearts left by the loss of James.

By 1850, the scale of what had occurred in the previous four years had become hugely visible to Britain and to the world. County Roscommon alone had lost, through death and emigration, wholly one third of its population. The degree of devastation varied around the country but, in total, about three million were gone. While both Lord Lorton and William Wills-Sandford had engaged in clearances through eviction, they nevertheless undertook personal initiatives to assist their remaining tenants. Subscriptions for aid to the poor of Roscommon, however, went unanswered by most of those of means.

It was Master Wills-Sandford who now impacted the lives of the Quinn family in a more direct and fateful way.

The master sat gazing into the roaring fire that warmed the library at Castlerea House. A dozing hound lay in a curl at the old man's feet. "Owen, I have decided that stronger measures are required to restore prosperity to the estate."

Agent Young stood respectfully and grunted in non-committal response, the hairs on the back of his neck rising in ire at the implied criticism. *What does he think I'm up to whilst he and the Madam are off in bloody Provence?*

William toyed absently with his glass of port, oblivious to his agent's long since empty glass. "It is a generally recognized fact, is it not, that the west country of Ireland has been overpopulated for decades in the run-up to this famine? And despite the shocking reductions of the last few years, we still have an overage of cottiers for what the land can profitably support."

Young listened with no little apprehension for what scheme his master may have in mind. "True, sir, very true," he responded.

The old man rose from his chair and paced before the cavernous opening of the fireplace. "I am decided now that assisted emigration is the only way forward. Otherwise, they will breed themselves back, and we will be just as bad off, if not worse."

The mention of assisted emigration snapped the agent into an even higher state of agitation. He set his glass down upon the sideboard and readied himself to insert a note of practical skepticism. "I admire your concern, sir, but—but subsidizing tenant emigration has been tried before, as you well know. Sure, Major Denis Mahon was turned on and murdered by the very tenants he tried to assist at Strokestown."

"Denis was a greedy fool!" Wills-Sandford barked back, reacting poorly to being lectured by his employee. "When his tenants wouldn't clear out of their own accord, he bought them out at five pounds a family, hoping to lighten his Poor Tax burden."

The Mahon family, related through marriage to Mrs. Wills-Sandford, had a large estate in the eastern part of Roscommon. Major Denis Mahon had been shot dead in his carriage near Four-Mile House on All Souls night, 1847. To rid himself of tenants, he had chartered the cheapest available passage—emptied timber ships returning to Canada. He packed six hundred families aboard, over three thousand persons, in conditions reminiscent of the slave trade. Hundreds died in the crossing to Quebec. Those who survived the journey were further decimated by fever during the weeks that followed. Conditions aboard the ships were so appalling as to trigger a sharp protest from the Canadian authorities to London. Major Mahon's notoriety for these paid evictions and their aftermath cost him his life.

Young ventured cautiously, not wishing to further antagonize his employer. "'Twas a sad affair all around."

"What I'm proposing is different, Owen! Assisted emigration must be underwritten with funds sufficient for the cottiers to survive their journey."

The agent shrugged in resignation. The old man's mind was made up. Besides it was his money to waste—or his wife's. "Very generous, sir. How would you like to proceed?"

Two weeks later at Mass, Father Keane read out a letter from Owen Young to all the tenants of the Wills-Sandford estate. On behalf of his master, the agent extended a monetary offer to those families who wished to emigrate. Not only the fare of proper passage but also a modest stipend for the journey was to be included. The remaining tenants of the estate debated the merits of the offer and considered their options.

The following week, Pat made the decision for the Quinn family. "We'll have the money," he said to Peter as the two labored in the turf pit. "Though I can't think of leavin' Ireland forever. If we go, it should be for a short while. When times are better, we'll return to Cloonfower."

Finan embedded his spade in the next layer of turf to be cut and swept the perspiration from his brow with his sleeve. The sun was getting low, and they'd been at it since morning.

"If it's just a short time you're thinkin', Pat, you'll not be wantin' to go to America. The distance is great, and the risks of the voyage are considerable. Then there's the cost of return. If you're determined to leave, best go to England, get some work, and come back when you've got a bit of money."

Pat stopped pitching the black, moist, brick-like chunks out of the pit. "I haven't any idea of where to go or what work I might do. I've only cut turf and dug praties since I was a lad. But, I'm thinkin' there should always be a call for laborers in England."

"No doubt. But you must watch yourself among those British bastards. Remember, me friend, they are the enemy, always have been, always will be!" Peter's face reddened as the thought of life in England began to enkindle his resentments. "They steal our land, and call us lazy. Outlaw our schools, and call us ignorant. They even drove us to these mud-wall cabins, and now they say we live like animals!"

"You've never spoken so fondly of the Brits before," Pat joked.

Peter jerked his spade free and returned to the work at hand, stung a bit by having his righteous anger deflated.

"Sure, laugh all you want, but you'll not be findin' yourself entirely welcome over there."

Pat sensed he'd gone a bit too far. "I'm worried of that too. Still, many have gone, and they've found work and wages." He put a hand on his friend's shoulder.

Surprised at the touch, Peter turned and looked at him quizzically.

"You've been the most generous brother possible, Peter. Now 'tis time for us to quit bein' a weight on your back."

"Now Pat, don't be goin' on our account. The decision is yours. But if you go, remember, you will always be welcome back at my door."

Chapter Three

Ashton

✠

Flanked by the river Tame, Ashton-under-Lyne was a town of thirty thousand, six miles east of Manchester. It was one of many textile centers in the county of Lancashire. Warehouses and mills spilled down a hillside to a quay on the Manchester and Ashton-under-Lyne Canal that paralleled the river on the south side of the town. Cotton, coal, and other industrial goods were shipped via this canal, its dirty gray-brown waters exuding the pungent smells of dyes and raw sewage. Between the canal and the equally polluted river, there was an area of grassy banks and the graceful ash trees from whence the town derived its name. It was here, on a peaceful Sunday afternoon in late summer of 1853, that father and son walked and talked.

Pat, not yet forty, tired easily these days. He stopped and surveyed a seat on the trunk of a downed tree. "Here, son, let's rest a bit, eh?"

Pat loaded his clay pipe while Michael playfully balanced himself on a fork of the long dead ash. Both father and son were dressed in the plain but proper clothes of Britain's working class. Collarless cotton shirts, woolen trousers held high by galluses, even cheap leather shoes were typical attire.

"Tell me a story about Cloonfower, Da," asked young Michael Quinn.

Pat raised his eyes to heaven in supplication. "Ah, Michael! How many times have we told you those old stories? Bejabers, you must know more about Cloonfower than any of us by now!"

The boy pulled at his father's arm. "Oh, Da, you know I like to hear about Ireland."

"Well, 'tis your seventh birthday! But shall we try a different story, lad? Maybe I'll tell you about our journey to Ashton? There's a good story for today."

"Aye, I'd like that."

Pat stood and scratched his head, counting back the years since their arrival. He took Michael's hand and they proceeded along the riverbank path, all mottled by the interspersed patches of shade and afternoon sun.

"You was comin' up on four when we took our leave of Castlerea and bid farewell to your Uncle Peter, Aunt Nora, and all our friends in Cloonfower. We had little more than what we was wearin' and, of course, the money from Master Wills. 'Twas a hard journey for Ma and you children, walkin' all the way to Sligo. Still, the weather was fine."

As they walked, Michael occasionally tossed sticks or stones out into the river. Pat chided the boy. "You're sure you want to hear all this, young man?"

"Yes, please, Da. I'm listenin'."

"All right then. . . . After several days, we gets to Sligo harbor. And a sorry sight 'twas after years of the hunger. But ships from England could be found there, and we chose a cattle boat as the fare was cheap. Rode the open deck with all them cows mooin' and stinkin' right beside us."

Michael cast his gaze toward the slow moving waters of the river Tame. "I think I can remember the waves, Da. Did the ship bring us to Ashton?"

"Arrah, big ships can't come to Ashton, lad, only barges. So, the next day, the ship puts in at Liverpool. I never did see so many people, all jab-berin' and millin' about. 'Twas like Castlerea on a market day, only bigger. Your Ma was carryin' Mary Anne, and John was bringin' you. Margaret and me had Roderick and our few bundles. We pushed along the crowded quay, not knowin' where the divil we was goin'."

"So how did you find Ashton, Da?" asked Michael.

Pat chuckled in contemplation of the comic scene from the past and how woefully naive he had been about the wider world. "I seen this funny lookin' gent, a fat man with long gray whiskers and wearin' a beaver hat. And wasn't he full of the blather for any who'd listen?

"'Work to be had, work to be had,' he called, as he gave handbills to folk who passed.

"'What 'tis it that the papers say?' I ask. The bugger laughed at me."

"'Can't read, eh? If it's work you're looking for, Mick, I'm the man to see.'"

"So I says, 'Where is the work, and what must one do?'"

"'There's need for cotton workers in Lancashire,' says he. 'Those young ones of yours, they're just the right age to get on at the mill.'"

Michael looked up from his examination of a furry, black caterpillar. "In Ireland, a mill is where corn is ground for meal."

"So it is, son, so it is. But in England, a mill is where they make cloth with a grand loom. And in Lancashire, there must be more of them mills than freckles on your face. Anyway, I says to him, 'What wage are you talkin'?'"

"'Four and six, for the young ones,' says he. 'For you, maybe fifteen shillings as a warehouse man. Your wife may have eight and six as a twister or a warper.'"

"Sure, I had no idea what he was talkin'. But, I took his paper and we moved into the city lookin' for someplace to stay."

The sun was beginning to sink toward the horizon and the wind carried a chill. They had reached the end of the island and turned back to the canal bridge from whence they had come. Pat continued his story as they crossed over and headed back toward the city center.

"We was warned by folks on the ship, 'Don't be givin' no money to any what promises work or lodgin'! There's many a rascal who'll talk you out of your shillings. They'll run off, leavin' you with naught but your rosary.'"

Michael's face took on a serious expression. "Were you not afraid, Da, that the rascals might take your money?"

"I don't mind admittin' it, son. I was a bit fearful, bein' in the thick of all them English. But glory be to St. Patrick! There was Irish voices on me left and on me right! I think Liverpool holds near as many Irish as Dublin."

He laughed at the ironic justice of it, the English nearly outnumbered by the Irish in their midst.

"'Twasn't long before a kind soul gave us directions to the North Ward. We looked for shelter, but, ach, the lodgin's on offer wasn't fit for your grandmother's goat! We took a patch in a dark and smelly court cellar. 'Twas all covered with straw, and that in bad need of changin', I'll say. 'Twas a right enough place to catch the plague! We didn't stay no more than a few days."

Michael wrinkled his nose and looked at his father with puzzlement. "So how did we get to Ashton, Da?"

Pat stopped and removed his pipe. "I'm comin' to that part, boyo, give a man a chance!" He rapped the now exhausted pipe against the heel of his shoe. "So I meets a blowser in the pub, a cotton worker from Preston. He lost his job there, no doubt for his love of the craythur. But now, he says, he's after tryin' again."

They turned into Cavendish Street and began to climb the hill, their pace slowed by the incline and the horse droppings that littered the cobblestone way. "'Just pick a town from your paper,' the man tells me. He was a Donegal man, so I listened to him. I smooth me handbill on the bar, the one I got from that fat fella on the quay. I says, 'Can you read the list of mill towns to me?' 'Well,' he says, 'the first city on the list is Ashton-under-Lyne.' As 'twas no great distance from Liverpool, that's where we pointed."

"Did you work in the cotton mill, Da?" asked Michael, pulling his father by the hand toward Wellington Street and home.

"Oh, begorrah, no. There's no use for an old turf cutter like your Da in the mill itself. I'm too big for scuttlin' about 'neath the looms. And me fingers, they be little use in piecin' the threads. So I waltzed bales of cotton off the quay to the Grey Street Mill."

Pat's hands were rough and calloused after years of handling a spade in the turf pits and lazy beds of Cloonfower. Not long after arriving in Ashton, he turned to the less strenuous task of hawking hot tea and biscuits from a cart at the mill gates.

Number 34 Wellington Street was but another two-story clapboard building, such as hundreds of others in the mill quarter. Each floor was divided between two families and whatever lodgers they might take in to help defray the rent. These houses were rough and bare, though of fairly recent vintage. Avaricious landlords had thrown them together during the great influx of mill operatives from rural England and, later, those from

Ireland. These shanties compared favorably, however, to the hovels in which most of the Irish had previously lived.

When they reached the top of the Cavendish Street hill, the two stopped to catch their breaths. "Da, when can I go work in the mill? I'm near as big as Roderick and he's a piecer. I want to be a piecer too and bring me shillin's home."

"Ach, there's time enough for that, young man. Your mother needs your help at home, what with baby Catherine. 'Tis a long day for a cotton man, Michael. You rise when the factory whistle blows and you're down to the mill before six. And the foreman, he's always lookin' at you, wantin' it done quicker, always quicker. You'll be havin' none of that, lad, least till next year."

As they approached Wellington Street, the babble of many voices reached their ears. A crowd of neighbors could be seen gathered in the street in front of their home. Everyone seemed to be in full cry, fuming with loud complaints and epithets over something having to do with the Orange men.

"What's this?" Pat muttered as he took Michael's hand and pushed their way through the crowd. At its center were Cate and a rough-looking young boy of nine or ten years.

"Mother, are you all right? What's all the foosterin' about?"

Cate turned and sighed in relief at the sight of her husband. Then she smiled as Michael ran to her side. "Pat, will you be lookin' at who's here? 'Tis me own nephew, Roderick, Hugh's boy. He's come all the way from Cloonfower!"

Pat looked suspiciously at the youngster. "He looks like he was dragged here by a runaway horse. How'd you come all this way, boyo?"

"'Twas Castlerea folk what brought me, Uncle Pat," the Finan boy replied softly. "Sailed together on the boat from Sligo. They was goin' to Rochdale."

"Might I ask what's happened to you, as you look such a sorry sight?"

The dark-haired boy was bruised and bleeding, his clothes soiled and torn. He glanced at Cate.

"They was set upon, Pat, whilst in Liverpool! The whole party of them thrashed by the lads of the Orange Lodge! Why the poor souls left here just minutes ago," she said.

"We just happened on it, sir. All at once, 'twas cursin' and cuffs," Roderick added.

Cate threw an arm around her nephew. "You are safe and welcome here, lad. Come into the house and let's knock some dirt off you."

The neighbors' outrage at the infamous Protestant hooligans of the Orange Lodge gradually spent itself. After the Quinn family entered the house, the crowd slowly dispersed. Cate immediately went to the quarried stone fireplace at one end of the living area. There was a large, black iron pot of water hanging above a grate of glowing coals. She ladled hot water into a basin, dipped a rag and lathered it with much brown soap. She then performed a scrubbing upon her nephew such as only an Irish mother can give. When she was satisfied, the beleaguered boy was shining, red as an apple.

"How is it you've come this long way, Roderick?" asked Cate as she sat him down to the hot tea Margaret had prepared for the lot of them. Little Mary Ann climbed into her lap.

"Aye, and what news have you of Cloonfower?" Pat added.

The boy hung his head and paused for a second. He answered softly. "Me Da sent me to find you. I'm sorry, Aunt Cate, but 'tis sad news. Uncle Peter died of the fever last month."

"Jesus, Mary and Joseph!" Cate blessed herself with the sign of the cross and pressed her daughter to her bosom.

Pat dropped the lighted taper he was holding to his pipe. "Ach, no! Peter! . . . God rest his soul!"

Roderick stared into his tea and began to cry. After a moment, he continued in a choked-up voice.

"Da thought I should come to bring you word, knowin' how dear you was to each other."

Cate dabbed at tears with her flour-dusty apron. "Me own brother, dead and gone! And me not bein' with Nora at such a time! When I think of all they done for this poor family. . . ."

"'Tis the truth, Mother," said Pat as he remembered his finest friend of all. His blue-gray eyes were wet and a lump lodged in his throat.

The Finan boy looked apprehensively at Pat. "'Tis also Da's wish, if you agree, that I be stayin' with you, till I might find work. Things are quite desperate now in Cloonfower."

Pat had been pacing back and forth before the fireplace. Now he stopped and frowned. "And when were things not desperate in Cloonfower?"

He slumped into his chair and sighed heavily. "Don't worry lad, we're happy for you to stay. . . . But we've already one Roderick in this house, and some days that's more than enough. Startin' now, we'll be callin' you Roddy, so I can tell yous apart."

Pat's rechristening of his nephew was a necessity, for the boy was close to the same age as Roderick Quinn, then nine years. To confuse matters further, there was a distinct family resemblance between them as well.

Roddy got on as a doffer at the Oldham mill where his cousins were employed. He paid a share of his earnings to his hosts and sent the rest back to his family. This only intensified Michael's desire to join the world of work. But for now, there were still precious months of unfettered childhood remaining.

The natives of Ashton had long held a negative view of the Irish. Back in the late '40s, the starving and disease-ridden refugees arrived in droves, creating much resentment and occasional violent reaction. Though the ragged stream was now ebbing, the factories of Lancashire were booming, their maws hungry for cheap labor. At best, the English accorded these new-comers a cool civility. It was the landlords, factory owners, and publicans who were happy to profit from the Irish presence in their community.

One festive occasion, however, brought the entire community together. Each Easter Monday the Ashtonians celebrated the pilloring of the "Black Lad." This ancient ritual commemorated the infamous Sir Ralph Assheton, the feudal lord of the manor during the early 1400s. His serfs held Sir Ralph in great contempt for his exorbitant rents and the merciless measures he employed in collecting same. The pageant consisted of leading the effigy of an armored black knight on horseback in procession through the town to the old market cross. There the delighted crowd would tear it to pieces and burn the fragments.

In 1854, the festival provided an opportunity for Roderick Quinn to introduce this rite to Roddy and Michael. On the day, the threesome threaded their way through the crowded, cobbled streets, seeking a good vantage point from which to view the proceedings. First in Bow Street, and then in Penny Meadow, the boys hunted without success. Wherever they turned there were hordes of onlookers; hawkers with their meat pies, nuts, and sweets; and numerous unsupervised children. Fearing that the parade would pass them by, the threesome clambered up a stone wall near the market square. There they clung precariously to their perch and waited in excitement for the arrival of Black Lad.

The revelers were eager, and many boisterous with drink. Everyone strained for the best possible view. Roderick shifted his position atop the wall, dislodging a stone from the crumbling mortar. The chunk, about the size of a grapefruit, fell into the crowd, striking a large, rather drunken English workman.

"Bollocks!" The offended man, red with rage, looked up at his presumed assailant. "You rotten little scabby! Are you trying to kill me?"

He grabbed Roderick by the foot and jerked him to the ground and into the milling crowd.

Roderick, in great panic, shouted, " 'Twas an accident! I meant no harm!"

The laborer's eyes flashed. "He's Irish, the little bugger! I'll teach you not to pitch rocks at honest folk."

The man and his mates began to kick the boy repeatedly. Roddy and Michael looked on in disbelief. They jumped down from the wall and attempted to make their way to Roderick. But as they pressed their way, they too became the targets of shoves and cuffs from the jeering multitude. It was barely a few minutes till the city constables arrived, but it seemed to have passed in slow motion. Most bystanders stared at the brutal attack; none made any move to intervene. When the police finally pushed the crowd back, the three boys lay crumpled in the dirt, bleeding and crying, though Roderick had lost consciousness.

"Come along now, rascals! Black Lad or no, we'll have no breach of the peace, especially by you Irish bastards."

One constable led the way, throwing Roderick over his shoulder. His partner drove Roddy and Michael along through the cobblestone streets and off to the city jail.

It was hours before Pat was notified to come and collect his boys. A magistrate had been summoned to consider the charges. When the corpulent official arrived, it was clear the interruption of his holiday was most unwelcome.

His judicial costume comically askew, he climbed with difficulty to the bench and peered down at the whimpering transgressors.

The arresting constable addressed the magistrate. "Breach o' the peace, m'lord, and possible assault by the one."

Pat looked up from tending to the now-conscious Roderick. "Sure, m'lord, the boy meant no harm. 'Twas an accident as the lads tell it."

The magistrate sat back and thoughtfully pulled at his beard. "Mmm. They would do. Five pounds fine for each count. I'll reserve the assault charge. But, should I find any of you in my court again, it will be reinstated forthwith."

Pat was stunned, his mouth agape. "Fifteen pounds, m'lord! Faith, I'd be horrid rich if you was to find fifteen pounds upon me person. I'll be cadgin' me neighbors for to raise such a sum."

The magistrate, glancing at his pocket watch anxiously, paid little heed to Pat's plea. It was clear he wished to be elsewhere, and he was determined to avoid further delay. "The constable will accompany you to your home and collect the fine. If it isn't delivered promptly, the boys must be jailed till it's paid. This court stands adjourned."

Pat scraped together the fine, but it was weeks before Roderick could return to his duties at the mill. Roddy and Michael were luckier. They quickly recovered from their cuts and bruises. One night as Pat tucked Michael into his bed, the boy's anger flared over the incident.

"Da, I hate these English. When I grow up I should give them lumps like they gave Roderick."

Pat smiled ruefully at Michael's youthful bravado. "Ah, the English! They're the crown of thorns upon the Irish people, son. But you mustn't return evil for evil, Michael."

But the boy wasn't listening. A lasting, bitter taste of the English would now pervade his thinking. After this experience, every ethnic insult, every minor injustice, fueled a deep hostility within him.

Throughout the spring, Michael pestered for permission to join the older children in the cotton mill. "I'm eight and a half now, Da. Most lads me age are already doffin' at the mills. Even girls make a wage, whilst I make none. 'Tisn't fair at all."

When he left the room, Cate put down the sock she was darning and turned to her husband. "We could use the extra shillings, Pat. Perhaps we should let Michael do his part. Mary Ann has become a good little helper with baby Catherine now."

Pat looked up in exasperation. Jaysus, 'twas for her sake entirely I've been holdin' the lad back. If she can now part with him, why am I to be badgered to death?

He called Michael and the barefoot boy padded silently back to his father's chair by the hearth. Pat thought he looked too young by half for mill work, barely filling the hand-me-down shirt and trousers he wore. With a glum face of dejection, Michael braced himself for another speech about "one day."

"All right, young man. Your ma and me have spoken on it. If you come with me tomorrow, I'll be takin' you down to Oldham. We'll see if they'll have you at all."

A smile quickly dispatched Michael's frown and his eyes reignited with delight. He rushed forward and threw his arms around Pat's neck nearly knocking the pipe from his father's teeth. "Oh, Da! Thank you! I must go tell Roderick and Roddy!" Before Pat could respond, the boy was out the door and on his way.

Michael's first visit to the Oldham Mill was an amazement to him. Of course, he had seen the outside of the factory many times, as he awaited his brothers and sister at the end of their workday. It was easy then to view their work as an adventure, an entry into grown-up affairs. When they described their duties as relentless drudgery, he naively passed it off. It was as if he were being told that biscuits were not tasty.

The Oldham mill, between Stamford and Fleet Streets, was of 1790s vintage, relatively small though constructed in four stories. In England, Michael's age was no barrier to the ten-hour workday prescribed by law for the women and children of the textile industry. Though a far cry from the unregulated conditions at nearby collieries, the mills offered their own taste of hell for the laborers.

Michael's older brother gave him an orientation to the facility several days before the start of his employment. John, fifteen years of age, was a handsome boy with a straight nose and a strong chin, who wore his brown hair combed straight back. He felt especially protective of his brother, indeed of all his siblings, ever since he succeeded James as the eldest son.

John started their visit down at the quay. "Now, Michael, be payin' attention. Here is where the cotton arrives from America." Large bales of cotton wrapped in burlap and iron bands stood before them beside the canal.

"'Twas here that Da worked when we first came to Ashton," Michael noted proudly.

"So it was. Now, after the cotton is moved to the mill, the baggin' is removed. Then they run it through a pickin' machine what takes out leaves, seeds, and such."

They walked up the hill to Fleet Street and entered the mill through a side door, into the dimly lit carding room. A shaft of afternoon sunlight streamed through the doorway, illuminating the airborne particles of fiber, turning them to gold dust.

"This machine has sharp metal tines," shouted John above the din of the carding machines. "They pull the cotton into long, smooth strands. But only the brave or the stupid work here!"

"Why is that, John?" Michael shouted back. "'Tis very loud and dirty, but so is all the mill."

John held up his hands before him. "'Tis the fingers, hands and arms that are lost here, lad. One mistake among those tines and this place looks like the back of the butcher's shop. You'll never find me workin' here!"

They climbed a grimy wooden staircase and entered a large room full of spinning bobbins and long rope-like lengths of cotton fiber.

"'Tis so hot in here, John. How do you stand it all day?"

"They put steam in the air," John explained. "'Tis necessary that the thread and yarn not be breakin' all the time."

Michael noticed that many of the workers were young girls, each with her hair tied up tightly under a kerchief. "To prevent their hair from being caught among the pulleys and leather belts powering the frames," John explained.

Michael blinked in disbelief. "Can one really do?"

"Aye. It used to happen all the time. Some was killed of it too. Now the company insists on the kerchief, and short beards for the men!"

They passed long rows of drawing frames, one after another. "The cotton slivers coiled in these cans will be rolled again and again to reduce their thickness. After several goes of pullin' and twistin', the slivers is called rovin' and is ready for the final spinnin'. That's where Margaret is."

They crossed the building and entered a separate room. Michael gaped in amazement at the maze of moving machinery and fiber. Spinning rapidly from bobbin to bobbin, yarn was lengthened and twisted into a thread ready for the loom. Margaret was working this day, but was not on hand when they entered. As they turned to leave, she came around the corner from a line of spinning frames, nearly colliding with her brothers. She was a short, somewhat plain-faced girl of nineteen. She, too, had her hair tied up under a kerchief. Her threadbare, blue smock was covered with oil stains and dirt.

"So, Michael, 'tis' a cotton man you're wantin' to be, is it?" She cupped his cheeks in her dirty hands and planted a big kiss on his forehead. They spoke briefly till Margaret, remembering her place, turned a glance toward her supervisor and scurried away. "Got to be off," she called in her wake.

As Margaret disappeared, the supervisor crossed the room to investigate this presence of unannounced visitors. His face betrayed his irritation. A tall, lean man with thinning hair, he had been at Oldham for thirty years. John introduced Michael and explained his imminent assignment as doffer.

This position, typically filled by young children, involved the removal of bobbins that had been filled with thread in the spinning room, and their replacement with empties. Crates of bobbins, both empty and full, also had to be moved to and from the spinning room to enable a continuous flow of work.

As they began to move away, the man caught Michael by the galluses. "Be sure to apply yourself, lad. Your brothers can testify, my standards are exacting. But, if you do what you're told, we'll have little commerce between us."

Michael nervously swallowed, "Yes, sir." He was uneasy about working under this stern fellow. He would have to walk a narrow line indeed. Still, he figured he could do as well as Roderick or Roddy had done before him. The supervisor looked up, peering out over his spectacles. Had he heard the slightest change in the rhythm of machine noise? John and Michael chose this as the opportune moment to take their leave.

Again they climbed a staircase, this one leading to the weaving area. If Michael found the carding and spinning rooms noisy, this room was nearly ear-splitting with the clatter of the looms. The reed arm banged the filling yarn tight within the warp. Harnesses, controlling the pattern of the weave, rose and fell with a dull *click-clack*. The shuttle skittered back and forth across the loom, from impact to impact. A low rumble came from the network of drives, gears, pulleys and belts that powered the machinery.

An ever-present cloud of dust and fibers accompanied this crescendo of noise. The lint-covered workers nearly gagged in their efforts to breathe, and found it necessary to spit frequently to clear their throats. Respiratory illnesses were the typical reward for long service in the textile mills.

"Before weavin'," John shouted, "warp threads, thicker and stronger than the filling threads, must be wound on those large wooden drums. They will feed a whole cloth's width into the loom. In weavin', there be none of us Irish, save for oilers, sweepers, and piecers. The weavers, and them what repair the looms, is paid the best wages. These must be English."

Michael nodded his understanding without comment. Such discrimination was so pervasive throughout English society, it carried little shock value to the Irish workers. Nevertheless, Michael subconsciously tallied such affronts with his negative perceptions of the British.

John, Roderick and Roddy were employed as piecers. Whenever a thread broke, the loom or spinning frame had to be shut down immediately. The piecer would mend the break as quickly as possible to allow the spinner or weaver to return his machine to operation. Since all employees were paid based upon the units produced, quickness and dexterity were essential. In a year or two, Michael could expect to attain the piecer's role and increase his earnings accordingly. For now, learning to doff bobbins in the spinning room would be challenge enough. At least Margaret would be there, he thought, to look out for him.

In addition to becoming a textile worker, Michael embarked upon a second new experience that spring. By government regulation all textile workers between the ages of eight and fourteen had to be released to attend school for two hours per day. Through the years, employers frequently and easily evaded this law. In some instances though, compliance was frustrated by the lack of schools available to the Irish immigrants. Most of the schools in England adhered to the tenets of the Church of England. No good Catholic would venture to, nor be welcomed at, such a school. And Catholic schools were rare.

Such was the condition that prevailed in Ashton until 1852, when Father John Quealy founded St. Ann's chapel and schoolroom in Newman Street. Now Ashton mill owners had no excuse but to release their Catholic child laborers for schooling. Margaret and John Quinn had benefited but briefly. They were now too old to be embraced by the schooling law. Michael, however, joined Roderick and Roddy at St. Ann's each weekday afternoon.

Cate Quinn was returning from Market Hall one morning. She was accompanied by Michael who assisted her with the shopping bundles. Cate was still a pleasant-looking woman, though now more matronly. Flecks of gray in her auburn hair betrayed her years of hard work, even though she had avoided service in the mills. As they passed through St. Michael's Square, they paused to rest on a bench before proceeding along Stamford Street. Cate sat and adjusted her skirts, happy to be off her feet for a few minutes. Michael chased a pigeon briefly, and then took a seat beside his mother.

"Ma, why must I go to school?"

"Michael Quinn!" She frowned at her son. "'Tis a fine thing to be educated! Your father and meself haven't a lick of learnin' between us, and sorry we are for that. 'Tis our shame that Margaret or John must be readin' for your father and meself."

"But did you and Da not go to school when you were young?"

"Glory be, child! We had no school in Castlerea. Such was only for Protestant children. The English lords took our schools from us ages ago."

Michael's eyes narrowed and his jaw set tight at this revelation.

"Now you and Roderick will learn to read and cipher and become educated young men," Cate said.

"The English have their education, Ma. What's so good about them?"

"Sure, there's many educated people in this world besides the English, young man. 'Tis not education what spoils the English."

Cate said this in a matter-of-fact tone, betraying no emotion on the subject to her son. She collected her packages and handed some to Michael. "Besides, when you are schooled, you may find proper work away from these dirty mills. Come now, let's be off for home."

Chapter Four

Famine Again

✠

The next few years brought many changes for the Quinn family and for the Irish community in Ashton. In the spring of 1856, Cate was expecting her eighth child. One evening sitting beside the fire, she interrupted her mending. "Pat, we need to be findin' a larger house, what with the new one comin' and all."

Pat frowned and silently busied himself with his clay pipe. He was a cautious man in matters of money.

"And you'll know," Cate said, "Margaret is a grown woman. She's due a bit of privacy in a house full of young men. . . . Perhaps we can afford a bit more rent, what with six puttin' shillin's in the pot. Don't you think so?"

He was at a loss to challenge her logic. "You make a good point, Mother."

Cate was waiting for more than rhetorical agreement. "Pat!"

He nearly fell out of his chair at this unaccustomed challenge. He raised his hands in surrender. "Enough! I'll make me a search this week and see what's on offer. The mill quarter is always crowded. Still, you never know what a clever fellow might be findin'," he said with a wink.

Cate smiled with satisfaction and resumed her sewing. "Thank you, dear."

A search was undertaken and shortly thereafter a more suitable residence was found, four blocks south at No. 58 Church Street. The move placed them within the newly established St. Mary's Parish. And it was there, in October, that the Quinn's last child, Elizabeth, was christened.

A considerable boom in the textile industry marked the next few years. For several decades, cloth had been the single largest export of the British economy. For raw material, American cotton was preferred due to its excellent quality. Indeed, the factory machines of Lancashire were specially tooled to utilize this grade of cotton. But events in America were about to disrupt this commercial symbiosis.

With the 1861 outbreak of the rebellion in America, President Lincoln imposed a naval blockade upon the Confederate states. The effect of this blockade was to interrupt the flow of American cotton, thus devastating the textile industry in England. While alternative sources of cotton existed in Egypt and India, these proved far inferior to the American product. Furthermore, their use would require the retooling of much of the textile machinery. The mill owners of Lancashire preferred to await a presumed early victory by the Confederate States of America. What came to be known in England as the "Cotton Famine" now began, and cotton workers by the thousands were made idle as the factories closed. Ashton-under-Lyne was hit particularly hard.

In the Quinn household, fourteen-year-old Michael, an experienced piecer at the Oldham Mill, found himself and his siblings unemployed. John eventually secured work with a government relief project, constructing drainage facilities in low-lying areas. Pat still had his hawker's cart, though he could no longer focus on the mill workers for clientele. Rather, he began selling housewares door-to-door in Ashton and nearby Stalybridge. Margaret became a cleaner at T. Brownson, the tailor and clothier at Old Square. But their collective efforts were still insufficient to replace the lost earnings.

In contrast to its posture during the potato famine in Ireland, the British government undertook, in Lancashire, substantial relief efforts. It eventually ordered cash payments to the destitute through local Relief Unions. While the payments were modest, and though levels of want and misery rose very high, starvation was averted.

One evening in September of that year, Michael accompanied John, Roderick, and Roddy to the Old Thatch Tavern in Littlemoss, a district northwest of their own neighborhood. The boys walked west along the Manchester Road, querying John about the gathering to which they were embarked.

Seventeen-year-old Roderick was the first to press for details. "So, John, are you goin' to tell us more about this meetin'?"

"Aye, and why 'twas necessary to keep it a secret from Da," added Michael.

"Arrah, I'll tell Da when I'm able," John answered impatiently. "Sure, I don't know a great deal yet meself. Me friends are after talkin' about it for a week now. 'Tis a society for the Irish called the National Brotherhood of St. Patrick. They'll be explainin' all about it tonight."

Old Thatch Tavern (Courtesy of Mr. Gary Jones, Littlemoss, Droylsden, UK)

It was nearly eight when they arrived at Littlemoss. The tavern was, in fact, a thatched building with whitewashed brick walls, built to look like a country cottage. John spoke to a man at the door and he waved them in. They stepped inside a room resounding of Irish brogue and thick with clouds of pipe smoke. The main room had a long bar on one side, and though tables and chairs normally would be scattered about, tonight the space had been specially arranged for the meeting. Tables were pushed aside to make room for rows of battered chairs. The latter were supplemented with improvised benches, boards laid across standing ale casks. The young men selected such a bench near the back of the room and waited somewhat self-consciously while the older patrons gradually migrated from the bar to their seats. The room was soon filled, and the air stunk of sweat, smoke and slops of ale.

"Look, Roddy, there's Mister Monahan from Oldham," Michael said.

"Aye, there's several from the mill here. I've seen others from the parish as well," his cousin replied.

Roderick and John surveyed the crowd, watching for the arrival of the speaker. Three well-dressed men, obviously organizers of the meeting, soon passed through the assembly to a table placed at the far end of the barroom. Among them was a large, impressive man in a black frock coat, looking somewhat more prosperous and important than his colleagues.

"That's him, I'll wager, the man from the Brotherhood," John said with an air of authority.

As the room was unbearably hot, the man removed his coat and collar. He stood in his white shirtsleeves and waited for a hush to fall upon his audience. Thick black hair and a short graying beard complemented his powerful frame, all producing a commanding presence sufficient to bring the boisterous gathering to order.

"Jaysus, will somebody open another window or two," he began. Chairs scraped the floor as several men sprang to respond. "Me name is Will Cleary. I'm come from Manchester to enlist you men in the National Brotherhood of St. Patrick. This Brotherhood was established last spring in Dublin. 'Tis our aim to unite all Irish men in the cause of independence for our native land."

A round of huzzahs welcomed the reference to what was already a popular cause within the Irish exile community. An old fellow in the front row raised his hand. "'Tis a Catholic organization then?"

"I don't care if you are Catholic, or Church of England, or Church of nothin' at all," Cleary replied. "If you be Irish and love your country, we'll take you."

The hard-bitten workers chuckled at his irreverent attitude and jeered the questioner. Cleary continued. "But to progress our goal, we must first educate all Irishmen to our country's plight. You should be knowin' somethin' of Ireland's history and culture, 'fore the Brits did their best to destroy it. Only when you know what's been lost can you judge the crime. You must feel the torment inflicted upon our people 'fore you'll be truly committed to the struggle."

A voice from the bar interrupted Cleary again. "You're not goin' to send us old fools to school, are you?"

The crowd erupted with laughter. The Quinn boys were enjoying themselves immensely. Cleary grinned and scratched at the stubble on his chin. He was visibly relaxed, seemingly ready to trade banter with the most obdurate audience. "Not at all! Not at all! Far be it from me to inflict such a burden as you on the young ones and their schoolmasters."

Another peal of laughter swept the barroom. A constant flow of audience moved from their seats to the bar and back again as empty glasses did dictate.

"No, what I'm talkin' is the establishment, here in Ashton, of a place where you can come to listen to the Irish press and speakers on Irish history, culture and politics. 'Twill be a center of learning providing unity and, eventually, strength."

Another laborer stood, his pinched face and apprehensive expression betraying a caution that he now voiced. "The Crown will be comin' down hard on them which is caught in secret societies and incitin' rebellion."

A chorus of boos and rude gestures greeted this ill-judged remark and its owner shrank back into his chair. Cleary raised his hands, palms out, and hushed the crowd. "Now, now. You'll not be asked to take a secret oath. Neither will you be breachin' any law. What you'll be asked to do is to support our cause, with your voices and your pennies. The monies collected will be to support your local branch and provide a bit of relief for them which are starvin' back in Ireland."

A grumble of misgivings signaled a shift in mood among the listeners. The inevitable objection was now raised above the din. "So how much do you want paid? There may be hard times in Ireland, but we've hard times of our own here in Ashton."

Cleary had known this issue would be the great obstacle he must overcome. "The joinin' fee be 6 p. After, 'tis 1p a week. Sure, such payments will not be easy, but there be no way forward without cost. If you can't afford the fees, then get together and share the burden, supportin' delegates from among you. These can represent your interests and provide you with the information."

There was much discussion and debate within his audience. Cleary quickly shifted the focus from matters of organization to Ireland's misfortunes at the hands of its British masters. This part of his story played well among the exiles. Their memories of famine and eviction were still fresh and bitter. Now that the Cotton Famine had come to Lancashire, they could see how generous was the relief on the cards for English workers. Such relief had been previously denied to the Irish during their Great Hunger.

By the end of the evening, Cleary had brought folks back to a level of substantial support, if not universal enthusiasm. The Quinn boys were sold on the Brotherhood and the just cause of Irish independence from Britain. Their conversation on the way home was buoyant, emotional, and occasionally heated. To the amusement of the others, Michael was the most agitated by what he had heard. "That fellow, Cleary, made me blood boil with his tales of how the Brits have had their way with our people for six hundred years."

"Aye, though he never did say what the Brotherhood would actually do about it," Roddy said.

Roderick brought it down to practicalities. "'Tis all well for us to pledge our support, but there's no way for us to be payin' such dues when three of us have no work."

"Just the reason why I did not wish to tell Da," John said. "I could pay the dues from me wages, but he'll be missin' me pennies, sure."

Mindful of the late hour, the boys hurried now through the gaslit streets. It was almost eleven when they filed through the door, apprehensive that trouble lay ahead. Pat and Cate were sitting in near darkness before the fire, waiting to confront them over their unauthorized absence. Though John was old enough to come and go as he pleased, the younger ones were clearly beyond their curfew.

Pat jumped to his feet and fixed them squarely with angry eyes. "And where might you lads be spendin' your evenin' just now?"

The collective gaze of the younger three fell upon John. After all, it had been his decision to maintain the secrecy of their mission this night.

John shifted his weight from one foot to the other as he weighed how defensive to be with his parents. Finally he decided to proclaim his mission proudly, without remorse. "We've been to a meetin' of the National Brotherhood of St. Patrick."

An impatient frown covered Cate's face. "I have never heard of such a society. No doubt you spent your time offerin' prayers to St. Patrick himself."

The boys laughed nervously at her sarcasm. John described the character of the meeting so as to appeal to his father's sympathies for all things pro-Irish and anti-British. He carefully skirted the issue of the requisite financial obligations. But to his chagrin, that detail was easily extracted from Michael.

Appearing to be slightly mollified, Pat sat down and looked at his boys. "Listen to your Da. I'm for Ireland's freedom as much as any old mick in Lancashire. 'Tis shameful our people are used so poorly by their British lords. And 1p each week would be worth the sacrifice if the Brotherhood could actually pull the splinter from our arse. But divil if I'll see me sons breachin' the law, and findin' themselves in jail."

John placed his hands upon his head in frustration, as if hostility might rain down from the heavens any minute. "Da, 'tis no breach of law—"

Wham! Pat pounded his fist upon the table for emphasis. "Enough! Your mother and I have lost one son already! By all 'tis holy, we shan't be losin' another!"

John saw a shudder pass through his mother at this allusion to James. Somewhat chastened, he tried again in a voice more pleading than before. "Da, there was no talk of insurrection! This fellow Cleary, he was altogether agin it—though the Brits deserve whatever mischief we can put on their plate."

Michael grinned at the remark till his mother flashed him a cross look. Rising from her chair, she turned her glare back to John. "You dismiss a whole people in a blink of the eye, don't you, boyo?"

Everyone was struck by this unexpected sentiment from the one person in the house who was usually so mild-mannered. She continued with passion, approaching him and waving her finger in his face.

"I've seen all manner of these English, in Ireland and here in Ashton. I've learned that there's good Brits and bad, just like there's good Irish and some that'd make Cromwell blush with shame."

John, still feeling the ire that Cleary fired within him, was defiant. "I've yet to meet the Brit that I'm happy to drink with."

"Then you've not met Uncle John, the pieman up on Market Street," Cate replied, her tone as determined as ever. "He feeds hungry Irish families from his kitchen and nary the bob he takes for it. 'Tis his own Christian charity!"

"I'll drink with such a man any day," Pat said rising again, this time to go to bed. "Now you lads be off with you! We've lost enough sleep on you for one night."

Cate turned away and added, "And don't you be wakin' the little ones, neither!"

The family storm dissipated in a few days. Pat reluctantly agreed that John might allocate the pennies required, and soon John was enrolled in the Brotherhood. But it was Michael who, among the others in the family, took greatest interest in the affairs of the society. He was easily incensed by the anti-British stories John recounted from the nationalist newspapers, such as the *United Irishman* and the *Connaught Patriot*. One such cause célèbre that year was an undertaking of the Brotherhood called St. Patrick's Pence. It provided funds to Irish peasants who faced destitution and a cynical proselytizing by some in the British-sponsored Church of Ireland. By this scheme, they were offered food, but only if they agreed to convert from their Catholic faith.

In the months that followed, the members of the Brotherhood learned the history of the Irish missionaries that brought the Christian faith and Greco-Roman learning to Saxon Britain and to many other European countries at the end of the Dark Ages. Further, they learned of the duplicity of the English, their violation of truces and their murder of Irish delegates invited to their "peace" negotiations. Speakers described the rape of the country by Oliver Cromwell, and the Penal period when Catholic worship was outlawed and priests were hunted like animals. They were reminded of the British government's indifference to its starving Irish subjects during the famine years. However, to be fair, they also admitted the shameful disunity among the Irish and the too-frequent betrayals by their own.

In the spring of 1862, the Brotherhood suffered a body blow when the Catholic bishops issued a ban on the National Brotherhood of St. Patrick. They argued it was a secret society fomenting revolution against the Crown. Refutations offered by the Brotherhood were dismissed out of hand. In Britain, the predominantly English Catholic clergy resented the competition for the affections and financial contributions of their flock. In

Ireland, the Brotherhood was in conflict with the Irish hierarchy's strategy of surviving through accommodation with British colonialism.

One night in May, John returned from a Brotherhood meeting in considerable despair. He quietly entered the house, finding only fifteen-year-old Michael awake and waiting to greet him at the late hour. "Are you up so late, young man? You'll have sand in your eyes in the mornin'."

Michael, dressed in his nightshirt, sat up in bed, appearing eager for details from his brother. "Ah, I just want to hear all about tonight's meetin'. What news is there from Dublin?"

John took off his coat and sat on the edge of Michael's bed. They spoke softly to avoid waking the others. "There's not much worth tellin', lad. The turnout for tonight's meetin' was very poor again. Them what came spent all their time fightin' among themselves."

"A typical Irish gatherin' you might say," Michael joked, obviously trying to raise his brother's spirits.

"Some are still complainin' the dues are too high, whilst others say they'll attend no more for the ban by the church. Some of us are unhappy that all we do is talk, whilst Ireland is no closer to independence. Most of me friends, they're not to be bothered anymore."

John stood and looked down at Michael, whose sad eyes seemed to be apologizing for the lack of fidelity among the others. "We're all tired of just talkin' independence," the boy agreed.

John began to undress for bed. "I've no fear for what the Church says about the Brotherhood. Our clergy has always done a better job of buryin' the Irish than helpin' them stay alive and free." In frustration, he threw his shirt, sweaty and smelling of tobacco smoke, into a corner. "'Tis so pointless, when all is talk and we've no results to show!"

Michael left his bed, his nightshirt flappin at knobby knees. He countered, "Someday, I'll join the Brotherhood, too! We'll not forsake the Irish people, will we?"

John mussed his brother's hair. "Right you are, lad. Now you be off to sleep." He pinched the candle and went to sit before the ashen memory of the kitchen fire.

John's spirits stayed low over the next few weeks. It wasn't solely the problems with the Brotherhood. Nothing seemed to be going right as far as he was concerned. Sometimes he'd snap at the most innocent comment or query. The whole family noticed, but nary a word was said in hopes this moodiness would pass.

Cate told her husband, "John's feeling the pinch, livin' as a bachelor in a house full of younger brothers and sisters. He's twenty-two years old! 'Tis time he made a family of his own."

Finally, John's situation cracked like an egg forced open by its newborn chick. One day in June, he came home from work early. Pat was off hawking his wares, and the older children were out of the house. Cate encountered him as he came through the door, his shirt torn and his eye blackened and swollen.

"Mother of God! What happened to you?"

John slumped into a chair at the kitchen table where his mother sat peeling potatoes. He explored his eye gingerly with his fingertips. "I lost me job. That bloody foreman, Applegate! He finally pushed me too far! I've told you how he enjoys makin' it hard on the Irish navvies. Today, he was in fine form, orderin' us about, callin' us dirty micks, and criticizin' our every task. By the time he came crabbin' on me, I'd had enough. When the lads finally separated us, we was both the worse for it. But I got dismissed."

Cate held her head in her hands. "Oh, John, how could you? You had your satisfaction, but that relief work was a big piece of the family's wages!"

He placed his hand on her arm. His fury spent, remorse overtook him.

"I'm sorry, Ma. I'm usually able to laugh off such as Applegate. But lately, I'm feelin' like I'm goin' daft. 'Tis like I'm one of them caged animals we seen at the fair at Daisy Nook. I didn't mean to put another burden on you and Da."

When Patrick arrived home and heard the news, he just muttered, "Divil!" Otherwise, he held his tongue. A morose silence prevailed at supper that evening, till it was broken by Roderick who unexpectedly pointed the way.

"If 'twas me, John, I'd be off to America. They got bags of work there for them what wants it. Of course, I know you'd be missin' the joys of livin' under the Crown. . . ."

John laughed out loud for the first time in weeks. "There's an idea. I could go to America!"

Margaret gasped and sputtered angrily, her eyes welling up with tears. "Aye, they've work in America, and war as well!"

With that, she abandoned her meal and fled from the room, and Cate hurried in her wake, obviously to console her daughter. The others looked at each other with puzzled surprise.

Over the next few days, John rolled the intriguing idea of America over and over in his mind. Then one evening, he announced his decision to his parents. "Da, I've decided I'll be goin' to America." Though he saw a look of shock on his mother's face, he continued. "Of course, I'll be sendin' me savin's to you and Ma so you shan't be hurt for long. 'Tis time for me to be leavin' home anyway. Sure, you can use the space here. The young 'uns are growin' so fast."

"Oh, John. You musn't be leavin' on our account," Cate pleaded. "I can't abide the idea of you bein' off in a strange country, and us never seein' you again."

John looked to his father for support.

Pat put down his pipe and addressed John gently. "Son, you're a grown man. You come and go as you see fit. America is a long journey, and not without its dangers. I've also heard there have been agents here from the American mills, but they're only lookin' for weavers and loom mechanics."

"Aye, Da. But where they want weavers, you'll find spinners and piecers as well. I'm happy that I'll find work."

"Of course, the decision must be your own."

Cate started to speak but was silenced by a look of caution from her husband.

John could not have articulated his deeper feelings, even to himself. But in his heart he knew America was the key to finding his own way forward. Roderick and Roddy championed the idea and would have gone too, if allowed. But Margaret was still dead-set against John's leaving, afraid, she said, that he might die, and angry at him for "turning his back on the family."

It was the end of June 1862 when John left Ashton-under-Lyne for Liverpool and then New York. He knew from the industrial recruiters that the textile centers in America were in New England. His own savings were supplemented by his father. This amount would cover the cost of passage and a few weeks' living expenses.

"Don't you be worryin', Margaret," John whispered in her ear as he bid goodbye one night. "I'll not be fightin' no war over there."

With Michael, he offered further consolation. "'Tisn't goodbye forever, I'm thinkin', lad. If the good Lord gives me luck, I'll not be the only one of us off to America. If not, perhaps I'll return. Either way, I'm sure we'll be together again."

Silent tears ran down Michael's cheek, but John was embarrassed at such open displays of emotion. All he could do was place his hand on the boy's shoulder. "When the time comes," he added, "you must take my place in the Brotherhood. We'll always have that between us."

The next morning, he was gone.

Michael was crestfallen. He idolized John, his ideas, his participation in the Brotherhood, and his courage in resisting his browbeating English foreman. Embarrassed to cry openly, Michael saved his grief for nighttime, when he privately mourned the loss of his hero.

Chapter Five

Amanda

✠

Life in Ashton gradually settled back into a routine for the Quinn family. During the time since the textile mills had been closed, Michael and his younger siblings were free to attend St. Mary's parochial school on a full-time basis. Michael was approaching the age of sixteen and would soon complete the modest curriculum, as had Roddy and Roderick. He was acquiring rudimentary skills in reading and in doing sums, but his enthusiasm for school fell well below his mother's expectations.

The necessary mixing with the native English children was part of his antipathy toward school. The English students, though fewer in number, were typically better dressed and better fed than the Irish. Given his unhappy exposures to the English, and the negative image of them portrayed by the Brotherhood, Michael kept his distance, as did his Irish classmates.

But his resolve in this regard was threatened by the arrival of Miss Amanda Robinson, whose family had recently moved to Ashton from Birmingham. Michael was completely unhinged by Amanda's beauty. He watched her frequently during class, admiring her long light brown hair and her smooth golden complexion. She stood out prominently among the pale, freckled Irish girls. She had dark brown eyes and a small, slightly pouty mouth. Though only fifteen, she had a fine figure that drew attention from all the boys.

Michael's dilemma was further compounded when she was assigned to his reading group. When she was first called upon to read a passage from their text, her unmistakable English accent hit Michael like a splash of cold water. How could this goddess of the glen come besmirched with the wrong nationality? His mind tried to dismiss her, but his eyes and his heart would not take supervision. Visions of Amanda intruded upon his every waking moment. No words passed between them and, as far as Michael knew, his glances went unnoticed.

One day after class had been dismissed, Michael was asked to take his turn replenishing the inkwells. From the schoolroom window, he noticed Amanda leaving, somewhat delayed in joining her girlfriends as they headed for Stamford Street. As she hurried to catch up, she tripped and fell in a sprawl across the hard-packed dirt of the schoolyard. Michael was transfixed. He had watched her run and he had seen her fall. There was no adult on hand at the moment, only himself and the few young children at play.

Michael rushed from the schoolhouse, but approached Amanda cautiously, as if she were a wounded, yet dangerous, animal. With all his heart, he wanted to scoop her into his arms and kiss away each scratch and scrape. He knelt beside her, but he couldn't make himself reach out to touch her. A muffled sob passed her lips.

He gently whispered to her. "Are you all right? 'Twas a terrible fall. Shall I call Sister?" He looked at her crumpled form. Her dress was smudged with the brown dirt of the schoolyard. He couldn't help staring at her legs, which though covered modestly in stockings, were fully displayed in her dishevelment.

Amanda raised her head with great effort, her senses returning with their burden of pain. She pulled herself up into a sitting position and looked at her inquisitor. As her vision cleared and Michael's face came into focus, she saw tears tracking down his cheeks. His expression was one of tormented compassion. She recognized him now—tall for his age and skinny, like most of the boys in class, with light brown hair, a strong jaw, a straight thin mouth, and eyes of blue.

Hurried footsteps approached. The click of oversized rosary beads beating against one another announced the arrival of Sister Mary Magdalene. She pushed Michael aside and proceeded to give aid and comfort. "Ach, you poor, misfortunate child. Come inside, and let's give those scrapes a bit of water. Can you walk at all, dearie?"

Michael stood back and watched them disappear into the school. He felt so stupid that he had been helpless in the moment of crisis. With sadness and self-reproach, he walked slowly up the Wellington Road. Glancing back toward school for a moment, he turned and disappeared into Oldham Road.

In the school days that followed, Michael noticed his once secret glances were being returned. Embarrassed at being caught out, he would look away and pretend to be simply surveying his surroundings. In time, however, there were moments of shared fixation ending with a shy smile from each.

Michael became distracted and jumpy as he anticipated that somehow he might find himself in conversation with the beautiful Amanda. He was daydreaming a lot and his appetite was off. Never hugely expressive, Michael turned back all queries and pretended that the earth had not shaken beneath him.

As the end of the school term approached, Michael was becoming desperate. Once he completed his studies, there would be no obvious way to meet Amanda, and he hadn't a clue as to where she lived. He had to act soon. But he still hadn't devised a satisfactory strategy. As is often the case in such matters, the female had to take charge.

One day after class, Amanda stopped by Michael's seat as the students filed out. "I believe you dropped this," she said as she handed him a bit of folded paper and then continued out the door.

Michael was gobsmacked. He knew he hadn't dropped anything. He stuffed the paper into his trouser pocket and hurried outside. As he passed into Stamford Street, he sought out a quiet spot. The note was fairly burning up in his pocket. He sat on the steps beside St. Michael's Church and pulled out the note.

> *"Michael Quinn, I would welcome a few moments to speak*
> *with you. If you are agreeable, meet me at the boathouse on*

Crime Lake, in Daisy Nook. I shall be there Saturday from one o'clock. Amanda Robinson."

He couldn't believe it was happening. His mouth felt dry. He reread the note over and over to be sure he wasn't imagining this turn of fortune. He knew the venue. Several times he had attended the Easter Fair at Daisy Nook with his family. Indeed, it was not far from Littlemoss, where the Brotherhood meetings were held.

Waiting for Saturday was the challenge. When it did come, Michael made himself scarce after breakfast so as to avoid queries or household chores. He marked his time with a few friends till past noon, when he offered them an excuse and departed. He turned the corner and walked hurriedly up the Manchester Road.

What ruse had Amanda devised to get free of her family? What would she say and how should he respond? It was nearly one o'clock when he reached the boathouse. It was a white, two-story, Tudor-style

Crime Lake (Ashton-under-Lyne and Mossley, *1995 The Chalford Publishing Company)*

structure, with exposed wooden beams and braces. She hadn't yet arrived, which he proved to himself by circumnavigating the building three times. It was a pleasant day, though none too warm when the scudding clouds blocked the sun. Ten minutes passed before he saw her approaching along the path beside the lake.

She was with someone! A girl of about the same age, chatting away in animated fashion, walked beside Amanda. As they neared the boathouse, the two parted. Amanda waved goodbye to her companion who stifled a giggle.

Without thinking, Michael blurted, "Who's your friend?"

Amanda frowned and placed her hands on her hips. "A gentleman would say hello or wish one good day on first meeting. But if you must know, that's my cousin, Melanie. She and I were given permission to come to the park together. She will read quietly under some tree till 2:30 when she will collect me to go home."

Michael grimaced and struggled to gain a semblance of social grace. "Sorry, Miss. I am happy to see you and meant no disrespect."

Amanda dropped her reproaching demeanor. "Oh, Michael, I know you didn't. And I am glad to see you too. Ever since the day I fell, I have been curious about you and how it was that you cried for me."

He looked down, embarrassed at being confronted for his tears. "Did I really cry, Miss? I was ever so sorry for your trouble."

"Please do call me Amanda." She smiled mischievously. "Perhaps your pity also causes you to look my way frequently in class?"

Michael broke into a shy smile as well. "Yes, Miss. I mean no, Miss—I mean Amanda. Sure, lookin' at you is not difficult."

They walked, and gradually Michael's panic subsided. He stole side-glances at her; at her yellow dress, so clean and free of wrinkles; at her hair so neatly parted; and at that white silk bow.

They talked of school and their families. He told her of his career in the mill, now cut short. After a while, they sat face to face on a bench by the lakeside. "How is it, Michael, that you Irish stand apart from the rest of us in class? It's been nearly a full term, and no word of greeting has passed between us. Your group seems so unfriendly."

Michael took slight umbrage at this charge. His voice rose with emotion. "Arrah, Amanda, friendly is the Irish way. 'Tis shameful I guess, but Irish and English, we don't see eye to eye."

She placed her hand on his and argued, "Well, I'm English and I think we see eye to eye quite well. And now that you live in England, doesn't that make you a bit English too?"

His eyes narrowed as his temper was pricked again. "I'll never be English, never! I'm Irish, and glad of it," he barked. Then he reigned himself in. "You're different from most English, Amanda," he added in a softer tone. "You smile and have no hatred in your voice. Other folk are not so kind. I was in the mill for six years, workin' beside many English. They was happy to walk all over us, if we let 'em. And when we didn't, they'd give us the gate. 'Tis the English way."

Amanda shook her head in refusal. "Oh, I just want us to be friends. I don't want to worry about other people and their unkind ways."

They turned and stared in silence at the boaters on Crime Lake. Punts from the boat rental lazily glided along on the smooth gray waters, carrying young couples like themselves. The serenity of the scene stole away Michael's sense of indignation. But he had given Amanda much to think about.

Michael spotted Amanda's cousin wandering down the hill toward their bench. "Divil, 'tis time for Melanie already." He turned to Amanda. "I would see you again, if you please. Not in class, I mean someplace where we can talk."

"I want to see you again too. But today was difficult to arrange." Amanda paused for a moment and then smiled. "I am allowed some time each day after school to visit in Stamford Street with my friends. Shall we meet there on Monday?"

Michael's face beamed. "That's grand! But where on Stamford Street? I mustn't miss you in the crowd. . . . I know! Let's meet in front of Chadwick's, at the Delamere crossing?"

"Yes, I know the place. Till Monday, then."

Michael stood and watched as she crossed over to where Melanie was waiting at a respectful distance. Glancing back, Amanda waved cheerfully and then departed. The giggling Melanie would have annoyed Michael, but he was in far too joyful a state to let thoughts of her interfere. As he walked back to town, he felt elation and a new sense of freedom. He was at peace with the world.

That evening, Michael caught a ration of grief from his mother and father for his prolonged absence. But it was a cheap price indeed for the rendezvous at Daisy Nook. The harder part was waiting till the next encounter. It seemed that Monday would never arrive. When it finally did, his hair was neatly brushed, and he was wearing a shirt usually reserved for Sunday Mass.

Michael caught an occasional glimpse of Amanda during class. But she avoided making eye contact. When class ended, they each left school in their respective groups. Only upon reaching the town center did each disengage and make their way to Stamford and Delamere. Again Michael was the first to arrive. He fingered the few pence in his pocket that he had been hoarding for a special occasion. Now he considered that he might treat Amanda to a sweet.

When Amanda arrived, she took Michael's hand in hers, and they strolled away from the shopping district so as not to re-encounter any of their classmates. They walked west, into a quiet, somewhat affluent, residential neighborhood. Soon they found themselves on beautiful Jowett's Walk, a street of grand homes flanking a placid, well-kept, grassy square. As the afternoon was sunny and warm, they sought refuge in the shade of a venerable tree just inside the square.

"I have never known anyone like you, Amanda. The girls at the mill was different. I don't know why, but they all seemed sharp. Desperate, I guess, for their piece count. Never friendly, like yourself."

Michael spoke these words shyly, unable to look into her eyes. He toyed idly with a green stem plucked from the turf. Nimbly, he pulled it into knots emblematic of the piecer's trade. Amanda watched in thoughtful silence for several minutes. "I sometimes wonder what my life would be like if I had worked away my childhood like you and your mates. I'm afraid I know little of the world in which you live. And yet, I am very comfortable in your company."

*Above: Stamford Street near the crossing with Delamere
Below: Jowett's Walk* (Ashton-under-Lyne and Mossley, *1995 The Chalford Publishing Company*

Not knowing how to respond, he took her hand and kissed it. Then he reached over and kissed her softly on the lips. They basked in the mutual affection, and the moments passed comfortably as they talked on and on.

Amanda paused as if there was a thought she wished to add but needed to select the proper words. Then a look of shocked recognition crossed her face, as a cloud might blot out the sun. Michael turned to look behind him.

Along the Walk to the east, a one-horse open carriage approached with a sole passenger, a man in frock coat and black silk hat. Amanda jumped to her feet in nervous agitation. "Father!" she gasped.

Michael rose as well, his knees a bit weak and his stomach suddenly queasy. The carriage was reined to a halt on Jowett's Walk, opposite their resting place. Like Amanda, her father had an olive complexion, but this was accented with jet-black hair and eyebrows. Though clean-shaven, the dark shadow of a heavy beard was upon his face, and that face was a storm about to break upon them. He stepped down from the carriage, still clutching the whip, and strode toward the waiting couple. He grabbed his daughter firmly by the arm and seethed, "Get in the carriage, Amanda!"

Amanda started toward the carriage, then cast her gaze at Michael, to whom her expression seemed a wordless, aching farewell.

Robinson advanced toward Michael. The boy instinctively stepped back a pace as he eyed the whip. "We meant no disrespect, sir. We—"

The angry father looked disdainfully at Michael's rough clothes. "Young man, count yourself lucky to avoid a horsewhipping. My daughter is not available to Irish dross! Unless you want the law to come down to you, I suggest you forget any ideas of making further acquaintance of Amanda. Be off, and show your face no more!"

He turned to leave, his lecture apparently spent. But then he paused and added, as if to himself, "I was a fool to place her in the same school with you mill rats." He re-entered the carriage, leaving Amanda barely visible on his opposite side. With a snap of the whip, he urged his horse forward. Michael watched the carriage till it turned out of the square and disappeared.

"Anglo-Saxon toff," Michael cursed, his fists clenched tightly. "Acts like I'm the bleedin' dirt under foot."

Despite his initial fear and shock, Michael was now incensed by the familiar disdain of the established order. His anger combined with a feeling of desolation, and the dream of friendship with Amanda seemed foolishly impossible. On the walk back into town, he rehearsed to himself the ripostes he should have made to her father.

On Tuesday morning, Amanda was not present at school. Nor did she return in succeeding days. Each morning Michael's faint hopes withered further. Finally he admitted that she was gone and he would never see her again.

After the school term ended, Michael joined his father in hawking housewares. With this help Pat extended his route to include sections of the nearby towns of Mossley and Dukinfield. Roderick was working in the relief projects, though not under John's old foreman.

In September, Michael and Pat arrived home to find the family much distraught. Roderick passed them at the door with nary a word of greeting. Inside, they found Roddy with reddened eyes being clutched by Cate.

"Me da has called me home to Cloonfower," the boy explained. "He says that with work so scarce in Lancashire, 'tis no longer fair to you nor advantageous to us."

Cate would not speak of it and left the room. In the last nine years, Roddy had truly become a member of the family. For her, another son was leaving home. But the parting was especially hard for Roderick. He and Roddy had become the best of friends. It would take weeks for Roderick to regain his customary good spirits.

In the spring of 1863, the Quinn family received a postal packet from John. They all huddled round the table as Margaret read it aloud.

Dearest Family,

I hope you had not given up on hearing from me. It did take a time to get settled here and find work. I got to New York on the 13th of August. The voyage was very rough. I got sick, as did many others. We were mostly Irish, from Ireland and England.

I journeyed by rail from New York to Boston. The countryside here is green and prosperous, though the cities are rough, as in England. There were no textile mills in Boston. The folk there said I should try Lawrence or Lowell, which were not far. Me and a few other Irish, we picked Lawrence to try first. It is just as in Ashton, though the mills are big and new. I found me a job, a piecer again! The mill is called Atlantic. They have a boarding house for the operatives, but it is full. I found me a room at 49 Meadow Street. It's a long walk to Atlantic from here, but I must take what I can get.

The people here have a low opinion of us Irish, just like in England. But there are so many of us in Lawrence, I fit in all right. The pay is better than in Ashton. And there is the Irish Benevolent Society here. They have helped me with this letter and with the bank credit that is enclosed. If you take it to a bank in Ashton, they will give you money that I have saved for the family.

Because the United States is all at war, the mills are sore pressed to meet the call for cotton and wool cloth. Jobs are going begging for experienced operatives. If Roderick and Roddy still wish to come here, my foreman says he can get them on at Atlantic, sure.

I will send more money, as I am able. I miss you, every one. Perhaps Roderick or Margaret will write a letter and give me the news.

> *Your loving son,*
>
> *John*

Cate was crying, and Pat was not far behind. When Margaret put down the letter, Cate turned to her husband, her voice choking with emotion, "Ach, Pat, will we never see our boy again?"

Roderick interrupted, his face aglow with enthusiasm, "Da, did you hear what John said about me comin' to America?" He danced about his parents, demanding their attention. "Can I go? Please, Da, can I go? John doesn't know about Roddy. But I can go, can't I?"

Roderick's words sent Cate into a further wave of tears. "'Tis not enough that John is gone o'er the sea, now you want to leave us too!"

Michael stood at the door listening to Roderick's appeal and his mother's reaction. His emotions were a jumble: sadness at this reminder of his loss of John and that John had made no mention of him in the letter, envy at Roderick's apparent invitation, and pity for his mother and father.

"Now, mother, nothin's decided yet," Pat comforted. "We'll be talkin' about it later. Roderick, hush yourself! Margaret, give your da a look at this here paper for the bank."

The debate was re-engaged the next day. Roderick pestered them all. "When I get to America, I'll be after sendin' money too. Then you'll be gettin' quid from both of us. That makes sense, don't it, Da?"

Weeks of torment ended when Pat's patience with Roderick was exhausted. "If sendin' you to America is the only way to hush your gob, by Michael the Archangel, be off with you. Then maybe I'll see some peace again."

Cate was not happy at all, nor were Margaret and the little girls. But Michael kept himself quiet. He reasoned that if Roderick went, and was as successful as John, then his chance would surely come too. And it was to America that he was increasingly attracted. He wanted no part of settling into the rough margins of English society when the promise of America beckoned. And he wanted no further reminder of the social gap between himself and such as Amanda. Yes, let Roderick go. I'll be next.

Chapter Six

The Crossing

✠

That autumn, another letter arrived from John.

> "*Roderick arrived safely in June. He is now employed at Atlantic Mill, a piecer too. This mill is different than those in Ashton. Here, one may rise to spinner or weaver, given time and good cess. Such is now my first thought. Should I be a twister or a spinner, our savings will increase greatly. As our fortunes improve, Roderick recalls it was his idea to come to America. Though it was, I'm thinking he left his humility in Ashton.*"

Given such encouragement, Michael undertook his own campaign to join his two brothers. One day, as he pushed the cart of pots, pans, and kitchen utensils through the streets of Stalybridge, he broached the subject with Pat. "Da, as John and Roderick have found good work in America, 'twould be a shame were I not goin' there as well. The money the three of us could be sendin' home would be most welcome."

Pat turned to his son, pushed back his cap, and sighed. "I know you're all afire to be off to Massa . . . that place."

"The province of Massachusetts, Da."

"Begad, what a strange name! I know your brothers are doin' well enough for themselves. Still, I'll be knackered how to give your ma any comfort in it. The poor woman, she's been sendin' her heart to America piece by piece. If you leave, all our sons will be gone."

Michael's face fell. But Pat saw his reaction and quickly clarified his own position.

"Oh, I'll not be standin' in your path, lad. But you'll have to be patient. 'Twill take a bit o' time for your ma to come to grips with it."

Michael broke into a wide grin and quickly assured that he would bide his time. Pat walked to a low wall beside the road, sat, and pulled out his pipe. With an iron nail he scratched at the coat of ash that lined the bowl. "Look here, son, I've been thinkin'. If you boys can help us get the quid together, perhaps the whole pack of us should be followin' to America. 'Twould be a comfort to your mother, and wouldn't I like to shake this English dust off me shoes as well?"

Michael could hardly contain his delight at his father's words. He left the cart and threw his arms around his da. "Oh, wouldn't that be grand, to be together in America, all of us?"

"Aye, but nary a word to your ma, or anyone else! 'Tis our secret!"

Next to emigration, Michael's great passion was the National Brotherhood of Saint Patrick. Now seventeen years of age, Michael took up membership in his own right. He began attending meetings and making the subscription payments out of his own earnings. He tried to discuss issues of Irish liberation with his father, but to no avail. Neither of his parents could conceive of any change in the status quo. Only with his Brotherhood friends could such dreams be shared without inhibition.

The Brotherhood had experienced a bit of a revival in recent months. George Archdeacon, the charismatic leader of the Brotherhood in Liverpool, had sparked renewed activity and recruitment throughout Lancashire. By February 1864, there were seventeen branches in the region, and more in the offing, despite continued opposition from the Catholic hierarchy. But the Brotherhood was also on the cusp of a sea change, this time from within.

On a cold, blustery evening in March, Michael set off to the monthly meeting at the Old Thatch Tavern. Several members about his age were waiting outside when he arrived and then they took their places together. A speaker from Liverpool, Francis Riordan, was to address the meeting on this occasion. He was a short fellow, but the fiery speaker's presence was big. He wasted no time in shaking things up.

"Men of Ireland," he growled in a deep, almost angry voice. "'Tis time for Ireland's independence! The Brotherhood of St. Patrick has built a grand following among the Irish. But talk of history and culture will no longer suffice. From today, our work is organizin' the birth of an Irish Republic."

A wave of surprise and excitement passed through the assembly. The chatter among the members reflected varying points of view. Some were taken aback by this sudden, radical shift of policy. But many, like Michael, were encouraged that, at last, talk might be replaced by action.

"You will have heard the name Fenian," Riordan continued. "'Tis used to refer to the nationalist cause. Our proper name is the Irish Republican Brotherhood and our leader is James Stephens. In America, Colonel John O'Mahony is organizin' thousands of Irish exiles to come to Ireland's aid, once the American war is over."

Riordan paused and gave the crowd a knowing wink. "Good job Mr. Lincoln is providin' our lads free military trainin' and battlefield experience!"

A question from the floor interrupted the laughter of the crowd. "Are you tellin' us that the Brotherhood of Saint Patrick is no more? And are we replaced by this Fenian thing of yours?"

Again, murmurs raced through the audience. Riordan ran his fingers through his head of red hair and heaved a sigh. "'Tis a fair question. The Irish Republican Brotherhood has replaced the old organization in Liverpool. Many other St. Patrick branches will follow our lead. But we cannot force you to do so. 'Tis your branch, to do with as you will. But, if you truly long for the day that your country gets off her knees and takes her rightful place as a free nation, you will cast your lot with us."

Shouts of affirmation erupted. Clearly, the more aggressive line offered by their Fenian visitor had widespread support. After the meeting Michael and his friends stayed on to listen and drink ale. They noticed Riordan mingling and working the crowd, and were thrilled when the Fenian made his way to them. "Well, lads, what say you? Are you ready to do your part?"

Riordan was friendly enough, but he had a way of looking one right in the eye, as if he was gauging the character of his target. Michael felt somewhat intimidated at first. Then he thought of his brother John and the frustrations they had shared regarding the Brotherhood. "If me brother John were here, instead of in America, he'd be askin' where you was two years ago. As for me, I'm happy to be a Fenian, if that will help Ireland."

Riordan grasped Michael's hand. "I can't be responsible for the past, son. But together, we can help make the future different."

The others in the group also voiced their support for the Fenian cause. "John Bull won't come along happily," remarked one of Michael's mates.

The Fenian laughed dismissively, "Could be the force of Irish arms may bring him around."

"Mr. Riordan," another inquired, "what does the word Fenian mean?"

"You must not have the Irish tongue, lad. Perhaps your da will recognize the word. The ancient Gaels would say Na Fianna. These were the royal guards who, in times past, protected the Ard Ri, the High King of all Ireland. I guess Fenian is as close as the English tongue can get to Fianna."

As Riordan turned to go, Michael put a hand on his arm. "You say the IRB is in America already?"

"I'd wager there's more Fenians in America than in Ireland," he replied.

Michael was elated at the thought. Soon, he would be with his brothers. Together, they would help enkindle the flame of Irish freedom. "That's grand news," he said, holding out his hand to shake again.

Early in June, Pat received more money from John and Roderick, enough to finance Michael's voyage to America. His son had been making his own preparations for the journey. Over the past two months, he and his father had worked hard to win Cate over to the idea of his leaving. She was not happy, but reluctantly accepted it as inevitable. She grabbed her son around the neck and pulled him close. "Oh, Michael, I pray the good Lord will be watchin' o'er you," she whispered into his ear. "Someday, in His kindness, I'll see me boys again."

As he kissed and comforted her, he wondered if her words and her acquiescence signaled an awareness of the secret plan to bring the family to America. Pat never suggested though that she'd been told.

Michael felt his emotions swelling as he progressed through the sea of hugs and kisses of goodbye. His younger sisters, Mary Ann, Catherine, and Elizabeth, were saddened at the thought of losing another brother. Still, they were young and excited for him to be embarking upon such an adventure.

Margaret had always opposed all thoughts of emigration. But now, a young man of Ashton was courting her and soon she would be putting down roots in England. All this distracted her from her old fears and lessened the sting of her brother's leaving. Still, there were tears to fight off as the two embraced self-consciously.

Michael gave a final hug to his da. The old man could barely speak as the tide of emotion overwhelmed him.

"Don't be sad, Da," Michael whispered. "Remember our secret, eh?"

"Aye, lad, I'll have me sons again someday."

The 22nd of June was gray and threatening rain. Michael set out early on the first leg of his journey, to the city of Manchester. He could have taken the train, but chose to husband his modest financial stake and walk the towpath along the canal. The canvas bag that held his belongings was not heavy as his possessions were few. He waved to the tillers of the slow moving barges he passed. They reminded him that he could make the entire journey to Liverpool by canal boat, but he decided not to spend the added time. From Manchester, he would indulge himself the rail passage to Liverpool.

He arrived at Manchester's Victoria Station well before noon. The one-story, one-platform station was one of the largest in Britain and somewhat overwhelming with its crowds and its bustle. While he awaited his train, he sat in the large, rather dark waiting room, watching the many diverse passersby. He snacked upon the simple lunch of boiled beef, bread, and cheese his mother had put up for him. The smell of her bread brought on a twinge of homesickness for the family and home he was leaving behind.

It was early afternoon when the Liverpool train departed. Michael had often seen steam locomotives hauling freight to and from Ashton's Park Bridge Ironworks, but this would be his first ride on the rails. He took a seat, alone and next to a window. With a lurch, the cars slipped past the platform and out under the darkening sky. Soon raindrops blurred the green countryside that rushed past his window at an exhilarating speed. The other passengers seemed unfazed by their progress, but for Michael, who had imagined this adventure for years, it was a marvel. It was raining steadily when the train reached the city. The pendulous, pelting clouds were well suited to the scene into which he now entered.

The busy port of Liverpool seemed full of homeless folk, beggars, and menacing street toughs as Michael walked from Lime Street Station. The English were quick to attribute Liverpool's social evils to the Irish influx of the preceding twenty-five years. Indeed, the city's population was now nearly a third Irish, and in some wards they were the majority. This was certainly the case with Vauxhall, a district north of the center that hugged the banks of the Mersey.

Michael huddled beneath his upturned collar and tried to ignore how wet he was getting. No stranger to the sordid urban life, he judged that the ills of Liverpool differed from those of Ashton only by degree. He knew well to avoid the array of con artists preying upon unsuspecting travelers. There were hawkers for rat-infested boarding houses; emigration agents who sold passage on non-existent ships; and hustlers who would seize one's bags, carry them to one's destination, and then demand onerous fees for the service.

Michael dodged the rapscallions and made his way into Vauxhall. The wet cobblestone streets reflected the glow of the occasional gas lamp as a premature darkness fell upon the dockside district. He rejected numerous lodging opportunities as too grotty or menacing. In early evening, he selected a modest tavern in Dickson Street, offering accommodation in rooms above the bar.

A grizzled barman in a dirty apron met Michael upon his entry. "You'll be sharing the bed," he confirmed, "unless, of course, you wish to pay double?"

"No, no, I'm happy to share," Michael replied as he offered his coins. He stowed his bag under a table in a quiet corner of the smoky barroom. A pint of bitter washed down a supper of kidney pie. A few sailors occupied the bar, but they were relatively subdued after hours of steady drinking. After his meal, Michael carried his canvas sack up the narrow, dark, and creaky staircase that led to the room indicated by the barman.

It was a cramped space, made smaller by the dormers overhead. Cobwebs and dust appeared to date to the founding of the inveterate establishment. A forlorn, wooden bed nearly filled the room, its sagging straw mattress covered only by a thin, stained blanket. Michael spread his coat upon the far side of the bed, surrendering the near side to his prospective bedmate. A basin and pitcher of water provided some relief from the road dust and soot he had collected through the day's travel. When he finally extinguished the candle lamp, sleep would not come. His mind whirled through the imagined promises and dangers that lay before him. About eleven, he conquered the noise from downstairs and began to doze off.

The door burst open. In the dark, Michael's night vision discerned the silhouette of a man framed by the doorway and swaying upon unsteady legs. The intruder conducted a discourse full of Irish brogue and maritime jargon, which was apparently directed entirely to himself. He tossed his sea bag into a corner and collapsed on the bed. A panoply of odors, none of them favorable, accompanied his arrival. But in short order, the fellow's ramblings were replaced by sporadic snoring.

Michael had lived in close quarters all his life and was quite capable of ignoring such assaults upon his senses. Still, his sleep that night seemed all too brief. He rose before dawn and dressed quietly. The prospect of making the acquaintance of the sleeping sailor held little appeal, and there was much to accomplish this day. He emerged from the now-quiet tavern and found a street vendor hawking hot tea and sweet cakes in Waterloo Road. Michael consumed his breakfast, then walked on in the drizzle of Merseyside.

The air became increasingly foul as he approached the quays. Damp scents of soot, coal, tar, and spices married with the smoke belching from the stacks of the steamers idling at wharf side. The scene was also visually complex. A jumbled array of docks extended for miles along Liverpool's riverfront. Some of these were active and sturdy, others launguished in sea moss and rot.

Michael began his search for a vessel bound for America. As there were no guideposts to assist the uninitiated to their destination, he waded into the stream of travelers, arriving and departing with their baggage. Cargo slings swung from derricks to the chugs and gasps of steam-powered winches. A stevedore cautioned Michael against stepping into the hydra of ropes that lay about. "Step lively, bloke, lest these lines catch you up and haul your bones to the heavens."

In the famine years, the ships carrying the Irish to America were mostly timber ships from Canada and the U.S. Since there was no significant freight business from England to North America, these vessels would otherwise return empty. The shippers' motto had been "better bogtrotters than ballast." Now the flow of emigrants through Liverpool came from all over Europe. Together with the carriage of the post, these travelers supported a steady stream of vessels across the Atlantic. The conditions were distinctly improved over the crowded and filthy timber ships. Still, for steerage passengers, the voyage was a gauntlet of turbulent seas, crowded and fetid accommodation, and contagious disease.

Michael queried several dockworkers for a New York vessel, but they were too busy to stop and dispense directions. Later, he found an elderly shipping agent in a brown corduroy coat and a flat cap, sitting outside a dilapidated shack of an office. He puffed furiously on a clay pipe that refused to stay lit in the damp air. Michael set his bag down. "Please, sir, can you help me find a ship bound for New York?"

The old Englishman looked him up and down and chuckled. "Another Mick off to Americay, are you? I don't understand it."

"What don't you understand?" Michael asked politely.

"For all the Irish we send over there, we seem never to run to short supply here. But never mind."

Michael privately cursed the insolence of the fellow who, having had his joke, now assumed a matter-of-fact tone. "Try the Inman Line. They run many a vessel to New York. From the looks of you, you'll not be havin' the price of a compartment on a Cunard vessel. You'll find the Inman agent down on Queens Wharf." Michael thanked the agent and continued on his way from quay to quay.

As the morning passed, the press of the crowds became greater. About 11:00 a.m. he spied a sign reading "Queens Wharf." There he found several wooden shanties along the pier where various shipping lines booked the passenger trade. Passing through the crush of people and baggage, Michael came to the stall for the Inman Line. The agent inside was serving a queue of prospective passengers. Michael took his place in line and waited.

The largest steamers were not docked at the wharf, but rode at anchor in the depths of the river channel, where the ebb and flow of the tides posed no limit on their coming and going. The passengers of these vessels embarked and disembarked by means of a landing stage. It was a wooden platform riding offshore upon iron pontoons. It was said to be capable of accommodating forty thousand standing passengers at a time. The floating platform was tethered to the riverbank by two iron bridges, one served those embarking, the other those disembarking.

When it came his turn to be served, Michael found himself before a thickset gentleman in black frock coat and vest, who was seated on a high stool before a clerk's desk. He wore the muttonchop style of side whiskers and was topped by a derby hat. A pencil rode above one ear and a large black ledger sat before him. The agent's florid face bore an expression of world-weary resignation. He seemed to Michael to have steeled himself against the next stupid question from an ill-prepared traveler.

"Well, boy, what's yours today?"

"I'm after a vessel for New York, sir. Steerage class, if you please."

"If I please, eh?" he mocked. "Next available, is it? That would be the *City of Limerick*. She sails on Monday morning at eleven. But you must be here at dockside by nine-thirty to be processed for departure."

"Nothing earlier?" Michael had hoped to leave promptly, and this booking would entail a three-day wait.

"That's the very next for New York. You may wish to try another destination. We've one for Quebec tomorrow morning."

"No, New York it is."

The ticket cost the Sterling equivalent of $19.00 (U.S.). Michael dug down into his trouser pocket and retrieved coins from a knotted handkerchief. He was unused to carrying, never mind dispensing, such sums.

"Here's a list of kit, food and such, you must have with you. None will be boarded in steerage without the necessities."

The agent took Michael's fare and inscribed his name in the black ledger. Then he pounded a ticket vigorously with a red ink stamp and handed it over.

Michael moved away slowly, wondering how he would pass three days in the vortex of Liverpool. After resigning himself to the delay, he proceeded to the High Street, where he would shop for the provisions required.

Monday morning was again wet and dreary. Michael carried his sack on his shoulder, trying to shelter beneath it. Some in the queue had umbrellas, but no one offered to share. Luckily, it was not a cool day, as he was drenched and quite uncomfortable. An inspector came along after half an hour, and Michael displayed his ticket and demonstrated the adequacy of his provisions. Then he and his fellow passengers were herded over the iron bridge to the landing stage. There, Michael got his first close look at the ship that would carry him to America. . . . it seemed huge to him.

The 1,529-ton S.S. *City of Limerick* was a hybrid vessel, employing a steam engine as well as sails. She was two hundred eighty-one feet long and thirty-four feet wide; and had an iron hull that was painted black, three masts rigged for a dozen sails, and a large single smokestack amidships. Steam alone would produce a speed of ten knots, but wind power would be substituted whenever conditions permitted. Since the westward journey would be against the prevailing winds, it would take a bit longer than a return trip. Still, the use of steam power had reduced the passage interval from the previous three weeks to ten days or so, depending on the weather. This voyage would take a bit longer, as there was an intermediate stop at Queenstown on the south coast of Ireland.

About ten a.m. boarding began, first- and second-class passengers being accorded first embarkation. Almost an hour

S.S. City of Limerick (Mail & Passenger Steamships of the XIX Century, *edited by Captain H. Parker &* Frank C. Bowen, 1928. Courtesy of TheShipsList.com)

later, those for steerage mounted a gangway and were directed across the open deck and down a wide wooden staircase into the hold.

Men, women, and children scurried into a long, narrow, dark cavern with a low ceiling of iron beams. They were in mad pursuit of the wooden bunk of their choosing. Each had their own criteria of selection: near the stairs, near the loo, by a porthole, away from the porthole. Michael hadn't considered the issue previously and was relegated to a bunk in the center-rear. After a period of settling in, the steerage passengers were asked to assemble for instructions.

A red-bearded ship's officer, in a uniform of blue and brass, called for quiet. In a distinctly Scottish accent, he read from a small blue book, *Her Majesty's Order in Council of 6 October 1849 – Preserving order and securing cleanliness and ventilation on board passenger ships proceeding from the United Kingdom to any of Her Majesty's possessions abroad.*

The fact that the United States of America hadn't been one of Her Majesty's possessions for almost eighty years seemed to have escaped the notice of both the government and the shipping line.

"All passengers will be required to observe the following regulations." The Scot went on to enumerate various requirements:

- All passengers will arise at 7:00 am and roll up their bedding.
- Male passengers, above age fourteen, will take turns in sweeping the deck and discarding overboard all rubbish and night soil.
- Preparation of breakfast will then be permitted.
- All persons will report in proper attire for Sunday services, promptly at ten a.m.
- There will be no naked lights or fires of any kind, save in cook-stoves provided.

"I must caution you all," the officer added, "that whilst on this ship, Captain Jones exercises absolute and unquestioned authority. Instructions from the ship's officers should be treated as having come from the Captain." After several minutes of questions, the passengers were dismissed.

On his way back to the steerage, Michael stopped a passing crewmember. "How is it you have both sails and steam for your ship?"

The friendly young man tipped his hat and smiled. "With sails we don't have to fill the ship with as much coal as would be needed to fire the boilers through the entire crossing. After all, coal pays no fare, whilst you passengers do."

The voyage commenced under dark skies and a steady rain—an inauspicious start. When they approached Queenstown, Michael took in his first sight of Ireland since he had left at the age of four. He presumed it would be his last. White spring lambs dotted the rich green pastures that ran right to the edge of the jagged, rocky shore. Queenstown was a small, whitewashed village set on the hillside above a natural harbor. Its unimposing appearance belied its role as port for the nearby city of Cork.

Michael paced the main deck as he waited for the Queenstown travelers to board. A short, middle-aged Irishman smiled as they passed each other.

"Ach, what a travesty," Michael observed.

The emigrant, who had also boarded at Liverpool, raised his eyebrows. "What's that?"

"A fine Irish town named after Queen Victorie!"

The Irishman chuckled and shrugged his shoulders. "Well, lad, the Brits stole everythin' else belongin' to Ireland. Why would they not be takin' away the names of our cities?"

In a few hours, the *City of Limerick* began the transatlantic phase of the voyage in much improved weather. The slate-gray waters of the Irish Sea had been left behind, exchanged for a beautiful blue expanse of the Atlantic. Strong winds, however, meant that one's only respite from the stifling atmosphere of the steerage compartment was the cold, steady blast of fresh salt air on deck. Many men from the steerage happily braved the main deck to enjoy a pipe of tobacco. Smoking below was strictly forbidden. It seemed to Michael as if the large black smokestack had begotten numerous, little white clay smokestacks, which then wandered all around the deck.

The days passed but slowly. Steerage was a maelstrom of coughing, spitting, lively banter, and wailing children. Michael found himself nearly always in a queue. . . . for the loo, for a cooking stove, for water. When not so engaged, he spent his time up on deck, as the smells below became increasingly unpleasant. No bathing facilities existed in steerage.

Late in the voyage, a fine summer's evening presented itself with calm seas, a slackened wind, and a gold and purple sunset off the bow. It was a welcome respite for the many who had been cooped up for so long. An old Irishman brought out a battered concertina. Soon, a young Scot produced a fiddle and joined him. As they commenced to play, a few brave souls began to dance. Before long, many of the passengers, young and old, bucked and kicked to a lively air. Children ran happily about the perimeter of the deck. A wave of unfamiliar contentment passed over the ship's company. For Michael, it was the first truly enjoyable episode since he had left home.

The fourteenth day at sea dawned bright and blue. Late in the morning, Michael paced the deck knowing their journey's end was near. He chatted up a young maid from Clare. She was a slight, pale figure with long, dark hair. He judged her far too fragile to be traveling to America by herself, especially after she confessed herself desperately homesick.

When he asked her reasons for undertaking such a voyage, she shyly admitted, "There was no choice about it. When me pa died, the farm became too much for me to care for. And divil if I was havin' any of them brutes from the village for a husband. So I am off to join me brother and his family in the city of Baltimore."

Michael smiled in admiration of the determined lass. "Good on you! It takes a strong heart to leave the old and make a new life far away."

"Aye, but what of you?" she countered. "I've five years on you, if a day. And here are you, doin' the same. Surely you must have fears of your own."

Michael cast his gaze at the unbroken expanse of ocean beyond the gunwale. Then he looked into the girl's gray-green eyes. "I am afraid, sometimes at night . . . when I'm lyin' in me bunk and 'tis dark all about. I listen to the ship slicin' through the waves or hear a baby cry. 'Tis then I think of me family what I left behind." He sighed heavily before resuming his customary optimism. "But, I'm happy to be leavin' England. 'Tis no place for an Irishman. Look at all these about, old folks, women like yourself, even little children. I guess if they can manage, I'll be doin' me bit too. Besides, I've me two brothers—"

A shout went up from a passenger across the deck. "Land! I see land! See, over there! We're in America!"

Michael's face illuminated with delight, and even the homesick girl managed a wee smile. Those on deck raised a cheer, and passengers from below scrambled up the stairs to get a first look at their new homeland. What they saw was the eastern tip of Long Island. It would take hours before they entered the bay encompassing New York harbor. Another of the ship's officers made the announcement that an inspection of each passenger's ticket would take place presently. Stowaways were a common blight upon the transatlantic trade.

Michael was mesmerized by the sights and sounds of the port of New York. From the deck of the *City of Limerick*, his gaze took in an imposing array of buildings, factories, churches and tenements. They blanketed the horizons, from Brooklyn on his right, to New Jersey on his left. And, most dramatically, before him was the island of Manhattan, a small finger of land, seeming with every square inch spoken for. The many tall buildings huddled behind a picket of docks and sailing vessels. Above it all, chimney smoke and sea mist imparted to the city a blue-gray hue. Steam whistles and chugging motors from the plentiful harbor traffic hailed their arrival. He lingered upon this scene until the order came to gather belongings and prepare for disembarking. So this is New York! John and Roderick came through here. 'Tis grand enough.

A landing stage was employed to receive the passengers and their bags. Once again, cabin passengers were served first. They were received by a great rusty barge and then pushed by a tugboat to the wharf at Castle Garden, just off Manhattan's Battery. Michael had to wait several more hours before his turn came to step again on terra firma.

Castle Garden actually looked like a castle. Built as a fortress to repel British forces during the War of 1812, the building was a large, circular bulwark of massive, red granite walls. Used in a later period as an opera house and theater, from 1855 the site was the inspection and processing center for the State of New York's Commissioners of Emigration.

A dozen indolent officers of the Emigration Commission and the Customs House stood about in small clusters chatting. Reluctantly, they suffered interruption to casually direct the arrivals toward the reception hall. Hoisting his bag, Michael navigated the pressing, anxious crowd and proceeded through a narrow passageway flanked by high wooden fences. At the end of this walkway, passengers and their bags were separated, the latter being checked into a large baggage room. An agent took Michael's bag, marked it with a black grease pencil, and presented him with a claim check. With the men and boys, he was then herded to a toilet block and washroom. It was a large room, well stocked with soap, water, and rolls of clean towel,

Above: Castle Garden—exterior view from the Battery
Right: Interior of Castle Garden (Day in Castle Garden, Harper's Monthly, Volume XLII, 1870)

free for their use. After his long passage from home, through Liverpool, and across the sea, Michael welcomed this opportunity to restore some degree of hygiene.

Ushered to the rotunda of the Castle, he joined another queue to await the scrutiny of dual inspectors. One was on sharp lookout for the sick and disabled. These would be separated for treatment at Commissioner's Hospital on Ward's Island, in the East River. The other inspector registered Michael's name, birthplace, and destination, making confirming reference to the ship's manifest.

It was early evening when Michael was passed through, so he made no attempt to venture into the unknowns of the New York City night. Rather, he decided to take shelter in the waiting room of the rotunda. Gas lamps hanging high above the floor illuminated the huge room filled with rows of hard wooden benches. Two large iron stoves, between four and five feet high, sat at opposite ends of this great room to afford heat in winter. No need of them, though, on this fine summer evening.

The growling of his empty stomach reminded Michael that his last bits of food were in his checked bag. A commissary of sorts was available, where simple fare could be had for twenty-five cents or less. He hurried off to the currency exchange to replace his shillings and pence with dollars and cents. It was a fairly administered service that the Commissioners rendered.

"Good ya caught me before closin'," the agent chided. "Outside the Castle, there's a nest of sharpsters. They be ready to prey on them unschooled in the true rates of exchange."

"Aye, as in Liverpool," Michael nodded in reply.

After dining upon soup and bread, he returned to the waiting room. The discordant mix of languages and costume here fascinated him. While many were Irish, Prussians and Dutch seemed to predominate. Most of the nationalities, including Swedes, French, and Italians, were unrecognizable to Michael, but shared hardships and aspirations bound all together in reasonable comity. Though each group tended to stake out their own area, he noticed no conflict among them.

The next morning Michael awakened with an aching back, the reward of sleeping on a crowded, wooden bench. After breakfast, he visited the "booker," an agent of the Railway Association, whose job it was to advise on routes, sell tickets, and direct passengers to their appropriate rail terminal. Should Michael have needed it, there was also a bureau of correspondence, where immigrants could compose messages or have directions written out for them in English. There was also a labor exchange, where employers and applicants could be matched. But all Michael wanted was to purchase a ticket to Boston and be on his way.

One more wait to collect his bag from the baggage room, then he made his exit from Castle Garden. Outside he was met with a sea of purveyors: hacks, food vendors, moneychangers, and runners for the boarding houses. Striding purposefully, Michael waved off all solicitations and made his way into the city.

Castle Garden was originally sited on a small island, or more accurately a pile of rocks, just off the foot of Manhattan. Over the years, it had been connected to the Battery by landfill. Michael walked the short isthmus, then through the Battery, to find himself at the foot of Broadway. He swung his pack over his shoulder and proceeded north, lingering momentarily at the improbably bucolic Bowling Green. There, New Yorkers sat, strolled, and enjoyed the warmth of the summer morning in the verdant patch across from the majestic Customs House.

Michael's immediate destination was the terminal of the New York and New Haven Railroad.

"Go up Broadway and then turn east at City Hall Park," the booker had told him. "The station is at the meeting of Chatham and Centre Streets."

The buildings along Broadway towered over Michael, whose previous experience was with the two and three-story structures of Ashton. He had only fourteen blocks or so to walk, but the cobblestone streets were clogged with people, carts, dogs and horses, all slowing his progress. The shouts of the hawkers and the smells of strange foods roasting on smoky carts mingled with a babel of languages that filled lower Manhattan.

As he made his way, Michael noticed the tricolor bunting, American flags, and army recruitment posters that bedecked many of the buildings. These, and the many Yankee soldiers in the streets, reminded him that the United States was a nation very much at war. As he approached the rail station, he passed numerous veterans who, he assumed, were making their way back to homes and families. Michael involuntarily gawked at the sight of those maimed in the war, wondering what it would be like to live without a hand or a leg. It was with good reason that Margaret was so strong that John and Roderick stay clear of the fightin'.

He mounted the station platform, clutching his precious rail ticket. A chalkboard was posted with the schedule of arrivals and departures. Michael stared at the listings in bewilderment. Needing assistance in deciphering the schedule, Michael looked about for whom he might ask. A bluecoat lounged against a lamppost nearby. As Michael approached the soldier, his gaze was drawn to a neatly pinned-up sleeve, where the fellow's right arm should have been. He hesitated at first, feeling awkward about inserting himself into the pitiful man's respite. The soldier was short and stocky, perhaps in his late thirties. His face carried a few days of stubble, but otherwise, he was clean and presentable.

"If you please, officer, could you advise regardin' which train be for Boston? All these trains seem to be goin' to New Haven."

The soldier guffawed at being accorded new rank, even out of igno-
rance. "Arrah, lad, I ain't no officer. Must be this here clean tunic they gave
me on leavin' hospital. Murphy's me name, Corporal Francis Xavier
Murphy. Me mother was a great one for the saints."

Michael began to apologize but the fellow paid no heed. "I'd offer me
proper hand but those damned Johnny Rebs stole it off me."

Michael was stymied by the soldier's loss, finally managing, "I'm sorry
for your trouble."

"Ah, not to worry. Now, about these trains, they all go through New
Haven. One must change there for Boston."

Michael breathed a sigh of relief. A seventeen-year-old in a strange
country, he was keen to get things right. "Thanks for your help," he said,
turning to go.

"Actually, I'm bound for Boston meself," Murphy added. "Shall we
wait together?" They found a bench upon the platform. "Don't I recognize
the brogue of a fellow Irishman?" asked the Corporal.

"I'm after leavin' England," Michael explained, "but I was born in
Ireland." He told Murphy of his family in Ashton and the brothers he
would join in Lawrence. When their train was called, Michael offered, "Let
me hoist that bag of yours."

But Murphy waved him off. "Nay, lad. I'm just now gettin' the hang
of doin' things with me left hand. I'd better get good at it, I've got the rest
of me life to make do."

The soldier swung his sack over his shoulder and nodded toward a car
down the line where there was less crowding. They climbed aboard and sat
together on bench seats surfaced with straw wicker. Michael put their bags
up in an iron luggage rack. With a cloud of steam and the clanging of a
bell, the penultimate leg of his journey began.

The train made several stops as it progressed up Manhattan Island.
They passed through the rest of the city, and a bit further, the density of
settlement became quite sparse. From then on, farms and the wooded hills
of upper Manhattan dominated their views. As they rode along, Michael
listened to the effusive Corporal Murphy recount how he had lost his arm
to a cannonball at a place called Cold Harbor, in the state of Virginia.

"'Twas just six weeks ago. General Grant got us into a whuppin' that
was pitiful to see. Them Rebs kicked the bejesus out of us. Me mates were

bein' killed, left and right. Others of them died in hospital later. 'Course, I ain't too pleased to be losin' me arm. But, I figure I'm gettin' a better bargain than they did—me life and a ticket home. By thunder, I want no more of soldierin'! Take me advice, boy, stay away from this damnable war."

Michael looked out the window, unseeing. He recalled his brother John's pledge to avoid this war in which he had no stake. "I'm happy to have no part in this civil war of yours. When I take up arms, 'twill be against me only enemy, the bleedin' British. 'Tis them and their rotten lords in Ireland what sorely deserve what you called a whuppin'."

Murphy slapped his remaining hand upon his knee and laughed aloud. "Don't you remind me of the Fenian boys back in the regiment! One war ain't enough for them. They wants to fight again as soon as they get done this one. Me, I've chewed the sweet out of bein' a military man." Michael put a determined scowl upon his face, causing Murphy to pause. "Of course, if fightin' Brits is your ambition, I suspect you'll be gettin' your chance soon enough. Why, there's even Irish lads among the Johnny Rebs, pledged to the Fenian cause! I wouldn't want to be in that company, with Irish Rebs and Irish Yanks marchin' side by side."

Michael nodded, but to him it made good sense that Irishmen, Yank and Reb would itch to turn their rifles on redcoats.

It took several hours before their train arrived at New Haven. It was late afternoon when they moved across to the platform for the Boston train. Michael was getting hungry again and found a food vendor's stall in the station, purchasing enough provisions to last him through the next day. He shared some of these with Murphy as they sat and looked out over the nearby New Haven harbor with its many sailboats and swooping seagulls.

Murphy spoke of his own emigration from Galway in 1847, in the teeth of the great famine. Once on the Boston train, he shifted the discussion to their arrival next morning in Boston. "Michael, you're a fine lad. God willin', I'll be havin' a son such as yourself one day. Why don't you come along to Charlestown in the mornin'? Me home isn't much, but me wife is right handy in the kitchen. It'll give you a bit of time to get yourself back on your feet."

Michael sat back in his seat, somewhat overwhelmed by the quick assessment and generosity of a near stranger. "'Tis a very kind offer,

Corporal Murphy. But I'm keen to go on and make an end of me travels. John and Roderick will be waitin' on me arrival. If I can get a train to Lawrence, I may see them yet tomorrow."

"That's fine, lad. I understand how you feel. . . . 'Tis the Boston and Maine line you'll be lookin' for. Now, 'tis a different station entirely. Just walk north through the Haymarket. Folks will show you the way. It shan't take long."

Michael pulled down their bags to rest their heads upon and moved to an empty bench behind. They napped off and on through the night, waking each time the train stopped at some intermediate town. In those moments of wakefulness, Michael turned his thoughts to homecoming, imagining what he would face later that day. He looked forward to the reunion with his brothers and finding fellow Fenians in America.

When they pulled into Boston, the sun was rising. As it promised to be a warm day, Michael stuffed his coat back into his sack. He was happy to busy himself with his belongings. It allowed him to deflect thoughts of parting from his kindly, misfortunate companion. When the time came to say goodbye, it was mercifully brief. A simple farewell and God bless was all that could be exchanged before they were carried off by the sea of humanity upon the platform.

The town of Lawrence, Massachusetts was still relatively new, one of the first pre-planned communities of nineteenth century America. Located

Lawrence, Massachusetts, circa 1854 (Collection of Lawrence History Center—Lawrence, Massachusetts)

at Bodwell's Falls, on the Merrimack River, it was founded to succeed Lowell as the premier city of the textile industry. By the time Michael Quinn arrived in Lawrence, fewer than twenty years later, no less than seven major mills had been constructed and more were on the way. The labor pool for the textile mills began with young people from the neighboring farms and villages. Then, increasing demand for workers coincided with the Irish famine years and a huge influx of Irish immigrants. As in England, the Irish faced great resentment and discrimination from the native population. For the newly arrived Irish, it was as if their old English nemesis was waiting for them in New England, in the guise of a Yankee.

Michael had been traveling for almost three weeks. It was late morning when his train arrived and he was tired—tired of sleeping rough, tired of wearing the same clothes, and tired of smelling like a goat. All he could think of was getting a bath and falling into a proper bed. From those at the rail station, he sought out directions to the section of the city where John lived.

It suddenly occurred to him that his brothers would be at work till six p.m. He walked the dirt streets slowly, almost idly, trying to pass some time. But his fatigue and hunger for an end to his journey pushed him on to the northeast neighborhood of two-story clapboard houses. Housewives hanging out laundry and youngsters playing in the street distracted him such that he missed 49 Meadow Street and had to backtrack to find it. The house was simple, but neatly whitewashed. It was set in a good-sized yard with mature shade trees and several out buildings behind.

He approached the door and struck the wrought-iron knocker. Through the lace-curtained sidelight, he could see a gray-haired woman in a flour-covered apron, ambling down the front hall.

"Yes, who is it?"

Michael stood erect and smiled pleasantly. "I'm Michael, brother of your boarder, John Quinn."

She made no movement to open the door. "He's at work now. Best come back this evening."

Michael looked up and down the quiet street. Where would he take refuge on the edge of the city? He was so damned tired. "If you please, Ma'am, I've come a very long way and have nowhere else to go. I'd be happy to do you some chores about the place, if I could just stay the afternoon."

The old woman hesitated, then unbolted the door and opened it a crack. She eyed Michael up and down, noting his youth and road-weary condition. Her face relaxed a bit. "I could use some coal brought in from the shed out back. You'll find the scuttle behind the door. You look a mess, but that will have to wait till the coal's in. No sense washing twice."

Michael discovered that this lady of the house was Mrs. Alice Munns. A Yankee widow, she was cautious of foreigners but also needed the revenue from her boarders. With over forty percent of Lawrence's twenty thousand citizens being foreign-born, and most of these Irish, she had to accept Irish mill workers as clientele. Her features and dress reminded Michael of the English ladies of Ashton-under-Lyne.

After carrying in the several loads of coal she required, Michael was surprised to find a hot tub of bath water prepared for him in a room off the kitchen. While he bathed, Mrs. Munns brushed his clothes, but to little advantage. When he was dressed again, she sat him at the kitchen table where warm roasted chicken, fresh-baked bread, and cold milk waited. For Michael, it was an experience close to heaven. His appreciation of the old lady doubled after dinner when she allowed him to wait in John's room. There a bed, a real bed, would dispel the deep fatigue that now was nearly overwhelming.

The summer sun was still high in the evening sky when Michael was jolted awake by a playful whack delivered to his backside. "Who's this gentleman of leisure tying up me bed?"

Michael sat up quickly, taking a few seconds to orient himself. Rubbing Michael's hair into further disarray, John applied the familiar teasing that was his way of showing fraternal affection.

"John! Jaysus, you gave me a scare. Sorry for settlin' in. The woman, Mrs. Munns, she said 'twould do no harm."

"She said rightly, no harm at all! 'Tis good to see you after, what, two years? You've got bigger since I seen you last." John sat on a straight-backed wooden chair and removed his shoes. "Twelve hours on me feet, 'tis quite enough. Now, what of Ma and Da and the girls?"

"They're fine, just grand. 'Course, they all miss you and Roderick fiercely, especially Ma. But their health, please God, is good. You will not yet know, but Margaret has a beau and is bound for the altar."

"Good for Maggie! Roderick thought such might be in the offin'." John bent down and brushed the cotton lint from his hair. "And what of your journey? I see you lived through the crossin' all right."

"The journey was fine, no misfortunes at all. Still, 'tis a far, far way and the length of it put sand in me eyes."

John went to the dresser and poured water into a basin. "Well, you had best get it out! Tonight, we're off to the Plains with Roderick. We'll be drinkin' your health and good fortune in America."

"Where does Roderick live? Mrs. Munns made no mention of him."

"Nay, lad. There was nothin' here. Mrs. Munns was full up, as the Americans say. But we've been plannin' for your arrival. You'll stay at Roderick's place. We'll have our supper now, and then be on our way."

The Plains was a predominantly Irish district, bordered by the Spicket River on the north, Haverhill Street in the south, and by Hampshire Street and Jackson Street on the west and east. Here, in this "little Ireland," many of the mill workers made their homes in the two and three-story tenements that typified the New England mill towns.

Unable to find housing close to the Atlantic mill, Roderick had settled at 57 Hampshire Street, a couple of blocks north of the Spicket River, at the edge of open countryside. It was after eight p.m. when John and Michael set off, and after the twenty-minute walk to Roderick's tenement, they discovered he was not in. A haggard neighbor woman from downstairs directed them. "He'll likely be at Fallon's."

Fallon's was a tavern situated in the Plains, occupying the ground level of the patron's house. Its atmosphere was thick with pipe smoke and the sooty tails emanating from the oil lamps overhead. The place was crowded

A Lawrence Saloon suggestive of Fallon's (Collection of Lawrence History Center—Lawrence, Massachusetts)

with mill workers and with the navvies constructing the new Arlington Mill on the north bank of the Spicket. Most had the dirt of the day still on them, and some appeared to Michael to have chosen drink over supper.

John and Michael found Roderick standing at the bar. He was in a group of mill workers being regaled by the off-color stories of Roderick's friend, Martin Mulcahey. When their laughter subsided, John called out to his brother. "Roderick! Look at what washed up on the shore this afternoon!"

Roderick turned abruptly and peered through the smoke. He recognized John's booming voice, but it took a few seconds to focus upon Michael. He strode forward and grabbed him in a bear hug. Michael felt a sense of relief to be reunited with both of his brothers.

Roderick seemed somewhat different from how Michael remembered him. He was still lean and of average height, his dark eyes more deeply set than Michael remembered. His slight jaw, his small mouth, and his long neck now combined in a less than fortunate visage.

"Michael! We've been expectin' your arrival any time. You seem none the worse for your journey."

"'Tis grand to see you, Roderick. All the family sends their love."

"Let's get a drink in you, for travelin' builds up a powerful thirst. You'll find the beer in this country is not the equal of a good English bitter, but the whiskey is as good as any."

Michael waved off the whiskey option. "Beer will be fine. I'm afraid a whiskey would put me to sleep and you'd have to carry me home."

"Let's get a table where we can talk," said John. "We'll not want to be shoutin' at each other all night."

They seated themselves in a back corner, where they could find relative tranquillity. After twenty minutes of exchanged queries, Michael turned the conversation to his keenest interest, the Irish Republican cause.

"We've heard of the Fenians," John responded. "They're as thick in Lawrence as flies in the privy. But we've been too busy workin'. Speakin' for meself, I've little energy for politics at the end of the day."

Michael was stunned. He rubbed his face as if he was experiencing a bad dream. "Wasn't it you what was complainin' in Ashton about your mates that was too busy to be bothered with the Brotherhood? And did you not hunger for action rather than talk of Ireland's independence?"

Roderick strongly countered, "'Tis different here, Michael. England and Ireland are far away. What's the point of being a Fenian in America? The struggle is back there, not here."

Michael burned with indignation, his voice rising as he answered Roderick's challenge. "Ah, you're wrong, Roderick. 'Tis from America that the hammer blow will come! There'll be Irish soldiers from the American war, money, and arms flowin' into Ireland from America. That's the whole plan of it!"

Placing a hand on each brother's arm, John tried to sooth flaring tempers. "Michael, let's not be foosterin' on our first night together," he said, acting the peacemaker. "Maybe you are right, or maybe it shan't be so easy. Anyway, far be it from us to criticize them that's tryin' to make somethin' happen on the ground in Ireland. We just haven't been involved since we got here. You'll see shortly, 'tis a full day's effort, just workin' and livin'."

Michael rolled his eyes in frustration, but held his tongue. He was not placated and promised himself that there would be no such excuses on his part. He had made a pledge to the Fenian cause before he left Ashton, and he felt it unthinkable not to fulfill that pledge. He forced a smile. "So what must I know of Lawrence?"

The brothers talked the next two hours pleasantly of home, of Lawrence, and of America. Near midnight, Roderick yawned. "'Tis late! Come now, lad, we must be off home. John and me, we've got to be at the mill before six."

Later, as he lay abed, Michael's mind was awhirl with plans for finding work, for investigating the local Fenian organization, as well as with thoughts of the family back in Ashton. Sweet exhaustion won out quickly though, and he slept the sleep of the dead.

Chapter Seven

American Fenian

✠

Michael awoke next morning to the sounds of carts and voices in the street below the window. He found himself in the deserted and unfamiliar room he now shared with his brother. Roderick had left for the mill over four hours earlier, and now the summer sun was high in the smoke-stained sky. It was already rather warm in the upstairs apartment. He looked around the cluttered room—a sea of tangled bedding, dirty work clothes, and personal effects. His own canvas sack was where he had slung it last night, in the only unoccupied corner.

"Ma would fall upon Roderick like a shriekin' banshee if she could see this pit what he calls home," he mumbled to himself as he recalled Cate's manic dedication to tidiness.

It was Michael's intention to visit the Atlantic Mill and get an introduction to the hiring agent. He would catch a brother during the dinner break and then address the hiring issue. He pulled on his least dirty clothes and with necessity's speed, navigated the back stairway that led down to a crude wooden privy in the backyard. Upon his return, he used the chipped basin, pitcher of water, and a sorely used straight razor he found in the kitchen. He figured there was still adequate time to get a bite to eat and see some of Lawrence before the noon whistle blew.

He walked straight down Hampshire Street, assured by Roderick that it would lead him to the gates of the Atlantic Mill. Mature poplars, maples, oaks and elms generously shaded the city's network of dirt streets carved out of woodlands and fields. Michael enjoyed the cool respite from the July sun. At Essex Street, he found the city's only macadam surface and a horse-drawn trolley serving this main business thoroughfare.

Essex Street, 1873 (Collection of Lawrence History Center—Lawrence, Massachusetts)

He tarried at a newsstand where the agent could have looked no more Irish had he been tattooed with a harp and a shamrock. His red hair, blue eyes and aging, freckled face were familiar and welcome. Michael glanced at the variety of journals. "Which of these will be carryin' news of the Irish folk?"

The agent interrupted his task and eyed him curiously. He placed a hand upon the stacks of newspapers before him, indicating each option. "Forget about *The American.* That'd be the Yankee paper. The only news of the Irish inside will be police reports of divils and drunkards taken in hand."

The agent imparted his literary criticism in a friendly, confiding tone. Michael listened patiently. "Then there's the *Sentinel.* That'd be a better choice. Ah, but you're wantin' the comin's and goin's of the Irish. It must be the *Pilot.* It carries dispatches from Dublin and London."

"The *Pilot* it is, then," said Michael, picking through the coins in his hand, trying to recall which were which.

Over breakfast in an Essex Street diner, he thumbed his way through the pages in search of news of the Fenians. There were notices of their activities, but these related to events in Boston. Of the Fenians of Lawrence, he found nothing. He folded the paper and gulped his last swallow of tea to the scream of the factory whistle—the poor man's timepiece.

Michael hurried back to Hampshire Street and down to the gates of the Atlantic Mill. Many of the workers were already in the yard within the gates, fleeing the claustrophobic atmosphere of the factory floor. Even the warmth of a summer's day would be refreshing after six hours in the hot, humid work areas. Workers opened their lunch pails or went home for dinner. A few would indulge the expense of a meal from a cluster of vendors' carts beyond the gates.

Michael scanned the crowd till his eyes fell on John, seated with some mates, eating and talking in the shade of the main factory building.

"Here he is now, the American sleepin' champion," his brother announced. John and his fellows laughed good-naturedly as Michael drew near. After a round of introductions and brief social chatter, the brothers excused themselves and strolled toward the gates.

"I'm keen to call on the hiring man today," Michael said. "Will you make me an introduction?"

John burnished an apple and nodded. "I'm happy to do. 'Tis a queer old Yank, name of Jack Clark. He hired meself and Roderick. The formalities must wait the back-to-work whistle, but a friendly "how are ya" can do no harm."

They searched about for ten minutes before finding the agent under a tree on the north bank of the canal. He was alone, sitting comfortably on the grass, puffing upon a fine briar pipe, his legs crossed at the ankles.

"Mr. Clark, may I introduce me younger brother, Michael Quinn. He's lookin' for work here at Atlantic. He was a piecer for years back in Lancashire."

Clark pushed back his leather cap and rapped his dying pipe against an open palm. "Another just off the boat, eh? Well, we're full up on piecers right now, fella. Put on three apprentices last week. You can drop back to doffin' if you like. Of course the pay is only 80 cents a day."

Michael shuddered at the thought of returning to child's work and wages. Clark noticed his disappointment and offered consolation. "You know," he said as he repacked his lunch pail, "an experienced piecer ought not want for work in Lawrence. Why not try next door?"

John thanked the agent and they walked slowly back through the gates. "'Tis a shame, Michael, but no great tragedy. The Pacific Mill is just next along the canal. They've a grand reputation for how they treat their workers. They even have a library and a relief society for workers what get maimed."

Michael hung his head in disappointment. "Work is work. I just never figured on not bein' with you and Roderick, here at Atlantic."

John slapped his brother on the back in encouragement. "Don't be troublin' yourself. When they call for piecers here, you can always come back. Besides, there's no tellin' if we'll stay at Atlantic anyway."

Michael looked at John with a puzzled expression.

"There's the new Arlington Mill bein' built up on the Spicket," John explained with a sly smile and a confiding tone. "I'm still lookin' to become a spinner or even a weaver. Maybe at Arlington, I'll be havin' me chance."

After John returned to the afternoon shift, Michael left Atlantic and walked west along Canal Street to the office entrance of the Pacific Mill. The Pacific was the largest and most impor-tant mill in Lawrence,

Pacific Mills, seen here in 1890 (Collection of Lawrence History Center—Lawrence, Massachusetts)

the flagship of the city one might say. With over three thousand staff sup-porting twenty-six hundred looms, the operation produced huge quantities of cottons, woolens and cashmeres.

The main building was a three-story brick structure, eight hundred feet long and seventy feet wide. At its western end, it was met at a right angle by a stone building that housed the boiler room, where steam was produced. Here, too, was the engine house, where waterpower was transferred to the network of gears, pulleys and leather belts that powered the frames. A smaller building, in the angle of the other two, was the blower house, from where hot, steam-laden air was carried into the workrooms to maintain a high humidity.

Michael had little difficulty in signing on at Pacific. All the mills were straining to supply the needs of the Union war effort. As an experienced cotton worker, Michael was a welcome addition to the rolls. His job as a piecer was to commence the following Monday morning. Having been unemployed for the last three years, Michael was greatly relieved to have a real job again. Though it was no great joy to be returning to the harsh conditions of the mill, there was comfort in the economic security of earning over a dollar a day.

He had agreed last evening to meet Roderick at Fallon's at the end of the day. It was only 4:00 p.m. when he arrived at the tavern, over two hours early. The place was devoid of workingmen. Its only custom at this hour came from the unemployed and the aged. A jaded bartender pulled a draught of lager without the usual pleasantries. Michael carried his schooner to a table near the window where he could watch for the approach of those coming from the mills. Honest daylight, even through smoke-stained windowpanes, exposed the dust and dirt of the barroom. The boisterous noise and laughter of the previous evening had been replaced by the hum of a few quiet conversations.

A gentleman entered the barroom wearing a black frock coat and a stovepipe hat. He cast an appraising glance around the room. Though his style of dress was refined, the condition of his clothes belied any hint of prosperity. His hat was slightly crumpled and his trousers were shiny from years of service. His coat would have welcomed a vigorous brushing. He was not young, and his expansive paunch testified he was not the laboring type.

He ordered a beer and selected a table close to Michael. He removed his hat, and mopped his pate of thinning hair with a well-used handkerchief. Looking in Michael's direction, he muttered, "'Tis a warm one today."

"Warm indeed," Michael replied politely but without great interest. He gazed out the window, lost in his own reactions to this first day in his new home. But the garrulous fellow would not be put off. "I don't think we've met, have we?"

Michael refocused his attention reluctantly. "Sorry, sir, what's that?"

"Your face is not familiar, and I know most all of them in this quarter."

"I only arrived in Lawrence yesterday."

The stranger's face broke into a beatific smile. He had found the object of his professional pursuit. "Ah, a recent arrival . . . from Ireland is it?"

"No, sir, from England. Me family's in England thirteen, no, fourteen years. I've come to join me two brothers what have been here for a time."

"And the name? Perhaps I know of them."

"Quinn, John and Roderick Quinn. Me name is Michael."

The man drew his hand across a whiskered cheek. "I don't recall them, though we have some Quinns here in the Plains."

"Ah, that's it, sir. Neither of me brothers is livin' in the Plains. John is in the northeast of the city and Roderick lives above the Spicket."

The stranger sighed. "Well, there's the explanation, sure. I would've known them if they was third ward people. I'm the ward captain for the Democrat Party, you see. Me name is Charlie Hogan." He offered his hand.

Michael left his seat, shook his hand, and pulled his chair toward Hogan's table. "Pleased to make your acquaintance, Mr. Hogan. I'm a bit ignorant of your politics in America. 'Tis it not the Democrats which are in rebellion?"

Hogan nearly choked on a swallow of beer. He mopped his chin with the venerable handkerchief. "Nay, not at all! Many's the proud Democrat what is loyal to the Union. 'Tis them in the slaver states what has taken up arms. Most Democrats hereabouts got no sympathy at all for rebellion. Faith, we're the friends of the workingman! You'll be discoverin' as much soon enough."

Michael pulled his chair closer yet. "If you please, could I ask another question or two?"

Hogan assumed a more erect and dignified posture. "And why wouldn't you? Fire away."

"You know of the Fenians? The Brotherhood is here in Lawrence?"

"Pshaw! They've a Circle for Lawrence alone! That's what they call the local organization."

Michael assumed an air of worldly experience. "I was a Fenian in England, though 'twas for a short time."

"A Fenian from the auld sod! And at your young age."

Michael now pressed his objective with renewed enthusiasm. "Who might you suggest I speak with to get on with the Brotherhood here, Mr. Hogan?"

Before Hogan departed Michael received full guidance as to how to proceed.

Roderick flicked his cap at the back of Michael's head. "I'll be right with you. I'm gettin' a beer. Are you ready yourself?"

Michael shifted in his seat with excitement as he quickly filled Roderick's ear with the day's events.

"Good job you got on with Pacific, Michael. 'Tis a shame you couldn't get a position at Atlantic, but, ah, it makes no real difference at the end of the day."

"I'll be fine at Pacific. Still, I'll miss workin' with you and John." Michael paused for a moment, considering whether to share his latest news with his brother. "Oh, and I sorted out the local Fenian Brotherhood. I'll be one of them soon enough."

Roderick gazed into his beer, unwilling to lock eyes with his brother on this issue.

"Mmm. Well, yes, 'tis your decision entirely," he admitted without relish.

Michael, his enthusiasm quashed, flared with frustration. "You could at least say 'Good on you' or some such encouragement. I'm already clear on the fact that you've no stomach for rebellion yourself."

Roderick wasn't keen to debate the question again. He raised his palms and leaned back. "Look, Michael, you live your life and I'll live mine! I've got better things to do with me time and me money."

At that moment, Michael decided to no longer challenge his brothers on the issue. He would represent his family alone in the pursuit of freedom for their homeland.

The next few weeks for Michael were filled with establishing himself in his new job at the Pacific Mill. His long absence from the looms made his initial efforts awkward and inefficient. His fingers were no longer quite so nimble. He had grown considerably since he last scuttled under a loom, in the dust and spittle, to mend a break in the threads. Everywhere he turned, it seemed, he found an elbow or a knee bumping up against the frame. This struggle to relearn his trade did little to enamor Michael to his foreman. Still, Michael was sure he was better off than the sweepers, oilers, and doffers.

After work Michael would meet Roderick on Canal Street for the walk back to the tenement. Sometimes, John would join them and the three would spend an evening together. Roderick and John had been pooling their savings to periodically send stipends to the family back in Ashton. Now Michael joined them in this practice.

In September, they received a letter from home, scribed by their sister Mary Ann. In it, she announced the family's intention to join the boys in Lawrence, once adequate funds could be accumulated. Employment was still scarce in Ashton, as the Cotton Famine continued. And Cate, she related, was still disconsolate over the absence of her sons. She had, therefore, readily agreed to the plan of emigration that Michael and Pat had shared months ago. It might take a year or more to accomplish all this, but the decision had been made. Only Margaret would remain in England, as her engagement was now well established. John and Roderick were thrilled by the news.

Most Sundays, the brothers would attend Mass at St. Mary's Church at the corner of Haverhill and Hampshire Streets. While none of them was hugely devout, their faith and their church were also important cultural fixtures, part of their identity as Irish in America. And like many Irish immigrants, they found their main social outlet within the Catholic parish. Periodically, one organization or another would organize a dance, a picnic, or some such event, usually as a fundraiser. It was at one of these, a dance, that Michael and Roderick encountered Miss Jane Hearst.

The Quinn brothers, Roderick, John and Michael

It was a chance meeting, one of those occurrences that gives rise to "small world" stories. It was a Saturday night, and the Quinn brothers were turned out in their best attire for a "Harvest Ball." John, being better established than the younger two, had acquired a fine outfit of beige nankeen trousers, a dark brown frock coat, and a yellow silk waistcoat with a matching bow tie. Roderick and Michael had only plain black suits and waistcoats. Still, they felt suitably resplendent for men of the laboring class.

Oil lamps hung brightly in the large basement chamber under St. Mary's church. The burning tapers gave off heat and the odor of soot in an already close atmosphere. The room was gaily decorated with sheaves, gourds, and pumpkins, in keeping with the harvest theme. The manful efforts of the musicians from the Irish Benevolent Society were nearly drowned out in the din of conversation and laughter.

Shortly after their arrival, John hurried off in pursuit of young Catherine Cunniff. She was a recent acquaintance whose family also came from County Roscommon. Roderick and Michael, neither much for dancing, retreated to the punch bowl. From there they would survey the female prospects of the evening.

Michael eyed the swirling dancers over the brim of a cup of punch. "Wait till our sisters get over here from Ashton. They'll be havin' a grand time at dances like this,"

Before Roderick could respond, a voice behind them piped up. "Is it Ashton, you say, Ashton-under-Lyne . . . in England?"

The brothers turned as one to confront the unseen speaker. A florid, fleshy gentleman and two handsome ladies were newly arrived at the punch station.

"Forgive me," the middle-aged man hurried to add. "I really wasn't trying to eavesdrop, but I could not resist your mention of Ashton."

Roderick bowed slightly to the ladies and turned to the speaker. "No offense taken, sir. I'm Roderick Quinn and this is me brother, Michael."

"My name is James Hearst. May I introduce my wife, Mary, and our daughter, Jane."

The ladies curtsied in unison. Michael and Jane traded glances and smiles, and ignored the ensuing conversation that passed before them. Jane was a younger vision of her mother. Both women were of greater than average height, with dark brown hair parted in the middle in the severe style of the day. Jane's face was girlishly pleasant, her mother's somewhat plain.

Roderick smiled and returned to the subject at hand. "'Twas Ashton-under-Lyne that was mentioned. And how does this interest yourself?"

Mrs. Hearst slipped her arm through her husband's. "Imagine our excitement at the mention of Ashton! Why, we have come just recently from the neighboring town of Mossley."

"I had lost my position as loom mechanic in the Cotton Famine," Mr. Hearst added. "An agent from Washington Mill enlisted me to come take up work here." He continued with a lengthy account of their journey from England and their settlement in Lawrence. Whenever he was able, Roderick interjected the briefest account of their own background and emigration from Ashton. As the band took up a particularly lively selection, numerous attendees broke into a rhythmic clapping and the Hearsts' attention was diverted.

"They're English," Michael hissed into Roderick's ear.

"They're Brits all right," Roderick answered softly out of the side of his mouth. "When he said he was a loom mechanic, that clinched it. Still, they seem friendly enough."

"Ah, but what are they doin' prancin' about the basement of St. Mary's?"

Roderick shrugged. "Sure, they must be Catholic themselves. That gives them as much a right as anyone here to prance about, as you say."

It took little time for the willful and socially forward Jane to settle upon Michael as her quarry for the evening. Before he knew what was happening he was among the dancing couples, Miss Jane clinging to his arm. Despite the close oversight of the Sisters of Notre Dame de Namur, who functioned as guardians of virtue for the evening, Jane drew Michael frightfully close as she led him through the rudiments of a waltz. His clumsy efforts to synchronize his feet with hers, and with the music, kept him from pursuing the vague sense of misgiving chafing his mind. It was only at the merciful end of the dance, upon returning Jane to her parents, that the thought of her British background recurred as a concern.

Roderick's attention was also fixed upon Jane Hearst, now in the arms of a more accomplished dancer. Her dark brown locks fell gracefully to her shoulders and she seemed to float about the floor in perfect rhythm with her partner. Too shy to ask for a dance, he nevertheless was attentive to her movements throughout the evening. As the festivities ended, both brothers knew they had not seen the last of Miss Jane Hearst.

As in England and Ireland, the Catholic Church in America was hostile toward the Irish Republican cause. Fenians had to muffle their political views within the social purview of the parish. But despite clerical opposition, the ranks of the Fenians continued to grow dramatically. This was especially the case with Irish-American soldiers, discharged from service against the Confederates, as they returned to the mill towns of New England.

Later that autumn, Michael was officially inducted into his local Fenian Circle. The meeting was held in the Bridgeman Hall on Oak Street, in the heart of the Plains. It was Dennis O'Sullivan to whom Michael had been directed by Charlie Hogan. A Fenian officer, Dennis was an affable man in his thirties, with brown hair and a neatly trimmed goatee. He greeted Michael at the door well before the formal meeting began. "You're entirely welcome to the Brotherhood, Michael."

They shook hands warmly and Michael's face beamed with delight. "I'll do me best for the Brotherhood and our people back in Ireland."

O'Sullivan nodded and called over several other Circle members. "This is Michael Quinn, boys. He was a Fenian man back in England, right under the nose of the Brits. How about standin' as witnesses, as I have him take the Fenian oath?" With murmurs of support, they gathered around and one of them handed Michael the Fenian flag, a green field featuring a golden harp and sunburst.

"Repeat after me," Dennis began. "I, Michael Quinn, solemnly pledge my oath, as a Christian and an Irishman, that I will labor with earnest zeal for the liberation of Ireland from the yoke of England and for the establishment of a free and independent government on Irish soil. . . . I will foster, defend, and propagate the aforesaid Fenian Brotherhood to the utmost of my power."

"Huzzah, huzzah," cried his new comrades as they shook Michael's hand and clapped him on the back. Michael gave O'Sullivan his initiation fee, which would be followed by monthly dues of fifty cents, nearly half a day's wage. But he was unfazed by the financial commitment. He was now eighteen years of age and in position in America and in the Fenian Circle. It was just as he had dreamt it back in Ashton.

More members arrived, filling the hall. Some were dressed in the improvised uniform of a prospective Army of Ireland, but most members were in their regular street clothes. Some were men of years, while others were as young as Michael, even younger. Their voices rang with jovial banter, delivered in varying degrees of Irish brogue. Gradually, they took their places in battered wooden chairs of various designs and vintage. The program this evening featured a speaker, Captain Tim Deasy of the Ninth Massachusetts Volunteer Infantry. After several principals strode out on the platform, the chairman called for order over the din of conversations.

"Sons of Erin! Tonight you will hear one of Ireland's own, now returned from the war against the Confederacy. Captain Tim Deasy was born in Clonakilty, in County Cork. His family came to Lawrence in the black days of '47. He was educated right here in Lawrence and has been a member of the Brotherhood since '59."

There was enthusiastic applause for the young man many members had known from his youth. Sitting in the place of honor, Deasy betrayed neither pride nor embarrassment during this introduction. He seemed older than his twenty-five years. He wore a large drooping moustache that nearly covered his strong jaw. His eyes were clear and focused.

Captain Timothy Deasy

Patriot — Irish American

Captain Timothy Deasy (Courtesy of the Lawrence Chapter of the Ancient Order of Hibernians)

Michael could feel his piercing gaze and watched him with great admiration.

"When the war broke out, Tim enlisted in the Union army, where he has been promoted repeatedly for acts of valor. When all the commissioned officers of his Company were killed in '62, he was made the acting Company

Commander. He fought gallantly in the famous battles of Manassas, Antietam, Chancellorsville, Gettysburg, and The Wilderness. He was wounded in May of this year at Spotsylvania. But despite his wounds, Tim returned to his unit in time to participate in the terrible battle of Cold Harbor. Now Tim has returned home to recover, and we'll all be wishin' him the fullness of health."

More shouts and applause came from the audience. The chairman turned, faced Deasy, and raised his voice to new heights. "But before he was mustered out, he enlisted many of his comrades into the movement. I'm askin' you all to give a grand welcome to a real Fenian hero, Captain Tim Deasy!"

The hall shook as the boisterous audience rose to its feet. Deasy slowly stood and acknowledged the tribute. He was dressed in his officer's blue tunic, with its gold epaulets and a double row of brass buttons down the front. He approached the chairman and accepted his embrace. Then, without notes, he proceeded to address the assembly.

"My Fenian Brothers, thank you for your kind welcome. Ed Devlin, thanks for puffing up my military reputation. But I'm not here to bask in praise of my service to the Union. In real war, glory means little compared to the suffering and sacrifice of the common soldier. No, I come to talk of a fight that is yet to be engaged, and of soldiers who are your Fenian brothers. They wait for the day when they can put their weapons and their experience of battle to use for an independent Ireland. If they will risk death to free the black man, can we not risk as much to liberate our own people?"

Michael had never considered this perspective. He could feel the energy and patriotic fervor swelling within the crowd and within his own breast. Why couldn't John and Roderick be here tonight? They'd see for themselves what role America will have in bringin' freedom to Ireland.

"We Irish have proven our loyalty and affection for these United States of America," Deasy continued. "After the sacrifices of Irishmen on the American battlefield, let no man call us strangers! And in return, America owes us her support in the struggle for Irish liberty. Then will Britannia lift her skirts, abandon her stolen estates in the Emerald Isle, and hurry back to England's shores."

Deasy reached down and unsheathed his sword. A stillness of apprehension fell upon his rapt audience. He held it across his outstretched hands, as if offering it to the crowd before him.

"Tonight, I say, prepare yourselves for the coming conflict. Be under no illusion, the force of arms will be required. Some of you will have to shed your blood for Ireland. Some may even lose life itself. Let your oath be heart-felt and your resolve firm. When the order comes to move, let no man of you excuse himself for duty to family or profession. Rather, kiss your loved ones and grab your gun. Irish brothers in arms will be there by your side, to train you and lead you to victory. Erin Go Bragh!"

Deasy stepped back, still offering his saber symbolically. The frenzied crowd picked up the Fenian anthem, a song Michael did not know. He listened closely to catch the words:

> We love the generous land in which we live,
> And which a welcome hand to all doth give.
> May God upon it smile and swell its fame!
> But we don't forget the isle from whence we came.
> Things may soon take a turn; There's no one knows;
> When the stars and stripes may burn against our foes.
> When Yankee guns shall thunder on Britain's coast,
> And land our green flag under the Fenian host.
> Oh, let us pray to God to grant the day,
> We may press our native sod in linked array.
> Let them give us arms and ships; we ask no more;
> And Ireland's long eclipse will soon be o'er.

The effect of the song was intoxicating. With officers like Captain Deasy, the cause would surely be won. Michael and his new comrades were ebullient as they dispersed for conversation and the light refreshments provided by ladies of the Irish Revolutionary Brotherhood. He was enjoying himself and lingered till the crowd began to dwindle. Then he edged his way close to where Deasy stood surrounded by various IRB leaders. One of them noticed Michael's presence and turned to him. "Is it Captain Deasy you're wantin'?"

Michael gulped, his voice betraying his nerves, "Aye, sir, a word with the Captain, if 'twould not be inconvenient."

"I'll see what I can do, lad. The name's John Breen. What's yours?"

"Michael Quinn, sir, Mr. Breen. That'd be grand."

In a few minutes, Breen returned with Deasy at his side. The soldier stretched his hand out in friendly greeting. "Well, my friend, I hear you'd like a word with me. What can I do for you?"

Michael bowed slightly in response. "'Tis an honor, Captain. I've recently arrived in your country. When I heard the introduction tonight, I could not help noticin' the mention of Cold Harbor."

"A nasty affair and a poor battle plan to boot," Deasy said dismissively. "I was there, though I'm sure I did our forces little good." Deasy's expression signaled his reluctance to be reminded of this unpleasant memory. He swept the room with his eyes as if he was eager to depart.

"Well, sir," Michael continued, "when I arrived in New York three months ago, a soldier of your army helped me. As you both are from Massachusetts, I was curious if you had known him. A Boston man he was, name of Francis Murphy. Lost an arm at Cold Harbor."

Deasy's face blanched at the mention of Murphy's loss; his voice turned low and gentle, all impatience gone from his demeanor. "Why, sure, I know Corporal Murphy. The blackguard probably saved my life a couple of times over the last three years. . . . I did not know he had lost his arm. What a great shame!"

Deasy appeared lost in his thoughts, so Michael made a move as if to retire and let the captain return to his colleagues. "Well, thank you for your time, sir."

"And what of you?" Deasy asked before Michael could move away. "You've lost no time in becoming a Fenian volunteer." He exchanged a glance of satisfaction with Breen.

Michael stopped, embarrassed that the discussion had turned to him. He fingered the bill of the cap in his hand. "I was a Fenian back in England, sir. It seemed only right to be joinin' up here in Lawrence."

"Good man! We'll need you, and more like you, before this is over."

They all shook hands and Deasy departed the hall. The place was nearly empty now; just a few of the IRB women cleaning up the debris. Michael and Breen stepped out into the dark of Oak Street. It was a crisp autumn night, and the chill felt refreshing after an evening in the crowded, stuffy hall. A waxing moon spilled its light through the trees that still wore their autumn display of yellows and reds. They walked together as far as the corner.

"Michael, you made a good impression upon Deasy tonight. It cannot harm you to have his acquaintance. He'll go far as a leader within the Brotherhood." He placed a hand on Michael's shoulder and looked him in the eye. "Let's stay in contact. The time is not long before the Confederacy will die. Then we'll see where Deasy and his mates take us."

A strategic underpinning of the Fenian cause was the considerable enmity that had developed between the United States and Great Britain during this period of the Civil War. Despite having outlawed slavery years before America, Britain still found its natural sympathy with the Confederacy. This was, in part, due to her dependence upon Southern cotton for its textile industry in Lancashire. Beyond this, Britain's commercial interests were threatened by the emergence of a very competitive American textile industry in New England.

The Fenians were happy to see America increasingly antagonized by British partisanship. At best, they hoped for active U.S. support when they launched their campaign against their ancient foe. At worst, they would count upon benign tolerance when Fenian activities took place upon American soil.

The winter of '64–'65 passed slowly for the Quinn brothers. Life was full of laboring and saving. But Michael and Roderick also spent considerable effort in furthering their acquaintance with Jane Hearst. At first these contacts were polite social calls upon the Hearst family, as they had learned that Jane, despite her appearance, was only sixteen. This limited their contact drastically, as James Hearst was a most protective father. Still, they saw her at parish socials and at church after Sunday Mass. As the months passed, Jane's preference for Michael became increasingly obvious to Roderick. Whatever the reason, Roderick made no concession and redoubled his efforts to find favor with Jane and with her father.

Michael became resourceful in circumventing the confines of parental control and in keeping Roderick at bay. But, it was Jane who was the most resourceful one. Her temperament was nothing if not hot blooded, and she seemed to enjoy defying her father's preference that she aspire to a higher strata of society. The brief interludes of privacy with Michael were usually of her design. It wasn't long before these occasions were marked by rushed flights of passion, heavy breathing and groping hands.

"Michael! We must stop," Jane would whisper as she bit his earlobe teasingly. The confusing and conflicting signals she sent his way were a source of frustration and annoyance to the healthy eighteen-year-old. How many times must he approach the precipice with her, only to be sent into disorderly retreat?

"Damn your eyes, Jane! You shan't be teasin' me like a lapdog with a treat. If you love me, let's marry and have each other freely. If not, don't be buildin' fires inside me like this."

Jane pulled away and pouted briefly. "Oh, father wouldn't consider it. . . . at least not till my eighteenth birthday. Besides, you're still a piecer and he would never stand for that either. We have no way forward but to wait. I'm sure you'll make spinner, or even weaver, long before I'm eighteen."

She was right, of course, and he knew it well. But he also knew he'd go crazy long before the two years passed.

America's great civil war entered its denouement that spring. The surrender at Appomattox was cause for great rejoicing throughout the Union. In Lawrence, church bells pealed the news, and public demonstrations broke out throughout the city. But the happy glow of victory would last only five days.

On a gray Saturday morning, Michael arrived at the Pacific Mill for work. As he crossed the North Canal, he sensed something was amiss. A presence in the air, like ozone during an electrical storm, made him strangely uncomfortable. As he got to the factory gate, Michael noticed that no one was going into the mill. Workers stood in clusters, their usual banter and laughter stilled. A woman walked past Michael, sobbing in great heaving breaths, tears streaming down her cheeks. What's all this?

Then he saw the front page of the *Sentinel*. Topped by black banners, it announced that the American President had been shot the previous evening in Washington and was not expected to survive. Michael knew little about American politics, but he had heard Lincoln's name since he was a boy. For years, the English had vilified President Lincoln for the blockade of trade with the Confederacy and the ensuing Cotton Famine.

Michael had also been informed at the Fenian Circle that Lincoln's administration had developed a winking recognition of the IRB in America. Private assurances of implicit support had been communicated to the Fenian leaders. Of course, political realists recognized that Lincoln supported Fenian recruitment within the Union army largely as an offset to Democratic Party influence among the rank and file. But there were few such realists among the IRB leadership.

As grief is a catching disease among the Irish, Michael and his brothers gathered that evening to drink to the memory of the martyred President. The atmosphere at Fallon's was greatly subdued. The low, sad conversations were broken only by an occasional outburst of emotional tribute. Roderick's friend, Martin Mulcahey, was one of those who stepped forward to mark the somber day. A short, stocky fellow in his early twenties, Martin was also one of the Fenian Circle to which Michael belonged. He was known, not only for his comical nature but for the fine tenor voice with which he was blessed. Accompanied by a gentleman playing a concertina, Mulcahey offered a melancholy rendition of an old Stephen Foster tune:

> *"Down in the cornfield*
> *Hear that mournful sound;*
> *All the darkies are a weeping –*
> *Massa's in the cold, cold ground."*

Despite their relatively short tenure in America, the Quinn brothers were not immune to the emotions shared by their American peers. Mulcahey's tribute left them slightly embarrassed at having to blink back the odd tear.

As the moment passed, John took a pull at his beer. "The man was a great one for the poor folk wasn't he? He made them black slaves free, but it cost him his life."

"I'm thinkin' the assassin was a British agent," Roderick speculated. "Sure, the English are no great lovers of the President—or of the Union."

"Probably paid by old Victorie, herself," Michael said. "Lincoln was the great hope for us Fenians. Now that the Confederate rebellion is put down, we were countin' on the Union for arms and such. Who's to say about this fella, Johnson?"

In July, Michael participated in his first celebration of the American Independence Day. With the time for Fenian action fast approaching, the Brotherhood went all out to capture public support and to recruit new members. Many of the Fenians wore uniforms of green caps, white shirts, and black trousers. Almost four hundred members marched together in

Lawrence's parade. As the contingent passed through the Plains, the Irishmen cheered lustily, while young ladies threw admiring glances at the gallant volunteers. When they marched in front of the city hall, Michael was shocked to see Jane and Roderick together among the spectators. Of course, he knew of Roderick's interest in Jane, and that they saw each other occasionally at parish events. But the sight of them made Michael's jaw tighten, and his pleasure in the parade quickly dissipated. The march continued, and all he could do was gamely return their waves.

After the parade had dispersed, Michael joined several of his Fenian colleagues over beers at Fallon's. During a lull in the conversation, he addressed a question to his friend, John Breen. Exiled from Tipperary with his family during the famine years, Breen was just four years older than Michael. But he had an extensive schooling that made him seem older and more confident, which greatly enhanced his leadership abilities.

"Would not the money spent on these fancy uniforms have bought greater advantage in arms and ammunition?" Michael asked.

Breen smiled and shook his head. "Look at it this way. A dollar spent on arms gets us just that, a dollar's worth. But a dollar spent on attractive uniforms will bring in a hundred, maybe two hundred, in contributions. The extra amount will buy more guns and shot than we could ever afford otherwise. You see, Mike?"

John Breen in later life (Courtesy of the Lawrence Chapter of the Ancient Order of Hibernians)

Michael was taken aback a bit by Breen's use of a nickname. Mike! It sounded so American, so casual, and unpretentious. Michael liked the sound of it.

"Ach, I guess that's why you and Deasy are leaders, and I'm only a private in the Brotherhood. I'd never have thought of the impact of uniforms in attractin' donations to the cause. Speakin' of Deasy, I didn't see him in the march."

Breen leaned over and spoke in a low voice, as in confidence. "Don't you know? Deasy is gone! He's been sent to Ireland as one of several experienced Irish-American officers to help organize forces on the ground there. Our time approaches!"

Breen's optimism seemed misplaced, however, when the ever-cautious Fenian leadership in Ireland procrastinated in setting the date for the insurrection. By September, British spies had done their work well and many members of the Brotherhood in Ireland were identified and arrested. Tim Deasy was one of those captured in their net. The Brotherhood members in America were bitterly disappointed, yet their leaders resolved to find a way forward.

One Sunday afternoon that fall, Michael was ensconced at home, absorbed in a serial in the *Boston Pilot*, "The Croppy – A Tale of 1798." It was an account of Ireland's last serious uprising, and Michael was greatly enjoying it. Jolted from his reverie, he went to answer an urgent pounding on his door.

"Michael, me lad, cast your eyes upon the newly appointed spinner of the Arlington Mill!" His brother John's smile came close to his ears. "A piecer no more!" he exulted.

Michael clapped his brother on the back and shook his hand. "Why, that's grand! You'd have been an old man indeed 'fore you made spinner in Ashton."

John laughed and nodded knowingly. "Aye, and pretty near that old if I stayed at Atlantic. Still, Roderick is an optimist. He's stayin' on. Once they construct the company housing block, I'll be moving north of the Spicket too. 'Tis a long walk to Arlington from Mrs. Munns' place."

"Sure, this is more money for the account! Ma, Da, and the girls will be here before you know it. I can't wait for that day to come!"

"Me, too. Grab your coat and let's go find Roderick. This calls for a drink, or two, don't you know!"

Chapter Eight

O Canada

✠

In late February 1866, Michael was leaving Mass at St. Mary's Church when he heard a voice calling, "Mike! Mike Quinn! A word with you?"

Michael recognized the voice, and turning to it, he saw John Breen waving his black bowler hat as he descended the steps of the church. As Michael waited for him, he took some pleasure in being hailed as "Mike." The nickname was becoming more comfortable, especially from Breen, whom he admired greatly. He had a way of making everyone feel important and heard. It was often remarked that he would make a successful politician, should he choose.

Breen weaved his way through the departing congregation. "Good job I caught sight of you. I was wantin' to invite you around for dinner this afternoon. Several others from the Circle are comin'. 'Tis just an informal meetin' to discuss a bit of Fenian business. Ma's makin' pot roast. You'll come, won't you?"

"Try to keep me away! A home-cooked meal will be most welcome. What time shall I arrive, then?"

"Come about three o'clock. I'm sure you'll enjoy yourself."

As Breen hurried off to his home, Michael remained standing in front of the church, a bit overwhelmed at the invitation. His youth and junior status among the Fenians made this an unexpected honor. He knew it was his friendship with Breen that propelled him into this select group.

Leaders of the Fenian Circle gathered late that afternoon at the Breen home in the Plains. After a grand pot roast with spuds and gravy, Breen and his guests retired to the parlor where an item of conversation was the newly elected mayor of Lawrence, Pardon Armington. Though a Republican, Armington was the first Yankee politician in Lawrence to run on a platform of improved working conditions in the city's mills.

"'Tis a case of the divil that you know," offered Tom O'Gara, a jovial but capable Fenian officer. "As soon as the Workingmen's Party began to organize textile workers, a Yankee candidate emerges as a 'friend of the workin' man.' If you ask me, 'tis a sop from the mill owners. They'll be happy to spend a pittance on reforms, whatever they are, if they can escape the ten-hour workday and increased wages!"

"Ah, Tom," Breen retorted, "the dullest Yankee politician knows how to count noses. These days, there are nearly enough Irish noses to carry a city-wide election."

Mrs. Breen quietly brought in tea and set it down upon a doily-covered side table, valiantly attempting not to cause an interruption to the discussion. But her plan was foiled as her son's guests fawned over their hostess. "'Twas a grand meal, Mrs. B.," Dennis O'Sullivan piped up. "Me wife will be jealous to hear of it."

"G'wan with such nonsense. Now, you gentlemen give a call if you're needin' more tay."

Breen used this diversion to carry the discussion elsewhere. "So now, Tom, will you give us the news of the special meetin' in Pittsburgh?"

O'Gara took a seat by the fireplace and searched his pockets for his notes.

"Aye! I was wonderin' when I'd have to earn me dinner." The others laughed. "Well, most of you will know that last month I went to Pittsburgh as a delegate from our Circle. And of course, 'twas all work and no fun at all."

"Had it been so, we could never have forced you onto the train," O'Sullivan goaded amid a round of chuckles.

Michael smiled politely, trying to avoid being conspicuous among his seniors.

"And like any meetin' of Irishmen," O'Gara continued, "there was a wee bit of disagreement. 'Twas the same issue what was debated at last year's convention in Philadelphia. Back then, you'll recall, William Roberts, the dry goods merchant from New York, put forward a proposal for invadin' British North America. The goal is to create in Canada an Irish government-in-exile. We could then bargain away our Canadian conquests for Ireland's independence."

At this reference Michael set down his tea and listened most closely. This was the first discussion of military strategy to which he had been made privy.

"And Colonel O'Mahony daren't touch it with a barge pole. He's keen that all resources be devoted to action on the ground in Ireland. So he allowed no vote upon the matter entirely."

"I hear the Colonel got himself trumped by a General this time," O'Sullivan cracked as he loaded his white clay pipe.

"Somethin' like that," O'Gara said. "'Fightin' Tom' Sweeney, a real general in the Federal Army, threw his support to Roberts. Together, they forced this special session to resolve the issue. And we, from Massachusetts, was right in the van, supportin' Roberts. Told 'em we'd rather be fightin' Brits up in Canada than take the risk of the British Navy plannin' a homecomin' for us back in Ireland."

Canada! Michael had never considered the possibility of fighting for Irish independence by attacking the British here in America. Sure, more Civil War veterans will be persuaded to participate if they need only march a bit further north.

"So now," Breen interjected, "Roberts is elected the national leader, replacin' O'Mahony, and Tom Sweeney's now our full-time Secretary of War."

"Just so," O'Gara said. "Sweeney and Roberts are after workin' up the plan to invade Canada. But Jaysus, the way they argue these military questions in the open, with press correspondents listenin' to every blessed word! They might as well send a copy of the minutes to Queen Victorie, herself."

"Any word of Tim Deasy, Tom?" O'Sullivan asked.

"Aye. It seems Tim was released from Bridewell Prison for deportation. I'm figurin' he'll return to Lawrence directly."

The evening's conversation spent itself after an hour. But all were enthusiastic at the prospect of Tim Deasy's return. Finally, the years of talk were over, and the day of action was sure to come soon.

In the days that followed, the Fenian Circle in Lawrence named itself for William Roberts and began collecting arms. There were posters in the shop windows of the Plains, urging the purchase of Fenian bonds for ten dollars each. Balls and fairs were held to raise funds. Over five thousand dollars and a hundred stand of arms were collected.

But Jane Hearst had serious misgivings about the looming war and its implications for Michael and herself. One day, as they stood in her parlor, she confronted Michael about it. "My father says the Fenians ought be rounded up and sent to Van Diemen's Land. He has little patience for talk of Irish independence."

Michael threw his cap onto the table in disgust. "Your father would say such a thing. 'Tis all grand bein' a loom mechanic the day he arrives, and all the Irish workers waitin' year after year for a chance at such a position."

Jane took his hand in hers. "Hush, Michael, they may hear you. . . . All this talk of the Fenian war scares me. What if they ask you to go? You might be wounded, or even killed!"

Michael was touched by her concern and he caressed her cheek gently. "I know it seems crazy to you, dear, but I've given me word, taken an oath. I can't shirk it just when Ireland's best chance for liberty is on offer."

Jane walked to the window, still unsatisfied. "What good will it do the peasants of Ireland, all of you marching on our peaceful neighbors in Canada? It makes no sense to me at all." She turned to face Michael. "I admit your devotion to your homeland is admirable, but it's certainly of no help as far as our plans to marry. Father will be greatly upset—"

Before she could finish, Michael crossed the distance to her, anger flashing in his eyes. He grabbed her arm and pulled her close, speaking softly but, nevertheless, with great forcefulness. "What your father thinks holds no power over me! When the Fenians are called, I'll go willingly, and with a grand smile on me gob. And when you're of age, we'll marry, with or without his blessing!"

Seeing the shock in Jane's eyes, he released his grip. She pouted and turned away again. All was silent. Though his anger was vented, he was unwilling to apologize. There was nothing more to say. "I must be goin'." He retrieved his cap and quickly strode to the door.

Michael's chances of being sent to war were increasing. General Sweeney had completed his plan for the invasion of Canada, and William Roberts had discreetly sounded out the potential for support from President Andrew Johnson. A mildly positive reaction was obtained. Words to the effect that "We would obviously have to recognize any fait accompli" were attributed to Johnson.

The opportunity for an uprising in Ireland had come and gone, as most Fenian leaders there had been jailed. This object lesson pressured Sweeney to push forward the timetable for his own invasion, even though he had received less than a quarter of the $450,000 he had requested. He had no artillery and very little cavalry. He had asked for ten thousand men, but had no idea how many volunteers would actually arrive at the designated attack points. But Sweeney, a competent field commander, preferred to take his chances on the battlefield rather than see the opportunity to strike dissipate in America as it had in Ireland.

A plan for a three-pronged invasion was envisioned. First, diversionary forces would embark from Chicago and Milwaukee. Their objective was to get the Canadian militia in Ontario to divide its forces. Secondly, a column of Fenians from Detroit and one from Cleveland would cross Lake Erie and move east toward Montreal. French-Canadian dissidents in that city had promised to rise in civil insurrection, preoccupying British forces. With Upper Canada cut off from Lower Canada, IRB General Sam Spear would deliver the main thrust from Vermont and northeastern New York. Sweeney called for a general mobilization of IRB forces for the 10th of May.

A few days later, these events began to tumble down upon Michael. Captain Deasy had returned from Ireland to take part in the invasion. At a meeting of the Robert's Circle, Deasy, dressed in civilian attire, briefed the members on the impending action. He paced back and forth like a caged animal. It seemed to Michael that the aborted mission to Ireland had only intensified the leader's appetite to engage the enemy.

"Gentlemen, you'll be pleased to know that 10,000 stand of arms have been purchased from the U.S. arsenal at Philadelphia, and we've 2.5 million ball cartridges from the arsenal in Troy, N.Y. Depots for arms and supplies have been established at numerous points along the border."

Michael listened closely, trying to manage the mix of eager anticipation and nervous dread that filled his heart.

"We are ready to play our assigned role. All Fenian forces in New England have been assigned to General Sam Spear. You'll be transported to Vermont with whatever arms and supplies we have gathered locally. Any of you who are still unarmed will be issued rifle and ammunition when you get there."

Tom O'Gara, now the elected head of the Roberts Circle, stood up at his front row seat. "We expect to send over a hundred volunteers from Lawrence, and a further three hundred from Boston. Of course, there'll be others from all over New England joining us at St. Albans, so we'll have plenty of company."

"That's grand, Tom, we'll need them all," Deasy said, turning to details of logistics. "On Wednesday morning, we'll gather at the station for the 6:15 train to Manchester. You are to dress in regular clothes and sturdy shoes or boots. You must conceal any arms or military items during the journey. We'll provide each a ticket to Ogdensburg, New York. If you are questioned, Ogdensburg is your final destination. However, we'll disembark at St. Albans and split up into small groups, maybe ten or fifteen men to a squad. Then we'll move off into the countryside to evade the British spies."

As the briefing continued, Michael noticed the many recent recruits in attendance. He leaned over and whispered to John Breen. "Some of these lads must be no older than fourteen or fifteen!"

"Aye," Breen nodded. "Still, it's down to numbers, isn't it? We are lookin' to send as many volunteers as possible to General Spear. I'll wager these boys will find a way to be useful."

As the meeting concluded, Breen grabbed Michael's arm. "Have you made any arrangements at the mill, you know, to return to your job?"

Michael shrugged and admitted he had not inquired. "If it's up to me foreman, he'll send me off and bid good riddance. Anyway, I'm tired of bein' a piecer. America's a place to be makin' your fortune. I'll never have anythin' to show for meself here, save a case of cotton lung."

"I hear you, Mike. Let's see what opportunities come along once the campaign in Canada is won. Sure, you are destined for more than a piecer's lot."

Michael broached the issue of a leave of absence at the Pacific Superintendent's Office, but he never got past the clerk, who directed him back to his foreman. When he screwed up the courage to put the question, the reply was as expected. "Quinn, if you are not here one day, you'd better be sick. If you're gone two days, you'd better be dead. On day three, I'll have a steady worker behind you."

Michael looked about at the familiar hub of noise and activity that was the weaving room. Guess we'd better be victorious.

After Mass that Sunday, Michael looked for Jane, hoping to walk her home. It was a beautiful spring morning and he was keen not to spoil it. Still, he knew he must tell her what was coming. As they walked the leafy street, at a respectful distance behind Mr. and Mrs. Hearst, he began with a warning.

"You must swear upon your immortal soul that you'll not be tellin' anyone of this, least of all your father."

"Oh, Michael! Of course, I won't tell your Fenian secrets."

"Right, but it is important. We know the day now. 'Tis official. We'll be leavin' Wednesday mornin'."

Jane raised her nose in contempt. "You know I despise this little war your friends have cooked up. I'll not pretend to be happy about it."

Michael rolled his eyes and struggled with his temper. "We've been through all this, time and again. 'Tis a military decision where we fight the Brits. Besides, Canada will be welcomin' us for chasin' the Queen's forces back to England."

When the Hearsts turned the corner, he pulled Jane into the alley behind a row of houses.

"Jane, please don't be angry. Shall we not have a kiss of farewell? If I do die, I want me last memory of us to be a happy one."

Jane pouted a few seconds, but ultimately threw her arms around his neck and gave him a proper goodbye. "Dearest, please be careful. I couldn't bear it if—"

"Don't worry Jane, I'll be returnin' to you all right. And we'll marry as soon as you'll be eighteen."

It went less well when John and Roderick learned of Michael's imminent departure with the Fenian volunteers. They tried mightily to dissuade him. On the night of the 29th of May, they met at Fallon's for one last go at it. Roderick struck the first blow.

"You know well, Michael, how Ma will react, her youngest son goin' off to war. And Da, why he still has his heart broke over James. Can you imagine what it'll do to him if you buy a bullet up there in Canada? And what does Jane think about this?"

"Let's leave Jane out of this, if you please," Michael snapped. "If all felt as you do, Ireland would be under the British heel forever! You never did give a tinker's damn for your own country!"

Roderick's temper flared in the face of Michael's attack. His normally pale complexion went red from the neck up. "America is me country now, Michael!"

John pushed in between them. "Enough of this, you two!" He looked sharply at Roderick. "We'll not be talkin' him out of the Fenian Army, so let's not have brother against brother. Michael, if you're bound to do this foolish thing, at least take your leavin' friendly-like. Let's not have such words on our conscience . . . in case anythin' terrible should happen."

Roderick sulked for a minute, then got up from the table. "I'm off for a piss."

When he was gone, John seized the moment and pushed a packet across the table at Michael.

"What's this, then?" Michael took the packet and carefully unfolded the paper. Inside, he found twenty greenback dollars. "Shite, John! What have you done? This must be from the account for the family. I can't be takin' money from that!"

"Just take it and shut your gob! I'll kill you if you let on to Roderick. You'll have no job when you're done with this feis up in Canada. So keep the money and use it well. Ma, Da and the girls will get here soon enough. Twenty dollars ain't goin' to delay their arrival hardly at all."

Michael felt a lump in his throat. He didn't know what to say. When Roderick returned, there wasn't much conversation left in any of them. They drank "the brothers" and walked out into the warm spring night. An awkward moment followed. After brief embraces and words of goodbye, they parted.

Michael wandered aimlessly through the streets of the Plains. One moment he was steeling himself against the unknowns of the battlefield. At another, he felt a wave of melancholy over the farewells bid to Jane and his brothers. Tonight, he missed his parents and his sisters more than he had for a long time.

The sounds of tenement life washed over him: a baby crying, a couple arguing, the ever-present drunks on the stoops, joking and singing. One of the drunks, in a quavering voice, softly sang "Kathleen Mavourneen":

Oh! Hast thou forgotten how soon we must sever
Oh! Hast thou forgotten, this day we must part;
It may be for years, and it may be forever.
Oh! Why art thou silent, thou voice of my heart?

The huddle of run-down tenements looming over dark, noisy, dirty streets wasn't a particularly attractive setting. Yet Lawrence had become home to Michael in the nearly two years since his arrival. He crossed back over the silent, black snake that was the Spicket and tiptoed up the backstairs to his room. He had no wish to awaken Roderick and risk reopening the wounds of this evening past.

Upon the black skin of the throbbing locomotive glistened morning dew, gilt by the rising sun. Michael was early to the station, having slept but little. He paced the platform lost in his own thoughts. He had no interest in seeking out conversation with the other volunteers nearby. When the call came, he boarded and found a quiet seat for himself and his old canvas sack. Ten minutes passed before the car began to fill.

One of the young, new, Lawrence volunteers stood before him. "Is this seat taken, sir?"

Michael was not used to being addressed as sir. But as a 19 year-old, he was happy to learn. "Not at all! Sit!"

The red-cheeked boy was tall and rather handsome. He smelled of brown soap. His head was nearly swallowed by the oversized, black felt slouch hat he wore. Michael looked him over, appraising the lad, as he stowed his belongings. "I'm thinkin' I've seen you at the meeting of the Circle, but I don't know your name."

"Powers, sir, James Powers. Me family lives near Stevens Pond, at the end of Manchester Street."

"Ah, sure . . . Powers. Are you old enough for warfare and such?"

James was taken aback. He straightened his posture and countered, "I'll be sixteen soon!"

Michael smiled and nodded in appreciation of such maturity.

"Still, I'm a bit nervous," the boy admitted. "I never even held a gun."

Michael recalled how superficial was his introduction to the Springfield rifle at a Fenian meeting months ago. He also thought back on his own case of nerves upon arriving alone in New York City and the Union soldier who befriended him. Now 'tis me own turn. "You can stick with me, James. We'll see this thing through together. Sure, I'm scared a bit meself. We must take our lead from the real soldiers among us, eh?"

When they changed trains at Manchester, John Breen came along the platform and stopped to chat. Michael introduced young Powers to his friend, then pulled Breen away to privately query him for news from the border.

"Ach, it's a bit desperate at the moment, Mike. There are federal agents at St. Albans after playin' the spoiler's game. Last week, they confiscated a thousand stand of rifles. They keep a sharp eye for any such contraband. I hear they've been bribed by the British."

"Look, John. This whole campaign ain't the best kept secret in the world. Why, the papers are full of rumors of our lads, massin' at cities along the border. Does General Spear think the authorities will simply let us pass?"

"Not entirely. We'll have to march around them. True, we are too many to hide, but our camps will be well outside the city."

Michael shook his head in disbelief at how much of their plan was grounded upon hope alone. After Breen had left, Michael turned and saw enthusiasm and expectation upon the face of young Powers. Putting aside his misgivings, he answered a screaming whistle and climbed aboard the train for Vermont, James at his side.

General Spear, already in St. Albans, would have wished for the problem of too many volunteers to hide. Instead, he found almost none upon his arrival. Unable to coordinate his attack with those of the Western and Central Divisions, he was forced to await additional men and materiel. More trains arrived, but with men lacking arms or provisions. And they wanted to be armed and led, or, at least, fed.

The Lawrence volunteers were split up at St. Albans, early on the 31st of May. Michael and James were among those assigned to the Second Infantry under Colonel Michael Scanlan. Scanlan's forces deployed to Highgate Falls, a remote, wooded area about ten miles north of St. Albans. There, a long and frustrating wait began. Word came of an IRB engagement with the British forces just across the border from Buffalo. An advance party of Fenian volunteers, led by Colonel John O'Neill, had defeated a larger British force at the town of Ridgeway. While this cheered the men a bit, days passed and still no orders came from General Spear.

By June 2nd, U.S. General Ulysses Grant had arrived in Buffalo, his Federal troops effectively preventing the majority of the Central Division of Fenian volunteers from crossing the border. Grant's orders were to detain the Fenian officers and seize all arms and munitions.

Several days later, a group of Fenian volunteers from Boston arrived at Highgate Falls. They had been in St. Albans for the last three days facing similar shortages of food and munitions. Their arrival at Highgate only magnified the supply problems. The days were filled with hunger and grumbling. Many threatened to return home. Officers were scarcely able to control their men, most of whom had been without provisions or shelter for nearly six days. Colonel Scanlan returned to Spear's headquarters to demand supplies for his troops. Only the arrival of food donated by the Fenian Circle of South Boston forestalled an impending mutiny.

U.S. General George Meade, victor of Gettysburg, was dispatched to Malone, New York. There he captured IRB Brig. General Michael Murphy's Irish cavalry, which had been driven back from Canada by a superior British force. To add to their woes, the Western thrust of Fenians from Chicago and Milwaukee had been aborted for lack of adequate transport across Lake Michigan. Sweeney's plan of attack was unraveling badly, and Spear had not yet moved his forces.

A swirling wind blew campfire smoke into the eyes of the Lawrence men huddling beneath a stand of pines in the light rainfall.

Martin Mulcahey, Roderick's Fenian friend, was the self-appointed voice of all their frustrations. "Damn the smoke! Damn the generals! And damn the blasted weather! If somethin' doesn't happen soon, I'm off for home. Me missus told me I was mad for comin' at all. Just now, I'm thinkin' she had it right."

Mulcahey, a great one for whittling to pass the time, slashed furiously at a stick with his penknife. His place at the fireside was littered with the shavings of countless twigs, dispatched to feed the struggling fire.

"Will you also go home then, Michael?" James Powers asked.

Michael mopped the rain from his face with his sleeve. "I can't, lad, at least not yet. If there's to be any action, I'll not be missin' it. Besides, 'twould be a bitter day indeed to go back and listen to me brothers jeer our poor showin' as soldiers. I'll stay to see what comes."

Powers pulled his knees up under his chin, his thin canvas coat soaked through. He stifled a shiver. "When I told me girl that I was after becomin' a soldier, she seemed right favorably impressed. We talked of me comin' home in a uniform and maybe marchin' in a victory parade, right down Essex Street."

Michael frowned, wondering if Jane would take any such pleasure in a triumphant Fenian return. He rubbed his hands before the fire in a vain search of warmth. "You may well do that, James. 'Tis a bit early to be defeated when we've yet to meet up with a single British soldier. Maybe tomorrow the orders to cross over will be in hand."

There was no need to wait until the next day. Late that night, orders to break camp were issued. With little more than a few crumbs of hardtack in their bellies, the men hurriedly assembled with their mostly unfamiliar weapons. Those men lucky enough to have them had cleaned their army surplus Springfield rifles, but none had actually fired them for the conserving of cartridges and caps.

Colonel Scanlan took his Second Infantry over the border toward the Canadian village of St. Armand. Michael and his comrades welcomed the march, stretching their cold, stiff muscles to cover the distance. The morning sun began to penetrate the clouds and dry out their clothing.

About midmorning, they arrived at St. Armand, encountering no defensive presence. The village was a small, muddy huddle of homes strung out along a dirt road. Children, dogs and chickens were the only forces arrayed before them.

A lieutenant ordered, "Quinn, you and Mulcahey form a squad to forage for food and supplies."

Splitting the task, Mulchahey took some men to the west side of the village, while Michael, James, and three others went to the east. The IRB had made great promises about the welcome they would receive from Irish-Canadians and disgruntled Quebecois. Actual experience this day was far off that prediction.

"Thieves! Murderin' thieves, you are! Go back to the States, or Ireland, or wherever you're coming from," cried a distraught Canadian housewife.

Michael attempted to sooth her temper. "I'm obliged to offer you receipt and promise of full compensation," Michael stammered. Backing his way out the woman's kitchen door, Michael turned and whispered to James, "Get them chickens out of her sight! I'll be joinin' you presently. Now go!"

With that the matron grabbed up her twigged broom and charged at the Fenian soldiers who ran off to rejoin their mates. "Compensation! I'll have my husband take our compensation, and he'll be armed with more than this old broom!"

When they found Mulcahey, he was equally crestfallen to learn that St. Armand was not a hotbed of sympathy for the Irish Army. "Ach, there's an Ulsterman down that lane who gave us only hot tongue and cold shoulder! The bugger's probably callin' down the entire Orange Lodge over the bits of food we took off him."

Twenty minutes later, Colonel Scanlan allocated a small force to secure the village and led the rest of the column north toward the town of East Stanbridge. Two hours into that march, a scout returned to the main body with word of approaching British cavalry. Quickly but quietly, Scanlan flanked the road with his forces, taking cover in the thick forest of evergreens.

James bit the tail off a paper cartridge and spat it away. Then he poured its contents into the muzzle of his rifle as Michael steadied the barrel for him. The paper and ball were rammed home with the iron ramrod.

"That's grand." Michael counseled as he turned to look to his own weapon. " Now, don't be forgettin' the cap or the bleedin' thing will be useless to you."

1866 Fenian invasion of Canada from Vermont (Based upon maps in Troublous Times in Canada by J.A. Macdonald)

Hoofbeats in the distance pounded in their ears and frayed their nerves. By the sound of it, a very large force was upon them. *Klick, kluck. Klick, kluck.* The noise of many hammers being cocked further stoked the fires of emotion for the neophyte warriors. Word was passed along the ranks to wait until the leaders of the column had passed by. Colonel Scanlan wanted no possibility of strategic retreat by the enemy. The British cavalry, resplendent in bright red tunics and khaki breeches, crested the hill and entered the unseen maw of their quarry.

"Fire!" The lieutenant's voice quavered as he shouted the order. Instead of one big bang of simultaneous discharges, a string of sequential reports lasted for what seemed to Michael a minute, but was only about ten seconds. He was momentarily mesmerized by the swirling morass before him—the smoke, the screams of pain, the rearing horses and fallen riders in the dirt road. He clumsily set to reloading his musket, casting a nervous eye now and again at the British. Those still mounted had scattered quickly, the head of their column pushing through to the south, the tail wheeling back north. Some of the downed British riders clutched at their carbines and searched out the unseen enemy.

As Michael set the cap on the nipple of his rifle, a second Fenian volley was ordered. The crossfire roiled the redcoats again, convincing the stranded that their best chance lay in timely surrender. Throwing their hands in the air, the Brits were engulfed by cheering Irishmen. Mulcahey dashed into the dirt road and scooped up the fallen standard of his vanquished enemy. He marched it over to the Colonel Scanlan and, with comic flourishes, bowed and presented the enemy's colors to his commander.

Scanlan smiled and handed the prize to an aide and ordered a tally of casualties. There were no Fenian dead or injured, and only a few British fatalities were recorded. But there were numerous enemy wounded and in need of immediate medical attention. Again splitting his force, Scanlan assigned a party to escort his British prisoners back to St. Armand. The worst of the injured were taken to a nearby farmhouse where they could be attended to by his regimental surgeon. The remainder of the Fenian column continued their advance upon East Stanbridge.

Success had also greeted an advance party of the Third Infantry, who had taken Frelighsburg without meaningful resistance. Having discovered a position of strategic advantage nearby, they dubbed it "Camp Sweeney." It was a natural fortress from which a vastly superior force could be kept at bay indefinitely. Word was sent back to Spear, requesting reinforcement by the main infantry and cavalry units.

The day had been a tactical success. The significant towns in the region were now under Fenian control. The main trunk railroad running east-west between Quebec and Ontario had been cut. With only a fraction of the men he had been promised, General Spear had made a very good beginning. But with cash on hand of only $20.15, Spear telegraphed Sweeney: "Give me men, arms and ammunition."

Spear was totally unaware that Sweeney had already been placed under arrest by Federal troops in St. Albans. But a messenger did arrive with other, more devastating, news. President Johnson had issued a proclamation against the Fenian hostilities, illegal under the Neutrality Acts of 1818. The day after this proclamation, the British ambassador to Washington agreed that Her Majesty's government would pay the $15,000,000 in reparations demanded by the U.S. This was compensation for losses incurred during the Civil War as a result of British complicity with the Confederates. A deal had been done.

It was nightfall in East Stanbridge and a threat of further rain had passed. Thanks to the foraging done earlier in the day, the men of the Second Infantry were enjoying their first decent meal since they left home. The sound of a harmonica from a distant campfire floated in the air. James licked the fat of roasted chicken from his fingers and wiped them on his trousers. "Do you think you killed any of those cavalry, today, Michael?"

Michael set down his empty tin plate and reclined in satisfaction with the meal and the day. "I can't be sure. I may have done. 'Twas entirely confusin', what with downed horses, gunsmoke and such. I had one of those Brits in me sights when the order to fire was given. But I can't actually say I saw him fall. I hope I got one, at least. How about yourself?"

James wrapped his hands around a warm cup of coffee as the cool of the evening descended upon them. "I don't know if I was aimed properly. I heard the lieutenant yell 'Fire,' and I pulled me trigger." He paused momentarily, as if lost in reflection. "If I did kill one, I hope he went quick. I've been thinkin' what 'tis like to roll about in the mud with a hot Minié ball in you."

This comment struck a discordant note with Michael. It was not that he hadn't thought about the results of their efforts during the ambush at Pigeon Hill. But he was prepared to kill as many redcoats as possible, and James's ambivalence, even regret, struck him as weak and unbecoming. He stood up to go for more coffee and waved his empty tin cup dismissively at the boy. "No need to be usin' up your sympathy on Brits. They never gave a second thought when doin' the same or worse to our people."

As he walked to the mess tent, Michael reflected further on the day's events. How many years has it been since the Brits was upended by Irishmen? God, 'twas wonderful to see! The boy's concern for the individual British soldier is all very noble, but such sentiment won't buy Ireland's freedom. I wonder what tomorrow will bring. More victories, I'm hopin'. I'll show John and Roderick what difference we can make.

Shortly after dawn the next morning, a rider arrived with a message for Colonel Scanlan.

"It is with deep regret that I must order your regiment to retire from the field. It is now clear that men and materiel have been interdicted. Our current positions are hopelessly exposed. O'Connor and Contri have evacuated Frelighsburg, and are headed to Musgrove Corner. I suggest you make your way to the nearest border crossing, without delay."

General Samuel Spear, Army of Ireland

As the order to retire spread through the camp, the reaction of the troops was one of incredulity and anger. The men struggled to comprehend what was happening. Some, like Michael, wanted to stay and fight, even without official sanction.

Mulcahey bristled, "We braved our first action successfully! The Brits have been bested on the field of battle. What feckin' idiot ordered this retreat?"

Verbal abuse was heaped upon the officers attempting to carry out the command. The men were through with any further pretense at military discipline. Nevertheless, the breaking of camp proceeded as acquiescence and despair spread within the ranks. Recognizing the need to collect the wounded and the small garrison at St. Armand, Scanlan ordered a forced march back the way they had come. Despite the best efforts of their officers, the column rapidly degenerated into the undisciplined movement of a herd rather than a military march.

Later that morning, as the men were leaving St. Armand, scouts reported the approach of three infantry companies of Her Majesty's Sixteenth Regiment. In the distance, a bagpiper could be heard setting the pace for them. A wave of panic swept through the Irish forces. They ignored the orders to establish a rear guard effort, and what had been a desultory walk became a Fenian footrace for the border. As they approached the border, they were met by a column of Royal Guards and Cavalry from Montreal. Their commander, Captain Lorn MacDougall, gave the order to charge the fleeing rebels.

Michael and a few comrades had their muskets charged and broke their run to turn and fire into the oncoming attack. But so few Fenians offered even this limited resistance, the effect was negligible. Without time to reload, those inclined to resist were quickly overrun. British cavaliers used the flat of their sabers as they slashed their way through the stumbling, scrambling refugees.

"Ach, me ankle! Michael, help!" He knew that voice. It was James. Michael turned to look over his shoulder. A British cavalryman had James on the ground, a carbine trained upon him. It was useless to go back. On Michael's every side, there was a redcoat threat. Bleedin' Brits! Time to feck off!

Michael's panic overtook him and he resumed his headlong run. He knew the border was just over the brow of the next hill. Mulcahey was ahead, waving wildly, urging them on toward the line and its supposed protection.

As the Fenians crossed over to the U.S. side, they were met by the United States Third Artillery Regiment under Lt. Colonel Livingston. Michael and his comrades headed for their lines seeking sanctuary. But Livingston barked an order and the U.S. forces gave way to the pursuing British cavalry. Michael dove into a clump of bushes as the sound of hoof-beats chased away the hope of escape. From this meager cover, he witnessed Irish rebels being run through by British sabers upon American soil under the disinterested gaze of Livingston. "That bleedin' bastard," Michael muttered in horror and disbelief.

Those spared British retribution were taken in hand by the federal soldiers and placed under arrest. A sergeant in a blue tunic reached into the thicket where Michael and several others were hiding and pulled them out. Michael and nearly two hundred fellow Fenians were marched off the few miles to Livingston's encampment to await their fate.

Chapter Nine

Taking Leave

✠

It was the 12th of June and it was raining again. Three painfully long days had passed since Michael had been captured along with the remnants of the Irish Second Infantry. The uncertainty of their fate at the hands of the Federals was on everyone's mind. None of the Fenians captured by the British north of the border had been repatriated. Rumors were circulating of planned trials and executions for those unlucky ones.

Michael's anxieties were compounded by visions of that final, brutal slaughter and by the memory of James's voice crying to him for help. He repeatedly rehearsed his behavior, justifying his inability to effect a rescue. He prayed for James's safe return, but his mind would afford him no peace. The boy's cry would not be silenced.

The U.S. Army's camp was a spartan, makeshift prison set in a farmer's meadow several miles west of Franklin, Vermont. The comings and goings of the federal soldiers, their horses, mules, wagons, and the nearly 400 Fenian prisoners had churned the ground into a bouillabaisse of mud and muck. Though the prisoners were given the freedom of the camp, sentries guarded the perimeter closely. Rain showers sent the rebels scurrying into a thick stand of maples on the edge of the meadow. But these were newly leafed in palest green, affording scant protection against the elements. The sick and the wounded were sheltered in lean-tos constructed of tarpaulins and saplings. It was there that Michael fled and volunteered his services.

The evening meal was called. Michael turned his collar up and walked out into the gentle rain to join the queue of prisoners. A large iron soup pot, protected by a sheet of canvas, hung over a bed of sputtering coals. The beans plopped into tin plates by a sullen federal private were watery and nearly cold, but not to be rejected. Michael took his portion and returned to the lean-to where he sat down on the damp, matted grass. A stranger, plate in hand, joined him. He was dressed differently from the rest of the Fenian cadre. His tall, laced leather boots reached nearly to the knee and rough corduroy trousers were stuffed into the tops. A red, flannel shirt and a leather vest completed his costume. He looked about thirty years of age and wore a dark, close-cropped beard.

"We've not met," Michael ventured. "I'm Michael Quinn. What unit are you from?"

The stranger threw his head back and forced a derisive laugh. "My army? She is shit! The brave Quebecois would not leave their warm beds on the day of destiny."

Michael pushed his beans back and forth with a tin spoon. "Ah, right! I remember now. You French were after joinin' us in chasin' the Brits out of North America. You mustn't feel bad. Many's the Irishman who swore he'd fight but somehow went missin' when the call finally came."

The Canadian nodded in silent agreement as he consumed a mouthful of beans. "It is as you say. Forgive me, *mon ami*. I am called Guy Beaupre. I am special courier to your General Spear from *mes frères* in Montreal. It was my sad duty to report to the General their failure to rise up against the enemy. Then, of course, the bluecoats arrived."

Michael was amused by the stranger's accent, which rendered shit as "sheet" and Guy as "Gee." "I've never met any Frenchies before. Is it true that you've no more time for your British masters then we Irish?"

Guy gave another brief, sardonic laugh as he set aside his empty plate.

"*Les Anglais,* they are the most arrogant people in creation! For them, it is certain that God gave them their empire, and only He may take it away." He paused to wipe his mouth with his shirtsleeve. "But, of course, one must concede they are well organized and most determined. *C'est dommage! Mes frères,* they are not so blessed in this way."

Michael angrily scratched at the two-week-old stubble on his face. His last shave had been in Lawrence; indeed, his last bath as well. Now between the want of hygiene and an attack of lice, it was hard to be comfortable with himself, never mind with his neighbor. He responded ruefully, "Your friars can't be no worse than us Irish at marryin' our words and our deeds, or keepin' a secret of our plans. Still, there was the treachery of the American President. 'Tis hard to fight a war when men and supplies are seized before the battle begins."

"*Enfin,* Michel, what will become of your crusade for Ireland's independence? Perhaps a fresh start may be made from Europe? Could it be that France will again join in your struggle?"

Michael's mouth became a short, stiff line of anger and despair. His voice lost its animation. "'Tis altogether shameful that we have failed our Irish countrymen. I hate to admit it, but perhaps my brothers were right. At the end of the day, we are here and they are there. I'm afraid I've had me fill of glorious deeds what are only talk."

They sat for a while in silence, which allowed Michael to regain control of his emotions. "What of your own plans, Guy? Will you return to Montreal if we are released?"

"*Mais non!*" he sighed heavily. "I am afraid my depart from Montreal, it was not a happy one. I spoke freely of my anger and scorn. Now those of the weak knees will not be easily reconciled. Shall we take some *café?*"

They found their way to another queue where thirty or forty prisoners were awaiting coffee. "Perhaps I will join my older brother, René. He's a trader in the *région sauvage.*"

"Is there any fortune to be made in such wilderness?" asked Michael as he huddled against the drizzle.

"*Oui,* there is great opportunity. But it is not for the weak or the lazy. René began as a fur trapper, but now acts as *commerçant,* trading supplies to *les sauvages* for the pelts. Perhaps you also will voyage west and see for yourself."

A federal private declared the coffee ready. "All right, boys, come cut ya a slice of black."

Michael and Guy took their tin cups of coffee and hurried back to the shelter of the lean-to. Michael was considering Beaupre's comment about going west. "Guy, I'm still doin' the piecer work, which I first took up when I was eleven! There are days when I think I will go crazy, thinkin' about what might be me destiny. I'm sick to death of the mills and cotton and the English gettin' the good jobs. I want a go-ahead job, one with prospects. All the stories one hears of America make one desperate for his own fortune."

Guy did not know how to respond. They sipped their coffee in silence till they were recalled to duty with the injured.

The next morning the sun returned, bringing welcome warmth to camp. Banter and foolery among the idled men increased as the rhythms of daily activity—chopping wood, cooking, washing, hauling water—became a diverting routine. About noontime, the sounds of horses and wagons approaching the camp brought all to a standstill. Prisoners gaped as the U.S. Army brought remnants of the Fenian Third Infantry into camp. Michael searched the faces and recognized a few as Lawrence volunteers. Until the new prisoners were registered and deployed, however, the guards kept them at a distance.

Later that afternoon, Michael wandered through the ranks of the new arrivals anxiously seeking news of James Powers. But those who remembered the lad had no knowledge of his whereabouts. As he wandered through the camp, Michael passed a tent pitched at the edge of the woods. Emerging from the flapped entry was his good friend, John Breen. He was limping and had to steady himself with a stick.

"John!" Michael splashed through the puddles between them.

"Hey, Mike! It's grand to see you've come to no harm."

"You're injured!"

Breen bent down and rubbed a painful right thigh. "Arrah, it's nothin' to worry over. I fell off my horse as we retreated from Frelighsburg. Guess I'm not the rider I thought I was."

Each of them told stories of their respective, truncated efforts across the border. "'Twas a nasty sight," Michael admitted with some embarrassment.

"We was runnin' before the British cavalry and fallin' over ourselves to avoid the sabre or capture."

Breen quickly changed the subject. "I heard the Yankee soldiers talkin' this mornin'. They say the prisoner population here has outstripped supplies. It seems they cannot feed us beyond tomorrow. They'll have to start releasing prisoners, if no more supplies are delivered."

Michael was cheered at the prospect of possible release. "What happens now to the IRB and to the cause of Ireland's freedom?"

Breen's countenance hardened and his eyes lost their focus. "A soldier doesn't quit the war after one battle. The struggle for an Irish republic will continue till it succeeds. I expect we'll be forced to direct our efforts back to Ireland, since Johnson has clearly sold us out."

An awkward silence followed. Breen's limping walk chastened Michael to give his friend some comfort. "Let's sit down. I'd like a bit of advice."

They returned to the tent where Breen listened to Michael pour out his concerns. "I wish I knew what to do, John. I'm willin' to accept the chidin' me brothers will give for our poor showin' against the Brits. 'Tis not me pride I'm worried about. But goin' back into the damned mill . . . I'll be endin' me days as a coughin', weezin' fellow, old before me years. Should I not strive for more?"

Breen poked at the sodden ground with his stick. "What about the cause, Mike? Will you walk away from the Fenian oath you took?"

Michael's back straightened. "I'm a republican, and so I will remain. But me brothers are here and soon me parents and sisters will come too. I can't go off to Ireland now, at least not without some hope of success. The last few weeks haven't exactly given us a high regard for the Irish Army."

Breen's face winced at the criticism. He loaded his pipe with tobacco from a leather pouch. "I can't fault what you say, Mike. And your reluctance to go back to the mill is quite understandable. But you're an able man, and we need men such as yourself to rebuild the Brotherhood after this great setback."

Michael's voice now assumed a note of energy and optimism. "John, some here have been tellin' me of great chances to get on, out in the western territories. If I can make a bit of money, I'll be able to come back to Lawrence, marry Jane, and help me family as well."

"I'll be sad if you leave the Brotherhood. . . . But, if you're thinkin' to get to the frontier, your timin' could not be better."

Michael turned to look at his friend, his eyes flashing with interest. "What have you heard?"

"It seems General Grant has decided that the best way to rid himself of this misbegotten Irish army is get us all home as quickly as possible—by rail. No questions asked! You just tell them where you want to go, and they will write a military rail pass to get you there. A free trip to the frontier may be on offer, if you're sure you really want it."

Michael jumped up from the campstool. He could hardly contain his excitement. He wanted to rush off to find Beaupre. "As me own dear father would say, 'Glory be to St. Patrick!' When—how will they begin?"

"I don't know, but it seems they cannot wait much longer."

Michael placed a hand on his friend's shoulder. "John, you've been a grand friend these last two years. I'm more than grateful for all you've done."

"Ah begorrah, lad, what have I done at all?"

But Michael would not be put off. "I'll not be forgettin' your many kindnesses. But, can I ask one more of you? Will you tell me brothers, John and Roderick, of me decision. Tell 'em I'll write, once I know exactly where I'm goin'. And ask them to tell Jane I'll be back for her as soon as I'm able."

Breen extended his hand. "Sure, I will. Now get on with you. You've got plans to make."

The sun-battered cars of the Chicago, Burlington, and Quincy Railroad rolled across the flat, monotonous farm country of central Illinois. It was already a hot summer in the Midwest, and by midmorning the passengers were mopping perspiration from their faces. Only the rush of air from open windows offered some of them modest relief. The crudely furnished cars rocked in syncopation to imperfections in the ribbons of iron beneath them.

Michael gazed out upon the passing scene of green woodlands, geometrically defined fields of crops, and modest agrarian hamlets. Such had been their fare for most of the journey from St. Albans. Across the back of western New York, down through the hills of Pennsylvania, on through Ohio and Indiana, he and Guy had traveled, changing rail lines frequently.

There was no dining car. At occasional station stops, while water and coal were taken on, they piled out quickly to buy their food and drink. There was no time to tarry as they had to reach their final destination before their rail passes expired in two more days.

Michael got up to stretch. Ach, me back is breakin' on these wooden bench seats. It was midafternoon and he had been sitting for three hours. He flexed his knees and rolled his head to work out the kinks in his neck.

Guy looked up from a doze. "Michel, are we *arrivé* in Missouri yet?"

"We've another hour or two till we reach Palmyra, never mind our final destination." He chuckled to himself. Final destination! What is me final destination? This journey reminds me of me first time on a horse, the fair in Daisy Nook when I was ten. Da said, "Just hold on and see what happens!"

He looked down and studied the widening opening in the sole of his right shoe. His old factory clothes had worn badly through the campaign in Canada. He hadn't spent the twenty dollars given him by his brother John, but that time was coming soon. His own savings were nearly exhausted. Wherever I'm going, I must find a job pretty quick! He walked to the rear of the car to a cask of drinking water mounted there.

Palmyra, Missouri, was where they would change to their eleventh and final rail line, the Hannibal and St. Joseph Railroad. It would take them to the city of "St. Joe," as other passengers called it. There, on the east bank of the Missouri River, railroads and settled communities would give way to primitive, dangerous Indian country.

A white-haired conductor passed through the car again. Ever since they boarded in Chicago, Michael noticed how he eyed them with suspicion. Guess he's wonderin' how civilians should be travelin' on a military pass. Michael nodded to him politely, finished his drink, then returned to his seat. Guy was now fully awake and sitting up straight.

"Want some crackers and cheese, Guy?"

"*Merci*, Michel. Was it yesterday, rather than this morning when we ate last? My belly, she cries so loud she wakes me from my sleep."

Michael laughed out aloud at Guy's complaint, in light of his impressive ability to sleep anywhere, anytime. He reached into his sack and pulled out the food they had purchased as they changed trains in Chicago. As both were hoarding their funds, the diet was meager.

"Guy, what is this place where your brother René does his trading?"

"Fort Union, in the territory of Dakota. There, the Missouri, she receives the Yellowstone River." Guy took his ration gratefully. "But I think he will move his business to a new fort called Buford. René, he ask me many times to join him in the fur trade, but I never could leave Iberville . . . until now."

"So, you will find a riverboat at St. Joe for the journey to Ft. Union?"

"*Oui*, it is a journey of many days. You come with me, no?"

Michael, looking a bit sad, said, "A long passage by steamer will take all me money and more. When we get to St. Joe, I must find work."

Guy nodded, but he was clearly disappointed. He turned his face to the window and the conversation ended awkwardly.

Early on the morning of the 18th of June, they disembarked at St. Joe. A kerosene lamp cast a pool of light at one end of the platform. Sunup was still two hours away, and they both were desperate for a proper sleep. Guy opened the door of the station's unlit waiting room. Dark bundles, vaguely visible, were scattered about the floor like tossed dice. A closer inspection revealed travelers like themselves, snoozing away. Michael and Guy quickly exploited the improvised dormitory.

The city of St. Joseph, like St. Louis, Independence, and Nebraska City, was a jumping-off point for wagon trains headed west. Founded in 1843 by the trader, Joseph Robidoux, St. Joe had seen repeated waves of emigrants: Oregon settlers, Mormons on their way to Utah, '49ers eager for California gold, and later, those bound for Pike's Peak in Colorado.

Distinguishing St. Joe from her competitors was her history as eastern terminus of the Pony Express and the transcontinental Western Union telegraph line. Wagon train traffic had slowed during the Civil War and again most recently, due to the Indian war along the Nebraska and Wyoming sections of the great overland road. Though the danger from the Indians persisted still, it had subsided somewhat after the U.S. Army deployed more forts and soldiers to guard the route west. Traffic was now building again toward its final peak. The Union Pacific Railroad was being constructed a hundred and fifty miles west of Omaha. Before long, it would displace the mule and the oxen.

When dawn arrived, so did the station manager. He quickly expelled the "bunkers" cluttering his waiting room floor. A flurry of bags, blankets, and bodies pushed out into the already warm and brightening morning. Michael and Guy made inquiries among their fellow exiles regarding sources of food and inexpensive lodging.

"If ya kin afford a dollar," said one, "try the Huxley House. It's just spittin' distance from here. Old Philander Huxley will fix ya up with board and bed."

"Michel," Guy confessed, "I am ready to spend a whole dollar for a big breakfast and a real bed."

Michael grinned in contemplation of such luxury. "I'm right behind you, Guy. Shouldn't we be considerin' a bath as well? It may be difficult to get meself hired, smellin' as I do."

They crossed east, through the rail yard full of freight cars lined up for the river landing. At Eighth and Seneca, they found the Huxley House and surrendered a dollar each to Mr. Huxley. Soon they were seated at a crowded dining table replete with ham, scrambled eggs, flapjacks, and porridge. The rich aroma of fresh-brewed coffee wafted from the sideboard. Fellow boarders cheerfully chatted and offered advice on the finer points of interest in St. Joe while Michael and Guy made food disappear. Mrs. Huxley, who was serving the breakfast, instructed Guy where to apply for steamer passage up river.

A middle-aged man, dressed in buckskin, was seated directly across from Michael. His head was shaved entirely bare. When a curious fellow diner asked about this, he explained it was to discourage those who might wish to take his scalp. As he finished his meal, the frontiersman queried Michael as to his destination.

"I've no thoughts on it yet, sir," Michael replied. "Me first task will be to find work here in St. Joe."

"Well, son, there's plenty of work here in St. Joe. Me—I'm uncomfortable in such thickly settled places. Too darn many folks, all pushin' and rushin' to God knows where. I just come to cities to turn around my freight wagons and then I'm back out on the prairie."

After breakfast, Michael and Guy were shown to their rooms. A bath might be had, they were told, but it would take some time for water to be heated. "You take the first bath, Guy, I want to get a newspaper and see what the opportunities are."

Michael walked out into the increasing heat of a summer day. By the time he had covered the few blocks to the river, he had broken into a full sweat. Tall green cottonwoods and river willows at the water's edge soon gave way to the landing. There, rail cars were being off-loaded of freight by muscular, black stevedores, glistening in the streaming sweat of their labors.

He proceeded north along the levee, marveling at the continuous, noisy flow of wagons, carts, and animals, all moving huge quantities of freight to the ferries and riverboats lining the riverbank. The cracks of teamsters' whips punctuated a stream of coarse language urging oxen and mules through what seemed impassably crowded and dusty streets. The smells of hardworking men and animals filled his nose.

Michael found a store a block in from the landing, where he purchased a copy of the *Morning Herald.* He glanced briefly at the job postings but was soon distracted by the sights, sounds and smells of St. Joe. In the distance, he spotted the tall steeple of what looked like a Catholic Church. *I may find me some Irish there and, perhaps, they'll have advice about jobs hereabout.* He continued to the corner of Fifth and Felix where he entered the dim, candlelit transept of the church. It was refreshingly cool inside and, in the late morning, the church was virtually deserted.

He sat for a few minutes of quiet reflection, which brought on a rush of memories. He saw visions of home life in Ashton—his mother, father and sisters going about their daily routines. He recalled his passage to America and the hope-filled strangers from unfamiliar places. He could see Jane's face, and he pondered nervously her reaction to the word that he wasn't coming right home from the war. Ah, the war! Who could call such a war? Here he was, on the very edge of civilization, far from his family; far, too, from his beloved Jane and his brothers. It was difficult to believe all that had transpired in the last two years.

He left the church by the main entrance and, in passing, glanced at the sign in the front. "Saint Joseph's Catholic Church. Rev. Thomas Scanlan, Pastor; Rev. James Power, Assistant."

"James Power!" Michael blurted the words aloud in spontaneous reaction. It was Power, not Powers, but the closeness of the name riveted Michael where he stood. A wave of anguish washed over him. He felt weak in the knees. He sat down on the step in the shade of the building. He could hear again the desperate cry for help addressed to him below St. Armand. Tears welled up as he contemplated what fate may have already been dealt his Fenian friend.

"Is something wrong, my son?"

Michael was so startled he jumped to his feet. The voice on the steps above him was familiarly decorated with an Irish accent. He looked up into the eyes of a middle-aged man, dressed in a black cassock and a biretta. "No, Father, well . . . yes, Father. Just a bit of sadness came over me, Father."

"I'd be glad to help if I can. I'm Father Scanlan. Judging from your speech, I've a fellow Irishman on my doorstep. And from your appearance, this sadness isn't your only care at the moment." The priest took a seat on the step next to Michael. In a few moments he had extracted the story of the Fenian defeat in Canada and the capture of the fifteen-year-old James Powers.

"Sure, it must be a sign from the Almighty, Father," Michael said, "the name's nearly the same."

"Ah, but what's he saying? God has many ways by which to speak to us. The important thing is that we be listening."

Michael felt comfortable in confiding his concerns. He finished with his current search for opportunity on the western frontier.

"There's plenty of jobs here in St. Joe," Scanlan said. "You're a bit slight to be a stevedore. But I'm sure you can get on as an apprentice in one of the trades. Still, you must be warned: there's a railroad building west of the river. When it's completed, St. Joe will be in for hard times. The wagon trains shan't be coming here for their supplies and passengers. I'm afraid we'll lose the best of our trade."

Michael glanced at the sun and, remembering the hour, rose to leave. He thanked the priest for his guidance. "I can't say what I'll be doin' now, Father. But whatever 'tis, I'd be grateful for your blessin'."

The priest traced the sign of the cross on Michael's bowed forehead. "God bless you, Michael. I'll say a prayer for you and your captive friend. Perhaps you'll do the same for me?"

With a wave of farewell, Michael hurried to retrace his steps to Huxley House.

That afternoon, he bathed luxuriously, remaining submerged till his fingers and toes began to pucker. Then, with supervision from Guy, he managed a fair job of trimming his nascent beard. "It'll do me no harm to look a bit older to me prospective employer."

Guy sat on the edge of Michael's bed and picked up the newspaper lying beside him. "What have you found in the postings, Michel?"

"There's a number of notices for laborin', and some apprentice openings. But this priest I met told me that the railroad will ruin me chances here in St. Joe. I'm thinkin' maybe the job of teamster is best. It carries me further west at another man's expense."

That evening at dinner, Michael engaged the buckskinned lodger he had met at breakfast. "From your comments this mornin', mister, I'm thinkin' that you're a teamster."

The man's brow furrowed and his eyebrows knit together. "Bullwhacker, boy, bullwhacker! Some folk figure it be all the same, but 'taint. No, sir. A teamster, he handles horses, or maybe mules—nasty work, that. But a bullwhacker's gotta have the strength to wrastle the yoke onto a wild Texas steer with blood in his eye. Better have the persuasion of a lawyer to get the beast to move at all." The grizzled plainsman conducted this discourse through a mouthful of cornbread. "A bullwhacker don't ride his beast nor his wagon. He does his travelin' on foot and prefers it that way."

Michael was amused by this description and also by the fellow who offered it. There was an obvious pride and affection for his trade that the stranger conveyed, even if it came wrapped in humorous trappings. Upon learning that Michael was giving thought to entering the freighting trade, the frontier veteran shoved his hand at him over the bowl of mashed potatoes.

"My name's Jim Bowe, son, B-O-W-E. Most folk calls me Jimbo. Glad to have met up with you. If you got pluck, you'll find no better company of men than the bullwhackin' crowd. Have you signed on to any outfit yet?"

"I'm just after lookin' at notices listed in the *Herald* today. Tomorrow, I'm figurin' to apply somewhere. There's a big outfit here—Russell, someone, and Waddell."

Bowe nodded and reached out again. "Majors! Pass the gravy, son. Russell, Majors, and Waddell. Yep, they're the big outfit hereabouts. Got hundreds of bullwhackers on the rolls, and mighty particular 'bout their rules and regulations, I'll tell you. I worked for them back in fifty-eight. Didn't like it. Some may do, but I like a little slack in my tether."

Michael savored the beefsteak in front of him and winked at Guy, who politely audited the flow of counsel from Jimbo's usually full mouth. "Is there an outfit that you would recommend?" Michael asked. "Bein' a newcomer here, I'd greatly appreciate any advice."

Jimbo took a pull at his cup of black coffee and wrinkled his nose. "Well, now, I dunno. You see, I haven't hauled from St. Joe since the Nebraska City cut-off opened back. . . . Let's see, I suspect that was in '60 or '61. I forget. 'Course, I hear things from the fellas on the trail—who's happy, who ain't, who's got the toughest wagon master, that kind of thing. I'm only here to see my wife, as she is poorly at the present time."

"Your wife, she does not live with you?" Guy asked.

"Naw, she threw me out near ten years ago. If I could be said to live anywhere, I guess, it's out on the prairie. But I haul out of Nebraska City, mostly."

Michael was frustrated. Pushing his empty plate away, he leaned forward and looked Jimbo straight in the eye. "Perhaps in Nebraska City, there will be a good outfit for me to join?"

Jimbo sat back in his chair and grinned. "Well, that changes things if you throw Nebraska City into the pot. Why, I'd be pleased to speak for my own boss man, General Coe. That's General Issac Coe, as in Coe & Carter. A fair man, the General—gained his title and high reputation in the Nebraska territorial volunteers during the Civil War. Always treated me square. And he only hires the best wagon masters. Bein' that you're green and all, probably start you out at only fifty dollars a month. 'Course you have to cover the cost of your kit at the end of the trail."

Michael grinned. Fifty dollars a month is almost twice the wage I was paid at the mill. And I'll be outdoors, breathing decent air instead of dust and fibers. If only I can get on with such a freighter as Coe & Carter. Soon I'll have money for the family and, of course, to make Jane me wife.

Guy was nearly as enthused as Michael. "Michel, if you go to Nebraska City, we can ride the same steamer upriver!"

"When you goin', Frenchie?" asked Jimbo. "I'm near to leavin' here myself. My old woman ain't gonna die, least not this time. I'd welcome company if you got half a mind to try Nebraska City."

A pact was agreed and all shook hands on it. As a courtesy to Guy, Jimbo consented to wait for the next paddle wheeler bound for the Upper

Missouri and Ft. Union. The delay was slight, as river traffic was heavy at this time of year. A steamer, the *Peoria City*, was scheduled for Wednesday morning and that suited all three. Michael used the extra day at Huxley House to wash and hang out the single change of clothes in his travel sack.

Departure was early, before daylight broke over the high hill where the peacocks of St. Joe's high society took roost. In the dark, the muddy Missouri swept past like a stream of camp coffee, black and thick. The lights of the city of Ellwood danced and shimmered in reflected images on the waters near the western shore.

Jimbo led Michael and Guy up the stairs to the hurricane deck. "We'll be sleepin' up here, Mike. The fare is less than half and there's no hint of rain. If we get surprised, we can crowd in with Guy, here."

Guy, whose journey would be much longer, had opted for a private cabin. He feigned outrage at the notion of sharing his room and they all laughed. Later, the reality of the searing midday sun drove them below into Guy's small but shaded cabin. While Guy could enjoy promenading the covered upper deck with the other full-fare passengers, Michael and Jimbo had to lay low. With nightfall, however, the illicit traffic flow was reversed as young pilgrims from the cabin class made their way to the hurricane deck, preferring the cool night air to their hot, stuffy cabins.

Next morning, the three companions polished off the last of the biscuits and ham steak Mrs. Huxley had packed for their journey. "What will we do first when we arrive in Nebraska City?" Michael asked.

The question made Jimbo's face crack with a smile. He snorted his response. "We'll go back to sleep, my greenhorn friend. We'll likely make our landing about 3:00 in the mornin'."

"I'm sorry, Jimbo, I meant what must I do to get me employment arranged at Coe and Carter?"

"Aw, don't you worry, son. I'll take you straightaway to the company corral and we'll look up the General."

In the wee hours, the *Peoria City* made landing. To continue their sleep on the hurricane deck would be futile, due to the clatter of freight being unloaded and loaded. Jimbo led Michael ashore and up into a grove of trees on a low hill, to the left of the wharf area. "We can doze a bit up here, till sunup," he assured.

"Aye, but I'll want to be around to bid farewell to Guy before the steamer pushes on."

Shortly after dawn, they returned to the wharf and found Guy waiting for them. His face betrayed his reluctance on departing from such amiable company. Michael offered his hand to Guy. "I wish you good fortune with René."

Guy ignored the gesture and pulled Michael into a firm embrace. "And to you, *mon ami, bon chance* with the freighter's life. If she don't please you, you come visit Guy in Dakota, no?"

"I might well do that, Guy. Thanks for bein' a grand partner in our travels."

"*Au revoir*, Michel, and to you too, Monsieur Jimbo."

"Keep your hair, Frenchie," said Jimbo, as Guy walked back up the gangplank.

Chapter Ten

Becoming a Bullwhacker

✠

"Come on, Mike, let's answer the grub bell!" Mike and Jimbo walked back up the hard-packed dirt street from the wharf and across First Street, scattering the early birds pecking at the bits of grain spilled upon the ground.

"I reckon we all could use a proper breakfast."

Mike grunted his hearty concurrence and picked up the pace as they entered the awakening Nebraska City. The Cincinnati House wasn't fancy. But it well met the needs of Nebraska City folk. Fresh coffee, ham, eggs, and flapjacks were most welcome after two days of meager fare on the river.

"Eat your fill, Mike," Jimbo advised as he loaded sugar into his coffee cup. "No tellin' when the grub'll be this good and abundant again."

Mike raised an eyebrow at this remark. "Your meals on the trail are a bit sparse?"

"Well, there's usually enough to fill you, but I get tired of sowbelly and biscuit after a while. And 'land o' Goshen,' can they burn coffee beyond all resemblance!"

They made short work of their breakfast, and then sauntered leisurely through the streets toward the company corral at the south edge of town. The heat of the sun felt good on their backs till the morning chill was gone. The only offensive aspect was the plethora of "road apples" and "cow pies" littering the track they followed. If there's one thing that could be said about a freighting town, it was that the livestock seemed to own it more than the humans.

Coe & Carter was one of over sixty freighting companies operating out of Nebraska City. It was not the largest, certainly, but a good-sized firm in an industry where many small outfits of one or two teams participated. Like other freighting companies on the Missouri, they were straining to accommodate a busy season that, at its peak, would place up to one hundred and fifty wagons a day upon the Overland Trail.

As they approached the large corral, Mike complained that the air was full of assaults upon the olfactory. But Jimbo assured that he would learn to tolerate and ultimately forget them. From a distance, the scene was mostly clouds of dust from which emanated the streaming oaths of the bullwhackers and the bawling protests of recalcitrant beasts. On closer examination, Mike could see bullwhackers, each with an ash yoke on his shoulder, walk through a sea of Texas longhorn bulls to cull out the individual animals of their teams. Beyond the corral, a field of freight wagons was being sequenced into trains and prepared for loading.

Mike found there was no fastidious attention to grooming among the bullwhacking fraternity. Their life on the road across the wild prairie produced a notable acceptance of long greasy hair, scruffy beards, and dirty, dilapidated attire. A broad-brimmed hat topped the usual outfit of flannel shirt and black or brown woolen trousers tucked into high-topped leather or buckskin boots. A cartridge belt supported a knife and sheath, as well as a holster and revolver. Jimbo explained that the company would later provide its teamsters with rifle, caps, and cartridges with which to protect their trains from Indian attack.

As Mike and Jimbo approached the company office, a florid man in gray whiskers, about fifty years of age, ambled out into the yard. He was in white shirtsleeves, black vest and trousers. He carried a wad of waybills in one hand and waved his straw hat at Jimbo with the other. General Coe addressed Jimbo in the residual accent of his original Connecticut home.

"About time you came back from Missouri, James. How's your ailing wife?"

"Her spleen be healthy, that's all I know," Jimbo replied with a grin. "I brung you a raw recruit, General. Meet Mike Quinn, late of the Army of Ireland in America."

Mike extended his hand to a firm, vigorous shake. "I am pleased to meet you, General Coe."

The General removed his hat and swept his sleeve across his sweating brow. "I've been reading of the exploits of you Irish volunteers, young man. It seems you boys took quite a thrashing."

Mike struggled to maintain his composure. Keep smilin', lad. I need this job and mustn't sour things in political debate. "There's often more to a story than what's written in the newspapers, General," he responded with diplomacy.

"Well, since James brought you to me, he must have seen promise. Welcome."

After a few minutes of social chatter, Coe called out to a passing employee. "Sam, come over and meet another recruit for your crew. This is Mike Quinn. James brought him up from St. Joe. Show him around, will you? Then we'll have James take him to the outfitter."

Mike looked up into the dark eyes of the tall, powerfully built wagon master. He wore a buckskin shirt and a planter's hat and carried a huge bullwhip. His expression signaled neither welcome nor hostility. If anything, he seemed preoccupied with his duties, regarding this encounter as an obligatory distraction. "Sam Blake. You'll be assigned to my train, along with Jimbo here. Come with me. We'll start at the corral."

Mike gave the others a nod of farewell as he walked off with Blake. He could feel a knot forming in his gut. While the General had been good-humored and friendly, Blake's manner was crisp and businesslike. Mike hoped he was up to the challenges he now faced. Remember, things could be worse. You might be back at the Pacific, skitterin' under the looms in the heat, dust, and gobs of spit.

As they approached the corral, Blake began his orientation. "Each set of wagons has its team of six, eight, usually ten yoke of bulls, dependin' on the load. They're assigned by name to the bullwhacker for that team. There be several classes of bulls—leaders, which take the front. These can be a mite smaller and are picked for reliability and intelligence. Then there's wheelers, last in line, strong and steady but needn't be bright. In between you have your pointers, or swingers. That's where we break in new bulls what lack discipline. Within a yoke, each bull is assigned to nigh side—that's left, or off side—on the right. You'll not wish to get them mixed as they be creatures of habit. Tomorrow, we'll get you goin' with your own team, yokin' and hitchin'."

Mike looked out into the corral full of longhorns, each weighing around four thousand pounds and standing nearly six feet tall. He shifted his stance in nervous contemplation. "Why do you use cattle rather than horses or mules, Mr. Blake?"

"Call me Sam. Horses and mules are faster, but less sturdy over the long pull. Also, you have to carry their feed grain, while these bulls do mighty fine eatin' the grasses along the trail."

They walked around back of the corral to the freight wagons. These were huge wooden crates mounted on a carriage. Its wheels were over five feet tall and rimmed with iron tires nearly six inches wide. The wagon box of well-seasoned hardwood was eighteen feet long and four and a half feet wide and deep. Over the wagon box were set wooden bows and the white osnaburg covers to protect the load from the elements.

Mike knelt and examined the undercarriage of a nearby wagon.

"Our wagons is mostly Murphys, from St. Louis," Blake continued. "But you may find a Studebaker or two in each train. We want the best wagon we can find for haulin' eight thousand pounds of load through rough country. As this be your first run, you'll have just one wagon and six yoke. Once you get used to handling the teams, you'll pull three wagons with ten yoke."

The ground around them was covered with wooden yokes, bows and piles of chain. Beyond the wagons, bullwhackers were busy snubbing wild steers to the hubs of wagon wheels before attempting to place yokes on them for the first time. The din from the animals made it hard to hear everything Blake was saying.

"You'll find that the bullwhackers are generally a decent lot, but they'll rub a greenhorn till he's sufficiently polished. Don't let their rough manner put you off. If you keep your mouth shut and pull your weight, you'll fit in fine."

Blake called out sharply to one of the crew breaking new steers, and made it clear his supervision was forthcoming. Then he turned back to Mike. "You go with Jimbo and get your gear. Meet me back here at dawn tomorrow for yokin' and hitchin' school."

Before he could turn away, Mike interjected, "Sam, what might be our destination?"

"We're headed for Denver." With that, he hurried off, leaving Mike awhirl with new information and trepidation. Denver! He had no idea where it was. As he returned to the office to collect Jimbo, his mind conjured up images from newspaper accounts he had read, of mountains, snow, and gold mines.

The outfitter's store was back in town, a large emporium of clothing, accessories, and weaponry for use on the frontier. Jimbo guided Mike to the requisite gear: a new slouch hat, a blanket, a gutta-percha raincoat, boots, clothing, and a "war bag" in which to carry it all. Jimbo handed Mike a used Colt's revolver, a .44 calibre Army model with an eight-inch barrel and cracked wooden grip. "Here, you'll be needin' this. Don't never be without it while we're on the trail."

"I'll be needin' some instruction from you in loadin' and shootin' this. I've only handled a musket rifle before," Mike admitted, "and that was all too briefly."

"Don't worry, Mike, they're all of a piece."

Lastly, they collected a worn leather holster and a leather pouch of cartridges and caps. The whole lot was put on the account of Coe and Carter.

"Come on," Jimbo urged. "Let's get back to the company. Maybe we can still get a nestin' place in the hay barn."

Mike hesitated at the door. "I'm needin' to send a telegraph message, Jimbo. Can I meet you back at the company?"

"Why sure, give me your kit. I'll see you back at the barn."

Mike searched out the Western Union office and, drawing from the small amount of cash he had left, he sent a message to Jane back in Lawrence:

Apologies for unplanned departure. Bound for Denver. Letters to postmaster will reach me there. Will return when finances permit. Best wishes to you and brothers. Affectionately, Michael.

Mike suspected his telegram would not be received warmly, but it was better than the silence he had maintained since setting out from St. Albans in what seemed ages ago.

It rained hard that night. The next morning, Mike rose in the pre-dawn and pulled on his new trousers, shirt, and boots. He left Jimbo snoring in his bedroll in the haybarn. Grabbing his new hat, he headed out to the corral, now a sea of mud. The gray eastern sky was beginning to brighten. He was early; the cattle were not yet in the corral. A couple of bullwhackers sauntered by on their way to a low campfire in the wagon yard.

"Get your grub first, boy," one advised. "You'll not last the day save you get somethin' in your belly."

"Right. I'll do that." Mike dogged their heels over to the undersized wagon used for carrying food and preparing the crew's meals. Gradually more and more bullwhackers showed up, and presently bacon, biscuits and coffee were allotted to each by the thoroughly shabby camp cook named Jasper.

A bullwhacker joked as Mike made his way through the grub line. "Don't get too close to Jasper, son. He's like as not to cook you for supper."

The others laughed, while Jasper grumbled something about being tired of feeding a bunch of ingrates. Mike smiled nervously, collected his portion, and searched out a relatively dry spot under a nearby freight wagon where he could sit and eat. The biscuit was large, and a poorly cooked slab of bacon was sandwiched within, hanging out of each side and dripping hot grease. It wasn't elegant, but it was hot and filling. Mike washed it down with a tin cup of camp coffee, burnt, strong, and awash with grounds.

He offered words of thanks to a bewildered Jasper, turned in his cup, and headed back to the corral. His breakfast felt suspended somewhere between his gullet and his stomach. As the sun pushed over the hillock, a rider on horseback brought the bulls in from the pasture and herded them into the corral. Then Blake showed up with seven other greenhorns in tow. "School" was about to begin.

Without introductions, he pointed to a nearby pile of yokes saying, "Each of you grab a yoke and bring it here. There's bows and keys there too. Get one of each."

Each novice toted a forty-pound yoke over one shoulder and carried a wooden bow in his free hand. Two wooden chuck keys hung from leather strips held firmly in each man's teeth. Blake pointed out a specific animal for each recruit and opened the corral gate.

"You'll yoke the off-side animal first. Once you've got that done, let the end of the yoke down to the ground and come get another bow and keys. I'll fix you up with the nigh-side critter."

Pandemonium ensued as the eight recruits entered the corral and proceeded to wade through a herd of a hundred and fifty or more bulls, to seize their assigned beast. Mike, mindful of the threatening horns, dodged and weaved. The animals, smelling strangers among them, bawled and eluded them as best they could. A cry of pain sounded as someone's toes got stepped on. Mike cursed in frustration as his yoke fell into the mud and manure. But he took a little comfort that it was not he who proudly signaled a successful yoking, only to be informed by Blake that he had captured the wrong animal. Still, Mike wasn't doing much better than the rest. He fell, was pushed, got stepped on, and dropped his yoke several more times.

"By the cattle of Cuchullain!" Mike crabbed through clenched teeth, as he chased and caught, lost and chased his quarry. It was thirty minutes before he finally got the yoke over the steer's neck and the bow from below up through the holes in the yoke. After setting the keys to hold the bow in place, he let the other end of the yoke down and staggered toward the gate. He wasn't the first to get his second bow, but at least, he wasn't one of the last.

They spent all morning getting the hang of the yoking process. Mike found it difficult to recognize his assigned animals by their size, color, and markings. Gradually, his efforts improved, but not much. This is a skill that will require some time in mastering, he decided.

In the afternoon, they learned how to connect a long, thick chain to an iron ring atop each yoke with a clevis. The chain then ran from the lead, through each yoke to the wagon. They also practiced hitching the wheelers beside the wagon tongue.

It was a long, muddy, smelly, tiring day, with few breaks for food or water. "You boys will have to do a heap better than this tomorrow," Blake warned. "We're headed to Denver on Monday at sunup. I'll not tarry while you chase your team around this here corral."

The night-herder arrived to turn the bulls out to graze and water in the meadows nearby. Mike and his fellows limped away, covered in drying muck. The heat and their efforts had played them out.

A skinny, young man with a pockmarked face spoke in disgust. "I ain't chasin' no more bulls for that fella. There's got to be better work back in town, and I aim to search it out!"

"Aw, fiddledeedee, Elmer, you use up pretty quick," replied another recruit. "Me, I'm goin' to stick it out. No dumb animal ever got the best of me yet, horns or no. What about you, fella?" He addressed Mike, who had been silently auditing the grumbling exchange. "You comin' back for more?"

Mike stopped walking and faced the group. He forced a smile and replied, "I figure the first day on any job is likely to be the worst. I guess I'll stay at it. Me belly still likes to be fed regular. I'll see you tomorrow."

With that, Mike headed for the haybarn to look up Jimbo, who was to spend the day breaking new bulls to the yoke and the hitch. He wasn't back yet, so Mike washed up and changed clothes. Then he took his muddy clothes and boots to the well pump and did his best to restore them to a semblance of acceptability.

Later, Jimbo listened to Mike's account of his day at "school." He tried to offer some solace for the disappointing start. "Can't let them beasts get you down, Mike. Today, you was a stranger to them. Tomorrow they'll know your scent and be more agreeable. Like most things, it takes time and doin' it over and over."

"Is Sam a tough wagon master? He sure seems hard to please so far."

Jimbo sat down on a rough wooden bench and removed his boots. "Aw, Sam's all right. Sure, he's tough! That's what you want in a wagon master. Tough might just save your life out on the trail. What with Injuns after your hair, and the risks of high water crossin's, or stampedin' cattle, or prairie fires, you'll be happy to have a fella like Sam givin' the orders."

The next day seemed to Mike to go a bit better. At least, Blake went easier on him and the other six young men who returned, a reward for their perseverance if not their skill. In the afternoon, he introduced them to the bullwhacker's principal tool, the bullwhip. In his left hand, he held its three-foot hickory stock, while coiled in his right was twenty feet of braided rawhide. It was tapered gradually to its tip, where it ended in a thin strip of buckskin called a "popper."

"We call this the 'persuader'," Blake announced. "You'll find it is needed regularly to remind your team who's boss. 'Course these whips can do plenty of damage, so you'll not actually lay it on your bulls, except on rare occasions. Just a flick above the ear is usually all that's needed."

Wheeling the stock upright, he rotated it in a circle with both hands above his head and paid out the length of rawhide. He then jerked the stock forward. The whip extended itself full length, in the direction the stock was pointed. A wave rolled out along the whip towards the popper with increasing speed. The popper cracked loud and sharp, like a rifle shot.

"With a bit of practice, you'll be able to discipline a stubborn steer without injurin' him or disturbin' his yoke-mate. You fellas try this awhile. Just don't kill each other doin' it. Tomorrow, you'll get your own whip when you are assigned to your wagon. Say all your goodbyes tonight, as we'll be leavin' here right after sunup."

Mike was feeling less than confident as the junior bullwhackers dispersed late in the day. After the locals had left for town, he walked back to the haybarn, shaking his head. Two school days only! I'm still near hopeless with the yokin', and it'll be a miracle if I ever do master that whip. Sure, I hope my bulls know more of freightin' than I do.

Chapter Eleven

Sailing the Sea of Grass

☩

It wasn't exactly sunup when they pulled out the next day. Though the night herder brought the cattle in well before dawn, the yoking and hitching took much longer than usual. Even though this day's performance was better than in the two-day bullwhacker school, it was still a problem. The experienced bullwhackers were hitched and waiting while the new boys seemed as lost as a hungry calf in a corral full of bulls. A few veterans finally provided grudging assistance in getting them hitched up.

Mike and his peers were dispersed through the length of the train to allow the experienced whackers to set the pace. With the order "git up," Mike struggled to get his team under way. *I know "gee" means turn right and "haw" means go left, but damned if me beasts have been told this before.* After a few more urgings, his team, blessedly free of wild, half-broken steers, fell in behind the wagon in front of them. It was nearly eight-thirty before the train left Nebraska City and the muddy Missouri River behind them.

A bullwhacker and his outfit (Library of Congress)

Walking beside his nigh-side wheeler, Mike gradually calmed himself. His bullwhip was a useless ornament, given his lack of skill. But he carried it anyway, so as not to let on to the bulls.

The rustle of heavy chain and the creaking of wagon-boxes and wooden wheels were constant. Occasionally the crack of a whip or a colorful oath from the lips of a veteran whacker would fill the air. And there was dust, lots of it, kicked up by hooves and wagon wheels. It got in Mike's eyes, ears, and mouth. It made him gag and spit till he ran out of wet. Pity the poor lad, he thought, who's got the last team in this train . . . or worse, the day-herder, drivin' spare bulls, mules, and horses, far to the rear.

An early morning drive and another in the late afternoon was the typical pattern of progress for a bull train. However, given their late departure, Blake delayed the morning break by almost two hours. Around noon, they pulled off the trail and positioned their wagons in an oval created by alternate teams heading left and right in arcs that brought the first and second teams together side by side. This contiguous assembly of wagons would serve as a corral for yoking and hitching. It would also be their fortress if a defense against hostiles were required. The teams were unhitched and released to graze and water through the heat of midday.

"Bulls don't do well pullin' in the heat," Jimbo had explained earlier. "Come to think of it, neither do I."

As if one yoking and hitching effort a day was not enough, the new bullwhackers again delayed the afternoon departure, but less so than they had that morning. It was late and nearly dark before they pulled into Wilson's Bridge, their first camp on the "cut-off" trail. They had made a mere eight and a half miles, about half the standard day's drive.

The night herder, or "nighthawk," took charge of the animals. The bullwhackers, grouped into four eating crews, were assigned to forage for fuel for the campfires or dispatched for water at the creek. Mike was given the latter task and sharply warned to always draw upstream of the animals. He soon found that toting two buckets of water nearly a half mile was not the best way to end a day of walking and wrestling cattle. But at least the first day was nearly behind him. Crawling under his wagon immediately after supper, Mike laid out his blanket and collapsed in total exhaustion.

It seemed like only a few minutes before the rumble of hooves and the nighthawk's call of "Bulls in!" woke Mike. "Divil, it can't be feckin' mornin' already." He turned over, involuntarily resuming his slumber. But Blake came down the line of wagons, pounding on their sides. "Roll out! Roll out!" he barked to his whackers.

Mike threw back his blanket and crawled from beneath his wagon. His whole body complained of kinks and aches. Even his feet protested as he pulled on his boots. Jaysus, no time for breakfast! Hardly time for a piss! Get into that corral and start yokin' and hitchin'!

The morning's efforts were an improvement over the first day, as the new recruits were more familiar with their beasts and vice versa. By the time the sun broke on the horizon, the train was on its way from Wilson's Bridge. The road was wide and the hard-packed dirt made a smooth, easy surface. Along the sides of the trail, Mike noticed a stream of litter—a dresser here, a kettle there, a broken coffee grinder dumped by the side of the road.

"Them pilgrims is always over-packin' their wagons with useless stuff or fancy furnishin's," Jimbo explained later. "It all gets tossed out when the fools see they gotta lighten the load for their poor teams. I seen everythin' from feather beds to iron stoves. It all gets picked over by the locals. I 'spect many a pilgrim tear were shed over them lost treasures."

Beyond the wide road and the trail of litter, Mike beheld the dramatic sight of the eastern Nebraska prairie. An ocean of big bluestem grass, over three feet high, rolled in green waves as the wind raked it back and forth. It was into such lush areas that the herders drove the bulls during their encampments. Mike recalled Blake saying how the animals did thrive on such fare, and that he always finished the first trip of the season with animals fatter and healthier than when he set out.

The train for Coe & Carter was not alone on the trail. A crush of wagon trains clogged the road. Most were headed west, but an occasional train was encountered returning from the frontier. When the line of march curved a bit, Mike could look ahead to the front of his train and beyond, to other trains further ahead. Their white canvas appeared to him like sailing ships upon a sea of grass. Reminds me of vessels in the Mersey, as I left Liverpool. God, Liverpool! One day soon the family will pass that way and see those sights as well.

When Blake called for the morning halt, it was close to 10:30. They had made about six or seven miles. Rather than camp close by other trains, wagon masters sought their own stopping points so as not to contend for fresh grass and clean water. The bullwhackers were ravenous for their first meal of the day. They had been on the trail for more than four hours, and the summer heat was wearing on animals and men alike.

After they had eaten, Mike and another bullwhacker, Billy Mayhew, scavenged for bull chips to fuel the next campfires. Firewood was hard to come by in this stretch of the trail; earlier travelers had long since gleaned what grew along the creek beds.

"Make sure you get it bone dry, Mike. It's a foul job to gather and burn cow pies what ain't yet ripe."

Mike kicked at one of the hundreds of targets along the trail and befouled the toe of his boot. "I see what you mean."

Billy was tall and brown as a kidney bean. Nearly twenty-three, he had already been bullwhacking for five years. He and Mike had become pals in the last few days, working and eating together in the same crew. They swapped past histories as they returned to camp with full gunnysacks.

"How'd you get to be a bullwhacker then?" Mike asked.

Billy stopped and pushed back his hat. "My family lived on a farm in Missouri. Pa and me was always in a ruckus," he said with a cryptic smile. "Virgil, my brother, and me, we slaved for that man, but he weren't never satisfied. Ma would take no sides. One day, I got mad and told Pa he could keep his farm chores. He grabbed a hold of me and beat me like a red-headed stepchild!"

Billy hunkered down on his haunches and wiped his brow with a bandanna. Mike dropped his sack and sat down to give Billy's story his full attention.

"I guess that's when I determined to leave home. But the war was on then and it was dangerous to be on the roads alone. Pa was set against slavery, save that of his own sons. Said it was a stain upon the Christian conscience. And so I believe today. Anyway, his views became well known in the county, and they brung down punishment on our whole family."

Mike winced at the thought of where this account was apparently leading. The telling of it was affecting Billy's manner and put a quaver in his voice. The young bullwhacker looked off to the distant horizon, as if visualizing the scene he was describing. "Missouri was boilin' over with slave and free factions. Bushwackers and vigilantes, on both sides, took up the fight. You never knew which of your neighbors might secretly snitch to such a gang. One night in the spring of '64, John Thrailkill and his bloody rebels was out burnin', lootin', and murderin' them what supported the Union. They come and sacked our farm. Pa and Virgil was whipped and beat bloody. . . ."

Billy turned his face away from Mike. He blinked back tears and paused a minute to gather his composure. Mike wanted to put an arm around his shoulder, but he dared not. He waited patiently till his new friend could continue his tale.

"They was dead," he choked finally. "I'd 'a been too, but I was visitin' with a neighbor friend. I didn't give a hoot about Pa, but Virgil. . . . A few days later, I found Ma dead in her bed. Died of a broken heart, I suppose."

Mike shook his head, struggling with the images of brutality and pain. It made his grievances with the British pale a bit in comparison. After an uncomfortably quiet minute, they rose to head back to the corral.

"I'm awful sorry for your trouble, Billy," Mike said as he hoisted again the heavy bag of chips. "So then you left Missouri?"

"Yeah, I took Pa's horse and headed west. Never went back, never laid claim to the farm. Come to Nebraska City and signed on with Coe & Carter."

"Have you been to Denver before?" Mike asked.

"Twice. I go there, get let go, work my way back to the river, then head out again."

"Let go?" Mike's voice was full of alarm. "Why did you get let go?"

Billy grinned. "Aw, Mike, it ain't like it sounds. It's just a manner of speakin'. See, there ain't much freight headed back east. So, the company wants to let go as many men as they can at the end of the drive. They pay a little dearer if they can discharge their whackers upon delivery. It's cheaper than payin' them for the return journey. They usually sell off most of the wagons and teams too. I always take the better wage and find a way back on my own."

"I assumed I'd be comin' back with the train," Mike said as they stumbled down the hill above the bull train encampment. "Jimbo never talked about what would happen after we got to Denver."

"Guess he figured it best that you make up your mind once you've had a full taste of the bullwhacker's life."

Mike wondered what he would do after reaching Denver. Best take the higher wage, I'm thinkin'. The more I make, the sooner I'll be gettin' back to Jane. If I want to work for the General again, I'll be findin' me some way to do.

Gradually the rhythm of the days became familiar and more comfortable: a morning pull, the midday stop, an afternoon drive till dusk. Most days were sunny and hot, but an evening breeze usually cooled things off for easy sleeping.

A party of thirty-two men supported the twenty-five teams in the train. In addition to the twenty-five bullwhackers, there was the nighthawk, two day-herders, three spare hands and the wagon master. These were organized into mess crews of eight men each. Mike and the other new recruits were assigned, one or two, to each mess crew. The other bullwhackers were friendly enough, though they always made a point of calling them "greenhorns." If there was an extra chore that needed doing within the mess, there was no doubt who would be assigned.

One gruff old fellow took Mike in hand to instruct him in the use of the tar bucket, which always hung under one wagon in each team. Its contents were used to grease and lubricate each wheel hub every few days. The red-bearded veteran bullwhacker took pains to criticize Mike's efforts. "Not so much! Ease up or you'll use up your tar 'fore we even get out of Nebraska."

Mike complied and ignored the pain of rebuke. He'd faced worse back in the mills. After the second go, he got so he could set the jack, pull the linchpin, remove the wheel, tar the hub, and put it all back without more than a cautious stare from his tutor.

Mike was interested to see how Blake spent most of his day—riding ahead of the train, sitting upon his gray mule, searching out the best grass and water for the midday and nighttime encampments. He would exchange reports with other trail bosses about high water crossings, hostile Indians, and such. One hundred and ten miles from Fort Kearny, the bull train approached Beranger, a campsite on the Big Blue River. There, Mike overheard that the Army was holding trains at the fort until groups of thirty teams or more could be organized for joint travel and common defense.

That night, they encamped a bit west of the Big Blue. Each mess group selected its cook, and a good one, once found, was almost never deselected. Mike's mess crew was so blessed, and this evening was treated to beans, cornbread and honey, instead of the usual biscuits and bacon.

After supper, some of the boys broke out cards. Mike strolled off to find Jimbo, who was in a different mess crew. It had been days since more than a "howdy" had passed between them. As Mike approached the campfire of Jimbo's crew, a whacker cautioned, "Watch it fellas, we got another greenhorn in our midst."

The group laughed and Mike decided to play along. "Aye, and 'tis a good job that I am green. Sure, that's the only kind of horn they make back in Ireland." More laughter ensued and the tension of the moment evaporated.

Jimbo left his place at the fire, and the two climbed up the side of a grassy knoll above the corral. There, as the darkness deepened, they lay back and scanned the heavens. An evening song came from the cicadas chattering in the willows along the creek banks.

"Sure is a pretty sky this evenin'!" Jimbo remarked. "Look at all them stars up there. Makes a fella feel kinda puny, don't it?"

Mike didn't respond immediately. Physical exhaustion and memories flooded his consciousness. After a moment, he rolled onto his side and leaned upon one elbow, returning to the present. "I'm reminded of the stars I seen on the ocean crossing a couple of years ago. The skies back in Lawrence are usually so smoky, you don't get such a view as tonight."

Another minute of contemplation passed. "You never have spoke too highly of that Lawrence place you're from, Mike. Why are you so fired up to get back there, anyway?"

Mike smiled at the suggestion of returning to Lawrence. "Ah, 'tis not the place, Jimbo. I have me a girl back there. Her name is Jane. We're to be married when I return."

Jimbo laughed lightly and sat up. "Well, when's that? If you love her, why don't you just high-tail it back there now and be done with it?"

"Ah, 'tis not that easy," Mike cautioned. "I can't go back till I make me fortune."

"Your fortune?"

Mike's expression grew serious and determined. "Aye. I shan't go back before. You see, Jane's father will never agree if I can't provide what he figures to be a proper livin' for his daughter."

The night had driven dusk away, the cicadas were quieted, and only occasional noises from the herd disturbed the serenity. Mike's mood suddenly turned dark, and he thrust his goateed jaw forward defiantly. "Someday I'll show that buggerin' Brit what I can do. Here on the frontier, a man can rise quickly if he's willin' to work hard and seize on the opportunities."

Jimbo looked down the hill at the line of low campfires beyond the corral, and Mike's gaze followed. The other whackers were peeling off, one or two at a time, heading for their bedrolls.

Jimbo took a deep breath and sighed. "Them's great ambitions, son. I hope you can get that fortune of yours in good time. I ain't never got me a fortune. Guess I'm just a plumb fool, dodgin' the civilized life. But, I'm happy enough bein' nursemaid to a passel of longhorns, long as they gee and haw for me."

Mike looked quizzically at his friend. "Didn't you ever hope for a bit more, Jimbo? Why, sometimes me head is full of wishes and wants, things so many folk in America have. Me family never lived in a proper house. They're always wonderin' is there enough in the pot for everybody. We all had to dance the tune of the line supervisor in spinnin' or weavin'. I want more than that for Jane. She should have fine things. I've promised her as much."

Jimbo stood up and yawned, "Guess I'm ready to turn in." He ignored Mike's question.

"I've tasted bein' poor," Mike said as they walked back to the corral. "I'm thinkin' that bein' rich is worth a try!"

The pull to Ft. Kearny took another six days over the still green, undulating plains. Forty miles out of Dogtown, the bull train reached the Platte River. They would follow its south bank clear to the mouth of Cherry Creek in the city of Denver. Though the men joked that the river was a mile wide and an inch deep, it was neither. But whackers preferred a good yarn to a boring fact. The river water was brown with mud and there were numerous islands and sandbars, many large enough to support a grove of cottonwoods and willows.

Here, the Nebraska cut-off joined the original trail from Independence and St. Joe, coming up through northeast Kansas, along the valley of the Little Blue. The traffic became heavier yet and the trail widened considerably. A snarl of freight and emigrant trains made the daily search for good grazing and watering spots a considerable challenge for Blake.

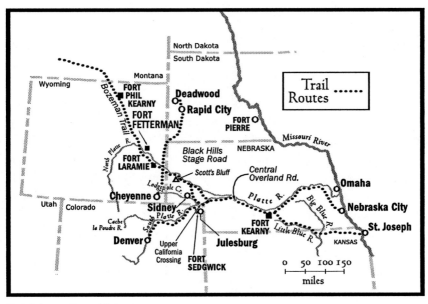

Freighting trails and forts

Dogtown was an ugly little settlement, part road ranch and part Sodom and Gomorrah. Its scrappy wooden shacks were eight miles from Ft. Kearny because the U.S. Army wouldn't tolerate them being any closer. Dogtown's traders, gamblers, whores, and ne'er-do-wells did their best to engage pilgrims in various and sordid transactions with well-practiced blandishments. Blake knew better than to set down near Dogtown. He would encamp well downstream.

Still, their arrival at the environs of Ft. Kearny represented a landmark reached. A brief stopover was, therefore, cause for a modest celebration among the hardworking crew. Blake would make the required check-in with the military authorities controlling movement further west into Indian territory.

After morning encampment with its meal and chores, he addressed all but a skeleton crew of the day-herders and spare hands to guard the train. "You men what want a taste of the fort and its sutler's store, come with me. But, by no ways get yourself into any ruckus with them bluecoats. They've little affection for bullwhackers, and I'll not be spendin' General Coe's money bailin' you out of the stockade. There's tame Injuns here as well. They'll be beggin' whatever you have, so beware. We'll return to the train an hour before sundown."

Up the dusty road through Dogtown, Mike and the rest of the crew walked behind Blake and his mule. As the freighters paraded by, a few well-worn whores came out in their bloomers, hooting and cajoling the men to tarry awhile. "Hey fellas, how about a spell of high times?"

Mike laughed self-consciously as other whackers hooted back. Some waved to the girls and told them that, left to their own devices, they were hot on the idea. Perhaps they would stop on the return trip.

When the crew approached the fort, it was crowded with wagons, teams, freighters and pilgrims, all awaiting permission to proceed west. In the distance above the fort, Mike could see the reeds, flowers, and cattails that covered the banks of the Platte.

Blake dismissed his men with a reminder about not wandering off. Then Mike and his fellows swarmed off to the northwest corner of the fort. The sutler's store, Mike thought, was as lively as a beehive knocked from the tree. Emigrant children eyed the penny candy, while their mothers admired the colorful fabrics for dresses, curtains and such. Pawnee women carried away purchases of flour or cornmeal in the folds of their upturned skirts. In the shade of a nearby tree, bullwhackers smoked, drank, laughed, and told tall stories.

At the store entrance, Jimbo turned to Mike. "Don't go off. I just wanna get me a good plug of tabbaccy."

Mike was happy to while away a few minutes with a cool cup of lemonade dipped from a bucket wrapped in wet burlap. The clerk took his price and reminded Mike to surrender the tin cup prior to leaving the store. After his drink, Mike wandered outside to listen to the whackers and wait for Jimbo.

Jimbo emerged a few minutes later, accompanied by a tall, thickset man wearing a flat-topped planter's hat and smoking a cheroot. Jimbo waved a hand at Mike. "Come here, I wanna introduce you to this fella."

Mike approached and smiled. The stranger's gaze upon him made him feel like a horse up for sale.

"Mike Quinn, this is Mr. John Gilman, a friend of mine and sometime competitor of General Coe. J. K. and his brother, Jeremiah, hired me after I left St. Joe. But they sort of got off on other business, so I went over to Coe & Carter."

"It seems Jimbo knows about everyone freightin' along this road," Mike observed.

Gilman laughed pleasantly and shook Mike's hand with a firm grip. "He knows us all, and our sins too. But don't believe everything he tells you about Gilman Brothers."

"Are you off to Denver also, sir?" Mike asked.

Gilman shook his head. "We're just done with government contracts over at Fort McPherson, construction mostly. Got a road ranche out by Cottonwood Springs. I'm on my way back to Nebraska City for a load of supplies."

Jimbo grumped, a mock scowl upon his face. "J. K. is after me to leave Coe & Carter and join up again with his outfit."

"I'll make you a fine offer, Mr. Bowe. After all, it ain't disloyal. Why even Levi Carter's agreed to come in as a partner."

Mike tilted his head to one side. "Is Mr. Carter leaving the General to join Gilmans?"

"Haw, haw," Jimbo laughed. "That's a good one, eh, J. K.?"

"Not at all," Gilman said, smiling broadly at Mike. "Levi Carter is an old friend, hails from New Hampshire as do us Gilmans. Together, we're starting a new company to supply timber to the Union Pacific Railroad. We need teamsters, good men like Mr. Bowe here, to haul ties from the hills to the end-of-track." Gilman winked at Mike. "Say, perhaps you'd consider joining Gilmans? How old are you anyway?"

"Almost twenty," Mike announced proudly. "Thank you, but I shan't leave a job halfway through. But, I wish you luck."

"How far has the railroad got, J. K.?" Jimbo asked.

"I hear they're less than thirty miles east of here, making good progress as the weather remains dry."

"Any Injun trouble?" Mike asked, mindful of the Indian threat frequently discussed among the bullwhackers.

Gilman shrugged and dropped his spent cigar to the dirt, crushing it with the toe of his boot. "The Sioux raided some stations out our way a couple of months back. But, these days they mostly steal horses."

Gilman chuckled to himself. "Reminds me of a good story. It seems that Chief Spotted Tail and his Brule warriors paid a visit to the railroad camp up at Grand Island. Came for a look-see at the "iron horse." So, the Union Pacific folks gave them a tour of the train and a little ride. But then, Spotted Tail suggested a race between the train and their fastest ponies, which, of course, they did lose."

Mike and Jimbo grinned at the scene described.

"Now, Spotted Tail, he's a bit put out," Gilman continued. "So he calls for a demonstration of archery from one of his best bucks. This fella shoots sixteen arrows in a row through the hole in the handle of a shovel stuck in the ground sixty feet away. Finally satisfied that his honor is restored, Spotted Tail makes to move on. But before he can get away, the Irish construction superintendent says something that Spotted Tail don't exactly appreciate. The boys said their argument was a real show."

All three laughed at this failure of Indian-Irish diplomacy. But Mike was intrigued by Gilman's business enterprises and shifted the discussion back. "When do you start your railroad contract, Mr. Gilman?"

"When we get the bid," he replied with an air of self-assurance, "we'll start supplying the tracklayers between Gothenburg and Julesburg. The company has our quote, and it's near a sure thing. We're kind of friendly with Jack Casement, the boss of tracklaying, so that helps. You won't reconsider, will you Mr. Bowe?"

Jimbo shook his head as he bit into his new plug of tobacco. "Naw, I gotta get this train to Denver. Besides, I ain't sure the General would take kindly to me pullin' up my stakes quick-like."

"Very well. Glad to meet you, Mike."

As Mike and Jimbo walked off through the camp, Jimbo grumbled. "Ain't that a fine thing, tryin' to unhitch us both from the General in the middle of a drive?"

"Is he not a good boss, Jimbo?"

"Aw, J. K.'s a fine fella. . . . So's his brother. I'd have worked for them forever 'ceptin' they cut back on the freightin' to do construction for the government over at Fort McPherson. J. K. knows his Injuns right well too. Speaks the lingo of most tribes in these parts. When winter puts a stop to freightin', he and Jerry head south to trade supplies to the Sioux and Cheyenne. Yep, Gilmans is good folk, but I wouldn't leave the General."

Mike was surprised to see the many Indian braves at the sutler's store. Dressed in buckskin leggings and loincloths, they lounged about the grounds, socializing with one other.

"Are there not hostilities between the Injun tribes and the settlers?" he asked Jimbo.

"Sure, there is! But these here redskins is Pawnee. They done settled down, peaceful-like, in recent years. Natural-born horse thieves, they is, quick and quiet as a field mouse. They do well as scouts for the army. And believe me, they got no use for the Sioux, nor the Cheyennes neither. Them's the tribes what raised the ruckus hereabouts last year."

After several hours of touring the camp, the crew rejoined Blake for the return to their wagon train. Before leaving, he gave them his news.

"Boys, we're gonna have some company between here and Upper Crossing." Though he shared this in a matter-of-fact manner, it was easy to see that Blake was a little more than annoyed. "The army has teamed us up with an emigrant train of Mormons headed for Utah. They'll drive with us, but we'll camp separate. You boys mind your manners in front of their womenfolk. And no nighttime adventures, if you know what I mean!"

Having tasted a few sups of "oh-be-joyful" during their stay at the fort, the whackers gave out with grins, laughs, and promises of decorous behavior.

"I only hope I can get you past Dogtown," added Blake as he spurred his mule forward.

As far as Mike could see, the attachment of the Mormon train to theirs was more formality than fact. The Mormons kept their distance, and only the outriders passing back and forth betrayed their presence. For three days, they pressed on together following the Platte. They arrived at Plum Creek having seen no signs of hostile Indians. This was a relief to all, as the valley of the Platte would now begin to close in, with high bluffs on the north and south banks.

In three more days, they reached the Gilmans' road ranche, east of Cottonwood Springs. A sign reading "Woodchoppers wanted – Good pay" could be seen at the side of the trail. In the morning, two of the greenhorn bullwhackers were gone, likely to cut ties for the railroad. "I ain't surprised," Blake commented at the morning halt. "Hard to keep our new boys interested when Gilmans are payin' high wages." Wagon masters must anticipate some losses within the crew, Mike learned, and Blake had prudently brought a couple of extra hands from Nebraska City.

As they made their way along the trail, Mike counted how many of the road ranches were deserted, burned out in the Indian raids of the last year. These stations ain't much to look at, even when spared by the Sioux war parties.

Ackley's Ranche was typical of its kind, a sod house of three rooms and a roof of pine poles covered with turf and mud. It offered hotel accommodation, stables for one hundred twenty-five horses, and a corral large enough for sixty wagons. Such stations did a good business with the emigrant trains, but it took serious trouble to drive a freighter into a road ranche.

After Ft. Kearny, the plains took on a mostly brown coloration, as the tall, rich bluestem grasses of eastern Nebraska were replaced with blue grama and buffalo grass. Shoots grew to only a few inches in height and were quickly browned out by the hot, dry summer on the western plains. The grass was highly nutritious though for buffalo and cattle. It retained its food value even during the winter, when grazing animals could paw through the snow to find green, succulent shoots below.

It was mid-July when the two trains approached O'Fallon's Bluff, its name reminding Mike of the saloon back in Lawrence where he and his brothers would often spend an evening. The Platte had forked twenty-five miles back, near the old Jack Morrow road ranche. Continuing on the south bank of what was now the South Fork of the Platte, there was only sixty-five miles remaining till they reached the Upper or "Old California" Crossing. It was here folks headed for Oregon, California, or Utah would ford the South Fork and turn northwest.

After dinner, Blake called his crew together for a little chat. "Men, we'll make the Crossing come Friday, if there ain't no breakdowns. The Mormon wagon master has asked for the loan of a few teams to give extra pull through the quicksand at the ford. It'll cost us a day."

One of the bullwhackers voiced dissatisfaction at the delay, but most accepted the rules of the road. Jimbo had schooled Mike in the principle that a courtesy extended might someday be needed in return. On the frontier, everybody needs help sometime.

Blake ignored the disgruntled one. "I figure we can make good use of the time, what with greasing hubs and such. Those of you with wheel spokes shrunk up can use the time soakin' them in the river. Jimbo, Mack and Eddy will muster your teams with the Mormon train just after sunup on the day. The waters ain't so high, so with any luck, they should all be across in six or seven hours."

"Just my luck," Jimbo complained later to Mike. "When we finally get a day to lay back on our haunches, Sam volunteers my ass to pull Mormons to the Promised Land."

"I'm happy to come along to help," Mike offered. "Do you think Sam would let me?"

Jimbo shook his head in disgust. "Sam don't like to change an order once given. Besides, your wheels could use some soakin'. But thanks anyway, pardner."

On Saturday morning, the nighthawk left most of the herd at pasture. They had camped the previous evening west of Julesburg, Colorado, not far from Fort Sedgwick. Julesburg, all ten new frame houses of it, had recently been rebuilt several miles east of the old Julesburg, which had been laid waste the previous year in a bold raid by Spotted Tail.

The men and teams assisting the Mormons had been gone four hours or so. Mike and five other whackers were up at the riverbank, soaking wagon wheels they had tethered to the trunk of a big cottonwood tree. Such periodic treatment was important to counteract the drying and shrinkage that could destroy a wagon wheel if neglected. They were about a mile downriver from the crossing point and a quarter mile above the encampment. While three of them played cards in the shade, Mike and the others dozed beside the river.

The sound of pounding hoofbeats interrupted their reverie. Mike looked up and saw a teenaged boy, mounted on a chestnut mare, tearing down the riverbank, waving his hat and calling out through a cloud of dust. "Help! . . . An accident! We need help! . . . A teamster's got gored!"

A senior whacker in the group jumped to his feet, taking charge as he hopped about, pulling on his boots.

"Mike, climb up with this fella and take him to the campsite. Find Sam. We'll go upriver to see what's up. Git!"

Mike grabbed the boy's hand and swung up onto the bareback of his mare. He pointed over the boy's shoulder and shouted, "That-a-way!" The boy dug his heels into the flanks of his mount and they raced toward the corral. As they approached the camp, Mike called out to Billy Mayhew, who was walking by, tar bucket in hand. "Billy, where's Sam! There's been an accident up at the Crossing!"

It took a few seconds for Mike's words to register. "I'll get him directly!" Dropping the tar bucket, Billy turned and jumped a wagon tongue, disappearing within the corral.

Visibly shaking, Mike and the Mormon boy dismounted. Before they had tied the mare to a wagon wheel, Blake was running toward them, followed by Billy and several other whackers.

The Mormon boy, clearly distraught, poured out his story in clumps of words. "One of your whackers . . . his horse stepped into a hole . . . middle of the river . . . throwed the rider upon a longhorn leader. The horn poked straight through, front to back. My Pa and the others pulled him free and laid him out on the north bank. Poor fella is bleedin' somethin' fierce."

Blake turned to one of his trusted veterans, "Get to Fort Sedgwick, Jimmy. Tell 'em we need their medical officer double-time quick!" One of the whackers hurried a saddled horse and Blake's mule forward. Jimmy took the horse and headed east at full tilt. Blake and the boy headed north, toward the crossing.

Mike, Billy and the others milled and mulled and worried. "Who got it is what I want to know," Billy said.

"If it's as bad as the boy makes out, he's sure to be a goner," replied another.

Mike walked the perimeter of the corral, sat, stood quickly, and walked it again. Dear Jesus, it mustn't be Jimbo—not him!

Through the afternoon, none of the men had eaten, their appetites dulled by the despair and apprehension that enshrouded the camp. It would be hours before they'd know the outcome. Just before sundown, Jimmy returned to camp, horse and rider sapped by their high-speed mission of mercy. As the men came out to meet him, the whacker slid from his saddle and handed the reins to Mike. "It's Jimbo. He never stood a chance. The army doctor came, but there was nothin' to be done. Said he lost too much blood. Sam, Mack and Eddy are comin' in directly with the body."

Mike felt his face shatter. He turned away before his tears became public. Though he had only known the man for thirty days or so, Jimbo had been a pillar of support and encouragement. Mike retreated to the box of his lead wagon, feeling that, once again, he was on his own.

Morning clouds cloaked the mourners in a gray mist, as they stood under a copse of trees near the river where a grave had been dug. Except for the day herders, the entire Coe & Carter crew was present, as were the wagon master and a few pilgrims from the Mormon train. They stood silently, hats in hand, waiting for the loquacious preacher from Julesburg to quit. As things broke up, Billy groused to Mike, "Hell, he didn't even know Jimbo."

Blake called an afternoon drive that day, though Mike couldn't remember hitching up his team. He found himself walking beside his nigh wheeler, heading down the South Platte, into Colorado Territory. His mind played over the times he had shared with Jimbo and the sense of companionship he felt. He felt anger too. These whackers are a queer lot! Last night, nobody told stories of Jimbo! Not a proper wake, at all! Mike wondered if he shouldn't go back to Lawrence at the end of the drive. At least then he'd have Jane and his brothers to extinguish the deep loneliness that pervaded him.

There was the smell of rain in the air. The afternoon sky took on a green-gray hue and pendulous thunderheads amassed like an army in formation. The wind kicked up and blew sand into their faces. When the storm broke loose, the thunder and lightning were like nothing Mike had ever seen before. "These cattle are spooked to the point of stampede," Billy said as they completed the move into corral position.

Mike too noticed the wild-eyed look among the herd. Rather than turn the bulls out and run the risk, Blake ordered them left yoked, lead pair snubbed to the wagon in front. Spare animals were kept inside the corral, snubbed or hobbled.

"We'll water and graze them come dawn," he barked. "You men get to cover. We eat cold tonight."

Mike and his mates, drenched in the downpour, retreated to their wagons, taking shelter among the loads of freight. The rain continued driving for hours, drumming upon the canvas above their heads. It was a long night, with little sleep for most.

In succeeding days, Lillian's Ranch, Fort Morgan, and all the other milestones on the way to Denver made little impression on Mike. The daily grind of walking, eating clouds of dust, swatting flies, cajoling longhorns, and sidestepping cow pies made the time pass in an undistinguished blur. At least, Mike thought, they were moving faster now without the Mormons tied to their tail.

The valley of the South Platte widened into a browned-out plain whose edges fell over the distant horizons. A strip of green vegetation more than a hundred yards wide ran down its back, marking the path of the river from which they would not wander far. By the time they reached Fremont's Orchard, the silhouette of a distant mountain range loomed like a phantom out of the hazy western skies. Blake called them the Rockies. Mike repeatedly cast his gaze in their direction as they pushed on to Cherry Creek. Each day, he could see more clearly the magnificence of the snowcapped peaks. He'd never seen such mountains before, only the green, low mountains of western

New York and Pennsylvania on that rail journey that seemed so long ago. The Rockies was a sign that soon they'd be in Denver.

The general grief caused by the loss of Jim Bowe at the Upper Crossing was gradually replaced by a grudging acceptance. Mike heard Blake encourage this transition one evening. The evening meal was over and many of the crew were lingering over one last coffee before turning in. A young bullwhacker asked Blake if he'd seen many men lost on the trail. He wasn't much for speeches but he answered this question loud enough for everyone to hear.

"Hell, every day on the trail is full to the brim. Most times things work out, but sometimes you get a run of bad luck. A fella's gotta choose what memories to hold on to. As for me, I choose to let them bad memories go."

Mike was encouraged by Blake's advice and was beginning to look forward again by the time they pulled into Denver. Billy helped too that morning, slapping him playfully with his hat.

"Come on, Mike, let's get these critters home. I got a powerful appetite built up for a Denver welcome—real food, catchin' some sleep, and all the gaiety I can stand!"

Chapter Twelve

Moving Up

✠

The bull train's final destination was the Elephant Corral, built on the east bank of Cherry Creek. More than a corral, Robert Teats' operation included a hotel, a gambling hall and a saloon. On site, too, he hosted tenant businesses—a general store; a stage line; a blacksmith; a freight forwarder/storage; Denver's first livestock exchange; shops for hardware, clothing, and paints; and even a diner called the Louisiana Lunch Room.

The initial task was to navigate their bull train through the crowded city, south to the corral's main entrance on Blake Street. This was no mean feat as men, wagons, and teams from other trains seemed to want to occupy the same space at the same time. For Mike, inserting his team into this maelstrom was not so much an act of personal courage as simply a matter of not wanting to become separated from the rest of his train. It was chaotic and loud as a passing locomotive.

Once inside the corral, they deposited the tons of supplies from each wagon with C.E. Cook & Co, a co-located freight forward and storage company that would unload and record the delivered goods. It had been a prof-

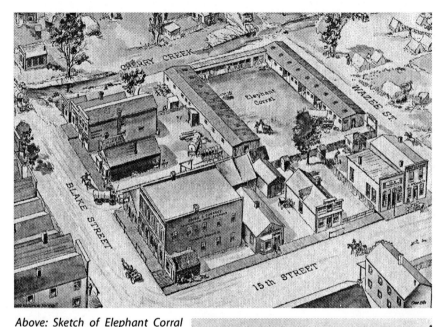

Above: Sketch of Elephant Corral and related businesses
Right: The Elephant Corral, Denver (Courtesy of the Colorado Historical Society)

itable run for General Coe. Flour was going for $20 for a hundred-pound bag in Denver. At these prices, one wagon could generate $1,200, yielding 300% profit on this one commodity alone. Other freight delivered included salt, bacon, beans, sugar, crackers, "airtights" of condensed milk, coffee, clothing, shoes, and mining equipment. While the margin of profit on these items would vary, Denver's voracious appetite for such goods would ensure a lucrative return on each.

As Mike's wagons were emptied, Blake was standing by with instructions. "After you get your rig parked and your beasts penned, meet me at Cook's for the payoff."

Mike and his colleagues needed little encouragement to finalize these tasks and get their pay. When they returned, Blake was ready with the wages each was due. The line of whackers resembled a class of schoolboys about to be dismissed for the summer break. Laughing, shoving, and calls of excitement made it a lively wait. Mike had earned nearly seventy dollars. But then there were deductions for his kit that the company had funded back in Nebraska City. In the end, he netted thirty-five dollars for the forty-odd days of bullwhacking.

Most of the whackers moved off promptly upon being paid, the saloon and gambling hall at Elephant being a strong temptation. Originally launched as the Denver House, it was an essential gathering place for all classes of frontier society. Here, miners, freighters, trappers, and stockmen came to drink at a bar that ran the length of a city block. For the adventurous, a half-dozen gaming tables operated around the clock. Occasionally, a patron would get outside of too much "Taos Lightning" and find himself on the wrong end of a revolver. Should the worst ensue, the management cheerfully sponsored the burial arrangements.

After being paid, Mike and Billy went to the saloon to discuss how next to proceed. Mike was amazed at the size of the place. As they entered the dirt-floored room, a boy came by with a sprinkling can, dousing the floor to keep the dust from rising. They pushed their way to the bar and Billy ordered beers. "Sam's takin' a few whackers back to Nebraska City with a load of dried buffalo hides. But I ain't in no rush. It's only August and the trail won't close till the first snow. What about you, Mike?"

"I don't figure on goin' back to the river just yet. I'll be lookin' for somethin' here in Denver. As long as the pay's good, I'll not be a slugabed."

They leaned on the bar and watched the varied parade of humanity come and go. Mike saw Sam Blake enter the saloon and waved him over. "I'd like to buy you boys a drink." Blake said. "I figure we all earned one on the company."

Billy and Mike were happy to accept another beer. The bartender poured Blake a whiskey, which he downed in a gulp. "Mike, you've got the makin's of a good bullwhacker," he said. "I'd be pleased to have you in my outfit again, once you get back to the river."

Mike was gratified at praise from such a demanding source as Blake. He lifted his beer to him. "Thanks. But I'm thinkin' I'll see what opportunities Denver may offer." He put his beer down and added, "Someday, I'd like to get me own outfit."

Billy let out with a cynical laugh. "Pretty soon, Mike's gonna want to hire you, Sam, to be wagon master for his outfit. Haw, haw!"

Blake smiled, but it was not a smile of derision. "Never hurts to think big." He motioned to the bartender for another whiskey. "You could pick up a few used wagons here in Denver. 'Bout the end of the season, they'll come cheap. . . . maybe ten dollars for a well-worn rig. But, you'll need more capital for bulls and such. Suppose I put a flea in the ear of the agent over at Burton and Higgins. That's the auction house here. Fella's name is Johnson. Maybe you can work for him and, in time, put together a stake."

Mike was stunned at the generosity of Blake's offer. "I'd be obliged if you would do."

"Right, I'll speak to him in the mornin'. You can go by his office anytime after that." Blake drank again and shook hands with both of them. "Billy, I'll see you in Nebraska City."

"Yeah, Sam. Thanks for the drinks." As Blake walked away, Billy looked at Mike like he was crazy. "Are you really goin' to try to raise your own outfit? Why, you just got started in the bullwhackin' business."

"And why should I not? As Sam said, it can't hurt to try. Besides, I'm here to make me fortune, not just march at the backside of a bull for the rest of me days. I'll be goin' back to the States for me girl. . . . and hitchin' up, as you say. Then I'll talk her into comin' out here."

Billy shook his head in disbelief. After draining his beer, he slapped Mike on the back. "Well, if you can pull it off, bully for you! Now, let's get squared away at the hotel. We're keepin' Denver waitin' for our company."

The hotel at Elephant was nothing grand on the inside, despite the impressive brick exterior. Its patrons included cowboys, miners, bullwhackers and various frontier riff-raff. The rooms were small, stuffy, and none too clean. Clients shared a bed, and Billy and Mike agreed to split such accommodation. Besides it being a bit close, the rambunctious nature of the patrons was a major impediment to a good night's sleep. Gunshots and rebel yells were familiar markings upon each passing night. By day, however, the place was nearly serene. Soon, Mike and Billy were well fed, well rested, and reasonably clean. Still, they were recognizably bullwhackers by their appearance, if not the persistent smell of cattle on their clothing.

On Monday morning, Mike called upon the agent at the livestock auction house. A South Carolinian and veteran of the Confederate Army, Clevis Johnson was a pleasant, if somewhat preoccupied, foreman for Burton and Higgins. Mike found him at the stock pens, holding a pencil in his teeth, taking a count of his beasts.

"Sam Blake speaks highly of you. That's good testimony."

Mike nodded, unsure how to respond.

"I do need a stock hand. Pays $12 a week, and we keep the Sabbath."

"What will be me duties as a stock hand?"

"Mostly what you was doin' for Sam, hitchin' and unhitchin' teams, shiftin' wagons. You'll also be drivin' stock from the corral to the grazin' lots and back."

It was promptly agreed, and Johnson put him to work immediately. Mike was more than pleased. With this income, he figured to cover his expenses and put some aside for the purchase of wagons and bulls of his own.

After work, Mike called at the Denver Post Office. When there was no letter waiting for him, he was surprised and disappointed. Sure, Jane received me telegram from Nebraska City. I suspect she's in a terrible vexation, what with me goin' off to the frontier and not a word of warnin'.

The next day, he posted her a letter:

You will know, my darling, that we cannot marry before next autumn in any event. I'm sure your father will be pleased to give his blessing once I have my fortune in hand. I hope someday to show you this grand country in the territories. Till we are together again, be assured of my deepest affection.

Though the postal clerk assured Mike that his letter would go east on the daily stagecoach, and that Jane should have it in hand within a few weeks, Mike was still left feeling lonely and despondent.

That night, Mike and Billy again went out on the town. For a change of scenery, they tried the Stag Hall saloon but were unhappy with the place. Continuing up the block, they put in at the Mountain Boys Saloon and Bowling Alley. Mike had never seen bowling before and was quite taken by the game. They played and drank for about an hour, until Billy became bored. By the time Mike was ready to head back, Billy was pretty drunk on the home-brew he was sharing with a few prospectors from the Colorado gold fields. "You go on back, if you want," Billy said. "I'm for stayin' on awhile."

In the morning, Billy had not yet returned. That evening, he was laid out on the bed, looking a bit the worse for wear. "Well, where've you been off to?" Mike asked. "I was about to call at the jail or the morgue."

Billy rolled over and grinned sheepishly. "Aw, I'm all right. Nice to know you was concerned, though. Nearly talked myself into the gold diggin' business with them fellas at the bowlin' place. Sounded like a rich deal, but those boys weren't my kinda folk. Anyway, I'm waitin' to see if you get your own bull outfit. If'n you do, maybe I'll throw in with you."

In late August, Mike saw an advertisement in the Rocky Mountain News. It was a potential business opportunity of the type he might have dreamed. The Pacific Telegraph Company announced its intent to embark upon the construction of a direct telegraph line between Denver and Salt Lake. The company was the creation of Edward and John Creighton, the men who had been the driving force in the construction of the Western Union transcontinental telegraph route back in 1860–61. When it came to telegraph construction, the Creightons were the gold standard.

Mike learned that Pacific was hiring freighters to haul supplies, poles and wire along the new Salt Lake route. He went to their offices immediately to inquire, but the Pacific agent was not encouraging. "You'll need your own wagons and bulls, son. We provide the grub and a contract for a hundred and twenty days with right of extension."

Mike had saved some of his wages, but was still far short of the necessary investment. Though he could muster the capital for a couple of wagons, the teams would be beyond his reach for months. One day at the corrals, Mike saw a group of twenty to thirty bulls penned off from the rest of the herd. When queried, Mr. Johnson told him the bulls had come up lame and had been left behind by various wagon trains. "We aim to sell 'em to the slaughterhouse," he said.

Mike remembered that Jimbo had told him once how such animals could be salvaged. The technique called for cauterizing their bruised and bleeding hooves with a red-hot iron. After several weeks of recuperation, they could be put to the yoke again. Most freighters didn't use, or even know of, this tactic since they rarely had the time to nurse a lame animal back to health.

Without any hint as to his intentions, Mike asked Johnson if he would sell the lamed bullocks.

"Sure, you can have them," he confirmed, "for the beefsteak price, of course. They're only in the way here."

"Might I pay you on account, Mister Johnson? I can give you half the amount now and then the balance within thirty days."

The foreman stroked his long black moustache and frowned. "Well, I don't know, Mike. Burton and Higgins don't usually deal on terms of credit. Cash business is our custom and gold dust is preferred."

Mike persisted. He knew he had proven himself to be reliable and hardworking, and he suspected that Johnson admired his sense of initiative. After several days of haggling, Mike won him over. Taking the bulls to a remote grazing lot, Mike, Billy, and a few stock hands from the corral set about searing the hooves of the abandoned longhorns. Part of the deal struck with Johnson was that the animals might continue to graze on the Corral's lots. In a couple of weeks, Mike figured, they should be fit to pull the wagons he had purchased on the cheap—a battered Studebaker and one of the big Carson wagons. He was broke and in debt, but at least he had a few assets.

Returning to the Pacific Company, Mike took a haulage contract for the new telegraph line. By lowering his asking price, Mike was able to talk his way into several hundred dollars up front. With this, he went back to Johnson and paid off the balance on the cattle purchase.

"I'm afraid I'll be quittin' me job here, Mister Johnson."

The agent pulled the ever-present pencil from his teeth and laughed. "I ain't rightly surprised, Mike. I ain't sure I can afford for you to stay. You bargain like a fire-eater of the first order."

Mike was on his way. In four months, he had learned the rudiments of a trade and was now in the business on his own, all in time for his twentieth birthday. Won't Jane be surprised? A piecer no more, eh?

It was mid-September before Mike got his outfit rolling out on the route of the Salt Lake line. As he predicted, Billy agreed to hire on for the length of the contract. Mike handled the team on the Carson, while Billy took the Studebaker. With the wagons full of coils of wire and supplies, they accompanied a gang that would string the telegraph wire from pole to pole. They followed the crew setting the poles by a day or two. It was easy work for Mike and Billy. The pace was slow, maybe five or six miles a day. But the stringers were an odd bunch and chose not to mingle with the likes of bullwhackers. Still, Mike and Billy were happy to keep their own company.

Unfortunately, a few weeks into October the snows arrived. In what was to be a winter of legendary proportions, blizzard conditions blanketed the entire frontier. The line crew and freighters spent a week sitting it out, but soon realized the work must be abandoned for the winter. The Pacific's contracting agent announced that partial payoff and terminated contracts were the order of the day. In Mike's case, because of the advance he'd received, there was no payoff at all. "Billy, I've got barely enough to pay you through our return to Denver."

Billy grinned. "You can't run off a puke like me that easy," he said, using the familiar but derogatory nickname for a Missouri native. "I figure the snows have snuffed all freightin' hereabouts. I'll just stick, if that suits. Besides, I got you picked for a winner someday."

Mike was somewhat embarrassed at Billy's commendation, but he was eminently grateful as well. He clapped a hand on Billy's shoulder. "That's grand. I'm happy to have you stay."

So they turned back to Denver, bundled as best as they were able against the driving winds and drifting snows. Luckily, Billy had passed a few winters on the plains and knew how to provision well. Each wore two pair of woolen socks and a scrap of blanket within oversized buckskin boots. Such footwear was more pliable and allowed better circulation than stiff leather boots. Elkskin britches were worn over their woolen trousers, and buckskin jackets covered their blanket-lined canvas coats. All this heavy clothing offered good protection, but Billy complained, as the weather remained bitterly cold. "I'll be lucky if I get back to Denver without my feet turnin' to blocks of ice."

Frequently, they had to shovel a path through the snow for their bulls and wagons to pass. It took nearly a week of such laborious going before they got back to Denver. But being off the plain was not much comfort. With little money, wagons to store, and stock to feed, Mike needed to secure another freighting contract fast. However, a quick round of the warehouses and freight-forwarding agents turned up no business. At the post office, Mike found a long-awaited letter from Jane. He tore into the envelope as he left.

Dearest Michael,
It has been nearly five months since you set off for Canada with your Fenians. I was saddened that the end of that unfortunate adventure did not prompt your return to home and family. I worried for months, not knowing your whereabouts. Why have you imposed this separation upon us? Even John and Roderick have had no word from you.
I have told Daddy of your plans to make your fortune and return to Lawrence. But he gives little weight to such schemes, and I am unsure what I might say to reassure him. Please come home soon. Trusting that God will keep you safe, I am
Your devoted,
Jane

Mike trudged through the snow-filled streets. Back at his hotel room, he paced about, his thoughts preoccupied with how to respond to Jane's appeal. I do miss her so. . . . Now, she's after defendin' me to her father. . . . and I ain't been helpin' that much. I can't be returnin' to the states without me fortune! Jane's father will be laughin' his big, English arse off should I come home with empty pockets and talk of marryin' his precious daughter. No, I must do what I have set out to do. First, the fortune! I just got me wagons and teams. Best to put them to good use quick as I can.

The next day Mike dictated a telegram to Jane.

Jane,
Received your letter. Please be patient. I will not disappoint. Business shows great promise. Expect my return in autumn, in time for your birthday.
Love,
Michael

One night at the saloon at Elephant Corral, Billy Mayhew introduced Mike to a fellow named Reeves. The stranger appeared to be in his forties and seemed a friendly, seasoned frontiersman.

"He runs a road ranche west of Julesburg, up on the Platte River trail," Billy related. "He's in Denver for supplies and additional livestock. The weather caught him 'fore he could return."

Over drinks that evening, Reeves made an offer to Mike and Billy. "If you whackers want work, why not come back up the trail with me? I could use your wagons to haul contract supplies to the sutler at Fort Laramie. It's a one-time job, but there ain't nothin' else leavin' Denver till spring thaw."

Mike was noncommittal as the rancher talked on. When Reeves stepped away briefly, he turned to Billy. "I'm not keen on bustin' through snowdrifts again without a real contract. Still, this fella, Reeves, seems honest. And I've not a week's worth of fees for to corral and feed the bulls."

Billy nodded. "I'm satisfied to follow whatever trail you choose. A man's gotta eat." When Reeves returned they accepted his offer. On the 26th of October, they left Denver with him and his three herders.

Reeves was a strange fellow in some ways. He never did offer his Christian name. Indeed, no one seemed sure that his last name was truly Reeves. His herders mentioned something about a Confederate past but had no details. It wasn't unusual for folk to come to the frontier for a fresh start after the War.

As they drove up the valley of the South Platte one afternoon, Reeves examined, with visible concern, a dark bank of clouds looming to the northwest. Halting their drive, he assembled the crew. "We gonna get hit hard in a little bit. Let's get these teams unhitched. The bulls, mules, and horses we'll run into that draw, down on the Platte. Them trees'll offer a bit of shelter and keep 'em from driftin' with the storm. Let's unload this wagon and turn it over. It'll make a shelter for us."

The men worked quickly in the face of the advancing storm. Then Mike, Billy, Reeves and the three herders crawled underneath the overturned wagon, using their canvas "paulins" to shield themselves from the blasts of wind and snow. Though it was but midafternoon, a near darkness settled upon them. There was no way to prepare a proper meal. The herders shared dried strips of buffalo meat that were frozen hard. One had to suck on them for five minutes to thaw them sufficient to be bit into and chewed. Eventually, there was nothing to do but try to sleep through the noise of the howling wind.

By morning, the wagon was encased in snow. But the storm had passed and the clouds were breaking up. Billy kicked away enough drifted snow to crawl out from their makeshift cave. Reeves gave everyone an assignment. Mike and Billy's task was to break up the ice at the river's edge so the animals might drink. Later, when the breakfast fire was dying, Reeves taught them another trick from his bag of frontier know-how. He mixed ashes and bacon grease into a sticky, black paste. This he smeared on his cheekbones and under his eyes. "You all get some black too. The glare of the sun on this snow will burn your eyes till they feel like they's on fire. Might go blind in the bargain."

The others followed suit, then went to gather the stock. Mike found the horses stripping bark off the trees, they were so hungry. He and the herders doled out grain to them and the mules. The bulls were left to root beneath the snow for the grass shoots along the riverbank. It was afternoon before the wagon was righted and reloaded, and they could resume their journey to Julesburg.

Weather again closed the trails shortly after they got to Reeves' road ranche. The sod-wall cabin, outbuildings and corral offered little scope for meaningful work for Mike and Billy. But they performed such menial chores as they could in return for the board provided. Reeves poked at the fire that barely warmed one corner of the cabin. He was careful to limit his consumption of firewood, as it was likely that the supply would run out before spring. "You boys 'll stay the winter? You set out for here on my word and nothin' more. Seems only fair I board you till the spring."

Billy frowned at the projected wait. "What about gettin' them supplies up to the fort? Ain't that sutler goin' to be a bit put out about his goods?"

Reeves laughed and shook his head. "A man can only do what a man can do, Billy. Besides, Colonel Bullock ain't no fool. If the country's bound up in snow, he knows well why his goods are delayed. In the meantime, them supplies is our meal ticket."

Mike scratched his beard in frustration. We won't starve, but we well might freeze. Here I am, stuck for months without work, makin' no progress toward me fortune! Jane ain't gonna understand this at all.

As there was barely enough hay for Reeves' horses and mules, the bulls were released to forage as best they might. When the weather was too severe to be outside, which it was frequently, Billy and Reeves taught Mike the finer points of poker. Played for matches rather than money, the game was a diversion that grew on him day by day, easing his cabin fever. By spring, he could call a bluff with the best of them.

In March, the ice floes began to break up on the Platte. The cracking reports were extraordinary. Mike swore he had heard rifle shots, but Reeves assured him it was only the ice. Though the trails would not be open till April, the ranche needed grain, cordwood, and some other items immediately. It was decided that Mike, Billy, and the herders would go to Julesburg with several wagons, while Reeves would guard the ranche. With the weather improving, the threat of an Indian raid was again a real concern.

It was almost a day's journey to Julesburg from the ranche, and Mike figured they'd be back by nightfall the next day. They camped that night east of Fort Sedgwick and up close to the river. The ground was no longer snow-covered, though it was a bit muddy. But the weather was mild and it was a pleasant break to again sleep fresh under the starry cloak of night. It had been a long winter in the smoky, stuffy confines of Reeves' prairie castle.

The next day's transactions took longer than expected. Nearly every place they tried was fresh out of cordwood. They finally found a fellow who had just returned from the hills with a new supply, but the rascal was of a mind to charge an exorbitant price. Try as they might, Mike and Billy had little success at bargaining him down. Finally, they paid him dear.

It was late afternoon before they were loaded and ready to hit the trail. Mike knew they couldn't reach home before nightfall, and Reeves' herders began to cajole for a stop at Twelve-Mile Ranche. There, one could find a good supply of home-brewed whiskey and a game of chance—for money, not matches. Mike was sensitive to the others' appetite for a little fun. It had been a long, dreary winter. The most to be lost, he figured, was a few hours sleep.

At sundown, they halted at the way station. The wagons were strung out along the river, about thirty feet off the bank. They left the teams hitched and hobbled for security. One of the herders agreed to stand first watch. And so it went till near dawn, when it was Billy's turn to guard the train.

Mike pushed back from the poker table, tired and bleary-eyed. He had gone easy on the "tangleleg," but he sure was ready to crawl into the back of a wagon for a few hours. He walked across the cabin floor and peered through a dirty pane of glass. The rising sun was just brightening the horizon.

"Jaysus!" Mike pulled his revolver and headed for the door. Out by the end wagon was an Indian creeping on his hands and knees toward the tailgate. As he climbed into the wagon, a shot rang out and his head snapped back violently. The culprit sprawled out upon the grass. The herders and the proprietor of the way station poured out the back door of the cabin, hands full of weapons. Another shot emanated from within the wagon. It was clear Billy was closely managing his own defense.

As Mike approached, he saw two others Indians beyond the next wagon—one carried a rifle; the other, a tomahawk. Mike's first shots sent them off, shouting whoops of warning to others yet unseen. It was only when the other defenders arrived at the wagons that they noticed a Brule war party mounted and waiting atop a nearby hill. Mike was unable to get a clear view to count the warriors for they wheeled their horses about continuously, tossing off errant rifle fire from their distant position.

"Billy, are you wounded at all?"

"I'm still in one piece, but I come close to peein' in my britches before you fellas turned out for me."

Mike's grin in response was short-lived as his glance fell upon the dead brave lying behind the wagon. The exit wound in the back of his head was as gruesome a sight as Mike had ever seen. A dark, oozing pool of blood lay on the ground beneath the youth. His shiny black braid was flecked with pink bits of brain tissue. Mike turned away, feeling a surge of nausea.

"Come on," Billy shouted as he jumped down from the tailgate. "Them boys on the hillside appear to be plannin' a visit. Pull them grain sacks out the next wagon and throw them over the backs of your bulls."

Billy demonstrated as he laid hundred pound sacks over the flanks of the nigh-side and off-side wheelers. He then rested his Springfield rifle upon this makeshift breastwork. Mike and the others followed suit and positioned themselves to repulse the war party. As they did so, the first volleys were received from mounted braves looping past the line of wagons. But for the fact the bulls had been hobbled, they surely would have bolted at the sound of gunfire. As it was, they stamped, shifted, and bawled in anxious complaint.

The warriors showed little inclination for fighting at close quarters. They preferred to take potshots on the run. These tactics, and their lack of marksmanship, reduced the risks as long as the limited ammunition reserves of the freighters held out. Ten minutes on, with one bull down and a few others wounded, the whackers were becoming anxious. They were outnumbered three or four to one. Only the river at their backs prevented them from being surrounded.

A new source of gunfire erupted from the far left. Even the warriors reined up as they sensed a new fusillade raining down upon them. On a hillock nearby, Mike could see two additional riflemen laying down rapid fire with repeating rifles. Billy was positively jubilant. "I don't know who they is. But come on, come on!" He waved his hat at the retiring raiders.

In a minute, only the cloud of dust hanging in the air and a few more Brule corpses gave testimony to the recent conflict. The freighting crew moved off their defensive positions, and the road rancher waved in the two strangers with the repeating rifles. One was rather short and stocky, his companion just the opposite. Their buckskin clothing was dark with age, dirt, sweat, and blood. The taller of the two wore moccasins, while his mate was shod in leather boots. The road rancher stepped forward and extended his hand. "French Louie, you sumnabitch! I sure am glad to see you this mornin'. Who's your friend, here?"

The trapper sheathed his rifle and shook hands. "Meet Buffalo John. We're after thirty head of cattle these damn Brules stole off me near a week ago. Tracked 'em all the way from Cheyenne County to them hills over yonder. Woke up this mornin' to the sound of gunfire. Whose outfit is this anyway?"

Mike stepped forward. "We're workin' for Reeves, road rancher about ten miles up the trail. I'm Mike Quinn. This is Billy Mayhew. We're mighty grateful for your help just now."

"Yeah, we sure are," added Billy. "We don't know nothin' about your cattle, but we got a bull down. Seems only neighborly to invite you to breakfast on beefsteak with us."

As Mike described the scene later to Reeves, French Louie and Buffalo John had the animal skinned and dressed out by the time the others could get a good bed of coals ready for the spit. But Mike also had some explaining to do. "I'm awful sorry for the trouble, Mr. Reeves. Lettin' the boys talk me into stoppin' at the ranche was a big mistake."

Reeves waved off the apology. "Oh, I ain't fussed about that, Mike. You had to stop someplace 'tween here and Julesburg. I reckon you did better at the ranche than if you was caught out along the trail with no help about. If I was to get lathered up, it'd be over the price you all paid for my cordwood. So I'm out a bit of money and you're out a good bull. I hope he tasted good."

Chapter Thirteen

Hell on Wheels

☩

By mid-April, all remnants of the harsh winter had receded. As promised, Reeves undertook his delayed delivery of supplies to Ft. Laramie, with Mike and Billy providing much of the transport. The winter had not been kind to Mike's stock of bulls. In addition to the one killed during the Indian raid, three bulls had wandered off in winter storms and were not to be found. Most likely, Reeves said, they ended up in the cook pot of some Cheyenne or Sioux. Nevertheless, Mike was able to pull together two short teams of five yoke each and shift some of the freight from wagons to Reeves' pack mules.

They were encamped west of Mitchell Pass, on the bank of the North Platte. It was about a week since they left Reeves' ranche. The weather had been cloudy, with occasional spring rains, but they expected to reach Ft. Laramie in another four or five days, if the trail wasn't too muddy.

Night descended upon the prairie, and the high clucking call of a bob-white decorated the background gurgle of swift river currents. Normally freighters would douse their fire after supper, so as not to attract attention from Indian raiding parties. But their proximity to Fort Mitchell provided a sense of heightened security.

"What we goin' to do once we finish up with Reeves?" Billy asked Mike. "Don't seem this pull will last much more'n another few days."

"Can't say, Billy, but I've been thinkin' on it. 'Tis folly to stay with Reeves—he has no further use for us."

Mike poked at the coals of the campfire. He was mindful that the winter months had been a financial loss for Billy as well as himself.

"Let's see what fortune holds at Ft. Laramie. If things don't look up soon, you can follow whatever trail suits you. Still, 'twould be most welcome, should you stay on."

Billy nodded without comment. No verbal response was necessary. A bond had grown between them, and their loyalty to each other was well understood. After they put up the skillet and tin plates, Billy retired and Mike settled his bedroll next to the fire. He palmed a final cup of coffee against the chill as he stared into the bed of coals. He wondered about Reeves and his days with the Confederacy. What terrible tales he might tell if he were of a mind to do. Nothin' as bad as what Billy has endured, I'll wager. To lose one's family . . . Jaysus. I wonder if me own family is yet in Lawrence. . . . Could be they're waitin' on me arrival this very minute.

He drained his cup and, reclining, pulled his blanket over him. Ah well, I'll be seein' them in autumn . . . and Jane, of course. God, I miss that girl.

It took a while to fall asleep. He felt the soft brush of the wind against his cheek, and heard the rushing waters of the North Platte above the camp. Just as he started to doze, a coyote gave a howl. 'Twill be a long wait 'til autumn, he murmured as sleep overtook him.

Fort Laramie was the principal bastion of military protection on the Great Overland Road, sited a few miles below where a swift-running stream from the nearby mountains joined the North Fork of the Platte. The mountain men informally named a trading post there for a French trapper, Jacques La Ramee. In 1849, at the height of the California gold rush, the U.S. Army purchased it to protect the hordes of Americans headed west. Later, gold strikes in Montana and the creation of the Bozeman Trail put an additional burden upon the garrison at Ft. Laramie.

The spring of 1867 was a time of heightened tension between the U.S. Government and the tribes occupying the valley of the North Platte. A federal suspension of Indian rations, the approaching construction of the Union Pacific Railroad, and the unannounced creation of additional military outposts along the Bozeman Trail had incited the Lakota, Cheyenne, and Arapaho into a furious state. The tribes struck back the preceding autumn, killing sixteen soldiers and fifty-six civilians.

In December, a Lakota leader, Red Cloud, led a band of nearly fifteen hundred warriors and entrapped an army patrol near Fort Phil Kearny, up on the Bozeman Trail. Brevet Lt. Col. William Fetterman, a rabid Indian-hater and an impetuous officer, had gone out to find and punish those who had been attacking woodcutting parties from the fort. Fooled by the decoy maneuvers of Crazy Horse, Fetterman suddenly found his unit surrounded by a vastly superior force. Forty-nine whites, soldiers and civilians, were annihilated, many suffering gruesome mutilation at the hands of their enemies. Thus Indian conflict was the main subject of discussion at Ft. Laramie when the Reeves train arrived.

During his brief time on the frontier, Mike had readily absorbed the attitudes of the bullwhacking fraternity toward the Indian nations. As prime users of the Overland Road, freighters, pilgrims, and road ranchers expressed little regard for the red men who occasionally inflicted death and destruction along the route. Just the threat of such an attack was enough to spoil a good night's rest when out on the trail.

The subject arose again during an afternoon halt, but Billy Mayhew saw things a bit differently. "Maybe it's on account of bein' run off my place back in Missouri," he told Mike and Reeves. "But I figure them Injuns is gettin' run off of their lands too. Settlers and buffalo hunters have done shot up most of the game. Now here come these gandydancers layin' iron across the best hunting grounds in the west. I'd raise Cain too if I was Injun."

Reeves spat and barked a rebuttal. "Shit, Billy! It be common sense that the days of livin' off the buffalo is over. If they just set down on the land and farm it, or graze cattle on it, there'd be plenty to go around. But no, they gotta have the whole damn country for huntin' grounds. I tell you, if any of them Sioux bastards come at me, I'll be firin' so fast, they'll think it's rainin' lead."

Mike was quiet, deep in thought. He got up and emptied the last of the coffee into his tin cup.

"What say you, Mike?" Reeves inquired.

Mike resumed his place in the shade of a freight wagon. "Billy, I hear your argument, but I'll be sidin' with Reeves on this Injun business. You see, me own folk was run off their land too, back in Ireland. 'Course I was just a wee one at the time, but I heard all the stories. Some say 'twas failure of the potatoes what run our people off. But that's not so. 'Twas the Brits who decided to starve us out, so they could take our fields for grazin' soon as we was gone. They took the land and they took away our Irish tongue. Some of us even forgot whose country it was after all. So what did we do? Them that stayed took up new ways of livin' and workin'. Some of us moved on and found our way to America, Canada, or Australia. We had to drink the bitter cup of exile, just like them Injuns. But damn it, we did it! And sure, these Injuns will have to as well."

A look of mild shock appeared on Billy's face. "Damn, Reeves! For a quiet soul, this fella carries a sharp edge on his knife!"

The rancher laughed and nodded. "He's well spoke in his views, Billy. I s'pect that, after another ambush, you'll be singin' the same hymn as us."

Mike was unimpressed with Fort Laramie. He had envisioned something like Fort Kearny, or perhaps a bit bigger. The military compound sat upon a low, bare mesa, wholly devoid of trees. To approach the fort, they first had to navigate a squalid encampment of various tribes, mostly Lakota, with a smattering of Cheyenne and Arapaho. The population of this village was greatly diminished at the time by the continuing conflict between the army and hostiles from each of these tribes.

Reeves referred to the inhabitants of this village as "loafers." It was a derogatory term given to them by their own hardline tribal brethren. The hunter/warrior society held in great contempt those who preferred a bare subsistence on the fringes of the white man's economy.

Beyond this periphery of tipis, dogs, and children was the clustering of buildings that comprised the fort. No longer encompassed as a walled fortress, Fort Laramie included about thirty rough structures that were mostly strung

Fort Laramie in 1868 (Photo by William H. Jackson, Courtesy of the L. Tom Perry Special Collections, H.B. Lee Library at Brigham Young University)

along the edges of a large, central parade ground. Across the parade ground was a long, single-story building, part adobe and part clapboard. This was the sutler's store. It was the center of commercial, political, and social activity for hundreds of miles in each direction. Colonel William Bullock had operated this establishment for years now. In so doing, he had acquired a considerable standing with Indians and military alike.

After being directed to a warehouse for off-loading their freight, Reeves and his party returned to Bullock's store for refreshment, news, and the scent of any business opportunity. Bullock was a tall, imposing figure, who looked to be in his mid-fifties. His prematurely white hair and full white beard gave him the stately appearance of a frontier Moses. But it was his steady gaze and keen attention to all around him that signaled his substantial business acumen.

He welcomed Reeves with warm familiarity, and he seemed genuinely pleased to make the acquaintance of the others in the party. Mike and Billy shook his hand, but soon moved off to survey the variety of food, clothing, weapons, and tools on display. They sampled the whiskey, which they found rough but welcome. Dried buffalo and antelope strips, crackers, and a large cheese wheel were also attractions to those seeking relief from the unvaried fare of bullwhackers' cuisine.

Later that afternoon, Reeves found Mike and Billy idling about the parade ground. "Colonel Bill tells me the railroad is expected to push through Nebraska and into Dakota Territory by late this year. Fella name of Van Tassel come through here last week lookin' for men to lumber railroad ties with him down in the hills. I also heard that Wells Fargo is lettin' wagons and stock go cheap as the railroad shuts down the stagecoach business in the east."

Mike thanked Reeves for this important news, and that evening, he and Billy talked it over at supper. The glow of the fire sent their shadows dancing across the white canvas of their wagons. Mike mopped up his beans with a piece of biscuit. "Far be it from meself to be loggin' for this fella Van Tassel. But it's got me thinkin' about where we might find our next stake."

Billy heaved a sigh of relief. "Damn, I'm glad to hear you say that. I figured sure you was gonna give up the freightin' game, just so you and me would be eatin' regular. That loggin' business is an awful tough line of work!"

"I'm sure you are right. But hear me idea first, and then tell me what you think. When we came through Fort Kearny last summer, I met a friend of Jimbo. Gilman, I think his name was. He told us he was goin' into business to supply railroad ties to the Union Pacific. Tried to get Jimbo to sign on. Asked me as well."

Billy threw his hands in the air. "Ain't that about what this Van Tassel fella is lookin' to do?"

Mike smiled reassuringly. "Ah, Billy, spare me a minute to spill it out. Sure, this is different. Gilman didn't want us for loggin'. He was after hirin' freighters to haul his ties to where the railroad was needin' 'em. 'Twas bullwhackers he was seekin'."

"You figure to sign on with this Gilman fella?" Billy asked, somewhat mollified.

"Maybe . . . I'm thinkin' on it. If we was to go back east, we might also pick up some cast-off wagons and stock."

"We're needin' bulls," Billy retorted. "But mostly, we need a contract."

Mike pulled a stick from the kindling and traced a crude map in the dirt. "If we go back to Julesburg with Reeves, I'm thinkin' we'll find Gilman's outfit somewheres east of there."

"It's some better than eatin' our bulls and usin' our wagons as firewood," Billy conceded.

And so it was agreed. Soon they were back on the trail and moving fast with empty wagons and well-grazed bulls. They left Reeves and his herders just outside of Julesburg. It was a bittersweet parting, given the kindness and help the road rancher had rendered for over six months. As Mike and Billy's grubstake had dwindled, Reeves had been generous with his supplies. The boys were anxious to move along, but agreed to one last evening of poker and "tangleleg" before taking their leave.

Early the next morning, they were off in a daze, with pounding headaches and unsteady stomachs. Still, they hurried their teams. The prospect of steady work implied steady meals. Besides, Mike was painfully aware that his fortune was yet unmade. Surely, Jane would soon be losing patience, perhaps even regarding him as a ne'er-do-well. Thoughts of her, and his long absence from home, goaded him as he retraced the road he had traveled last summer for General Coe.

At Alkali, they encountered their first sight of the railroad laborers pushing their way west for the Union Pacific. This initial crew was a grading party, Lewis Carmichael's movers of earth and rock. They could see a foreman, astride a mule, monitoring the operation along the north bank of the Platte as their small bull train passed on the opposite side. Mike and Billy were struck by the hoards of men, animals, and equipment. There were mule-driven scrapers, drivers, herders, and laborers with picks, shovels and wheelbarrows. They were raising a cloud of dust that could be seen for miles. That evening when they made camp, Billy agreed to play nighthawk while Mike went across the river to make inquiries.

The north bank of the Platte was lit with scores of campfires. In the purple afterglow of sunset that still painted the western sky, Mike found a good fording point and waded ashore. The graders were a sight unto themselves—big, strong fellows, mostly Irish immigrants, many veterans of the War Between the States. Their clothes were filthy dirty, suffering from the abusive wear and tear of their labors. The lilt of their various accents, some in mirth, some in complaint, others in anger, had a haunting effect upon him. Sounds like millworkers at the end of day.

The graders lounged about their campfires, playing cards, talking, singing, cursing, or fighting, according to their mood. Clearly, there was a supply of alcohol in camp to sooth the aching bodies and numb the bored minds of the weary cadres.

Mike approached a man standing by himself, enjoying a pipe of tobacco. "Excuse me, sir, I'm looking for the superintendent."

The man looked at Mike with a mix of curiosity and suspicion. "He ain't about now. Gone to end-of-track for a hooray with the bosses. You don't look like one of us, though you sound Irish enough. What is it you're wantin' with the super'?"

Mike brushed the trail dust off his sleeves. "I guess I do look a sight. I'm a freighter. Got me teams over the water there. I'm huntin' for the man who's supplyin' railroad ties. His name is Gilman."

The railroad man's face lit up in recognition at the name. "Ah, now. He's at this same powwow where Carmichael has got to. General Jack has got 'em all dancin' the carpet." He shuffled his feet playfully in a jig, suggesting what might happen in the morning. "'Tis 'bout the schedule. We're runnin' a wee bit behind." He removed his hat and scratched his balding crown. "Lost a heap of days to the hard winter. Much of what we built last fall was torn to bits by river ice and floodin'."

Mike's gaze and attention wandered.

"Sorry. I do go on—so me wife says."

"Can you tell where this end-of-track may be? I'll be goin' there directly in the mornin'."

"Sure, 'tis a movin' target, lad. Last I heard, they was a few miles east of O'Fallons."

It was full dark when Mike got back to camp. Billy was with the herd and Mike bedded down quickly. They would talk about this in the morning. Right now, he had to rest up for the second watch.

The end-of-track was moving continually as the Union Pacific pushed west from Omaha. The railroad bosses demanded that it progress at maximum speed, as the miles of track completed determined the price paid by the Federal government. And it was an urgent race against the forces of the Central Pacific Railroad, which was approaching from California through the Sierras. It was nearly a two-day drive before Mike and Billy found the end-of-track, about five miles west of O'Fallon's Bluff.

If the graders' camp was a town, the end-of-track qualified as a city, a big city. The total construction workforce, including the graders, exceeded eight thousand men. It was a veritable army, and General Jack Casement, a forceful, if diminutive, veteran of the Civil War was its leader. He and his brother Dan ran the construction effort like it was their private army. Everyone was assigned and trained to a specific task and dared not fail in its execution.

Moving at two miles or more a day, the whole operation was designed to roll forward constantly on the freshly laid tracks. There were dormitory cars for the laborers, though in good weather most men preferred to sleep outside on the roofs or on the ground. There were also dining cars, a baker's car, a butcher's car, kitchen cars, flatbed cars stacked high with rails and ties, stock-feed cars, a saddler's shop, a carpenter's car and a blacksmith's shop. Numerous supply cars held everything from fish-plates and rail "chairs" to cable, rope, wrenches, wood, switch stands, sledgehammers, shovels, food and water. Everything they needed was mobile and continuously replenished by supply trains from the rear.

Billy and Mike found a road rancher to mind their stock while they visited the end-of-track on the warm mid-May morning. When they arrived, they found the work site aswarm with activity.

"Comin' through! Out-a-me-way!"

Jumping back at the imperious command, the two teamsters retreated to a safe distance from which to watch in fascination as the tracklaying crew performed their magic with speed and precision. The roadbed, having been built up or graded down weeks before by the graders, was now dotted with rail ties hauled forward in mule-drawn wagons. From the newly

A crew of "gandydancers" constructing the Union Pacific Railroad, 1866 (Photo by J. Carbutt, Courtesy of the Union Pacific Historical Collection)

laid track came a light "lorry" car, drawn by a single mounted horse approaching at a near gallop with its burden of forty iron rails. Quickly, the rider unhitched the horse and led it away. Two men rushed forward and, barehanded, seized the end of the 560 lb. rail and pulled it away. By twos, ten others followed, till the thirty-foot rail was free of the car. Then this team advanced at a run to the point of placement.

"Down," commanded a foreman, and the men carefully dropped the rail into position onto the little iron "chairs," while the next team approached with the companion rail. No more than thirty seconds had elapsed before the first crew was hurrying back for another rail. Gaugers scrambled between the rails to ensure a four-foot, eight-and-one-half inch spacing was maintained. Once this was complete, the spiking crew stepped in to drive ten spikes home for each rail, three strokes to the spike. Finally, the bolters came to wrench into place the fishplates that linked one rail to the next. Once empty, the "lorry" car was tipped off the track to allow a new load of rails to be advanced onto the fresh track. Then the empty car was tipped back onto the track, to be galloped back to base for replenishing. So it went all day, as each task leapfrogged its way down the line at a breathless pace.

Mike gaped at the sight before him. "Glory be to Saint Patrick! I thought the bullwhacker's life was a busy one."

Billy elbowed him in the ribs. "So, you don't figure on becomin' a gandydancer, eh, Mike?"

"No, but we are in desperate need of payin' employment. Let's go hunt up Gilman."

They walked back along the right-of-way, through a sea of men, wagons, and railcars till they came to the base of operations. There, men in business suits and bowler hats bustled in and out of the rolling offices of the Union Pacific and the Casement brothers. It took several attempts, before Mike was able to apprehend a clerk.

"Gilman? Yes, he's here—somewhere. Saw him first thing, but now— try the big tent over there."

Mike and Billy strode purposefully over to a white canvas tent whose double door flaps were tied back, inviting ventilation. As Mike stepped into the opening, a large man in waistcoat and rolled up shirtsleeves nearly ran him down coming out.

"Whoa! Sorry, I'm in a hurry," he muttered as they each retreated a step.

"Me apologies, sir," Mike blurted, as the man continued by. "Mr. Gilman?"

The man stopped and turned. "You've found him. What's your business?"

"I'm Mike Quinn. We met last summer at Fort Kearny. I was bullwhackin' for General Coe then, and you was lookin' for teamsters to haul ties. I was committed at the time, but now we're lookin' to sign on, if you can see your way clear."

"Oh, yeah, I seem to remember you. Sorry, I got my teams. I'm full up."

Mike was stunned. He and Billy had traveled for close to three weeks just to get on with Gilman & Carter. As Gilman walked away, Mike added, "I'm sure you'll remember offerin' to hire meself and Jim Bowes."

Gilman stopped. "Jim Bowes!" he said returning to Mike and Billy. "I heard he got himself killed last summer."

"'Tis the sad truth. Got gored by a bull on the Upper Crossin'."

Gilman relaxed a bit. "He was a damn fine fella and one hell of a bullwhacker! I was sorely vexed to hear of his demise." Gilman removed his hat and mopped his brow with the sleeve of his shirt. "So, I tried to hire you away from Coe and Carter, did I?"

"Yes, sir. We've bulls and a couple of wagons at a road ranche a ways up the trail. You'll not regret givin' us a chance."

Billy stepped forward. "We're good workers, sir. Don't stir up no trouble."

Gilman looked as though he might relent. "Come on in here for a spell," he said, pointing back to the tent. "Could be I can use you. Let's talk."

The three entered the tent where tables were barrels straddled by planks, and campstools of wood and canvas provided the seating. The office was a sea of paper—maps, bills of lading, and correspondence. The sun, high in the sky, illuminated the interior through the rough canvas fabric. Though an occasional breeze found its way through the doorway, it did little to relieve the considerable heat building up inside.

As they sat, Gilman relit the butt of a cigar that had been left in a dish beside his chair. "Boys, we've been bringin' in ties, mostly cedar, from the hills above the Platte. That worked fine when we started out at Gothenburg. But the further west we go, the more we're usin' cottonwood, which ain't real good for ties, unless it be burnettized. Even then, it ain't wonderful."

"What's that?" Billy asked, trying to hold up his end of the discussion.

Gilman gave him a patronizing look. "We take a big iron tank, about a hundred feet long. We soak softwood ties in a hot zinc bath and then let 'em dry. Makes 'em acceptable while we're on the run for Casement. Probably won't last more'n a year carryin' traffic. The nearest supply of good hardwoods, as we move west, is in the Black Hills, between Fort Laramie and the right-of-way. We're just gettin' ready to move most of our loggers and freight teams over there."

Mike shifted anxiously in his chair. "We're keen to go, Mr. Gilman. Fact is, we're about run through our grubstake. We came here figurin' 'twas the best chance to make a haul. Do you think you might use us?"

"Well . . ." Gilman stood and stuck out his hand. "I'll put you on and see how it works out. Let me get my payroll book. I'll see you don't starve between here and the Laramies."

After a few days, a large team of loggers and freighters arrived at the base camp from the Nebraska hills. Bringing their teams in line with the others, Mike and Billy headed back up the Platte. This time, however, their path followed neither the North Platte nor the South Platte trail they had traveled to Denver. This new trail ran due west out of Julesburg, up along the banks of Lodge Pole Creek, and into the Dakota Territory, which included Wyoming.

At Crow Creek, soon to be renamed Cheyenne, they swung north, following the Chugwater Creek until they reached the stands of cedar, mountain pine, and hemlock in the hills between the forks of the Laramie River. The logging parties were constantly in jeopardy of Indian attack, as the Lakota and Cheyenne were currently in full cry. A mail party had been ambushed west of Laramie a few weeks back. More recently, nine railroad workers had been killed along the right-of-way in western Nebraska. Mike, Billy, and the other freighters spent their time patrolling the hills. Gilman had issued them new Henry repeaters to strengthen their defenses.

The first loads of ties and telegraph poles were ready for shipment by mid-June. The latter would be used to relocate the Western Union's line alongside the railroad right-of-way. The trip back was a slow one, the loads being heavy and the trails less developed. It was well into July when they arrived at the new base campsite at Julesburg.

"This ain't the same town we left behind," Billy said, gawking at the sights.

Mike grunted in agreement as he pushed back his hat and stared in amazement. In the time since they had passed through on their way to the Black Hills, the town's population had surged from fifty souls to four thousand. The streets were clogged with soldiers, herdsmen, teamsters, gamblers, whores, and merchants, and, of course, the railroad gangs. From tents and prefabricated shacks came the roar of laughter, profanity, and hooted invitations to drink, try one's luck at three-card monte, or invest in female companionship.

Flush with the pay from their first haul for Gilmans, Mike and Billy explored the "roaring town," cautiously protecting their earnings. They made their way to the Germania House. Here, a pretty decent meal could be had for fifty cents. The place was crowded, and sharing tables was the order of the day. They found themselves dining with a pleasant Julesburg native, Dr. Heimberger. After a few pleasantries, their companion leaned close and spoke softly, as if in confidence.

"You boys said you just came in from the trail? If I may offer a bit of friendly advice, best mind what you say or do here in Julesburg. Things have got out of hand lately. We wake up each morning with dead bodies in our streets, the results of the night's mayhem! Most are gunshot, others knifed. All have empty pockets."

Mike and Billy looked at each other and nodded. "Sure, we appreciate the warnin'," Mike replied. "The docksides of Liverpool and New York don't hold a candle to such as this."

Billy grinned at Mike's exotic references. "'Spect mindin' one's own business is the healthy way," he said. "You bein' a doc and all—must keep you mighty busy, patchin' folks back together."

"Busy, sir, but not always paid," Heimberger replied sardonically as he returned to his bowl of soup.

The vast payrolls being expended by the railroads had attracted a horde of drifters, drummers, sharpsters, and strumpets. They well knew that thousands of rail workers would be hungry for nighttime diversion after days of unrelenting toil. The most extravagant of the many dens of iniquity was the "Hell on Wheels," an oversized tent measuring one hundred feet by forty. Its patrons hoofed about on a wooden dance floor while provided with modest orchestral accompaniment. At the periphery were gaming tables and multiple bars offering watered whiskey at fifty cents a shot.

The competition came from Father Ryan, a priest from Columbus, Nebraska, who preached against all the profanity and dissolution in Julesburg. He also had a tent and provided rail ties to sit on, but the hard-bitten residents of the boomtown largely ignored his best efforts.

Mike, Billy, and their freighter colleagues at Gilman & Carter had little time to participate in the revelries of the town. Shortly after they had rested from their journey, Gilman had them headed back to Wyoming for another load of ties. This time, however, they would only have to return as far as the next base camp, which was planned for Sidney, Nebraska.

One day in early August, as they came down the trail, they met another Gilman & Carter outfit coming up the trail with empty wagons and important news. Their wagon master, a friendly fellow from Illinois, could hardly contain his story.

"Damn near war broke out," the wagon master started. "Seems that gamblers was squattin' on railroad-owned lots at Julesburg and refused to get out when General Jack says so. Union Pacific was offerin' the lots for $50 to $250, but ain't no one buyin' while the gamblers stay on. Fair warnin' was given, a couple of weeks back, with no reply. So Casements issued weapons to their crews and brung 'em into town about dusk. Then all hell broke loose."

Mike's crew leaned in, so as to not miss a word.

"Yeah, them railroaders like to kill near every gambler in sight, straight out. Put 'em all up on Boot Hill, with the murdered folk."

"Sounds like it were a good time for us to be gone!" Billy commented to Mike.

They were also told of the new town of Cheyenne springing up at Crow Creek. Planned by the railroad as the next base station after Sidney, it already had several hundred inhabitants in its first month of existence.

"Everywheres that railroad come, there's bullwhackers and freightin' outfits put out of work!" the wagon master cautioned. "Why, the whole valley of the Platte is near empty of bull trains, be they freighters or pilgrims."

"I met a gent at Julesburg, last time," Mike agreed. "He was only three days out of Philadelphia. Don't suppose any wagon train can compete with the likes of that."

By the time they reached Sidney, the end-of-track, moving at two miles or better each day, was already at Potter. As expected, the camp followers were present in force, minus a few score of gamblers. "Hell on Wheels" and the dance hall, "King of the Hills," had safely advanced to Sydney and would stay until base camp shifted again.

"You boys made a good turn," Gilman acknowledged as he handed out their pay. "Keep things movin' and we'll make two more hauls 'fore winter sets in."

Mike smiled as he shoved the envelope of bills into his shirt. They were making good money. When they finished the season, he'd net over $500. He was also keen to wrap up for the winter and catch a train east. *With me earnings, I'll have a respectable start on me fortune. 'Twill be enough to marry and buy wagons and bulls for next season!*

He felt guilty that he'd not corresponded with Jane for months now. In October, she would attain her eighteenth birthday. Soon, they could look forward to a reunion and a long winter during which to mend hurt feelings. *Best send a telegram now. She'll be expectin' some word of me return to Lawrence.*

He wandered about Sidney, searching out the telegraph office. There, he carefully composed a brief message.

Dear Jane,
Business progresses well. Return may be delayed till November. Will
celebrate your birthday then. Hope you enjoy best health.
Affectionately,
Michael.

There, it was sent. Now he could leave for the hills with his mind settled and a planned schedule for his return. *Won't it be a wonderful Christmas, all of us together again?*

Chapter Fourteen

The Break

✠

The bull trains dispatched by Gilman and Carter had good reason to be on guard against Indian attack. All summer Red Cloud's "Bad Faces" band kept the pressure on the forts of the Bozeman Trail, while Spotted Tail's Brules and their Cheyenne allies made the railroad right-of-way their main focus of attack. Their success was limited, however, by the Army's increased use of breach-loading Springfields, and by the withering fire of repeating rifles, still mostly in civilian hands. Nevertheless, the scale of the Indian uprising had convinced the Johnson administration in Washington that the manpower and costs of a full-blown military campaign would be prohibitive. Already a federal peace commission was at Fort Laramie soliciting negotiations with the hostile tribes.

"Circle wagons! Corral up! Prepare for Indian attack!"

They were still four or five days below the Laramie forks and the timber fields. On this third trip to the Black Hills, Mike had been appointed wagon master. His urgent commands were now quickly passed down the train from teamster to teamster. Empty wagons were drawn up into the tight oval corral of defense.

Billy Mayhew hurried to where Mike was leaning over his Henry rifle. "Good you're keepin' a close eye, Mike. How many of 'em do you figure there be?"

"I'm thinkin' there's thirty braves, maybe more. They're down in that ravine behind the hill. See, you can make out their dust just above the rise."

Leaving their teams hitched and hobbled, Mike and the other bull-whackers crouched behind their wagons and awaited the advancing warriors. When the Indians broached the rim of the hill on the eastern flank, a volley of shots spewed forth from the corral. The lead riders in the Indian party wheeled their mounts amid cries of surprise. Dirt exploded at their feet as lead poured into their position. Quickly the Indians retired, staying out of sight. The bullwhackers ceased firing, reserving their precious ammunition.

A bugler's call emanated from the ravine. It was followed by a white flag of truce waved from the barrel of a rifle, which was carried by an Indian dressed in breechclout, leggings, and a blue military jacket. An officer of the United States Cavalry accompanied him. Together, they cautiously walked their mounts toward the bull train's position.

"Hold your fire! I'm Captain Luther North, U.S. Army. We only want a parley!"

"Come ahead, but slow," Mike called back. He turned to Billy. "What the deuce is this all about?"

North and his flagman moved closer, hands held high. "My party is not hostile. Our companies are Pawnee."

"Sorry for the lack of hospitality, Captain," said Billy as he reached for the reins of the horses, allowing the visitors to dismount. "We're a bit jumpy out here in the back country."

Mike ordered the others to lower their rifles as he approached the Captain. "'Tis me own fault entirely, Captain," Mike said. "I didn't get a real good look at your outfit before you dropped into that ravine. Sure, I can't tell one tribe of Injuns from another, hostiles from friendlies. Any of you been hit?"

The Captain maintained his expression of reproach. "No injuries, as far as I know. But you folks must take greater caution in the future. What out-fit is this anyway?"

"We're a timber outfit for Gilman and Carter, goin' to the Black Hills for another load of rail ties. I'm Mike Quinn, wagon master."

North looked at Mike with an appraising eye, obviously perturbed. Mike too was suspicious of the young officer. *This Captain North ain't much older than meself.*

The officer pulled his yellow kerchief and mopped his brow. A bullwhacker passed a cup of spring water to North, but made no such gesture to the Pawnee. "We've been chasin' hostile Sioux since May. My brother, Major Frank North, is back in Nebraska with the rest of the Pawnee soldiers, defendin' the railroad gangs." North sat on the tongue of a wagon and gulped down the water. "There's been another massacre, this one west of the Plum Creek station. Happened about a month ago. Cheyenne warrior, name of Turkey Leg, and his braves cut out a run of telegraph wire. A telegraph repair crew was dispatched by handcar that same night to mend the break. The Cheyenne jumped them as they come up on a barricade."

"Any survivors?" Mike asked.

"Five was killed, but one poor soul escaped carrying his scalp in his hands. Later that night, the Injuns derailed an eastbound train. Both the engineer and a fireman was burned to death in the wreckage."

A buzz of angry sentiment rose as the bullwhackers voiced reaction to the tale of carnage. "Bloodthirsty savages!" one spat. "Did your brother get a hold of 'em yet?"

North shook his head sadly. "The last I heard they had not. These hostiles are not easily brought to heel. One of my Pawnee scouts put an arrow into Spotted Tail's brother last month. Son-of-a-bitch pulled the arrow right through his side, strung it, and fired it back before he dropped dead. That's the kind of fightin' we're up against."

North and his Pawnee scout mounted and made ready to leave. The bullwhackers thanked the Captain for fair warning, and that night, Mike put on additional lookouts, a practice they continued while in the timber fields and on the return trip to Cheyenne.

The end-of-track was still a ways east of Cheyenne in mid-October, but was expected there within a few weeks. Unlike Julesburg, the settlement was not yet the "roaring town" it would soon become. But the former Crow Creek had grown to well over a thousand inhabitants since its founding in July. The city now boasted a newspaper and regular performances by the Julesburg Theatrical Troupe.

When Mike and his train arrived in town, the Gilman & Carter office was still back in Sidney. While there was possibly enough time for another timber run before the winter weather set in, the whackers demanded to be paid for this last trip before undertaking another. Mike and Billy were of the same mind. But Mike had another reason for waiting in Cheyenne. He was hesitant to go for another load of ties so close to when he should be heading back east. There was no way that Jane would understand a further delay in his return, even if it were beyond his control. In the meantime, he would wait for the Gilmans and enjoy the distractions of life in the base camp.

The following week, the company relocated to Cheyenne, and Gilman settled accounts with his bullwhackers. Mike pocketed his wages, then shook hands with his employer.

"Will you not reconsider and bring another load in?" Gilman asked.

Some change from when I was beggin' this fella for work. Mike scratched at his accumulation of light brown whiskers and smiled. "I'd like to oblige you, Mr. Gilman, but 'twould cost me a wife. But I'll be returnin' by spring thaw. I'd be pleased to haul for you then."

Before Mike could leave the tent, Gilman pulled a packet of correspondence from his valise. "Hold on a second. I brought up the mail from Sidney. . . . seems to me there was something for you in here." He rummaged for a minute before extracting a battered envelope. "Yup, here's the letter."

Mike accepted the letter with relish, thanked his boss, and walked out into the dirt streets of Cheyenne. He would wait to read it in private, as it was likely from Jane. He and Billy had camped south of town, in good pasture where Indian attack was unlikely. When Mike arrived, Billy passed the day-herder job over and left for town to collect his own pay packet.

Mike sat in the box of one of the wagons and pulled the envelope from his canvas jacket. Despite good sunshine, the autumn air on the high plains was cool, and it seemed the wind would never quit. He looked at the envelope. It was thick. A long letter, he noted with pleasure. The postmark indicated that it had been sent from Lawrence the first week of September. Must have sat about Gilmans' place for near a month. He tore the flap open and unfolded the pages.

'Tisn't Jane's handwriting at all! He went to the last pencil-scrawled page and found Roderick's signature. Then he turned back to the beginning:

Dear Brother,

Jane shared with us the good news you will soon be home again. It seems so long ago you left for to go to Canada with the Fenians. John and me will be well pleased to welcome you home. But, not so pleased as your mother and father. They and the girls did arrive here in June. They have took a tenement over on Elm Street and are well settled. Da is still looking for work, but Mary Ann and Catherine have got on at the mill. Elizabeth is now in the school at St. Mary's. All have asked news of you and do send their kind greetings by this letter.

John remains spinner at Arlington. He now boards at the company house. He and Catherine Cunniff have announced that they will marry sometime next year. I now have made spinner, at Atlantic, since almost a year ago. I keep the lodgings at Hampshire Street, which we did once share. The district above the Spicket is well grown since Arlington Mill opened.

We are happy for your good fortune in the freighting business and that you are able to make the journey home. Jane sends her good wishes to you. But she asked me to write this letter, as we have a matter you must know before you return. Jane has decided to break her engagement, given your long absence."

"What! She cannot—" Mike sputtered, every muscle in his body tensed with anxiety.

You may guess that in seeking news of yourself, Jane did call on myself from time to time. In this way, we did come to develop a deep affection for each other. As Jane is now almost of age, I have spoken to her father about our eventual marriage. You will, no doubt, be distressed. I hope you will understand this turn of events was totally unforeseen. Perhaps in time you will come to accept what has happened. It is our desire that your visit be a happy reunion. We all look forward to the day.

Your brother,

Roderick

"The divil you say! Me own feckin' brother . . . he's stole me bride! Son of a bitch! Sure, didn't her father say yes. . . . feckin' Brit!"

Mike balled the letter and threw it into the back of the wagon box. He looked up into the endless dome of blue, clouded only by tears of rage. Is this really Jane's decision? Perhaps. I did run off and leave her for eighteen months with naught but a couple of telegrams. . . . No, Jane's not the villain here. 'Tis Roderick!

Mike ran his hands through his long shaggy hair. He could almost feel himself bursting with a violent anger. "What in jaysus' name do they figure! Shall I be comin' along home, just as happy as you please? And then, what? Congratulations to you, Roderick, you stole me girl—so now won't you be happy together? What a bleedin' sin 'tis!"

Close to sundown Billy returned to camp but found no sign of Mike. The bulls had drifted well down range. Despite his load of a few whiskeys, he saddled Victorie, the mule Mike had won in a poker game and derisively named for the British monarch. Billy set out to regather the stock. Mike didn't come back that night, or the next day either. Worried for foul play, Billy hired a bullwhacker friend to tend the stock while he set off for town.

The grayish-white tent saloons around Sixteenth and Ferguson were pretty much all-night operations. The one Mike picked proved to be an exception. About 4:30 a.m., the two bartenders decided to throw out their last lingering client who was passed out at the green felt-covered poker table. Each grabbed an arm of the young bullwhacker and pulled him out into the street.

It was reasonably quiet at that hour. Those who were about took little notice of one more drunk lying in the street beside the plank sidewalk.

But a skulking figure prowling the dirt streets, staying in the shadows, sensed easy opportunity. His tattered gray coat and checkered trousers were only matched by the grime that clung to them. He was unshaven, and a shag of ill-cropped hair stuck out weirdly from under his dented bowler. He was enthused to find his prey in such a vulnerable state.

16th Street Cheyenne, Wyoming, 1868 (Courtesy of the Wyoming State Archives, Dept. of State Parks and Cultural Resources)

May not have much money, but I'll get a price for that revolver.

He rifled Mike's pockets with practiced dexterity. Then sitting on the sidewalk, he began to remove the tall, bull-hide boots from his victim.

His first vague wisp of consternation came as a fragrance wafting on the night breeze. A scent of lavender soap, a substance truly foreign to his prior experience, now perked his senses. A note of alarm germinated in the dullard's brain upon the familiar click of a pistol cocking. The rustle of satin accompanied the kiss of cold metal upon his skull behind the left ear.

A voice, softly feminine, yet pitched low and dusky, warned, "This piece fires but once. But I figure no need for another go at this range."

Caught sitting and from behind, the vagrant despaired of drawing Mike's revolver from his waistband, cocking, and turning to confront his challenger before being dispatched to glory. Instead, he froze in mid-tug of Mike's right boot.

"You stinkin', low-down, buffalo-fucker! Ease back slowly. I'll want his revolver—handle first. Plus, any weapon of your own. I promise you, any funny business and you'll have a bit of lead in your noggin."

He broke a sweat. Shaking with fear, he handed back Mike's pistol. Then he heard a second cocking behind his head.

"I da . . . don't have no pistol of my own, ma'am. Got no weapon at all."

"I don't believe you. Pull your own boots and let's see."

The drifter pulled his boots, exposing a scabbard strapped to his right calf, housing an eight-inch poignard.

"I suppose that pig-sticker just slipped your mind. Hand it back—and slow."

Once having complied, he slumped in subjugation and awaited further orders from his captor. "All right now, get up." As the mouth of the Williamson derringer was removed from his matted hair, he exhaled a sigh of modest relief. The yet unseen mistress of his destiny jabbed at his butt with the point of his own dagger. "Be off with you. And don't let me see your face in Cheyenne again. Won't be healthy for you if I do."

Sprung forward by the prick of his weapon, he scurried away up Ferguson Street, rubbing his injured haunch, howling in complaint.

When Mike awakened some hours later, he found himself lying on an iron frame bed bedecked with real sheets and a blanket. The feather pillow under his head smelled sweetly of perfume. Beyond the open flaps of the tent he now occupied, he could see his clothes hanging over a guy line. His mind raced about, looking for the thread of events that led him to this juncture.

His mouth was dry as the dust in a mummy's pocket, and his head pounded like the sledge of a gandydancer. He was loath to even raise his head, but the urgent necessity of a piss got him up. The tent was crowded. In the foreground was a walnut dresser, its surface covered with bottles and notions. Beyond was a sea trunk and scads of women's clothing hanging from ropes strung the length of the tent. He saw a chair, a table and an oil lamp. Seems no one's home.

He stubbed his naked toe upon a chamber pot, which he quickly put to good use. When he went for his clothes, he found them damp. They'd been washed near beyond recognition. With his current attire limited to underwear, he had to admit he was marooned. Best be goin' back to bed.

When he next awoke, it was nearly midday. Someone was moving about in the tent. He opened one eye. He could see a woman, her back turned to him. She was fastening the garter that held a black stocking in place. With one foot set upon the seat of the chair, she smoothed the fabric from bottom to top in a long, languid motion that Mike found arousing. Must be a show girl.

He politely coughed, pretending to just awaken. She turned to face him, letting her blue satin dress fall to mid-calf. She was blessed with long tresses of shiny black hair that made her blue eyes a surprising contrast. She had a full, rounded figure, in keeping with the prevailing standards of feminine pulchritude. What might have been facial beauty had been sabotaged by a white slash of scar across her right cheek.

"So, you're awake, are you? S'pect that head of yours like to fall off. Now that you've tried my bed, you might introduce yourself."

Mike started to rise, but his scant clothing gave him second thoughts. Instead he sat up, pulling the blanket about him. "I used to be Mike Quinn. Today, I'm unsure. Who might you be? And how do I come to be in your bed?"

She pulled the chair and planted it backwards in front of him. She straddled the seat and rested her arms and chin upon the chair back. "Folks here call me Sally, but my given name is Sarah, Sarah Kincaid. I guess you be here as I didn't figure on leavin' you in the gutter to be picked over like carrion."

Mike looked into her deep blue eyes and lost his train of thought.

"Cat got your tongue?"

He recovered and asked, "How'd you get me here?"

"My boy, Matt, done fetched you back here."

"You have a son?"

"No, God no! Matt's my nigger. He works for me, you know. . . . I trust you preferred my bed to lyin' in the mud and havin' your boots stole off your feet!"

"Sorry ma'am. Indeed, I'm thankin' you. Sure, you even laundered me clothes, didn't you?"

Sally snorted her reply. "Well, I weren't gonna allow you near my bed, all covered in mud and horseshit as you was." Sally turned to glance in the mirror and pat her hair into place. "I s'pect you be hungry. Get your clothes on and we'll go put on a feedbag."

Mike rose gingerly from the cot, holding the blanket in place and inching toward the line where his clothes hung drying.

Sally snickered and taunted, "Will you quit actin' so damn prissy! I've seen more men naked lately—ain't likely to be swoonin' at the sight of your moth-bit drawers! You men are all a hoot."

They ordered dinner in the small, temporary quarters of the Chicago Eating House. It was situated near the railroad right-of-way. A more permanent manifestation of the eatery was under construction next door. The patrons were seated in a prefabricated structure, while all cooking and preparation took place in a tent out back. Mike's stomach was queasy, and he could only stare at the sawmill gravy, eggs and biscuits. Sally, though, had no trouble with her dinner.

"My husband, Ben, and me was raised down in Arkansas—river town name of Osceola," she offered without being asked. "Ben, bein' handy with cards, figured he'd make some money off the railroad folk up here. We left home last fall. . . . brung Matt with us. Matt was my daddy's nigger till the war's end. When daddy died, Matt come to work for Ben and me."

Mike listened, but his attention was distracted by the pounding in his head.

"We rode the riverboat as far as Omaha and then come the rest by train. . . . Joined the end-of-track when they was just east of the fork of the Platte. Ben was doin' good at the tables, and we bought the tent and had some furniture shipped in by rail.

"Is your husband away somewhere?" Mike asked.

Sally held out her cup for coffee from a passing waitress. "You could say it that way. Ben's up on Boot Hill, back in Julesburg—murdered by them damn Casement brothers." Sally slammed her coffee cup down on the table at the memory of it. A bit of coffee splashed upon the table. "Only reason I ain't shot dead, I was hidin' in the sea trunk."

"Sorry for bringin' sad times to mind," Mike said sheepishly.

"Aw, I've got over Ben. We was more business partners than sweethearts. He did his gamblin' and, me, I went to whorin'."

Mike gulped at his coffee to gain a few seconds to compose himself. He was shocked by Sally's candid acknowledgement of her line of work, though he wasn't naive about prostitution. He had seen it in Lawrence and in England before that. On the frontier, one couldn't but notice the openness with which the trade was plied. So far he had escaped the attentions of prostitutes out of devotion to Jane. Now that particular incentive seemed well behind him.

"We had a reasonable pile of money, till the Casement gang picked Ben and the others clean. So hey, what about you? I hope you don't sleep in the gutter regular."

Taking his time, Mike described the events that led to his two-day binge in Cheyenne. Sally listened closely, ignoring the rest of her dinner. She probed for details, but Mike didn't feel she was coming on nosy. He poked at his dinner and, finding it cold, pushed it away. "I'll not go back. Sure, there's nothin' in Lawrence for me. S'pect I'll go up to the Laramie Forks once more before the snows fly."

"But, Mike, what of your ma and pa? Will you not miss seein' them again—and your sisters too?"

Mike looked away from Sally. "I'll be doin' better by them if I make me fortune. They don't need one more mouth to feed, poor as they are."

Sally shrugged and pulled on her coat. "It's your decision. Come on, you can walk me to work." They stepped lightly into the muddy street. Mike turned and looked closely at Sally. He was fascinated by the animation in her face and the sparkle in her eyes. As they reached the plank walkway on the other side, he asked, "'Tis none of me own business, but I'm curious how you come by that scar."

Her demeanor turned cold and stiff. She looked at Mike with resentment in her eyes. Then her face softened again and she sighed. "It do look awful, huh? One of my johns, son of a bitch—went at me with a knife when I told him to get."

Mike shook his head in sympathy. "Your beauty's still there. Besides, the scar, 'tis likely to fade in time."

"Keep talkin', bullwhacker. I'll take all the sweet talk you got."

Miss Crowley's whorehouse occupied two floors in one of the newly constructed buildings in town. As they reached the rear outside staircase, Matt, a Negro in his early twenties, was sitting on a step waiting for Sally. He was short and stocky, his bare feet like two great calluses. His head was a tangle of matted black wool. He looked at Mike with suspicious recognition, barely nodding as Sally introduced them to each other.

"I hope I see you again, Mike. Now you know where to find me, don't be no stranger."

Mike sauntered down Fifteenth Street. The rail bed, on his right, was graded and awaiting the tracklaying crews. As his approached Dodge Street, Billy

Mayhew came around the corner, nearly bumping into his partner. "Where the hell you been, Mike? I figured you got a bullet in you when you didn't show up at camp."

"Ach, Billy! I'm sorry. I didn't mean to go off like that without tellin' you. I got some bad news from home."

Billy's face fell. "Someone die on you?"

"No, no, nothin' like that. It's just that I ain't goin' back east after all."

"Aha! That woman of yours done been cheatin' on you, right?"

Mike stiffened, embarrassed at having his private affairs discussed. "Somethin' like that. Look, let's let it go. Anyway, I could have had a bullet in me, save for the kindness of a lady here in Cheyenne."

"Well, you can tell me all 'bout it on the way back to the herd. I got Frank Lawson mindin' things while I was ahuntin' you all around town."

That evening as they sat at the campfire, Mike's spirits were very low. While intrigued by Sally Kincaid, he was still feeling gut shot at the loss of Jane and the cancelled trip back to family and friends.

"Say, Mike, did I ever tell you 'bout my first trip up here in the high country?" Billy asked.

Mike shook his head and sighed. " I don't remember you sayin' nothin' about it."

"It was my first run to Denver. We was at Latham Station, where the Cache la Poudre River hits the South Platte. Our 'cookie' come up with a case of somethin' sounded like whoopin' cough. Anyhow, I drew the short straw to do the cookin' for the boys. I wasn't much worried though. I'd fixed meals for myself plenty before that."

Mike poked aimlessly at the fire with a long stick. "Yeah, your cookin' has always been fair enough."

Billy grinned and continued his tale. "So, I figure to make flapjacks and bacon for breakfast that first day. And the boys all thought they tasted plum delicious, so I was feelin' pretty good about it. But come the evenin' halt, most of the boys came in complain' 'bout bellyaches. By the time supper was fixed, the whole crew was cramped up with some sickness. And fart! 'Land of Goshen,' they was fartin' up a whirlwind. Soon, they was cussin' me, said I poisoned 'em with that breakfast. I reckon I must have done, as I was feelin' poorly too."

Mike's face began to glimmer with a smile at the thought of a whole camp of bullwhackers doubled over and breaking wind at each other.

"The wagon master storms up to me and says, 'Whatcha put in them damn flapjacks, Mayhew?' I says the usual stuff, you know, flour, salt, molasses, bakin' powder. . . . 'How much bakin' powder?' he screams at me. I says 'bout two full measures, same as I learnt from my Mama back in Missouri. 'Well, this ain't Missouri,' he says. 'We be at over five thousand feet here on the plain. Bakin' powder will blow us all to hell at this elevation. You're supposed to cut back.' Well, ain't nobody told me about it. Besides, I ain't the regular cook anyways. Then, he says, 'Yeah, and you ain't never gonna be neither!'"

Mike burst out laughing, which set off Billy, and they both laughed till they cried. Billy waved his hat in pantomime. "Yeah, I darn near died of windburn that night."

"I believe I'll cook breakfast tomorrow," Mike offered through tears of laughter, rather than of sorrow.

Mike did not fall off to sleep easily that night, or for many nights thereafter. He nursed the pain of rejection and the loss of his sweetheart. Mostly though, he wallowed in his resentment of Roderick and the betrayal perpetrated by his brother while he was away and unable to defend his interests. Me success will be me revenge. When I have me fortune, they'll learn who has lost and who has gained.

Chapter Fifteen

Making Business

✠

The city of Cheyenne welcomed the arrival of the end-of-track on the 13th of November with music, flagwaving, and a general turnout of the population. The first passenger train from the east came to town the very next day. The Union Pacific paused its construction only briefly, pushing west until the twelfth of December when the first blizzard hit. Then the graders and gandydancers returned to Cheyenne to ride out a long, hard winter at base camp.

Luckily, Mike and Billy got back to Cheyenne well before the trails closed for the season. They loosed their bulls on a range north of town and put up their wagons, and Victorie the mule, at the Elkhorn Corral at Reed and Eighteenth Street. Then off they went to Gilman and Carter to receive their pay.

Mike took a room at the Rollins House. Afterward, he wasted no time calling upon Sally Kincaid. In a few weeks, such visits became a daily routine. As their friendship grew, he insisted they keep their personal relationship apart from her business transactions. "A man ain't much of a man if he has to buy the affections of his lady," he told her.

To which Sally huffed in mock outrage, "Don't be puttin' me outa business yet, pardner."

Mike suspected she was pleased with this arrangement. Before a month went by, they were lovers, spending winter afternoons together after taking dinner at the Rollins House. In the evening, while Sally was on duty, Mike and his bullwhacker friends would play poker at the Headquarters Saloon.

The harsh winter weather had only a slightly moderating effect upon the violence and crime in Cheyenne. A roaring town was just that, whatever the weather. But the snows were more effective in shutting down hostile Indian activity. In September, the peace commission from Washington had secured a tentative truce with the Brule at North Platte. But Red Cloud and many Oglala refused to come in and meet with the commissioners. First, they demanded, the bluecoats must remove their forts from the Bozeman Trail. Second, the Powder River territory must revert to exclusive Indian control. The commission returned to Washington empty-handed, and the Indians settled into their winter camps. Another severe season fell upon the high plains.

Mike and Billy hurried their labors on the new buildings at Fort Russell, the recently established Army installation northwest of town. Their job was neither long-term nor lucrative, but it covered their living expenses during the winter shutdown. The threat of a March snow loomed darkly in the west, and they were anxious to get back to Cheyenne before it began to rip. A rail spur between the camp and town had been put in place in December, so commuting was as simple as begging a ride from the "hogger" on the supply train.

They were "flying light," in that they had missed dinner, so they headed directly to Tim Dyer's Hotel and "Tin Restaurant" on Eddy Street. There, oil lamps and the warmth of a cast-iron stove took the edge off the dark of evening and the swirling gusts of snow. The large dining room was already crowded when they arrived, but the adverse conditions outside encouraged them to wait.

Mike noticed two gentlemen departing from supper and immediately recognized one of them as J. K. Gilman. Mike tipped his hat and greeted them as they passed by. "Good evenin', Mr. Gilman."

"Well, hello, Mike! And Billy! How're you fellas makin' out?"

"Not to complain," Billy responded. "We're doin' construction for the army. It ain't much, but it'll keep us till the thaw."

Gilman stood aside for his companion. "Let me introduce you to Levi Carter. Levi, these are two of our best bullwhackers from last season, Mike Quinn and Billy Mayhew."

Carter was a lanky, quiet gentleman, decades senior to the rest. "Pleased to make your acquaintance, Mr. Carter. Billy and me are keen to get back to it for you gentlemen this spring."

Carter glanced at J. K. with surprise. "Why I'd like nothin' more, fellas. But things seem to have gone awry for Gilman & Carter."

J. K. hung his head, obviously embarrassed at Carter's candor. He placed a hand on Mike's shoulder. "I'm sorry, fellas. I just received the news a few days ago. We lost our spring bid to Pacific Lumber."

Mike groped for words, reeling with the shock of this announcement. "Guess we're after findin' ourselves a new outfit," he said.

Carter took Mike by the arm. "I didn't mean to surprise you with bad news." But Mike and Billy were too stunned to reply. Carter and Gilman buttoned their coats against the elements and left just as the headwaiter arrived, announcing that a table was available. Mike shrugged as they followed him across the dining room.

"Damn, we're just about used up," Billy commented as Mike scanned the menu.

"We'll find something, pardner. I'm not givin' up on me Irish luck. Let's eat. I'm fairly famished, meself."

As winter turned to spring, Mike and Sally Kincaid continued to see each other almost daily. But Sally's profession had become a source of irritation to Mike. Like an investigating tongue constantly seeking out the sore tooth, he couldn't leave it alone. Discomforting thoughts of her wanton trade bedeviled him. He tried to repress his objections for many weeks, but he was like a frayed cord, ready to snap at any increased tension.

It was April, at a time when the movement of supplies and men betokened the recommencing of rail construction west of the city. A party of buffalo hunters was in town, eager to take hides from the still significant, if dwindling, northern herd. It had to be done before the weather warmed and the buffalo began to shed their winter coats.

One of the hunters, a fellow named Rankin, arrived at Miss Crowley's whorehouse after an afternoon in Cheyenne's saloons. He wandered into the first-floor parlor where clients chatted up the girls over watered whiskey. He acted pleasant enough at first, apparently in no hurry to make a selection for the evening. The madam, Jennie Crowley, an attractive redhead of middle age, greeted him. They talked and laughed briefly while he was ordering a drink. But when Sally entered, Rankin's hungry eyes met hers across the crowded room. He wasn't an ugly fellow; but to her mind, there was something unsettling about his darting glances and the trill of his nervous laughter. As she made her way to the bar, he approached her. "Perhaps, little lady, you will take a drink with me?"

She noticed that his clothes smelled funny, but couldn't identify the faint odor of animal slaughter. "Sure, mister," she lied, "but my evenin' is spoken for already. You might prefer to drink with one of the girls who's still available. If you want, I'll speak to Miss Crowley, over yonder. She'll be happy to fix you up with someone you'll like."

He smoothly took her arm in his and whispered in her ear. "I ain't attracted to none but you, miss. Let your john wait. His lateness has cost him his turn."

Sally squirmed to free herself from his grasp. She was used to managing unruly clientele, but Rankin was strong and determined. He easily subdued her defenses. She looked across the room, trying to catch Jennie's eye. She knew Jennie to be a strict taskmaster of her girls, but she was also highly protective.

Having seen Sally's distress, Jennie quickly crossed the room to confront the stranger. "Mister, I think you best leave. We—."

Whack! Rankin's swift backhand swatted her across the room into a heap of crinoline and tears. The other patrons were stunned and turned on Rankin, but he froze them, drawing his Whitney .36 Belt Revolver. He would brook no interventions from outraged citizens.

Sally's Matt was washing glasses back in the kitchen when he heard Jennie's cry of pain. He poked his head around the corner just as the hunter pushed Sally upstairs ahead of him. Balling his apron, he tossed it aside and rushed out the back door. He knew Sally needed help and he was bound to fetch it. Darkness had descended upon Sixteenth Street, and kerosene lanterns winked the only light from the tents and storefront windows along the way. Where's dat marshal's office? I seen it once . . . but . . . Ferguson or Eddy Street? He raced into Eddy Street and turned north. Dyers' Hotel and Restaurant loomed on his left. Damn, dat's where Mike Quinn like to eat his supper. . . . maybe he can help?

Mike was indeed at supper. As the waitress poured coffee, she said, "There's a nigger out back, askin' for you." He presumed it must be Sally's Matt. He went through the kitchen and out the back door. In the alley he found the young man, highly agitated, pacing back and forth. "Hey, Matt, what—?"

Before Mike could finish his query, Matt spilled forth his dire description of Sally's plight. They ran back down Sixteenth to Crowley's place of business. Mike was huffing and puffing by the time they entered. He found Jennie in a swoon on a red velvet settee in the still-crowded parlor. Patrons and the girls of the house hovered and fretted about the madam. Mike drew his revolver and moved cautiously up the staircase.

"Hold it, fella!" Mike turned and faced a bulky stranger with a black brush moustache coming through the front door. He was carrying a .44 calibre Winchester carbine. Mike was inclined to accede to the stranger's request even before he discovered the metal badge that decorated his leather vest. He holstered his pistol and waited.

Marshal J. T. Rutledge raised his hand, silencing the eager occupants of the parlor, each of whom wished to press his or her own version of events to the lawman. Whoever slipped out to summon him had already provided Rutledge with the essential outline. "Which room, Jennie?"

"Fourth on the right, J. T. But please be careful. He's a spiteful critter. He'll kill her an' you, if he's able."

Mike stepped in front of the marshal, a determined look in his eye. "That's my girl up there—let's do this together."

Rutledge smiled and rested the barrel of his carbine on his right shoulder. He looked Mike up and down appraisingly. Pulling Mike by the sleeve, he drew him close. "Mister, there is somethin' you can do for me."

After a hushed set of instructions, Mike nodded and left by the front door. He climbed the outside staircase out back, then edged across to the roof of the porch that ran around three sides of the building. Quietly, he inched along. As he approached Sally's window, he could hear her cries and the slaps she received in response. He waited without showing himself.

"Open up in there!" he heard the marshal shout. "I want that woman unharmed."

"Get away, Marshal! There ain't no problem here," Rankin snarled.

Rutledge paused briefly. Then resting the mouth of his .44 against the doorjamb, he promptly blew a hole in the doorframe where the lock cavity had been. The door swung open. Looking left, he could see Rankin upon the bed, straddling Sally's prone body. She was frozen in fear as he held his revolver to her head. "Come no further, Marshal, or this gal's blood'll be on your hands."

Outside, shivering in the evening chill, Mike was ready. When he heard the rifle blast, he counted slowly: one, two, three, four, five. Then he reared back and kicked in the window with his full force. The sound of breaking glass attracted Rankin's attention and the buffalo hunter turned and fired. But Mike had stepped away from the opening as Rutledge had instructed him. Rankin's revolver found only a gaping hole full of night sky.

The marshal quickly strode to the bed and smashed Rankin in the temple with the stock of his rifle. He slumped to the floor and was promptly disarmed. Mike stepped through the window and hurried to Sally's side. She quickly covered her breasts, exposed when Rankin clawed the sleeveless dress from her shoulders. Sobbing heavily upon Mike's shoulder, she struggled to regain her composure. They both watched as Rutledge dragged his quarry out into the hall. Jennie, revived and relieved, rushed into the room. "Go on, Mike. I'll tend to her."

Mike hesitated, looking at Sally. But Jenny pushed him out into the corridor where the marshal stood over his prisoner. Mike saw the glow of an oil lamp being carried toward them from the far end of the hall. It was Matt. He held the light high so the marshal could see to bind Rankin's hands behind his back. Only after the buffalo hunter was led away did Mike notice a faint smile of appreciation cross Matt's face. Mike acknowledged him with a nod. "Let's go downstairs to wait."

The excitement had attracted a considerable crowd to the whore-house. Few, if any, of the evening's clientele had left, and now more were arriving. When Jennie returned to the parlor, she gave Mike a hug of relief. "Why don't you take Sally back to the Rollins House. She'll be better if she's away from here awhile. I've got a business to look to."

Sally met Mike at the foot of the backstairs. She was carrying a small bag. He helped her into her coat and put his arm around her. They walked to the Rollins House in silence.

It was an awkward, restless night. When the glow of dawn brightened the room, Mike went down and ordered breakfast to be brought to the room. Sally only poked at her food, though she sipped some coffee. As they talked, her spirits improved. "It's goin' to be a pretty day. Why don't you get dressed and we'll take a walk uptown?"

"I'd like that, Mike."

He stood by the window, sometimes looking out, sometimes watching her at the dressing table brushing out her long, black hair.

"It ain't exactly me business, but I'm thinkin' this whorin' is too damned dangerous! You was nearly killed last night. Someday, things might not turn out. . . ."

She put down the brush, her body rigid with tension. He noticed, but plowed on. "You know that I love you. Will you not give it up for your own sake, if not for me?"

She turned and looked at him sharply, her raw emotions written on her face. "Is it the danger, Mike? Or perhaps you object to sharin' my favors with them that pays?"

He shrugged at the challenge. "A bit of both," he admitted quietly. "But there's better ways for a lady to be makin' her stake than by whorin'."

She turned back to the mirror. "None that pays as well! Even after Miss Jennie's cut, I'm still makin' more money on a given day than most men in Cheyenne—includin' you bullwhackers."

After half an hour, neither Mike nor Sally had yielded their position. Finally, she brought the argument to closure.

"Look Mike, you're a fine fella. But you don't love me, not really. You just think you do."

Mike was sitting in a chair and his head jerked up in shock at her accusation.

"You needed someone after that brother stole your gal—needed someone bad. I knew that from the first day we met. You ain't never said, let's get married. And I don't blame you. But I ain't gonna be no poor old woman. I been puttin' money aside and I got me a sizeable stake. When my whorin' days is done, Matt and me'll go back to Osceola. I'll have me a fine house again. I can't be givin' all that up to the first handsome fella that comes my way."

It was like a bucket of cold water had been thrown in his face. Mike went back to the window, embarrassed, unable to return her gaze. Sally stood up and collected her things in the carpetbag. As she reached for her coat, he turned to her. "There's still the danger, girl. One day, a john will use his knife on you and you won't just be sportin' a scar."

She dropped the coat and looked at him fiercely, her face ablaze in fury. "I'll take my chances, mister! Seems I ain't the only one of us carryin' a scar."

The door slammed behind her. He immediately regretted the scar remark, but he couldn't move to call her back. He sat on the bed feeling sorry for himself. He looked around the small, sparsely furnished hotel room. His eyes caught the muddy trail boots standing in the corner. He stared at them a long time—mesmerized, remembering . . . Amanda, Jane, now Sally. He'd covered so much distance. But, there was so much further to go. . . . alone.

Chapter Sixteen

Wyoming Days

✠

In the spring of 1868, the Peace Commission from Washington was back at Fort Laramie, offering a treaty that, while confining the Lakota and Cheyenne to two great reservations, would bar encroachment by miners, settlers, and pilgrims. In return, the government promised to abandon its forts along the Bozeman Trail. From late April through early July, many of the Lakota chiefs signed on to the Treaty of 1868 on behalf of their individual tribes. But it took until November before Red Cloud and some others could be coaxed to accept the Treaty. They wished to be confident that the Bozeman Trail forts had, in fact, been decommissioned before "touching the pen."

Despite these delays in peacemaking, 1868 was marked by reduced hostilities along the route of the Union Pacific. Construction resumed through southern Wyoming toward its eventual rendezvous with the Central Pacific in Utah. Mike and Billy were able to return to freighting, again finding employment with General Coe. But by late 1868, most bullwhackers were looking for other opportunities. The Union Pacific had replaced bull train freighting in much of the region. There remained only the carriage of supplies to Fort Laramie and Fort Fetterman, up on the North Platte River. And this business was far less lucrative.

Sitting in the lee of a freight wagon at Camp Carlin, the two partners fried up some breakfast and surveyed their meager prospects. The autumn weather was already cold. They huddled under buffalo robes beside the coals of their campfire.

"You remember that Colonel Bullock we met at Ft. Laramie with Reeves last year?" Billy asked.

"Aye, I remember him, the sutler's agent," Mike said as he turned the crank on the coffee mill.

"Maybe he'll give us some trade at the fort."

"Friendly fella as I recall. We'll surely wish to get on with him. But we don't know a soul at Fort Fetterman."

"I s'pose not."

Billy stood up and retrieved a coffeepot of hot water. After Mike dumped the grounds into it, he replaced it in the bed of coals. "Hell, let's get on up there and see what's the lay of the land. Maybe the Colonel will give us a boost. They say he knows every white man in the territory—and most of the red."

"Sure, if we do get on, there's plenty of wagons and teams to be had, right cheap," Mike replied. "I'm thinkin' we'll have a go with the Colonel soon as the weather permits."

During the winter shutdown, they took their mules and hightailed it up the Chugwater Creek. When they got to Fort Laramie, Bullock gave them a sympathetic hearing, but he was not all that encouraging. Sitting before the glowing cast-iron stove in the center of his store, he combed at his white mat of hair with his fingers. He seemed, to Mike, an older, sadder fellow this time.

"Boys, the government is fixin' to drive all the tradin' to the new Injun agencies over on the river. That's gonna dry up a good bit of business around here. 'Course the soldiers will still need provisions here and at Fetterman. But, that's less than half the trade we been doin'."

Mike leaned forward. He was desperate and his face showed it. "We know things are lean, Colonel. If you could just try us out, any business at all would mean a lot to us."

The Colonel got up and pulled a thick ledger from a shelf behind the counter. Mike and Billy waited quietly, looking nervous. After a minute of flipping pages back and forth, he closed the book, and returned it to its place. "Well, I'll see what haulin' I can find for you come the thaw. And I'll write out a letter of introduction to Wilson and Cobb. They do the tradin' up at Fetterman."

Mike grinned at Billy in relief. It wasn't much, but it was something. Their trip to Fort Fetterman yielded a promise of limited business on the strength of the Colonel's endorsement.

By the summer of 1869, they had a modest business going, delivering freight to the forts. While Fort Laramie took their supplies from Cheyenne, a new road to Fort Fetterman ran directly north from the railhead at Rock Creek, west of Laramie City.

In addition, the retail houses in Cheyenne were offering all manner of goods arriving from the east by rail. Conforth Brothers, Glenn and Talpey, and the firm of Liddell, Robertson, and Brown all required delivery of goods to the road ranches and small settlements springing up north and west of Cheyenne. Mike and Billy added some of this trade to their small operation, bringing on or shedding bullwhackers as the business experienced its ups and downs.

Civilizing changes were having a dramatic effect on life in Cheyenne. A newspaper, *The Rocky Mountain Star*, was serving a burgeoning population. There was a large military presence at Fort Russell, Camp Carlin, and at a new military outpost, Fort Sanders, near Laramie City. In 1870, the Denver Pacific Railroad arrived in Cheyenne, killing the bullwhacking business between Julesburg and Denver.

Though he could not help but resent the impact upon his chosen trade, Mike was pleased to see improvements taking place. Like most folks, he saw settlement and modernization as welcome progress. He was proud of the establishment of a Catholic Church at Twenty-First and O'Neil, on a lot donated by the Union Pacific. Even so, he was not much of a churchgoer. The freighting kept him busy and most Sundays were just another day on the trail.

Early that year, Mike and Billy were laid up at the Rollins House during poor weather. One morning, a stranger in a gaudy plaid suit, carrying a bowler hat, approached Mike at breakfast. "Mind if I join you, sir?"

Noticing that most of the tables were occupied, Mike gestured to the chair opposite him. "Not at all, friend, have a seat."

When not on the trail, Mike's appearance was reasonably genteel for a twenty-three-year-old. His once light brown hair was darker now and trimmed fairly short for a bullwhacker. Like the stranger, he too affected a full moustache and close-cropped beard. His collarless shirt was covered by a woolen vest and a businessman's coat. He did not, however, wear plaid.

As the stranger settled himself, the waitress came to take his order and pour coffee. Mike tried to resume his perusal of *The Rocky Mountain Star,* but was interrupted again.

"My name's Charley Collins. Visitin' your fair city from Iowa." They shook hands and Mike introduced himself. Then Collins leaned forward with a confiding air. "Actually, Mr. Quinn, I must confess that I know who you are. The room clerk directed me to your table."

Mike pushed his coffee cup back, set down his paper, and looked sharply at this dandy. "Really? What can I do for you, Mr. Collins?"

Collins' smile took on an ingratiating appearance, as he toyed with his coffee cup. "I'm with the Sioux City Daily Times. But today, I'm here on behalf of the Fenians, the Wolf Tone Circle, back in Sioux City."

Mike gave a weak smile, before returning to an expression of skeptical caution. "Arrah, you'll be knowin' of me brief career as a Fenian soldier back in '66."

"Precisely, sir. And that's why I'm here—to see you and others like you."

"Why don't you call me Mike? We ain't too formal here in the territories."

"My pleasure, Mike, and please call me Charley."

"As I said, Charley, what can I do for you?"

The impatient tone of Mike's voice caused Collins to adjust his posture to a more businesslike stance.

"Well, sir, I'm coming to that. You see, in '66 I fought too, under Colonel John O'Neill at the battle at Ridgeway."

"Sure, didn't O'Neill become the president of the IRB a few years back?"

"Aye, that he did. Now, he's got a colony of Irish settlers over in Nebraska. Anyway, we Fenians are organizin' another go at Canada."

Mike eyebrows shot up. "Whoa right there! What makes you figure I'm happy to get me arse kicked by the Brits again?"

Collins nervously raised both his hands, as if holding off a physical attack. "Oh, it isn't just us hawkeyes! We got Fenian brothers from all over, Kansas, Nebraska—even from Chicago. And they're all hot to serve under O'Neill again. We even got allies among the French and Injuns over the border!"

Mike folded his newspaper and made ready to leave. "I remember how the French rose the last time! Look here, Charley. I'm out here doin' me own business. I haven't been active with the Fenians since we was run out of Canada last time. Mind you, I've got no love for the Brits, and I'm happy to do whatever helps me countrymen back in Ireland. But I ain't no fool. As they say here, 'once burned, twice shy.' I'll be tendin' to me freightin' business, thank you."

But Collins was not done. "Ah, it's your freightin' business that we need—to carry munitions and supplies into Dakota!" He continued to press his case and Mike continued to resist.

When Billy arrived in the dining room, all mention of the Fenian invasion plans was dropped. Mike excused himself, leaving Billy and Charley to breakfast together. Mike neither saw nor heard of Collins again for the next year and a half. But late in 1871, Mike read in the newspaper that another Fenian invasion of Canada had failed miserably. The U.S. Army had arrested O'Neill and his band of volunteers on the Dakota-Manitoba border.

That winter, Red Cloud, Spotted Tail, and other tribal chiefs traveled to Washington to meet with President Grant and various federal officials. They complained about the inferior land and the lack of game at the new Indian agencies along the Missouri River. They demanded relocation before starvation and whiskey peddlers destroyed their people. Red Cloud was eloquent in voicing his complaint to the Secretary of Interior. "The white children have surrounded me and have left me nothing but an island. When we first had this land we were strong. Now we are melting like snow on a hillside, while you are grown like spring grass." Red Cloud made no mention of how the Lakota had previously seized these lands from the Omaha, the Ponca, the Kiowa, the Arikara, and the Crow, sometimes in brutal massacres.

Several months later, a promise was extracted whereby the government would search out a more suitable location for the agencies. Despite this concession, both sides continued to undermine the Treaty of 1868. The

Northern Pacific Railroad, under the protection of Army escorts, began to coopt the ranges of the northern buffalo herd for a new rail line west. Using commercial buffalo hunters, they savaged the livelihood of the plains Indians, killing one and a quarter million animals between 1872 and 1873. In addition, new military forts were established in the Dakota Territory. Sporadic raids against settlers were launched by renegade bands of Indians, while frontier newspapers and politicians pressed repeatedly for a further contraction of Indian lands in favor of mining and settler interests. Clearly, serious trouble was in the offing.

For years, there had been rumors of mineral riches in the Black Hills of Dakota Territory. These were not the black hills of the Laramie Mountains from where Mike and Billy had hauled rail ties in '67 and '68. These hills, older than the Himalayas or the Alps, stood on the western edge of the Dakota plain. They were given their name from the color of the dense forests of Ponderosa pine that, when viewed from a distance, looked black. For the Lakota, the Black Hills of Dakota, or *Paha Sapa,* was holy ground.

In 1871, reporter Charley Collins sensationalized an interview with the venerable missionary to the plains tribes, Father Pierre DeSmet. Under Charley's close questioning, the aging priest admitted his long-held belief that the Black Hills region was exceedingly rich in gold and other minerals. Collins' newspaper story made headlines throughout the United States, and Charley became fixated at the thought of gold riches. With his news accounts and others like them, rumors of Black Hills gold continued to grow.

Three years later, the administration of President Grant, acting upon the urgings of the settlers and miners on the frontier, authorized a survey expedition to the Black Hills under the leadership of Lt. Col. George Armstrong Custer. He was posted at Fort Abraham Lincoln, in the northern reaches of the Dakota Territory. On July 1, 1874, Custer set out with twelve hundred soldiers; a cadre of geologists, scientists, and miners; and a gaggle of newspapermen in flagrant, albeit authorized, violation of the Treaty. By mid-August, dispatches from Custer gave confirmation of the mineral wealth of the Black Hills, speaking of "gold from the grass roots down."

One afternoon that September, Mike and Billy pulled their wagons into Hook and Moore's Great Western Corral in Cheyenne. For days, Billy had been unnaturally quiet and serious. After getting the outfit settled, Billy approached Mike. "Let's get a beer. I got somethin' on my mind."

The saloon they chose was quiet. The late day sun flooded through filthy, flyblown windowpanes and onto the sawdust-strewn floor. Mike and Billy grabbed schooners of cold beer and selected a table in a back corner where they'd likely go undisturbed.

"Shoot," said Mike. "What's eatin' at you?"

Billy shifted in his chair, obviously uncomfortable with what he was about to say. "I got a letter, Mike. It was from Charley Collins. You remember Charley?"

Mike was immediately on his guard, suspicious of anything involving Collins. "I do, the Fenian fellow, newspaperman from Iowa. He keeps writing stories about gold and such."

"Yeah, that's it. He's organizin' a party to stake minin' claims in the Black Hills. Says that the best of the gold fields will be for them that's first in."

Mike shook his head in disbelief. "You didn't get this letter as a surprise, did you?"

Billy lowered his eyes. "Naw, I wrote him first, a few months back."

"Ah, I should have guessed! You've been talkin' gold in me ear for almost two years." Mike's impatience was under control, but just barely. He stared into his beer, feeling a deep sense of gloom overtaking him.

"It's downright depressin', Mike! The freightin's been in tough times since the railroad come through. You're the one always talkin' 'bout makin' your fortune. I figure I should make me a fortune too, if I can."

"Aye, neither one of us is gettin' rich just now." Mike waved his hand dismissively. "Jaysus, Billy, you know that 'tis one miner in a thousand what actually gets his fortune in the boom. How many have we seen, comin' back from Montana, with naught to show for their time and their trouble? Between claim jumpers and Injuns, don't be so sure you'll have your gold dust to spend."

Billy's enthusiasm would not be repressed. "Charley don't aim to get in late, and me neither. . . . Why don't you come with us, Mike? One year of pullin' placer gold and you could buy out . . . Pratt and Farris!"

Mike laughed and stood to fetch another beer. "If there be gold in them Hills, Billy, every mine, saloon, store, and livery will be needin' supplies. The freightin' business may not be much right now, but it'll be big business then. If you don't mind, I'll be playin' the cards I'm holdin'."

Billy left a week later for Yankton, where he was to meet up with Charley Collins. He took his share of the business in cash, leaving Mike in much-reduced circumstances. Selling wagons and bulls though wasn't as hard on Mike as losing his closest companion. Sure, I can hire other bull-whackers to take up the slack. But where will I be gettin' another such as Billy? Let him go bust his pick, hopin' to find gold without losin' his hair. I'm certain of one damn thing. Whether the miners is successful, or if they fail, they'll be needin' supplies—thousands of tons of supplies!

It took two more years before Mike was ready, two years of working, scrimping, and saving. Everything he made went to the purchase of wagons, bulls, and equipment. With every passing day, he felt he was closer to his dream. The ignominious defeat of Custer at the Little Bighorn gave but temporary pause to his plans. In retribution, the U.S. military applied unrelenting pressure against the Lakota/Cheyenne alliance. Negotiations for the "purchase" of the Black Hills would drag on through the autumn of 1876. But the Black Hills were open, on a de facto basis, and the army made no more pretenses to the contrary.

Chapter Seventeen

Off to the Gold Fields

✠

The spring thaw of '77 had arrived and, with last minute negotiations with the supply houses completed, Mike Quinn was finally ready to roll. Many bull trains had made it into the Hills the previous year, but Mike had not attempted a run before February, when Washington officially declared them open. It was not the lack of government permission, however, that had delayed him. Rather than earn the mere twelve cents per pound freighting fee, Mike chose to invest in the inventory of goods, where the real money was to be made. But he needed a lot of capital to cover the costs of such diverse items as India-rubber boots, mining tools, blankets, tinware, dried and canned fruit, yeast powders, clothing, harnesses, and saddles. All were items that would fetch high premiums in the mining camps.

Mike recognized the impossibility of funding this all by himself, so he took on a partner/investor. He had found Jim Clark in Cheyenne the previous autumn. Jim, also a roomer at the Rollins House, had come west from Ohio with a sizeable financial stake and a good nose for business. He was a friendly fellow in his mid-forties. His short, thickset body might not suit the bullwhacker's life, but Mike was happy to have his assistance in financing their inventory and then selling it at the maximum profit.

The two partners decided they would head for Custer, one of the first settlements in the goldfields—so christened well before its namesake achieved posthumous glory. Custer was the Black Hills outpost closest to Cheyenne and functioned as a southern gateway to the Hills. They decided it would make a good merchandising locale.

The bull train left Cheyenne in mid-March, while there was still snow in the Laramies. But Mike was not too worried about additional winter weather this late in the season. This would be Clark's first trip into wild country and his jitters were showing. They pushed north along the mail road that ran beside Chugwater Creek, Mike walking beside his nighside wheeler and Jim riding beside on his strawberry roan. "I've made this run so many times in the last eight years," Mike said, "me teams could find their way without me. 'Tis hard to imagine that we ain't gonna stop at the river as we usually do."

Mike flicked his twenty-foot bullwhip at the ear of an unruly, young longhorn making his debut at right swing, and Jim nearly tumbled from his horse as it shied at the cracking report. Mike quickly reached out for Jim's reins and calmed his mare. "Sorry, Jim. Guess that mare of yours ain't broke to bullwhackin' ways yet."

Jim gave a nervous grin. "Aw, she'll learn. But thanks for the hand." He rode along for several minutes without further comment. Then he asked, "You anticipate any trouble crossin' the river during spring thaw?"

"We might have last year, but now they're after buildin' a new iron bridge across the Platte, just below the fort." Mike tried to put Jim at ease without mentioning that the crossing would be the least of their worries on a trail that, beyond the river, would be downright dangerous.

"Jim, would you give me a hand and ride back an' tell Johnny to close up? I'm thinkin' he's droppin' back too far ."

Mike was running three teams pulling three wagons each. The lead wagon was the largest, maybe 7,000 lbs. of load. Hitched behind was a swing wagon rated at 5,000 lbs., and that was followed by a smaller trailing wagon carrying about 3,000 lbs. Mike had the first team of ten yoke. Two hired bullwhackers, the Morris brothers—Laban and Johnny—had the other teams. They were good hands, Mike judged, though not as experienced as he. At nearly thirty years of age, Mike viewed himself as an old hand in the freighting fraternity. The Morris boys, still in their mid-twenties, seemed a bit green to him.

Five days out of Cheyenne, on the well-traveled trail, they stopped briefly at Three Mile Ranche, a short day's drive below Fort Laramie. Two of Mike's longhorns had come up with sore hooves, and he chose to drop them here for pick-up on the return trip. As was usual practice, he had brought spare bulls to allow for such a contingency.

The men waited at the wagons, while Mike made the arrangements. Laban Morris was taller and older than his brother, Johnny, but they shared the East Texas accent and a love of pulling pranks, especially on greenhorns from the States. As he checked the hitches between his wagons, Laban noticed Jim admiring the evergreen forest and the steel-gray granite outcroppings of the Laramie Mountains, some forty-odd miles to the west. The looming Laramie Peak offered a distinctive profile.

"Pretty sight, eh, Mr. Clark? I think they show best in this mornin' sunlight."

Jim nodded and leaned against the lead wagon. "We don't have such scenery back in Ohio, Laban. Makes me want a look at the Rockies, but that'll have to wait till we get back from this trip."

"I hear them Black Hills is a feast for the eye," Laban continued. "S'pect they'll do, assumin' no run-in with Injuns or road agents."

Laban noticed Jim's eyes widen at talk of the impending hazards of the trail. Laban knew Jim wouldn't wish to show yellow in front of his employees. "You probably heard them nasty stories back in Cheyenne," he went on, "like the one about the Metz family massacre last year up in Red Canyon? A real tragedy!"

He gave Jim an expression of exaggerated concern. "'Course, there's many that's made it through since, but I'd still watch the horizons closely and keep my Winchester at hand above the North Platte."

Three days later, when they were encamped within sight of the Rawhide Buttes, Laban and Johnny decided to play further upon Jim's fears and see what rise they could extract. Mike was busy dayherding while the others ate their midday dinner.

"Johnny, did I ever tell you the story of how them buttes over yonder got their name?" Laban winked to his brother and got a nod in return.

"Rawhide Buttes! Don't think I ever did hear."

Jim looked up from his beans and bacon. "I'd like to hear a good story."

Repressing a grin, Laban embarked upon his prearranged sojourn into local history. "I heard it was back in '49, time of the big rush to Californy. Seems a train of pilgrims was camped a few miles below here."

Johnny sat down in the shade of a wagon, close to Jim, as his brother continued his tale.

"One day, they dispatched a few riflemen on horseback to hunt up some game for dinner. A young Eastern fella drifted up toward the buttes and stopped to water his mount at this very crick, right here. He was all hopped up with tales of hostile Injuns, and he swore to one and all in camp that he'd handle any what showed up." Laban paused to refill his tin coffee cup and gauge Jim's rapt attention to his account. He saw Johnny turn away to avoid laughing.

"So while he's watering his horse, he spies down the crick bed a lone Injun, dressed in buckskin, also down getting a drink. Quietly, he caps his musket. Slowly, he cocks back the hammer and raises up to take aim. . . . Pow! He fired and did dispatch his enemy to the happy huntin' grounds."

"You don't mean it!" Johnny said.

"Yes, sir! So now, runnin' forward for a look-see, he discovers he has killed himself an unarmed squaw. He can't believe it. He checks her pulse, but she is truly dead. Lookin' left and right to see was she alone, he turns tail and hurries on back to the train."

Jim looked pale and slack-jawed. He had quit his unfinished plate and was now leaning forward. "Surely, he couldn't hide his sin!"

Laban raised his hand, silently begging patience. "Around evenin', a party of fifty or sixty Cheyenne approaches the wagon corral and calls out the wagon master. With the pilgrims crowded around, they tell 'bout the murder of their woman. The Cheyenne demand the guilty bastard, or they'll lay siege to the whole damned outfit. After a time of arguin' and thinkin', the white folks decide to give up the little son of a bitch to face his justice. No sense riskin' the lives of all of them."

"Rightly so," Johnny declaimed.

"So the greenhorn gets pushed forward, much ag'in his wishes. His brave words 'bout killin' Injuns is all behind him now. He pleads 'twas all a big mistake.' Four nasty-lookin' redskins grab him and pin him to the ground. They strip him down while a big, strong buck comes forward with his huntin' knife drawn.

"Well, them pilgrims is starin' in disbelief. Women turn their children away as the lad screams out in agony. To the enjoyment of his mates, the brave with the knife sets to peelin' the hide off the boy. When he's done, there ain't a patch of skin bigger'n a button left on the poor fella. And that's how that clump of hillside over yonder got the name of Rawhide Buttes."

"Aw, shit," Jim lamented. "They didn't really skin him alive, did they?"

Laban spread his palms forward in disownment of the account. "That's the story as I heard it. 'Course it was long 'fore my time out here."

Throughout their journey north, Mike's outfit was being passed repeatedly by swifter traffic. Mule trains with smaller wagons and lighter loads moved rapidly with their burden of perishables dispatched to the Hills by such as Nagle's General Merchandise Company of Cheyenne. Another regular feature along the trail was the daily exchange of the Concord coaches of the Cheyenne-Black Hills Stage Line. Jolting and jostling their passengers in a big wooden cab, their speed was meager consolation for the lack of comfort.

"'Tis almost worth the clouds of dust we're eatin', to see them movin' safely to the Hills and back again," Mike observed to Jim.

All were relieved when they arrived at Hat Creek Ranche. Jack Bowman and Joe Walters ran the ranche as hotel, bakery, butchery, brewery, and black-smithy. It was actually situated on Old Woman's Creek in the midst of a flat, barren plain dotted with brown-gray scrub brush. Only a few scraggly trees were to be found along the winding creek bed. While most road ranches were no more than mud huts, the Hat Creek Ranche was a two-story log complex, one of the grandest establishments of its type. The bullwhackers took advantage of a welcome respite that evening, testing Bowman's proficiency as a brewmaster.

In the morning, the train ran the Alum Springs ridge northeast to boggy lowlands around the Cheyenne River crossing. High water and a muddy bottom would prove a challenge for their heavily laden wagons. But Mike was able to arrange assistance from nearby Dears Ranche in pulling their wagons across.

The next stage of the journey was through the Red Canyon. Here, narrow passages and craggy walls offered ideal harbor for bandits or renegade Indians. Only a few weeks prior, they had heard that the stagecoach had been held up and its driver, Johnny Slaughter, had been shot dead. As they crept through the looming canyon, Mike noticed the crew acting as jumpy as a long-tailed cat in a room full of rocking chairs.

It was, therefore, a welcome sight when they exited onto the rolling, brown-grass prairie flanked by steep hills of tall, green ponderosa pines. Coming upon a vista, they could make out the blue-black color of the Hills themselves. Mother Nature was showing her beauty in full measure, a marked contrast to the desert-like conditions they had left behind. After a few more days of travel, they descended along French Creek and arrived in the vicinity of the town of Custer.

Laban and Johnny stayed with the train while Mike and Jim walked into town to make discreet inquiries. They chose to be cautious since it was their intention to compete with Custer's existing merchants for the miners' custom. As their boots hit the muddy streets, they were surprised to discover that the numerous saloons, stores, and newly built houses were all remarkably quiet.

"Most of the excitement has moved north," an Irish-born saloon keeper sadly related to the new arrivals. "We still got some trade, as there's enough placer gold round Custer for us to survive. But 'tis only survival, no more."

It seemed that Custer had been eclipsed and Deadwood was now the premiere Black Hills boomtown. Confirming this assessment with others in town, Mike and Jim resolved to press on. "Our goods will fetch no great profit here," Jim concluded. "Anyone who took ownership would have to haul the goods to Deadwood anyway."

Mike readily agreed and they returned to the train to give the Morris boys the news.

The grasses in the Black Hills were like a gift from heaven for the bulls in Mike's train. Indeed, everything about the Black Hills conveyed richness in plant and animal life, as well as mineral wealth.

"Damn, did you ever see such a fine country?" Jim observed. "Hats off to

President Grant for wresting it from the savages. They've made no real use of these Hills, so civilized white folk might as well do."

Mike nodded as he cast his gaze from horizon to horizon. "I'm sure you're right. 'Tis a mighty rich country. I've a good feelin' about this trip. I've seen many a boomtown, you know, with the railroad. Julesburg, Sidney, and Cheyenne all jumped up like weeds in a spring garden. Deadwood Gulch may be a place where a fella can make a fortune and keep it."

Mike could scarcely contain the excitement he felt during the next few days as the train climbed up and down the steep gulches, passing through rich pine forest on either side of the well-worn, muddy trail. It was slower than hauling on the flat plain, but that only increased the anticipations of the entire crew.

On the 17th of April, they reached Strawberry Gulch, south of Deadwood. As Jim was on horseback, it was agreed that he should ride ahead and scout out the town for a proper place where they might encamp and establish their mercantile. Mike and the Morrises pulled off the trail so as to be clear of the heavy traffic, but they kept the teams hitched.

Jim returned, leading his mare to the shade where the men were waiting. "We're about a mile out of town. I don't advise takin' the outfit into Deadwood. The main street is full of wagons. So damned crowded that folks crossin' the street climb right over your wagon tongue."

Mike and the Morris got up from their respite, anxious to settle into a final encampment. "Did you find us a good spot?" Mike asked.

"There's a nice little mining camp called Elizabethtown. It's a short walk to the center, but quiet enough for us to place our load out of harm's way. There's good grass between two creeks up ahead. We'll have to ford the one called Whitewood. It's not tricky as long as we skirt the minin' claims with their sluice boxes. We'll not wish to crowd these miners as they're touchy about claim-jumpers."

Mike was anxious to get his bulls released. "Let's make for Elizabethtown right quick," he instructed Laban and Johnny. "These steep hills steal the daylight well before a regular sundown."

The green hills loomed high on both sides of the gulch so that the same effect delayed a proper dawn the next day. After breakfast, Johnny played dayherder while the other three men walked up Main Street, into the heart of Deadwood.

After its first year of existence, the city was a sizeable, bustling community. It encompassed some two hundred stores, three banks, two sawmills, a public bathhouse, two competing post offices, thirty hotels and restaurants, seventy saloons and gambling houses, a waterworks, a fire department, a church, a school, and a telegraph line to Cheyenne. Miners and madams, gamblers and grocers had streamed in from Yankton, Fort Pierre, and Sidney, as well as from Cheyenne. The population was nearly four thousand souls, and the rush showed little sign of abating.

For a town well removed from the path of the railroad, Deadwood was remarkably fitted out with touches of culture. There were five playhouses; though only one, the Langrishe Theater, confined its offerings to the dramatic arts. Its principal competitor, The Gem, supplemented such fare with dancing, drinks, and girls, grossing five thousand dollars a performance—twice that on a good night.

They ambled down the plank wood sidewalks and across the perpetually muddy, befouled streets. "I'll see you folks later," Mike said. "I'm after lookin' up me old partner, Billy Mayhew. He come up here two years back.

Deadwood, 1876 (Courtesy of the South Dakota State Historical Society)

For all I know, he'll be ownin' a fine gold mine and livin' the gentleman's life by now."

"Have you had no word of him since he left Cheyenne?" Jim asked.

"Not a single word. But then, we bullwhackers ain't much for writin' letters and such."

While the others went off to see the sights, Mike made the rounds of the hotels and saloons, asking for news of Billy. He tried the Bucket of Blood, the Bella Union, the Red Bird, and others, only to find that, if they knew of Billy at all, they hadn't seen him for a month. Mike even inquired with the assayers and banks, but no one had a lead on where he might be found.

Within a week, Mike and Jim had the mercantile up and running out of canvas tents down in Elizabethtown, or E-town, as the miners called it. Even though they were up against more established competitors, the burgeoning demand for goods outstripped the delivery capacity of the supply trains. Mike and Jim's goods were moving nicely. In their first month, they recouped their capital and made a handsome profit. Though Jim was the principal investor, Mike's financial position also improved dramatically. It was decided that Mike and the Morrises should return to Cheyenne for more goods. Jim would remain in Deadwood to arrange the construction of a proper building from which to operate.

As it was out of the question to travel the trails with large amounts of gold dust, Jim made arrangements with bankers Brown & Thum for accounts upon which Mike could draw from Cheyenne to pay for new merchandise. With that settled, Mike and the Morrises set out for Cheyenne in the first week of June, moving at good speed with empty wagons. They were back in Deadwood by the 1st of August, and happy to be able to offload into a rough, but commodious, clapboard warehouse that had replaced their tents.

That night, after settling in, Mike and the Morris brothers joined Jim around the campfire, tucking into beefsteaks, beans, and cornbread—welcome fare after weeks on the trail. When they finished, Jim took Mike by the elbow. "Top off your coffee, Mike. I want to talk with you, private-like."

They walked away from the fire, while Johnny rustled the plates and Laban returned to watch the herd. Mike sat down on the rough-timbered stoop of their new warehouse. A narrow slice of night sky between the hills was bright with moonlight, bright enough to see each other clearly.

"Mike, tomorrow you must look up the sheriff here in Deadwood, a fellow named Seth Bullock."

Mike looked up in puzzlement. "Sure, there ain't no trouble, is there?"

"No, no, nothin' like that. While you were back in Cheyenne, Bullock stopped by here lookin' for you. Said he had news of your friend, Billy. Wouldn't give me no details. I hope it ain't bad news for you."

"Thanks, I'm hopin' so too. I'll call on him first thing."

Jim chuckled, "Don't make it too early. I'm under the impression that this sheriff works well into the night."

"Right. I remember."

It was midmorning and already hot. Mike was sweating as he waited outside the jail for Bullock to arrive. The sheriff ambled down the sidewalk. He was an impressive-looking man, tall, lean, with a neat mustache. Mike stood and introduced himself. He noticed Bullock didn't speak like a frontiersman—surprising for a man who had come to Deadwood from the Montana mining camps. Rather, he talked softly, with proper English usage and a Canadian accent. His clear gray eyes smiled, even as his expression and manner were businesslike.

"I understand you're looking for a fellow named Billy Mayhew," Bullock began. "A friend, is he?"

"He was once—and may still be. 'Tis over two years since he left Cheyenne. We was pardners in a freightin' outfit. Do you know him at all? Is he all right?"

"He's alive, if that's what you mean. I'll give you a note and the address where you can find him. Do you know Chinatown?"

Mike left the jail with a scrap of paper in his hand and a thousand questions in his head. Why had Bullock been so cryptic? If Billy was alive, why had he not come to the warehouse himself? What was he doing in Chinatown?

Mike had seen plenty of Chinamen in Cheyenne, in the days after the railroad was completed. But he had never known one personally. Coolies from the Central Pacific Railroad construction crews—hardworking, capable fellows—had moved east looking for work. They generally kept to themselves in an enclave. But they aggressively sought clientele among the whites for their laundries, shops and eateries. Mike walked north on Main Street, above the center of Deadwood, finding Chinatown on a hillside to the east.

His first sensation as he approached was the fragrance of burning incense. It wafted down the winding alley, propelled by the same gusts of hot wind that lifted dust and scraps of trash into the air. He squinted his lashes together to protect his eyes. The numerous shops were ramshackle affairs, occasionally decorated in exotic red trim. Windows were brimming with unfamiliar goods— silks and sandalwood, ornately carved ivory and teak, and food items. The locals, scurrying busily through the street, wore queues of long black hair and loose, blue, pajama-like togs. Sloe-eyed youngsters played in the dirt at open doorways.

When he reached the appointed address, Mike felt apprehensive. He looked up and down the alley. He was the only Caucasian in sight. He double-checked the directions on Bullock's note against the crudely inscribed number on the door. He knocked, but no one came. He knocked again more loudly. A *swish-swish* sound of slippers padding down a hallway was faintly audible. The door opened a crack. Though Mike could see nothing inside but darkness, he felt the gaze of inspecting eyes.

"What you want?" The voice was aged and unfriendly, yet surprisingly musical. Mike passed the sheriff's note through the crack. The door closed and the *swish-swish* sound was heard again. He waited again in the noonday heat. It was five minutes, easy, before the *swish-swish* returned. "You come," the voice commanded, only slightly more welcoming than before.

Mike removed his dust-on-black hat and stepped into the gloom. Guided more by the padding of slippers than by anything he could see, he was led to the rear of the wood-frame building and down a flight of stairs that followed the slope of the hillside upon which Chinatown rested. A cave had been hewn out of the earthen bank below the staircase. It was pleasantly cooler in here. Mike's wet shirt imparted a chill upon his back and he put his hat back on.

Upon reaching the bottom, a room of generous proportions greeted them. It was lit with numerous flickering candles, casting just enough light for Mike to appreciate the fanciful, embroidered designs on the blue, silk robe of his wizened guide. The old man spoke in hushed vernacular with a colleague. When they finished their brief colloquy, the command, "you come," was repeated. Mike moved past what appeared to be rough wooden bunks in which he could dimly perceive single occupants. Some were sleeping—others took slow, deep pulls at long-stemmed pipes.

D'vil if that's kinnikinick these slugabeds is puffin', Mike thought. He had heard stories of opium and absinthe, though his personal observations of addiction were limited to whiskey. They moved down a row, from one pool of candlelight to the next. They were about halfway across the room when the old man stopped. "Mr. Billy here. You talk little while. I come back."

Swish-swish. The slipper noise diminished into the nearly black recesses of the cave room. Mike moved to the end of the bunk closest to its candlestick station. "Billy, is that you?" he asked in a hushed voice.

There was no response. Mike got down low and touched the sleeping figure on the shoulder. A groan passed the man's lips, and as he shifted position, one of those pipes clattered noisily to the floor. Mike froze at the noise, clearly a violation of the muffled atmosphere that pervaded the room. He jostled the shoulder again, more vigorously. "Billy, it's Mike! Wake up you sorry son-of-a-bullwhacker's bride!"

Another groan, and Billy murmured, "Go away! I be sleepin' now."

Mike wasn't to be put off. "Bullshite! I ain't sure these China fellas will be lettin' me back in this hellhole. Come on, will you? Wake up and say howdy to your pardner of eight years on the trail."

Billy roused a bit and looked up at Mike, squinting as if the candle was the brightest thing going in his world. His pale complexion and drawn visage were barely recognizable within their frame of brown hair and black stubble. His eyes were not clear and his hair was dirty, matted in an awkward array of cowlicks. Billy leaned upon one elbow in a tangle of blanket smelling of urine. He blinked repeatedly to focus upon the figure beside him. "Mike, is that really you?"

"Aye, 'tis me all right. What brought you to this feckin' opium parlor? I thought you and Charley Collins was gonna strike it rich stealin' Injun gold."

"Only stealin' done was white on white," Billy spat bitterly. He shook his head ruefully at the memory.

"What are you foosterin' about?" Mike persisted. "Tell me what happened before they kick me out of here!"

"God, my mouth is dry," Billy complained. "Is there anythin' in that bottle there?"

Mike reached for the brown glass bottle beside the candlestick. He sniffed the open top. Nothin'. Must be water. He handed the bottle to Billy who urgently guzzled and coughed a bit. More awake now, Billy began his story.

"Me an' Charley got out here early last year. Best part of this town weren't here back then. Mostly sluice boxes and tents up and down the gulch. Placer gold was what folks was gettin' then." He paused, swigged from the bottle, and coughed again. "Later, seams was found, and the real diggin' begin. Me and two other fellas staked a promisin' claim down at Cleveland and sunk a shaft. We was goin' good and producin' right fair dust, breakin' down ore with a sledge. Then we run out of timbers. As I'd done wood haulin' back when, it fell to me to fetch a wagonload of pine trunks from the hills. I was only away a couple of days. When I get back, the boys is gone. . . . with all the kit, gold dust, and everythin'."

Mike pushed his hat back and whistled lowly. "Jaysus, Billy, why would those polecats be leavin' a payin' claim?"

"I found out the next day. Fella in Eastern getup come by the claim with four hired hands in a wagon. Says I must clear out as he done bought the claim clean and clear. I says, 'You ain't bought it from me. I been here since the first chunk was laid.' But he pulled a paper what my pardners signed over to him. Paid 'em a handsome price, he did, and they skeedaddled."

Mike stood up to flex his knees, tired from squatting beside the bunk. He shook his head at Billy's sad story. "How did you get on after?"

Billy fell back on the bunk, his eyes closed tight. "I had my gold dust with me. . . . We always made a split once a week. Took my cache with me whenever I left camp. I s'pect I drank a good bit of it. Gave the rest to this Liu fella when he took me in here. He's a pretty fine gentleman, for a Chink."

"Well, let's get your poke and clear out of here. I've got work to do. Been doin' fair enough in the business lately. You've got a home with me. You don't need to smoke that shite no more."

Billy rolled onto his side, turned away from his friend. "No, Mike. I ain't leavin'! Won't be no bullwhacker again. I had a fortune in gold, layin' right in front of me, an' it got stole while my back was turned. Only time I can forget is when I'm tuggin' on that pipe."

Mike looked about the room, then bent down again and whispered in Billy's ear. "What's that Liu gonna do with you when your dust is gone? Your arse'll be in the feckin' ditch before your feet touch the ground. Let's be goin' whilst you have your wits about you."

"Mike, I ain't goin' back on the goddamned trail! But if you ever get your fortune, watch your back. Don't be like me. Don't even trust your grandma with your dust."

Mike slapped his hat gently against the blanket-covered haunch of his friend. "I shan't be back, Billy. Best you be comin' now."

"I'm stayin' put!" he firmly stated and pulled the blanket back over his shoulder.

Swish-swish.

Chapter Eighteen

Moving to the River

☩

Jim walked out of the mercantile warehouse as the sun was falling behind the ridge. "Hey, Mike! Did you find your friend?"

"Ach, Jim . . ." Mike looked away briefly at the hillside of ponderosa pines across the gulch. He could almost see Billy driving a team of bulls out of the forests between the forks of the Laramie. He pulled himself back to Jim's question with effort. "Billy's been found dead. The sheriff took me to see where they laid him."

Jim sat down on a keg of nails to rest. "I'm downright sorry to hear that, Mike. How did he die? Do they know?"

"Nobody's able to say." Mike quickly busied himself with a stack of bills of lading, so Jim dropped the subject.

Mike threw himself into building up the business, making two more runs to Cheyenne that fall to replenish their fast-moving inventory. With each run, their financial position improved substantially. Jim cheered their success. "You're finally making that fortune you wanted, partner."

Late in the year, the Morris boys announced they were keen to winter back in Cheyenne, and Mike agreed to do so as well, leaving in mid-November. "That way, you can set out for the Hills with fresh supplies as soon as the winter weather has eased up," Jim said. "I'll stay and work the mercantile through the winter."

Jim enjoyed the society of Deadwood. He made regular visits to town for meals, theatrical offerings, or simply hang around the parlor at the IXL Hotel for the conversation. He was no gambler and drank only to oil the wheels of social discourse. As there was no good way to heat the warehouse, Jim staked himself to a room at the IXL through the long, cold winter.

One evening in February, Jim found his appetite rather puny at supper. Later, while sitting in the parlor visiting with other guests, he felt quite warm. Beads of sweat broke out on his brow, which he mopped at repeatedly with his handkerchief.

"Say, Jim, you don't look too good. You all right?" asked one of the guests.

"I am feelin' awful warm. Must be sittin' too close to the stove." Rising to change places, he was struck by a sudden dizziness. Before he knew what was happening, the rug-covered floor reached up and grabbed him in an embrace. Fellow guests quickly summoned Jim Van Danaker, proprietor of the IXL.

"Someone get Doc Babcock over here, double quick," Van Danaker ordered, as he and several volunteers carried Clark upstairs to his room. The doctor took no time in showing up. Though he was a genial, middle-aged gentleman, he was also extremely efficient and business-like.

"Van, this is the third case I've seen in the last two days. We gotta get this fella out of your hotel fast," said Babcock after examining Clark.

"What's he got, Doc?"

"Unless I'm wrong, we're dealin' with smallpox here. We've set up a pest house over in Spruce Gulch, a miner's cabin where we took the other two yesterday. I'll send a wagon round back within the hour. Once he's out of here, burn his linens and clothes and wash down everything in his room."

The hotelier drew a deep breath. "We'll do as you say, Doc. But this ain't exactly gonna perk up my trade. Can we keep this 'tween the two of us?"

The physician pulled off his spectacles and wearily rubbed the bridge of his nose. "Suit yourself, Van. But it's only Christian that you notify his kin. You'll do that, won't you?"

"I don't rightly know if he's got any family, least not 'round here. There's a partner, though. I'll wire him in the mornin'."

It was several days before Mike received the news of Jim's illness. By then, the presence of smallpox at Deadwood was no secret. And though he was warned of the highly contagious nature of the disease, Mike made plans to ride up to Deadwood on the next day's stage. He knew Jim had family back in Ohio, but he had no details about them. Perhaps I'll find what I need in Jim's papers at the warehouse.

It was a miserable journey from Cheyenne. The stagecoach skittered and bounced over frozen ruts of mud and ice. Mike adjusted one of the buffalo robes issued by the stage line to its passengers.

"It's cold as a well-digger's ass in here," complained a salesman who was also traveling to Deadwood.

"Sure, I'll be takin' your word on that, mister," Mike replied.

The salesman was well dressed and eagerly sociable. But Mike was more interested in sleep than conversation. He pulled his hat down over his eyes.

The only respite from the cold was to be found at the occasional stop at a road ranche. Here travelers might enjoy a warming by the fire and a plate of sowbelly and beans washed down with a hot cup of coffee. But such stops were infrequent and brief, little more than the time to change teams and deliver any mail or freight for their host.

The stagecoach exited Red Canyon and climbed toward Custer and Hill City. It was just before dawn when Mike awakened. Without looking, he knew the salesman was poised to exploit the renewed opportunity for conversation. But having slept, Mike was now more disposed for a chat. He removed his hat and yawned.

"Damn, it's dark out there!" the stranger said. "Makes a body wonder how the driver holds the trail."

"'Tis of no concern to the driver or his team," Mike replied. "They've been makin' this run so often they might as well wear blindfolds. Besides, in winter, 'tis nearly always dark in these hills."

"That sounds like the voice of experience. You with the stage line?"

Mike pulled aside the canvas window curtain and gazed at the first glimmers of a brightening sky. "No, just a freighter what has traveled this road a bit meself. What's your line of business, friend, if I may ask? "

"Jewelry, all the gems and trinkets you might desire, or more likely, that your lady might desire. Came out here from Chicago. Been on the road about two weeks. You must have had some fine adventures, met some colorful characters out here on the frontier."

Mike fingered the brim of his hat as it rested in his lap. "You could say that, I suppose. Could be you've heard of Madame Canutson? She's a lady bullwhacker out of Fort Pierre, over on the river. Made her first run to Deadwood in '76 with only her wee baby boy for company. Stuffed him into the oven of an iron stove she was deliverin' to one of the hotels up here. Guess you could call that colorful."

As Mike spoke, the man's eyes grew bigger and his foolish grin grew wider. "Did you ever make the acquaintance of Calamity Jane or Wild Bill Hickok?"

This curious drummer is up on all the Black Hills folklore, Mike thought. "Wild Bill was dead and buried before I made me first haul to Deadwood. But we used to see Jane Cannary on the road now and again. I'll not say I'm knowin' her all that well, mind you. But we bullwhackers pass each other comin' and goin', and wave howdy. 'Twould be a sorry soul that would not pull up for a few minutes to share the news."

"Always like to hear of women coming into these frontier towns. Does my business a heap of good."

It was midafternoon by the time the stage reached Deadwood. Already the sun was sinking toward the hillsides that loomed over the town. Mike bade a polite farewell to his traveling companion and hoisted his warbag out of the boot beneath the driver's box. He checked for a room at the Overland, but they were full up. The clerk sent him to the Wentworth where he found accommodation and stowed his things. It was after dark before he arrived at Doc Babcock's. The doctor welcomed him as he cleared a chair in his cluttered office. Mike held his coat and hat in his lap.

"You'll not want to pay much of a call on your friend, Mr. Quinn. There's a great danger of contagion, and there's little we can do for you if you come up with the smallpox."

Mike choked back the anxiety that he knew would color his voice. "I'm sure you're right, Doctor. I'll be keepin' me distance, but I must know if Jim's gonna pull through." He recrossed his legs and squirmed in his chair. "What care is bein' given to these poor souls at the pest house?"

The doctor absently used the toe of one boot to clean mud off the other. He looked tired to Mike. "There's a woman. . . . She's paid no heed to my warnings, been there over a week, feeding and tending the victims. I don't rightly understand how she's not down with it herself. She'll be able to tell you about your friend."

Mike thanked Babcock and left. He was resolved to get out to Spruce Gulch first thing next morning.

That evening, as Mike entered the dining room at the Wentworth, he was taken aback at the sight of Charley Collins. It had been close to eight years since he met Collins in Cheyenne, but he recognized him despite the now nearly hairless pate. Mike was never fond of Collins, despite their common Fenian ties. Indeed, he viewed Collins as instrumental in the ruination of Billy Mayhew. He no sooner had decided to avoid Collins and his dining partner than he was noticed and hailed across the room. Mike sauntered over, barely masking his reluctance.

"Mike Quinn! What a coincidence to run into you here in Deadwood. Haven't seen you since Hector was a pup! Was it '70, maybe '71? Let me introduce you to a fellow freighter, Fred Evans."

Frederick Taft Evans rose to his feet to shake hands. Though Mike, at six feet, was fairly tall, and strong in a wiry sort of way, Evans' six-foot-four-inch stature and considerable bulk overshadowed him completely.

"I recognize the name. Pleased to meet you, Mister Evans."

"Call me Fred. Everyone hereabouts does. Won't you sit a spell and add to the chin music?"

Casting a quick eye about the room, Mike realized he was trapped. He was clearly alone and the dining room was virtually full. "I'll join you, if I can get a plate of supper."

As he sat, Mike studied the man who was the leading freighter in the Black Hills. He had piercing, deep-set eyes; dark, curly hair; and a bushy moustache and beard.

Collins seized the moment. "You know, Mike, I talked Fred into goin' to the Hills back in '75, when he was runnin' streetcars back in Sioux City."

Evans chortled in response, "Why don't you tell him the whole story,

Charley? Tell him how you got me arrested and my bull train burned to cinders by the U.S. Cavalry?"

Mike spoke up before Collins could respond. "You ain't the first Charley's talked into comin' to the Hills, Fred. But, you've recovered nicely, I'm thinkin'."

Evans looked carefully into Mike's eyes, apparently sensing a subtle challenge in Mike's remark. "I'll not complain. The freightin' business is growin' like a field of toadstools and we're growin' with it. I'll add that I'm not unacquainted with your own success with the mercantile. You and Jim Clark have done a good trade here . . . for gettin' a late start."

Mike noticed but ignored the chiding. "We were doin' well, till recently," he admitted. "Now Jim's come up with a case of the smallpox. Doc says it might be the end of the trail for him."

Collins broke in. "No, Mike! Sorry to hear that. By the way, what ever happened to Billy Mayhew? Is he back with you now?"

Mike's jaw tightened as he struggled to maintain his composure. "Haven't seen him since he left to hook up with you in the gold minin' game," Mike said grimly.

While Collins took off into a paean to the glories of the gold rush, Mike tucked into a beefsteak and a dessert of dried apples and cream. When he finished his meal, he pressed Evans about his freighting operation. "I see that you are no longer pullin' freight from Cheyenne and Sidney, Fred. Is the road from Fort Pierre so preferred? And what of the Sioux?"

Evans tugged at his beard slowly and thoughtfully. "Ah, we can handle the Sioux. There's the bounty on Injun scalps, and the Army has pushed the tribes out of the Hills and clear of the trail. . . . But there's several reasons why I chose the road out of Fort Pierre. You'll know that freight is more cheaply delivered by the steamboats out of Yankton. And by approachin' from the east, I'm able to serve both Deadwood and Rapid City, sometimes with the same trains. Bigger loads and more teams attract additional business.

Mike nodded, keenly interested in Evans' views. "Aye, I've heard that Rapid is growin' into a sizeable settlement."

Fred leaned forward and lowered his voice. "There's another reason most folks don't know yet. I tell you this in confidence, Mike. My contacts in the Army say that a new fort is planned east of the Hills, where the Sidney,

Bismarck and Fort Pierre trails meet. I'm bettin' this will make the Fort Pierre trail dominant within a year."

Mike wiped his mouth with his napkin, hiding his excitement at this news. Janey Mac! What a nose for business. . . . But why is he showin' me his cards? 'Tis the first time he's laid eyes on me!

Collins appeared to be licking his chops over the scoop for his Central City newspaper. "Fred, am I at liberty to quote you on that bit from the Army?"

"Not yet, Charley, but if you hold your horses, I'll see you get first crack at the story. Otherwise, my friends will deny it entirely." Collins' look of elation melted like the snow on a south-facing hill. Fred turned back to Mike. "You're probably wonderin' why I'm tellin' you all this?"

Mike smiled at Evan's ability to read his thoughts. "I was thinkin' it might not be me Irish charm."

"As I said before, I've noticed your mercantile operation. If Clark don't pull through, you might be wantin' to tie up with someone else. I'd be disappointed if you threw in with anyone but Evans Transportation Company."

Mike raised his eyebrows. Here was the biggest operator in the territory making him an offer that could vault him to the highest echelons of the business. Still, it was hard not to resent Evans' calm assumption that he would cut a deal before his partner's body was allowed to cool. *A man that can hire me quick, can fire me just as quick.* "That's mighty generous of you, Fred. But, at the moment, I ain't free to agree anythin'. I've got me a pardner still. Sure, he's at death's door. Indeed, he may already be dead, for all I know. But I'll not be featherin' me own nest at his expense. Now, with your permission, I'll thank you both for the friendly discussion. 'Tis been a long day."

They stood and Evans stuck out his hand again. "I hear you, Mike. Let it go for now. We'll talk again, maybe."

The next morning was crisp and clear. The snow carried a sparkling crust from the previous day's melt, and it crunched underfoot as Mike left the hotel. He went to the Whoop-up Corral and rented a bay mare for the short ride out to Spruce Gulch. He had the basic directions from Doc Babcock, but he was happy when he came upon a grizzled, old miner working a placer claim. "I wouldn't be so fast to find that pest house, if I was you, mister. But if your mind is set on it, take the next turnin' to the northeast."

After another ten minutes of following tracks in the lingering snow, Mike pulled up and tethered his mount to a pine sapling. A miner's cabin lay ahead in a clearing above the gulch. Hurriedly constructed, its roof was now swaybacked, like a well-worn horse. As he made to approach, the door of the cabin opened and a shabby figure in greasy buckskins and tall leather boots emerged carrying two chamber pots. The contents of these were dumped over the edge of the gulch behind and below the cabin.

Mike looked closely and a smile of recognition broke out on his face like the emerging sun after a summer shower. Glory be to Saint Patrick! That looks like Jane Cannary!

On returning to the cabin, the figure froze, alerted by a snort from Mike's horse. "Whatcha lookin' at, mister? Don't you know better'n to sneak up on a soul in these parts? Like to get killed if you ain't more polite." The voice—gruff, yet feminine; whiskey-soaked; and unfettered by Queen Victorie's English—confirmed Mike's suspicion.

"Hey, Jane, don't be takin' offense. 'Tis me, bullwhacker Mike Quinn, out of Cheyenne."

She dropped her chamber pots and put her hands on her hips. She had buckskin fringe running down each greasy sleeve and trouser leg. Her hair was stringy and disheveled. Even on those rare occasions when she was properly bathed and groomed, Martha Jane was no beauty. Given her current condition, she was not an easy chore for the eyes. But somehow the quirky grin and her easy camaraderie created an aura about her that was entirely disarming. "Son of a bitch, Mike, why didn't you say so? You know, things ain't right here? Go away, less'n you don't care 'bout catchin' deadly pox."

Mike started slowly through the snow toward the cabin. "You have a fella here—me friend and business pardner, name of Jim Clark."

Jane looked back at the cabin and then to Mike. "Did have," she said sadly. "Died yesterday mornin'."

Mike twisted his body away as the bad news hit him.

"Another one went out last evenin'," she continued. "Put 'em in the snow bank out back. 'Spect we'll get 'em buried proper when all this damned snow melts. I'm plum sorry for your loss, Mike."

It took a moment before he regained his composure. He turned back to Jane, his face grim. "Doc said he was in a bad way. He was a fine fella. . . . God rest his soul. Have any of his personal items, do you?"

Jane shook her head. "Didn't come with nothin' more'n the clothes he was wearin'. If you get a hold of Van Danaker at the IXL, he's probably got the rest."

"Aye, I'll be doin' as you say." Mike turned to leave but pulled up short. "Are you all right yourself, Jane? Can I send you anythin' at all from town?"

"Thanks for the offer. Doc Babcock's comin' by later. He brings me what's needed. Promised to bring a sky pilot too when the time comes. Guess that's now."

"Sky pilot? What might that be, Jane?"

"You know, a preacher, a man of the cloth, as they say."

"Ah, sure. Well, God bless. . . . See you back in town, or on the trail, eh?"

"There you go! I'll look for you." Gathering up her chamber pots, Jane went back to her unsolicited, unpaid mission of mercy.

Mike led his horse back to the trail and mounted for the trip back to town. All the way back, he turned over in his mind the bad luck that befell those to whom he became attached: James Powers, Jim Bowes, Billy Mayhew, Sally Kincaid, and now, Jim Clark. Poor Jim! Damn his luck! Is there no one special in me life who ain't goin' to walk out, or up and die on me?

It took almost a month for Mike to organize Jim Clark's affairs. First, he collected Jim's personal effects. At the warehouse, he found some papers dealing with Jim's people back in Ohio. A telegram of response from a sister requested that Mike ship the body to Ohio for burial, but Doc Babcock was against the idea entirely. The quicker buried, the better, he insisted. So Mike paid off Jim's obligations, bought out the warehouse and its remaining inventory, and had the bankers, Brown & Thum, wire Jim's share to the sister back east.

In the spring, Mike resumed his freighting operation. He engaged Frank Whitney, a fellow bullwhacker and ex-policeman from Cheyenne, to take over the mercantile and liquidate its inventory. The Morris brothers agreed to continue their tenure. Taking a cue from Fred Evans, Mike decided to begin hauling from the Missouri River settlement of Fort Pierre instead of returning to Cheyenne.

This port for steamboats was handling a large portion of the freight—more than four million pounds per year—destined for the Black Hills. Mike arrived in late April, when the river was nearly ice-free and steamers were again plying its waters with their burden of foodstuffs, clothing, housewares, and mining equipment. He engaged additional whackers in Cheyenne and Sidney to outfit a full train of twenty-five teams. Still, Mike's business paled in comparison to the larger firms such as Evans Transportation, Bramble and Miner, and Daugherty and Co. Each of these ran hundreds of wagons and had their own warehouses along the river.

There were twelve way stations between Fort Pierre and Deadwood. After an initial eleven-mile climb from the river basin to the top of the mesa, the trail was reasonably flat, until the final push through the Elk Creek valley with its sharply cut arroyos. Various creeks and the Cheyenne River presented seasonal challenges of high, fast water. But the biggest problem on the trail was "gumbo," the regionally characteristic form of mud, famous for sticking to anything, including itself. Proceeding along the trail in wet weather was a nearly useless proposition, as the caked-up volume of mud on the wagon wheels would grind the train to a halt. Pulling off into the grass made things worse, as grass and mud mixed to create a dense adobe-like substance.

Whenever Mike thought about gumbo, he'd recall the yarn told by Zack Sutley, the road rancher at the Cheyenne River crossing:

"One day last April, I come 'pon a freighter and his team stuck in gumbo up to the axles. He weren't able to move a inch in any direction."

Zack turned to his cronies hanging around his stove and winked. "Looks like you's in a hell of a mess, says I. But the whacker shakes his head and says, 'Not so bad, mister. Least when you consider the poor fella and his team what's under me.'"

Mike put up at a popular boarding house in Fort Pierre. Being new on this route, it took him a week or so to negotiate a full train's load for delivery to Deadwood. Big firms, like Fred Evans' company, had large contracts for the entire season. But there was plenty of competition among the smaller shippers.

The big news in Fort Pierre at that time was the construction of a railroad route from Yankton to Pierre. It would be a year or two in coming, but would further enhance the freighting prominence of the Fort Pierre-Deadwood Trail. Every winter, river ice prevented the steamboats from Yankton and Sioux City from delivering freight to Fort Pierre. Even in the spring, rain and melt sent ice cakes as big as railroad cars roaring down the river, sweeping away everything in their path. The steamboats had no choice but to wait it out. But once the railroad arrived at Pierre, freighting would no longer be dependent upon river navigation and would be feasible, pretty much year-round. Of course, a good snowstorm could still halt the bull trains, but such snowfall was not a continuous condition throughout the winter. Mike was now further convinced that moving off the Cheyenne Trail had been a smart decision.

Mike had lots of company in the heyday of freighting on the Deadwood Trail. Dick Mathieson, Jim (Scotty) Philip, Jack and Tom Hale, Charley Zabel, and Ike Humphrey were a few among the many small operators who would become friends for decades to come. The shared travails of wind, wet, mud and mosquitoes along the trail created a bond between them. And no man's need went unaddressed if a member of the freighting fraternity was passing.

As Fred Evans had predicted, freighting to Deadwood, to Rapid City, and ultimately to the newly established Fort Meade, was in a boom. In November 1880, the first train of the Chicago-Northwestern Railroad pulled into Pierre, ready to compete with, if not squash,

Sandstone monument to freighters of the Deadwood–Fort Pierre Trail. The inscription reads "Upper Deadwood Gold Pioneer Trail 1876 to 1911 Early Freighters Dillon, Mandan, Dixon, Shoemaker, Philip, Dupree, Powell, Mathison, Walpole, Quinn" (Photo by Delwin Jensen, South Dakota Historical Markers, 1974. Courtesy of Brevet's Press, Sioux Falls)

the thirty-six steamers delivering freight from Yankton. Competition was also heating up on the Deadwood Trail. The Northwestern Express Stage and Transportation Company, previously operating a route from Bismarck to the mining fields, shifted their whole network of wagons, stock, way stations, stables and granaries to the Fort Pierre route.

In anticipation of this threat to his dominance on the trail, Fred Evans secured contracts with merchants and miners to haul their freight in the upcoming season for $2.00 per hundredweight. In response, the Northwestern assisted the smaller operators like John Hart, Fred Dupree, Louis LaPlant, Dick Dunn, and Noah Newbanks in the formation of what they called "the Bull Union."

Spirits among the union members ran high as they railed against the financial squeeze that Evans was imposing upon them. Mike Quinn threw his support behind the union effort to maintain pre-existing prices. At one meeting, the normally taciturn freighter was encouraged to speak his mind. His outrage colored his face, and his jaw jutted in defiance as he spoke.

"If Fred Evans can drive me out of business at his whim, then I should've stayed in England and not traveled so far for the privilege. I'll not haul me freight for less than the $2.50 rate we been gettin'! And if Fred Evans ain't careful, he won't neither! "

Mike didn't need to spell out the details. Quickly the Bull Union mounted their opposition. It began when the yardmen at Fort Pierre refused to shift and load for Evans' trains. But Fred didn't rise to his position as the top freighter without being tough and willing to defend his patch. He went to the newly relocated Indian reservations at Pine Ridge and Rosebud and hired Oglala and Brule braves to act as scabs in the freight yards. To make sure no one ran off his new workers, Evans called upon his Army friends to dispatch soldiers to provide protection. Much to the consternation of the Bull Union, these tactics were successful. For a while, only Evans' trains were rolling and everyone else was idled by the strike.

The plight of the strikers became increasingly desperate as the weeks passed. Not only were Mike's teams idled, long-time customers in the Hills were getting impatient with the strike and threatened to throw their business to Evans, or to anyone who could deliver. To prevent this, Bull Union members, under cover of darkness, slaughtered a good number of Evans' bulls at the grazing grounds outside Fort Pierre. Mike never claimed any involvement in this action, but he never denounced it either.

Fred was not to be undone. He ordered his train downsized to the most essential freight and repacked it into a train that his remaining bulls could pull. As the train climbed the hill out of Fort Pierre, about a half-mile from the yards, the wheels popped off and the heavy cargo crashed down, breaking fallen axles. The Bull Union boys had removed the hub pins.

The strike was finally broken by two dramatic events. A mysterious fire swept through Fort Pierre in January 1881, which happened to engulf certain businesses whose owners supported the Bull Union. Then in March, the Missouri River overran her banks in the spring thaw, smashing steamboats and washing freight and animals downstream.

Mike and his Bull Union colleagues were left with a dilemma. Some of the freighters looked to establishing an alternate trail from Chamberlain, a small river port south of Fort Pierre. Others decided to drop their rates and try to tough it out. Still others sought out different ways to make a living on the Dakota frontier. Mike would have to choose one of these alternatives as well. After four years of rising fortunes on the Deadwood Trail, the bloom was off the rose.

Chapter Nineteen

Where the Buffalo Roamed

✠

It was a late afternoon in April 1881. The buffalo grass was again flush and green across the rolling Dakota plain. The cottonwoods along the Cheyenne River were beginning to leaf out. Mike Quinn's train, bound for Rapid City, was too late to ford the river before dark. At this time of year, a crossing could take hours, if not most of the day.

After selecting a camp with forage and water, Mike ordered the wagons off the trail and circled up for the night. He was looking forward to spending this evening at Zack Sutley's road ranche on the west bank. The official reason for his visit was to request the assistance of Zack's mules in the next day's crossing, but Mike also relished the notion of a proper supper in place of the three b's: bacon, beans and biscuits.

Leaving Laban Morris in charge, Mike nudged his mount down the steep, muddy embankment and into the swift-flowing Cheyenne. He was glad he had a good swimmer beneath him as spring rains had the river rolling. Tomorrow's fording would be a chore, but he chased the thought of it with the imagined aroma of spotted pup, his favorite dessert of raisins and rice. It might be on offer if Zack was in a good mood.

The highway outpost was remarkably busy when Mike arrived. Eastbound bull trains were encamped nearby, waiting to make their own crossing. Zack's hired hands were running fresh horses out to the coach of the recently inaugurated Northwestern Stage Line, which was carrying mail between Fort Pierre and the Black Hills three times a week.

The sun was going down and Mike hurried to a wash station to rid himself of a coat of trail dust. On his return, he passed by the glowing glass windows through which he could see the dining room lit for supper. The first thing Mike did, after settling himself, was place his request for spotted pup. During the meal, Zack stopped by for a few minutes of conversation, whiskey bottle in hand.

Zack was of medium build, also in his thirties, and already showing thinning hair above a high forehead. He compensated with a full, dark mustache above a clean-shaven chin. "My mules will be happy to pull you across tomorrow, for a fee. Spring time is good for business. I get full use of them mules, pullin' wagons through high water."

Mike looked up from his plate of chicken and dumplings and winked at his friend. "Might not be long-term employment. The talk back at Fort Pierre is that the Milwaukee Railroad will be in Chamberlain before year's end. Could be that a new trail to the Hills will whittle away at your business."

Zack poured two glasses of whiskey from the bottle, then raised his drink in a toasting gesture. "Ain't nothin' forever, Mike. Still, that new trail might get routed up this way."

Mike paused in mid-hoist of his drink, his interest suddenly peaked. "Sounds like you know more than what you're sayin'."

Zack drew close. His eyes reflected the glow of the oil lamp set between them. He smoothed his moustache repeatedly before answering. "Fred Evans has been talkin' to me about surveyin' the Chamberlain trail for him. If I'm happy it'll prove, he'll swing teams down from the Fort Pierre road."

"Evans!" Mike sniffed. "Everywhere I turn there's Fred Evans and his hundreds of wagons, and teams and whackers." Mike's face flushed with emotion. "'Tisn't enough, he near owns the Fort Pierre custom? Now, he's fixin' to drive his bloody empire down to Chamberlain!" He knocked back the whiskey, paused, and then smiled malevolently. "Still, he'll be gettin' a taste of his own cookin' one day soon."

"What do you mean by that, pardner?" his host asked. "You ain't thinkin' more violence from the Bull Union?"

"No, I'm tellin' you that Fred Evans, sure, all of us, will be put on the shelf soon enough by the railroads. Look, they're in Pierre today, and they're after bein' into Chamberlain. Won't be long 'fore they'll be bridgin' the Missouri and layin' track right into the Hills. Why, Jack and Tom Hale are already quit freightin'. And if things don't look up soon, this season will be me last. Should I be makin' me livin' forever walkin' the arse-end of a line of bulls?"

Zack looked surprised. "You wouldn't sell out and go back to the States?"

Mike shook his head and laughed at the notion. "Nay! Dakota is still the best place for a fella to make his fortune."

After polishing off a second helping of spotted pup, Mike got up to pour one last cup of coffee. When he returned, he found a late-arriving diner had joined him at the table.

"You don't object to a bit of company, friend?" the newcomer asked as he rose to offer a greeting. He was dressed in a white, collarless shirt, leather vest, and black wool trousers stuffed into buckskin boots. He gave a firm shake with a callused hand.

"Sit, sit. I'm just finishin' up, though," Mike replied.

"I am Pierre Duhamel, but you must call me Pete. My English, she is not so good, but I try to speak like an American."

The cook came and took Duhamel's dinner request.

"You must be from Canada," Mike said. "I had a friend a ways back, talked like you do. He was from Quebec, name of Beaupre."

"*Bien sur!* I too am from Quebec, but I am now in the territories of United States for more than twenty years. I come to Dakota from Colorado."

In a few minutes, Pete's meal arrived, and Mike decided to stay on awhile, interested to hear the stranger's story. "How'd you come to leave Colorado, Pete? Sure, that's rich country."

Duhamel nodded slowly, waiting to finish chewing a mouthful of supper. "Rich? It was plenty rich till a plague of grasshoppers, she comes and eats every blade of grass, every leaf. There is nothing left for my cows, so we must leave quick. We trailed one thousand head to a range on the Battle Creek. Madame Duhamel, *les enfants,* and me, we take a place in Rapid City."

"A thousand head! That's a lot of beeves."

Pete brushed his full dark beard to clear it of cornbread crumbs. "Not so many as you think, Monsieur Mike. The Sturgis-Goodell outfit has over thirty thousand head. Anyway, the winter, she kill many steers. I think I must get me some more Texas cattle soon."

They talked well into the night, shifting from coffee to whiskey. Mike admired the gutsy Duhamel, who had come from nothing and had made himself into a respectable businessman. As they shared their stories and opinions of frontier life, they found that they shared a strong conviction that cattle would replace gold as the chief source of wealth in the west river country.

"Every time I drive me teams through this grassland," Mike said, "I think, we should be puttin' beeves on this range. No question about it, me bulls thrive on the buffalo grass."

"Maybe Red Cloud and Spotted Tail will not be so happy with the cows of the white man eating their grass," Pete countered.

"Aye, there's that risk. But the Injuns won't be havin' all that land to themselves for long."

Duhamel grunted in agreement. As both men intended an early rising, the two bid each other good night. Before retiring, though, Pete encouraged Mike to come call upon his arrival in Rapid City.

The Duhamel home was a two-story frame structure at Fourth and Kansas City Streets. It was fairly new, and its white walls and green trim carried less than the usual coat of prairie dust. When Mike knocked, a young boy, whom he judged to be about ten, met him at the door. The lad had fine, brown hair and wore his galluses hanging at his sides. " My pa ain't here just now. My name is Alex."

"Alexander, who is it?" The voice from within was female, foreign-accented, warm and gentle. All of a sudden Mike was embarrassed, realizing he was dirty with trail dust and hadn't bathed or shaved since leaving Fort Pierre close to two weeks prior. Here he stood in the doorway of one of the few real homes he had visited in the last fifteen years. The sights and smells from within betokened a very different world.

The lad retreated and presently a woman appeared, wiping her hands with the apron upon her waist. Beads of perspiration stood on her forehead.

"Excuse me, ma'am. Pete, I mean Mr. Duhamel, asked me to call upon him once I got to town. I'm Mike Quinn, freighter out of Fort Pierre." He looked down, wishing he could disappear.

"Ya, ya, Mister told me about meeting you. He will come soon." She offered a wet handshake. "You are most welcome to our home. I am Katherine. It is Saturday, so I give bath to the children now." She turned to the eavesdropping youth behind her and pointed. "Alexander, it is now for you to bath. In the kitchen, quick."

"You'll forgive me appearance, ma'am. I seem to forget the days when we're on the trail. I was in such a dither to get here, I missed bathin' meself. Tell Pete I'll be comin' back, once I get proper for come-to-callin'."

"Oh, no, Mister Mike Quinn. You will come too. In my kitchen, I got plenty hot water. You come!" With that Mike found himself pulled forcefully into the house and shoved toward a kitchen steamed up with hot water and smelling of lye soap.

What Mike noticed first about Katherine Duhamel was her blue eyes, straight nose, and strong chin. She was taller than most women and wore her brown hair pulled back into a bun. Friendly, yet commanding, she provided Mike with hot water, towels and soap and left the room to him and the boy. As Mike washed, Alex was full of questions about the life of a freighter, as his father had been one before going into cattle. Mike enjoyed the boy's friendly enthusiasm, and they talked on after completing their Saturday obligation.

By the time Pete arrived, Katherine had the five children fed and the baby in bed. After a wonderful supper of roasted pork and sour cabbage, Mike and Pete stepped outside. The night was cool but clear. A waxing moon gave a glow to the white box houses that filled the streets on the burgeoning south side of town. Each box, with its yellow eyes of oil-lamp luminescence, presented a level of domesticity still new on this side of the Dakota plain.

"Madame, she does not like that I smoke in her house," Pete apologized as he handed Mike a good-quality manufactured cigar.

"She's a right fine cook. That meal was a real treat. Don't know as I've ever tasted such fare."

Pete beamed with pride. "Katherine, she cooks good. Her people, they come from Germany. They had a place on the Platte, northeast of Denver. That's where we met. But we talk cows, eh? I will buy some Texas cows like we say at Sutley's place."

"Aye, I'd like to invest in some cattle too. The freightin' business is gettin' mighty tough. But I still got contracts for this season. Can't possibly go to Texas till winter, I reckon."

Pete shook his head at the naif. "No, no, my friend. We don't go to Texas! Trailin' a herd from Texas to Dakota, she's a big job. We got plenty cows here already. They was trailed up here for to sell to the Black Hills butchers. But with the railroads at the river, we stockmen think to grow our herds here in Dakota and sell beef in Chicago."

Mike sat on the front step. "Some of me freighter friends have gone to cattle—Maurice Kelliher, Hale brothers, John Hart. I ain't so sure they'll be sellin' stock what they purchased within the last year or so. Do you know anyone what will sell from their herd?"

The older man chuckled and sat down next to Mike. "My friend, I know many stockmen. They will all sell, at the right price! One outfit, she runs a herd on the Lower Cheyenne, near where I place my own

Rapid City, South Dakota (Courtesy of the South Dakota State Historical Society)

cows. They are three brothers, name is Holcomb, marking the HO brand. I meet Bud and Gene down on the range. I don't know the other one, Fred. But they seem good boys and honest too. And they got plenty cows."

Mike rubbed his goatee, which desperately needed a trim. "Holcomb? Seems to me I know that name. Ain't there a hotel, here in town, name of Holcomb?"

"That's their papa. He runs the Holcomb House. And that's where we go to find them boys. We see if they do business with us. How many head you buy, Mike?"

"I'm thinkin' on that yet, depends on the price and terms. Most of me capital is in bulls and wagons. Still, there's a bit of cash at the bank in Deadwood. I might buy five hundred head, if the winter losses don't drive the price too high."

Monday morning, Mike and Pete went to the Holcomb House to see if they could talk business with the brothers. The boys' father, W. L., was at the front desk when they arrived. The white-haired gent worked a toothpick from one side of his mouth to the other, and then back, with remarkable agility. He paused only for a friendly, if brief, response to their queries. "Bud and Gene are up on Box Elder Creek, gents. Might be able to scare up Fred if you give me a few minutes to look around."

Mike and Pete retired to the empty dining room, finding coffee in a huge pot warming on the cast iron stove at one end of the room. They had just settled at one of the two long tables when a young man in a tall, wide-brimmed hat entered. He flashed a pleasant, boyish smile as he greeted them.

"I'm Fred Holcomb. Pa said you was here to talk business." After shaking hands, he threw his hat on the table and went to pour a cup of coffee for himself. "Though I'm the only one of us in town, I'm sure I can represent the HOs interests."

"Mister Fred," Pete began, "we want to purchase some of your cows, separately, as individual operators."

"How much stock did you fellas have in mind?"

"Maybe a thousand or more between us, depending on price."

Fred pushed aside his his hat and set down his cup. His expression suggested that something was bothering him. "Well, I ain't sure. We've had a bad winter and still don't know our full losses."

Mike chipped in, "We'll pay a fair price. Of course, no tick fever, no scrubs included." Pete glowered a bit at Mike for the interruption. But Mike had been working with bulls for fifteen years and would not be sidelined.

Fred raised his right hand as if taking an oath. "Don't worry, Mr. Quinn. If we sell, our terms will be fair. We won't cheat you with bad stock. But we might have to wait a bit to settle on price and delivery. Just a couple of weeks back, the Black Hills Live Stock Association agreed to hold a common roundup. You know, for countin', brandin', and separatin' the herds. The south end of the range won't begin its roundup till the middle of May. After that we'll know our winter losses and the health of the herd. I know a month of delay might not please you, but every stockman in the territory is goin' to tell you the same thing. We're all in this together."

Duhamel looked at Mike and nodded in agreement. "We understand, Mister Fred. If you got serious interest in doin' business, we'll wait till after the roundup. In the meantime, we take a look at some of your stock, no?"

Holcomb grinned widely at the suggestion and slapped his knee. "Why don't you fellas come with me to Box Elder today? You can meet Bud and Eugene and look over some of the herd."

Mike hastened to clarify his own position. "I thank you for the offer, but I'm happy that Pete be me eyes and ears for now. Me freightin' business won't wait. Don't want them bullwhackers of mine to run off."

He put out his hand as he rose to leave. He had a good feeling about young Holcomb. He was comfortable as well that he and Pete Duhamel had begun a friendship that could be most helpful in easing his transition out of freighting. When he returned to Fort Pierre, he began the search in earnest for a buyer of his freighting business.

The economics of cattle were too good to pass up. There was no cost of land or feed, as the herd would be placed on public lands. Herds were nearly unattended, so significant labor costs were isolated to roundups and the drive to a shipping point. The cost of Texas cattle was reasonably low, and the demand for beef was rising. Not only were the mining communities in the Hills to be served, periodic deliveries of beef to the Lakota reservations were a federal commitment under the Black Hills Treaty. And, with railroads penetrating the frontier, the stockyards of Chicago were a reasonable destination for one's fattened steers. There, meatpackers might pay as much as $35.00 per hundredweight, which meant an average of over $400 dollars per head. Clearly, this was good business.

By June, Mike had his herd of five hundred and fifty beasts branded and placed along the lower Cheyenne River, between the Spring and Rapid Creeks. He devised the "Easy SJ" as his brand: an S lying on its back on top of an upright J. He was now in the cattle business, but when the freighting season wound down, Mike still had not found a buyer for his bulls and wagons.

The prospects for a new road from Chamberlain to the Black Hills were developing rapidly. A route had been surveyed, and Fred Evans and various Rapid City merchants had funded improvements, such as bridges. For $22,000, the Milwaukee Railroad secured a two-hundred-foot freighting right-of-way across the Lakota reservation, and on the 6th of October, the first Milwaukee trains reached Chamberlain. Everything was ready for a major expansion of freighting via this new route up along the White River, past the Badlands, to Rapid Creek. The first major freight outfit to haul on the new road left Chamberlain on the 2nd of January 1882.

Mike was getting anxious. Contracts for the new season were overdue. He didn't want to stay on another season, but he couldn't leave his wagons or his bullwhackers idle either. Mike had recently returned from Deadwood and was laying over in Pierre during a blast of winter weather. Among the other guests at the hotel was the small freighters' nemesis, Fred T. Evans. Mike wasn't looking for conversation with the baron of Black Hills' transport, but one evening the pair ran into each other at the entrance to their hotel.

"Hello, Mike. I didn't know you were stayin' here. How about joinin' me for a drink? I'd like to talk some business with you."

Mike stepped back to allow Evans to pass. His face offered no welcome. "Sure, I'm thinkin' there's nothin' we have to say to each other."

Evans stood planted and held the door, gesturing for Mike to enter first. "Now, Mike, that ain't entirely fair. I know you boys are mighty sore at me.

Maybe I got a few reasons to be sore too. But there ain't never been anything personal about it. Come on, a little whiskey's just the thing for two old rivals."

After a bit more cajoling, Mike surrendered and followed Fred into the lounge. They seated themselves in armchairs flanking a radiant fireplace. The warmth of the fire thawed temperaments as well as bodies on this cold, blowy night. The hotel night clerk came in. "Yes, Mr. Evans? What can I bring you?"

"Hello, Frank. Some rye whiskey from my private stock." The clerk returned promptly with a bottle of Old Overholt and two glasses. "Just leave the bottle, Frank. We'll be fine."

After a few appreciative sips, Mike looked around the lounge. The place was empty save for one other patron who was slumped in an overstuffed chair across the room. The old fellow had dropped off over his newspaper. His snoring was interrupted occasionally when his tilted head fell to one side and awakened him with a start. He would then repeat the sequence.

"What business is it you're after talkin' with me?" Mike asked.

"I hear you're lookin' for a buyer for your outfit."

Mike rocked back in surprise. "'Tis a well-known fact, I guess. I'm quittin' the freightin' business as soon as I can get meself a proper offer."

Evans shifted his gaze from the amber liquid in his glass to Mike's cautiously narrowed eyes. " Suppose I was to make a 'proper offer,' as you say."

"Look here, Evans!" Mike voice rose with his dander. "You already own the biggest piece of freightin' between here and the Hills. Now you're after haulin' on the new road out of Chamberlain. 'Spect you'll drive the small operators off that road too. I figure you've no need of me wagons and bulls. I'm thankin' you for your fancy whiskey, but I'm not interested."

He rose from his chair and placed his unemptied glass on the side table. Evans bounded to his feet, his height and bulk blocking Mike's retreat. "Wait a minute, Mike." His tone was appeasing. "Let me explain some things."

Mike stood impassively, holding onto his hat and coat.

"Look, you know damn right well, there's a freightin' boom comin'," Evans continued. "Not just in the minin' camps, but in Rapid City and all these little communities springin' up here and there. Settlers are movin' into the west river country in droves. You smaller freighters will be makin' good money, and it ain't me drivin' you out of the business. Admit it, you're quittin' 'cause of the railroad. Don't need to be a bright boy to know that in a few more years the railroads will push all us bullwhackers to the wall."

"True enough. But, if you think such, what could you possibly want with me old wagons and herd?"

Evans gestured for them both to sit again, and Mike reluctantly complied. "The Milwaukee road is payin' $4.00 per hundredweight to shift traffic away from Pierre. In time, the Northwestern will have to match that rate. I've got me a new warehouse at Chamberlain, and I'm gonna build me a mill there to supply flour to the reservations. Frankly, I can use every wagon and healthy team I can lay my hands on. In three or four years, this will all go for junk, but right now it goes at a premium."

Mike felt his hostility draining away, but he was cautious too. "Sure, if that's the case, there should be plenty of buyers."

"Ah, if they got capital. These new rates will make you freighters healthy in time. But whose got the cash to buy you out now? Why ain't you had an offer yet?"

Mike couldn't find a flaw in Evans' logic. He always knew this fellow was two jumps ahead of the crowd. And despite the resentment Evans generated among his competitors, Mike had to concede a grudging admiration as well. He sat back in his chair and picked up the glass of rye.

"What might you consider a proper offer for your outfit? " Evans asked.

Mike rolled his eyes upward, mentally adjusting his pricing on the fly. "Well, I've got eighty wagons presently, and about two hundred and eighty bulls. I figure to ask $40,000. I keep me horses and mules."

"Will you have another drink on that?"

Mike paused for a moment, then allowed a smile to creep across his face. He held out his glass. "Why not?"

Chapter Twenty

The Ravenous Wolves

✠

*P*UBLIC NOTICE

There will be a mass meeting of citizens of Lawrence, Pennington and Custer counties in the courthouse at Deadwood Wednesday, March 15, 1882 at 2 p.m. for the purpose of taking such steps as may be deemed advisable to secure and utilize the 45,000 square miles of grazing land in southwestern Dakota known as the Great Sioux Reservation, unequalled in America for its nutritious grasses, sufficient to sustain one million head of stock. The benefits to be derived from this must be obvious to all. It will attract stockmen from all of the northwest. It will bring capital to our midst and give employment to a large number of people. It is the great inducement to the building of the railroads to the Black Hills. Let everyone who is interested in the greatest welfare of the Black Hills attend and assist in the movement.

They were all there, Mike observed—Richard Lake, Jim Woods, C. K. Howard, John Brennan, Tom Sweeney, Dave Clark and many more. Dressed in collars and ties, in black frock coats and all, these were the big boys. Among them were some of the earliest pioneers, the richest of the stockmen, and the leading businessmen in the Black Hills. Mike had agreed to attend at the urgings of Pete Duhamel and the Holcomb brothers. Not that they had to press him. Along with others in the cattle business, he was adamant that the west river country be opened up for increased grazing for their herds. That day, the Deadwood courthouse—a rough, clapboard structure unused to accommodating such crowds—was well tracked by muddy boots and melting snow. The press of humanity steamed the windows and required the doors remain open, despite the chilling temperatures without.

A series of declamations ensued, but little unanimity emerged as to how their goal should best be accomplished. Stockmen favored negotiating for leases of Indian land that would meet their grazing requirements. Farmers and merchants would accept nothing less than extinguishing the Indians' rights to a major portion of the remaining reservation lands. It would, they said, lead to a great advance of civilization and increased prosperity.

John Brennan, the Irish-born cofounder of Rapid City and the proprietor of the American House Hotel, argued vociferously. "Grazing leases will only convince the Injuns to reject reasonable offers aimed at full cessation. Then we'll get less settlement and more delay in the arrival of the railroad."

As a minor operator, with a herd of only two thousand head, Mike Quinn's opinion wasn't solicited in the formal meeting. And Mike was not one to press to be heard. But over a beer that evening, in the company of friends, he explained his position in a very matter-of-fact way. "I ain't awful particular how the range gets opened," he began. "If we can get them folks back in Washington to write a new treaty, I'm for it. If they can't, then leases suit just as well. 'Tis the time it takes which is the key. I'm wantin' sooner over better."

Other cattlemen at the table grunted their agreement with these remarks. But it was obvious to all that John Brennan, with his knit eyebrows and mock scowl, wasn't satisfied. "Mike, if you wasn't a good Irishman, I'd say you was a small-minded fella with no sense of the future. As it is, I'll just be thinkin' it quietly to meself."

Mike laughed and winked at Brennan. "I didn't think you let small-minded folk stay at your 'first-class' hotel. Perhaps I should move elsewhere?"

For Mike, building his herd; bringing in shorthorn, "white-faced" breeds from the east to improve the quality of his herd; achieving access to unfenced rangelands; enjoying good market prices and good shipping points were what interested him.

Mike lived part-time in Rapid City and part-time in Smithville, splitting his days between inspection trips to the herd and playing penny-ante poker with his cronies. Rather than buy or rent a house, Mike took rooms at the hotels. His personal possessions were so few as to fit into saddlebags. He could cook simple campfire grub, but preferred to take his meals in town in a hotel dining room. He described his lifestyle as simple, though critics might have used the word "cheap," as Mike was known for his tight grip on his cash. When he did spend, it was to invest in the business, his herd. Even after sixteen years, Mike's devotion to making his fortune remained strong.

Mike's life on the open range was marked by occasional dangers, some natural, others man-made. Hard weather, flash floods, cattle stampedes, and rattlesnakes were among the former. Conflict with the occasional renegade Lakota or an irate "sodbuster" comprised the latter.

In the fall of '84, Mike was supervising his herd in the gap between Box Elder and Rapid Creeks. It was an area that had seen much animosity between cattle interests and recently arrived homesteaders. Mike had spent a week living out of his warbag and bunking under the stars. One night, he awakened with a start, hearing his horse skittering crazily in a vortex around a picket iron.

"Arrah, Francie! What the divil are you frettin' on?" Mike rolled out from under his blanket and hopped his way into his boots. Approaching the sorrel mare, he kept a low, soothing banter going till he came in range of the hackamore by which she was tethered. Her eyes were wild and bulging, and she snorted repeatedly. Grabbing the cheek piece, he patted and petted her, but she refused to be comforted.

Mike surveyed the landscape to see what animal or person might be spooking his mount. Then he saw it—a thin vermilion line lying upon the northern horizon like a misplaced sunrise. It took a moment to register in his still groggy consciousness. Then he smelled the smoke—dry, acrid, still faintly defined as the wind was blowing gently from the west. Wildfire.

In a heartbeat, he ran for his saddle and soogan. The cattle on the other side of the hogback, his own and those belonging to his fellows, would be drifting rapidly southeastward, if not in a headlong stampede. They would save themselves. Right now, he had to retreat and spread warning to any folk in the path of the red licking monster storming across the sun-parched prairie.

"Damn you, Francie! Hold still, will you?" The prancing, frightened mare repeatedly slipped her saddle and blanket before Mike could pull the cinch. Only when his bedroll and warbag were finally lashed into place did he release and abandon the picket iron. He grabbed a shortened right rein and the left cheek piece to keep her from bolting, then swung himself into the saddle and urged Francie into a brisk trot. He was aiming for the river, hoping to encounter any ranging cowman or maybe a homesteader's cabin along the way. Every so often, pronghorns, coyotes, and cattle came charging by, running from the oncoming flames. He heard them more than saw them as they flashed past in the dark and the smoke.

It was dawn by the time he reached the river. Though the water level was fairly low, the banks were thronged with milling, nervous longhorns. Mike carefully picked his way among steers whose sharpended horns measured four or five feet across. A memory of Jim Bowes' goring flickered in his memory. Damn me eyes! That was a time ago! God rest old Jimbo. Best take care not to follow in his footsteps.

He maneuvered so as not to become enveloped within the herd. A sky of billowing smoke blotted out the beauty of a plains' morning. The fire was not far off, he reckoned. Mike struggled to keep his eyes open in the Hadean atmosphere. He spied a bandanna-masked rider fording his way through the maze of beef between them. He knew that the slightest provocation—a shout, or a gunshot might send this herd racing to where the devil decides, taking him and the rider with it. Mike silently hailed the figure with a slight wave of his hat. As the rider drew near, he pulled the kerchief from his nose and mouth.

"Ike Humphrey! Sure, I'm mighty pleased to find 'tis you out here. How far behind us do you figure she is?"

Humphrey, another freighter-turned-cattleman, coughed up a mouthful of smoke-laden spit and dropped it casually at the feet of his brown and white pinto. "I f-f-figure two miles, m-m-m-more or less. Lucky the w-w-wind ain't truly up."

"Ain't seen any lightnin'. How do you suppose this thing got started?" Mike asked.

"S-s-some goddamned sodbuster put a t-t-torch to the prairie on a-a-account of his fence line bein' p-p-pulled—or his dog come up d-d-dead. Aims to p-p-pay back the cowmen what done it. No grass, n-n-no beeves."

Mike flexed his gloved fists in frustration. "Far be it from me to figure the thoughts of such a man what would light up the entire range. Now it must run its course. Do you figure 'twill stop at the river?"

Humphrey dabbed at his watering eyes with the edge of his bandanna.

"Might. Meantime, we g-g-gotta push these critters further upstream. If we can k-k-keep 'em on this side of the river, they'll be a heap f-f-fewer lost."

It was dusk before they had moved the cattle beyond the reach of the inferno. The flames didn't jump the river, but the range to the north was burnt black.

That evening they searched for a safe campsite. "W-w-we need to find new grass for these beeves," Ike said. "Pushin' everyone's cattle s-s-south ain't no solution. We was already t-t-trippin' on each others' heels 'fore this h-h-happened."

Mike raised himself in the stirrups, stretching the stiffness from his legs. "'Tis already autumn. Maybe we should drive 'em to the railhead and ship 'em east. There's plenty of grass 'tween here and Bismarck. Them what we don't ship, leave 'em up above the Belle Fourche."

"M-m-makes sense to me. Still, it'll t-t-take weeks to sort out our head from the rest. Maybe, we can g-g-get other outfits to d-d-do a drive with us. Let the count be m-m-made at the railhead."

That night, Mike lay back against his bedroll and saddle. The campfire they shared was no bigger than what was required to boil the coffee. Enough of flame and smoke for one day, he figured. "Right now, I'm so weary, I can't think," he said. "Let's ride up to Rapid come sunup. Maybe the Live Stock Association will clear the way forward."

The arrival of hordes of new settlers, with their garden plots, barbed-wire fences, and occasional grass fires made the pursuit of additional range-land more urgent. Weeks later at the Black Hills Livestock Association meeting, the clamor for range leases was higher than ever. Lobbying efforts in Washington had secured the support of Senator Dawes, chairman of the Committee on Indian Affairs, though he insisted upon giving the Indians a say-so on the deal and a fair price to boot. But even with Dawes' successful sponsorship in the Senate, the bill to open the Lakota lands died later in the House of Representatives. So there was no joy for either those seeking grazing leases or for those preferring cessation.

Rail lines constructed to Pierre and Chamberlain were apparently blocked in their path west. But the owners of Northwestern Railroad, which had the service to Pierre, would not be deterred in their desire to penetrate the Black Hills. Over a four-year period, the company moved aggressively to circumvent the obstacle of the Indian reservation. Acting through a subsidiary—the Fremont, Elkhorn, and Missouri Valley (FE&MV) Railroad—they plotted a route that approached the Hills from the south. In 1882, they pushed their way across northern Nebraska to the difficult crossing of the Niobrara River, near Valentine. By 1885, the FE&MV had progressed to Chadron, Nebraska. Turning north, it entered Dakota Territory near the western border of reservation lands. On the 3rd of July 1886 the first train arrived at Rapid City.

The following day, Mike Quinn joined fellow cattleman, C. K. Howard, for an Independence Day dinner at the American House. To celebrate, the hotel had prepared for its guests bounteous portions of roasted chickens, cured hams, beefsteaks and locally grown vegetables. This they topped off with dozens of peach pies.

Mike's friend, Pete Duhamel, was absent from the festivities. He had sold all his cattle to the Buckeye Company in '84 and was now on an extended visit to Quebec, visiting relations.

C. K. had come into town from his ranch near Smithville. He was thirteen years senior to Mike and looked like a walrus with his gray moustache and baggy eyes. C. K. had operated a general store in Sioux Falls before he moved to the Hills. After a scourge of grasshoppers destroyed the crops in Minnehaha

County in 1876, Howard had liberally extended credit to his farmer clientele, earning him the nickname "Ox-Heart Charlie."

"Everywhere I go, the railroad is right behind me," Mike said, "from North Platte to Julesburg, to Cheyenne, to Pierre, to Chamberlain. Now they're fairly drivin' up to me doorstep here in Rapid. Everywhere they go they're bringin' in more nesters, carryin' more freight, and puttin' bullwhackers like meself out of business."

C. K. laughed and pushed away the leavings of a second helping of pie. "Last time I looked, Mike, you was herdin' nearly thirty-five hundred head, and not bullwhackin' at all. That don't look like "out of business" to me. Besides, with the new holdin' yards down at Brennan, this here's gonna be the easiest shipment ever," he said.

"As usual, me friend, you have the better view of things. Such is these modern times, for like the good Lord, they giveth and they taketh away."

That November, Mother Nature did some taking away, dealing a crushing blow to the Great Plains that continued right through till March. From Texas to Canada, lashing blizzards and icy temperatures ravaged the herds, especially in the northern rangelands. A thick crust of ice covered the buffalo grass and starved those animals that hadn't already frozen to death. Some outfits claimed losses of eighty to ninety percent. Though Mike Quinn shipped nearly two thousand head of cattle from Brennan that fall, he lost nearly a third of his remaining cattle in the "great die-up" in the winter of '86-87. After this devastation, many stockmen, including some large corporate operators, pulled out of the business in Dakota. Those who remained had learned a valuable lesson.

One evening Mike, Pete Duhamel, and Fred Holcomb met over cards at the Harney Hotel. Pete had returned to Rapid City in '87 and bought back the remnant of his old herd from Buckeye Cattle. A little grayer and a lot wiser, he was once again a significant presence within the stockgrower community, and at these friendly poker games.

"Rather than leavin' our herds to drift through the winter, they need to be placed on protected terrain," Fred said. "And we gotta put out stocks of hay here and there."

Pete nodded in agreement. "We should also replace these warm weather longhorns with heartier breeds from the States."

"Some folks have been lettin' their cattle 'wander' onto the reservation," Fred observed. "With most of the Injuns livin' at the agency, they might graze unnoticed for quite awhile." He turned his gaze upon Mike in silent accusation.

"'Tis God's green grass and, sure, nobody's usin' it at the present time," Mike responded as he reviewed cards freshly dealt.

"We need the grass, there's no denyin' it," Fred replied as he arrayed the chips in front of him in neat stacks. "But I'd be careful about runnin' herd on the reservation, Mike. You never know."

Mike Quinn was approaching forty-two years of age, still lean and wiry as his father before him. He wore his salt-and-pepper hair short, though it could get a bit shaggy during extended periods on the range. And he still fancied his moustache and goatee beard, also now flecked with gray.

Socially and politically he was a follower, not a leader. Still he felt his convictions strongly and would voice them freely when the time came. He was not a big talker, though he enjoyed telling a joke or a tall tale when within his circle of friends.

He had lived close to half of his life on the frontier. For twenty years, he had made no effort to contact his family back east, being wholly unaware of the deaths of his parents two years prior. Indeed, he would have no news, this year, of his youngest sister, Elizabeth, succumbing to consumption at the age of thirty-two. Occasionally he considered paying the family a visit, but always dismissed the idea at the prospect of confronting Roderick and Jane.

In business, Mike was less retiring. He knew what he wanted and how to get it. His hired hands considered him a fair man. They trusted his judgments on the trail, his knowledge of the cattle business, and his ability to survive on the open plains. Mike had even mastered the art of clipping off the head of a rattler with a stroke of his quirt as he rode through the lush beige carpet of buffalo grass. He handled a rifle as well as needed to bring down occasional game for his campfire or to chase the elusive gray wolf away from a defenseless calf. He hadn't turned his weapon upon another human being since his encounters with hostiles during his early bullwhacking days—and he preferred that it stay that way.

In the spring of 1888, Mike and half a dozen hired hands were out doing their own little roundup, checking winter losses and branding new calves. As part of the effort, an excursion to the reservation was required to gather "wandering" head carrying the Easy SJ brand. One afternoon, Mike and three of his crew were trailing about six hundred head near White Water Creek, well within Lakota territory, when they stopped to water their animals.

As he dismounted, Mike advised his crew, "Get the blood movin' agin in your legs and backsides, boys. We'll not stay long. I'm keen to get another couple of hours on the trail before dusk."

After watering their horses, the men stretched and strolled by the creek. Suddenly a pounding, drumming sound caused heads to turn. Over the hogback behind them, a cloud of dust arose, confirming that riders were approaching rapidly. The arrival of visitors made Mike's mouth go dry. As a trespasser, he was not happy to be caught red-handed—men, cattle, and all.

In seconds, a band of Lakota warriors, maybe a dozen in number, reined up, not twenty yards away. No longer attired entirely in feathers and buckskin, these braves wore a curious combination of Indian and white man's costume: factory-made shirts, breechclout and leggings or woolen trousers, felt hats, or black bowlers. Though their appearance had changed, their horsemanship and armaments were as threatening as ever. The party was fully armed with a diverse array of muzzle-loaders and repeaters that had somehow escaped confiscation by the bluecoats. If they needed to trade lead, Mike thought, these boys were open for business.

Mike and his mates stood, as if frozen, against the bank of the creek. Cattle were still knee-deep at the water's edge and the horses were tethered in the copse of trees nearby. One of the cowpokes started for his revolver.

"Hold, Jack!" Mike barked. "Let's be gettin' out of this scrape alive, if you don't mind." He turned toward the Lakota party, extended his open palms, and slowly stepped forward. His eyes raced from face to face, searching out a leader with whom to parley. The countenances of the riders ranged from blank to visibly hostile.

"*How, Kola* (Greetings, friend)," he said, his voice coming out embarrassingly high pitched.

An Oglala rider responded, shaking his rifle in the air. "*Washichun lyaya yo! Hiya Kola.*" (White man, go away! No friend.)

"What's he sayin', Mike?" whispered another of the hired hands.

"I've no idea entirely. But he used the word for 'friend.' Now hush your gobs for a minute, the lot of you." Mike slowly advanced.

A brave in a red shirt and black leather vest called out. "White man, no come. This is Lakota land."

The first speaker rejoined. "*Letan khigla po. Unniktepi kte!*" (Get out of here. We will kill you!)

Mike tried to make eye contact with the English speaker but the brave's pony wheeled and pranced. "We came for stray cattle. We're goin' back across the river, off reservation lands. We go now."

"White man lies," the red-shirted one countered. "Cows on Lakota land since moon of falling leaves. You cross river. Cows stay!"

"Arrah! Them cattle is me own. I can't be leavin' six hundred longhorns! 'Tis stealin' them, you are. And the bluecoats at Fort Meade will be angry."

"White man steal Lakota grass. Steal *Paha Sapa* (Black Hills). Bluecoats say no white man come Lakota lands. You go! Leave cows here."

The speaker turned to his companions, apparently summarizing his forceful rebuke to the trespassers; for when they had heard him out, there were laughs of approval, war cries, and much waving of weapons. Mike and his men were cornered and everyone knew it, whites and red men alike.

He turned back to his fellows, a stony, sullen look upon his face. "Mount up, boys, these Injuns got the upper hand. 'Tis a feckin' scandal, stealin' a man's herd right out from under him. We'll give them soldier boys a chance to run these fellas to ground and get me steers back."

The laughs and war cries of the Lakota followed Mike and his crew all the way to the river.

Although the inhabitants of the Spring Creek valley were duly exercised by Mike's tale of alarm, the authorities were not happy about his invasion of the reservation. The Indian agent at Pine Ridge was blunt in his response to Mike's complaint. "You are lucky, Quinn, that I don't have you arrested. Do you expect me to risk an outbreak of hostilities tryin' to recover cattle illegally placed on the reservation? Half your steers is probably eaten by now! I should count myself lucky to retreat with my hair, if I was you."

In the end, Mike's cattle were forfeit, though most his stock was not on the wrong side of the river. As the issue of land cessation was still active in Washington, Mike became more vocal than ever that its time must come soon. He and his allies didn't have to wait a great deal longer. On the 2nd of March 1889, President Cleveland, in one of his final official acts, signed the bill to throw open nine million acres of Indian patrimony. The howling hordes of settlers, stockmen, miners and merchants were duly pleased.

Mike found Pete Duhamel in Tom Sweeney's hardware store in Rapid City. A sign in the window beckoned, "Tom Sweeney Wants To See You!"

"Pete, hold on to your hat. Them fellas in Washington finally figured out how to get it done. The reservation is open! 'Course, the Injuns gotta agree it."

Pete's face lit up, his bushy eyebrows dancing. "At last? I know right where my ranch, she's goin' to sit. I been keepin' my eye on a parcel right below the Forks of the Cheyenne. I'll put a cabin up there and run my herd between Squaw Creek and Pedro. Of course, Katherine and the children, they will stay here in town."

Mike pulled a stick of licorice from a jar on the counter. "Aye, that's fine country. I'm thinkin' I'll be placin' me herd along the Bad River. Jaysus, I've waited to see the day. . . . What am I doin' buyin' candy?" He dropped the licorice back into its jar. "This calls for a wee drop of the water of life! I'm buyin'!"

Tom Sweeney laughed as he came from behind the front counter. "I'll have some of that too, Mike. I don't know which turn of events is more awaited, the cessation or you buyin' drinks!"

"Ah, the divil with you, Sweeney. But as your family was Irish, come along then."

By mid-August, the requisite approval of the Treaty by three-fourths of the adult male tribe members had been secured, but only by the usual tactics of misrepresentation, threats, and lashings of whiskey. At that point, the land rush for homestead claims and open-range grazing did well and truly commence. It was banner times for the white man, as the once proud nomads of the plains were pushed onto the poorest acreage about. Even the political structure of the New West crystallized later that year when the Dakota Territory was split and entered the Union as North Dakota and South Dakota.

Chapter Twenty-One

Demons of the Night

☩

No sooner had cessation occurred than the government cut the beef issue to the Lakota tribes on the six diminished reservations at Pine Ridge, Rosebud, Standing Rock, Cheyenne River, Lower Brule, and Crow Creek. General George Crook, the government's representative in securing tribal acceptance of the Treaty, protested to Washington the near starvation conditions imposed upon the Lakota. The Indians' response was, perhaps, predictable.

Fred Holcomb complained to fellow cattlemen at Frank Cottle's road ranche at Smithville. "My brother, Gene, has been losin' cattle and so have I. I know it's them redskins at Cheyenne River, comin' over to Sulphur Creek."

Pete looked equally disturbed as he paced back and forth. "Last month, my cowhands shot at a few bucks nosin' about the herd above Deep Creek. Don't know as it'll do much good though, with the tribes near starvin'."

Mike Quinn noticed that these remarks sat poorly with Jim "Scotty" Philip, but the man held his peace. His herd of cattle, together with buffalo he'd saved from the slaughter, was placed on the range north of the Bad River, near where Mike had his herd.

Mike sat paring a fingernail with his penknife. Must be Scotty's wife, Sarah, he reasoned. Half-Cheyenne and half French-Canadian, she might give a man a different view on the Indian question.

It was the late summer of 1890, and though the onrush of settlers was still in full cry, the rangeland gained through cessation had vastly improved life for stock growers.

James ("Scotty") Philip (1858–1910) (Courtesy of the South Dakota State Historical Society)

"I ain't lost but a head or two," Mike said, "but that don't mean I ain't jumpy. Seems the whole damned Sioux nation's caught this Messiah foolishness, dancin' in circles, wearing those blue-figured shirts what they think can stop a .45 slug. They must all be dinin' on locoweed."

Their host, Frank Cottle, sat mending harness. "You been to one of these ghost dances, Mike?"

"Can't say that I have. But I'd be keen to do."

Frank was a tall, lean fellow with a high forehead and an untrimmed moustache. Though only in his late thirties, his prematurely receding hair made him seem older than his years. He had taken over the Cheyenne River road ranche from Zack Sutley some years prior.

"Damned if it ain't a sight to see," he continued. "I was down to Pine Ridge back in June. Went to see Henry Dawson on some procurement business. When I got there, he takes me out to the White Clay Creek, where the ghost dancers have their camp. There was a couple of dozen sweat lodges too, where they take the purification before the ghost dance begins."

Frank stood, stretched, and ran his thumbs up and down his galluses, seemingly pleased to be the center of attention. "A fella name of Kickin' Bear starts it off. Says how Jesus is mad as hell at the whites for killin' him. He also ain't too happy that the huntin' grounds of the red men have been stole and the buffalo slaughtered. Jesus promised he'd bring back the ghosts of their ancestors. All us whites is to be buried under new earth and covered with sweet grass, trees, fresh streams and lots of game. But Jesus will only come and make these changes if they do the dance."

Fred Holcomb pulled an apple from a nearby barrel. "Ain't that the damnedest thing you ever did hear?"

Scotty visibly bristled, his Scottish brogue deepening with emotion. "Makes a lot of sense, Fred, when you've lost everything and haven't had much to eat!"

Fred gave a puzzled look, but made no reply. There was an awkward moment of silence, then Frank cleared his throat and resumed his account. "So anyways, after Kickin' Bear has his say, the whole assembly forms a circle and joins hands. They begin to movin' slowly, in a shufflin' step, and chantin' some kind of prayerful song. This they keep up, but increasin' the pace till they is jumpin' themselves near to exhaustion. Dawson and me left about the time it was peterin' out."

Mike looked up from his manicuring task. "That must have been a sight. Like to give a man the willies. I'm thinkin' we're gonna see big trouble."

"I agree with you, Mike," Holcomb said. "Be glad once roundup is over. The more cattle to market, the less we gotta stand guard over."

Rumors of potential mayhem, mixed with occasional cases of real violence, went on for months in both directions. The white community and the tribes lived in heightened fear of each other.

That September, Daniel Royer, a greenhorn dentist from Alpena, South Dakota, was appointed the new agent at Pine Ridge. Knowing nothing of Indian ways, he was soon in a complete panic over the ghost dancing. By November, his urgent telegrams to Washington brought the deployment to Pine Ridge of five companies of Infantry and three troops of cavalry. With the arrival of these military forces, the hundreds of ghost dancers among the Lakota panicked. Many retreated to a naturally protected mesa on the edge of the Badlands called "*O-ona-gazhee*," or "The Stronghold." From that location they could hold off a superior force indefinitely. In response, the Seventh Cavalry, Custer's old outfit, was dispatched from Fort Riley, Kansas, under the command of Col. James Forsyth.

In mid-December, Agent McLaughlin at Standing Rock ordered his reservation police to arrest Sitting Bull for encouraging the ghost dancers. When the old warrior's followers saw him being led from his cabin in chains, a skirmish erupted. In the melee, Sitting Bull was shot and killed by his captors. Panic and outrage crested among the Lakota population like the spring flooding of the great Missouri.

The Eighth Cavalry was dispatched from Camp Cheyenne to bring a Miniconjou Chief named Big Foot and his band of ghost dancers to Fort Bennett. To facilitate this in a peaceful manner, Colonel Sumner sent as his emissary John Dunn, a squaw man living among the Miniconjou. But Dunn warned Big Foot against going to Fort Bennett. Once there, he suggested, the males would be disarmed and sent to an island prison in the Caribbean. Women and children would be left behind to fend for themselves. This had the effect of stampeding Big Foot's band into a headlong rush into the night, south toward Pine Ridge.

Mike and one of his cowhands, Rico Sandoval, entered the battle-field from the north. They followed the same route used by Chief Big Foot and his Miniconjou five days earlier. The remnants of the recent snowstorm clung to the wind-blown grassland along Wounded Knee Creek. Here and there, splotches of dark crimson ice decorated the ground where blood had pooled and frozen. Viewed from the rise of a hill, these seemed to Mike like strange, dark winter flowers trying to push through the icy crust. Beyond, he could see twenty or so scavengers, civilians and soldiers, scampering about, retrieving their pathetic tro-phies.

The cowmen eased their mounts down the hill and onto the flats where the Indian camp had been. Mule-drawn wagons creaked and rum-bled past, loaded with the rigid bodies of Big Foot's people. Men, women and children, left for dead during the three-day snowstorm, were frozen in the grotesque postures of their violent death.

They sat their mounts while the morbid caravan passed. Their horses stamped and snorted, clearly bothered. Mike pulled at his short goatee in contemplation, while Rico shook his head and whispered, *"Madre de Dios!"*

"Do you figure a horse can scent blood when it be froze?" Mike asked.

"I don' know, Señor Mike. But my horse, he knows when things ain't right."

"Your horse must be pretty smart, 'cause things ain't right. These poor folk called this down on themselves. Got the whole territory up in arms. And for what, I ask you? All that dancin' weren't gonna bring back the buffalo, nor send white folk packin' for the east. Damn their eyes! 'Tis a crime, a bleedin' crime!"

A rider in a fur cap and a sheepskin coat rode down on them from a nearby hill. Reining up, he eyed them impatiently. "If you're lookin' for the boss, that's Dawson. He's up yonder at the pit." He pointed in the direction of the hill to which the wagons were headed.

Mike nodded and raised a hand in greeting. "Thanks, but we're just passin' through. Goin' to Pine Ridge."

The young man winced in embarrassment. "Sorry, I figured you was

The scene of the Wounded Knee Massacre (Courtesy of the Denver Public Library)

contract hands, come late to the job. I'm Eb Jones, scout for the Eighth Cavalry."

"We're after sellin' beef to Uncle Whiskers," Mike said. Got a herd up on the Bad River. We would've been here sooner but for the storm."

A sudden blast of frigid air hit them like a body blow, threatening to send their wide-brimmed hats rolling across the winterscape. Mike quickly clasped his John B. upon his crown with one hand. "Did they kill 'em all?" he asked.

"Mostly. Four Hotchkiss cannon swept the camp like a spring-tooth harrow. Then they worked the ravine over yonder where the Injuns run for cover." Jones indicated a weed-filled ditch immediately west of the Indian camp. "Lasted close to three hours. Somewheres near two hundred bodies, I reckon. Course, the freeze got 'em that weren't dead outright. It ain't a pretty sight."

Mike touched the brim of his hat. "Guess we'll get on. So long, Jones." He turned his mount and said, "Come on, Rico. Let's take a look-see."

They rode up the hillside past another wagonload of misfortunate ones. What they saw on reaching the pit was worse than Mike imagined. The contract laborers were unloading the wagons by pitching the rigid corpses into a long trench about five feet deep. Some of the bodies were naked. Workmen down in the trench tucked small children and infants into gaps in the heap as one might chink a cabin wall. A crowd of locals and bluecoats loitered about watching the proceedings.

Another body, a boy maybe ten years old, landed in the trench. His expression of distress was captured in frozen testimony to his final minutes. The workers picked up his awkwardly twisted body with gloved hands. He'd been shot in the back. Suddenly, Mike felt the gorge rising within him. His vision went bright. It was as if the light of a locomotive's headlamp had blinded him. Everything was blurry. His heart raced, and he felt sure he was about to pass out. "Rico, let's get out of here quick," he said urgently, but quietly. Sightlessly gripping the horn of his saddle with both hands, he spurred his mare, and Rico led the way down to the Pine Ridge Road.

Three days later, the deal had been done. Five hundred head sold for immediate delivery to the quartermaster at Pine Ridge. Rico was happy with their success. "Is good business, no? Five hundred head and a good price too! Why you no sell cattle to *los federales* every year?"

Mike turned in his saddle and looked at Rico with a patronizing smile. "Sure, it ain't bad for such as meself, amigo. But it's nothin' to the big outfits that supply the government regular. My herd ain't big enough to meet the needs of the reservation. The agent wants several outfits deliverin' thousands of animals each. What with all these soldiers in camp, I was lucky to find the hindmost teat."

They rode on quickly. The terms of delivery were demanding. Mike had wired a message ahead to his foreman, Seymour Dillon. Told him to get five hundred plus steers cut out and start them south. He and Rico would meet up with the outfit on the north bank of the White River, close to Interior. That night he made camp on the reservation, near Sharp's Corner. With all the hostilities of late, it made no sense to bed down out in the open. Mike found a French-Canadian squaw man living on the reservation and bought shelter in a lean-to and grain for their mounts.

The night was clear, the cold stinging. The stars were nearly as bright as the moon. Four hours before sunrise, Mike rolled back and forth in his soogan. His voice cried out sporadically but wasn't intelligible. Beads of sweat broke out on his forehead despite the freezing temperature. Mike felt a hand on his shoulder, shaking him into consciousness. "Mike! *Señor* Mike! Wake up! *Tiene una pessadilla.*"

"Bejabers! Wha'? Rico, is it yourself?" He looked up into Rico's worried face, framed by the serape draped over his head against the cold.

"You have a bad dream, no, *Señor* Mike?"

"Aye, that's it. 'Twas a nightmare. I, I . . ." Mike rubbed his head and took a swig of water from a skin jug. It was partially frozen.

"You no sleep good. I hear you now four nights."

"Makin' a fool of meself, am I? I ain't had a good night's sleep since we come down Wounded Knee Creek. I can't figure it. I ain't no stranger to death. Can't be, not out here. Seen many a fella gone to glory. Still, I get these bleedin' dreams. Sioux banshees maybe, I don't know."

"We both get some sleep now, Mike." Rico retreated to his bedroll and Mike lay back down. Outside the wind was making its rounds, carrying the sounds of night—the horses wandering on their tether, the howl of a coyote paying homage to a moonlit sky. I've got to get meself some sleep. The image of the Miniconjou boy resurfaced in his mind. That lad! 'Tis his face I seen in me dreams.

Each night since they passed the battleground at Wounded Knee, Mike had the same haunting vision. First the mass grave, then the casual dumping of frozen bodies. Finally, the young boy thrown onto the heap looked straight at Mike. It was as if the boy knew him, as if he had something to say to him. But he didn't speak, just looked at him with that frozen, anguished stare. Oh, the divil with you, Mike! Go to feckin' sleep. But Mike's nights didn't improve. He delivered the herd to Pine Ridge and returned to Smithville. And each night the vision played out, over and over again.

At the Duhamel's supper table later in the week, Mike was even more laconic than usual. He ate the estimable meal prepared for him, but he did not relish it as in previous times. After Katherine cleared the table, the two friends were left to their coffee and conversation.

"*Le cauchemar*, the nightmare, she continues, no?"

Mike flushed red in the face. "Ach, Pete, let's not ruin the evenin' and a fine dinner with me own troubles."

Pete put a hand on Mike's arm. "Mike, you must get some help! You can't lose sleep every night."

Mike sneered, waving his hand disparagingly. "Help? You mean a doctor? Jaysus, Pete, I didn't break me leg, bust me appendix, or nothin' like that. What's a doctor gonna do for me? I'd be afraid he'd put me in the looney bin."

"Maybe Father Streaten at St. Mary's, he could be of some help. He's a good man, I think."

"I'm sure he is, Pete. And no offense, but what's he know about me dream and what happened down on Wounded Knee Creek? I figure 'tis somethin' from there, some evil eye. Me mother used to warn us children about the evil eye." Mike laughed morosely at the memory.

"If you got a curse from some Injun, maybe an Injun might break it," Pete offered.

"Shite, I don't rightly know. It sounds crazy, even to me own self."

Then Pete slapped his forehead in sudden recognition. "*Quelle catastrophe!*

Why didn't I think of this before? You know the priest who was at Wounded Knee? What's his name, Craft or Croft or somethin' like that? He was there, at the fightin'. Got himself near killed by an Injun knife. You read this in the *Journal*, no?"

Mike smiled wanly and sipped at his coffee. "Aye, Craft is the name. I did read about him. He's in the infirmary at Pine Ridge. Sure, he's part Injun himself. Tried to bring old Big Foot and his folks in peaceable-like. Much good it did, I'd say."

"Mike, if he knows the Injun ways real good, maybe he help you with whatever you got."

Mike resisted the temptation to dismiss his friend's suggestion. He raised his cup in salute instead. "Well, old friend, I'll be givin' it a thought or two. How's that?"

Father Francis Craft was born in New York City in 1852. His paternal grandmother was full-blooded Mohawk. His father, a medical doctor, was full of fervor for the defense of the Union in the 1860s. His enthusiasm for things martial prompted him to have young Francis schooled in the manual of arms and acquire a degree of prowess with the rifle and the pistol. At the battle at Gettysburg, the boy was wounded while serving briefly as a messenger.

In later years, Francis attended medical college, first at Columbia University, then at Louvain in Belgium. From there, he offered his services as a mercenary to the French forces in the 1870 Franco-Prussian conflict. This military service was, for Craft, mercifully brief. Still, the young adventurer hungered for the glory of the battlefield. In 1871, he recruited a band of 250 mercenaries, mostly Irish-American Civil War veterans. Together, they traveled to Cuba and fought for the Cuban rebels seeking independence from Spain.

Back in the States, Craft converted to Catholicism, and then, in 1876, entered the Society of Jesus at West Park, New York. His desire, he stated, was to serve the bereft Native Americans. Conscious of his own Mohawk ancestry, he was determined to be "an Indian to save the Indian." He chose not to remain with the Jesuit order, however, and was ordained a priest in the diocese of Omaha in 1883. Bishop Martin Marty immediately assigned Craft to be the first Catholic missionary at the Lakota reservation of Rosebud, in the Dakota Territory. There, his marksmanship, horsemanship, and rapid command of Lakota language and culture quickly won him the admiration and respect of many among the Brule population. But his Catholicism and lack of deference also earned him the enmity of the Protestant Indian Agent and the existing Episcopal missionary at Rosebud.

By the time of Wounded Knee, Father Craft had been exiled from Rosebud and later from Standing Rock. It was his determined and sustained effort to establish an order of Native American nuns that earned Craft the opprobrium of his own church and the civil authorities. Such a proposal ran counter to the racial prejudices of most whites, even those whose Christian tenets should have conflicted with such discrimination. Indians were to be ministered to, but could not minister, even to their own.

Relegated to a lonely, impoverished mission at Fort Berthold in North Dakota, Father Craft and a half-dozen Lakota novices were living in deepest deprivation. However, with the Messiah Craze underway, Craft's experience among various Lakota tribes became a valuable diplomatic asset. His services were commended to the Secretary of War to assist the government in its attempt to pacify the Lakota tribes. He arrived at Wounded Knee the day before the slaughter.

"That's him there, in the chair by the window." Having responded to Mike's query, the young Army medic hurried off to other duties among the wounded. The infirmary was a long single-story building. The February sun created pale alcoves of light at the windows along the south wall. Cots of wood and canvas were arrayed like sentries down the length of the room. Some still held soldiers caught in the crossfire of the various Army units at Wounded Knee.

Mike observed the man a moment or two before approaching. The priest wore a long black cassock over buckskin moccasins. About his waist was a sash from which hung long strands of black rosary beads. His clean-shaven face was long, adorned with a dimpled chin and piercing blues eyes. He was younger than Mike and looked quite fit. From his neck hung a large metal crucifix that he tucked partially into his cassock at midchest. He was smoking a cigarette as he read from a sheaf of handwritten papers.

Mike came forward slowly, his face drawn and his eyes sunken. He wasn't precisely sure what he should say. "Father Craft?"

The priest looked up and smiled. "Guilty as charged, friend. How can I help you?"

"I'm not certain that you can, Father. I'm not sure anyone can, but I mean to find out." Mike introduced himself and pulled another chair to the

Rev. Francis M. Craft, missionary to the Sioux and survivor of Wounded Knee (Courtesy of the Denver Public Library)

window. The priest listened intently to Mike's story, occasionally asking a question or nodding his head in understanding.

"So, you see Father, it seems there be a curse upon me, or some such thing. Me life is entirely in tatters. I can't sleep at night and I'm no good by day. I thought that you, bein' knowledgeable of Injun ways, might have some way to help."

Craft lit another cigarette and smiled politely. "The church gives little weight to curses and the evil eye. My feeling is that you are under no curse at all, my friend. What is botherin' you comes from within, not from someone else."

Mike's jaw dropped slightly, his eyes opening wide. "From within? What could be inside me to cause such visions? And how is it the burial day at Wounded Knee was the start' of it all?"

Mike puzzled a moment, his gaze following Craft, who stood up and went to the window. The priest looked aimlessly at the desolate prairie. His breath left a blanket of moisture on the cold glass and obscured his view. "I'm having my own bad nights over what happened that day," he admitted. "Between being wounded and trying to minister to the dying, I didn't witness everything. But I saw some tragic scenes. Craft drew deeply on his cigarette and then exhaled. "I can still see them when I close my eyes."

Mike nodded, feeling strangely comforted that he was not alone with this problem. "Ach . . . the sight of them innocent women and young ones! How does God let such a thing fall on 'em?"

Craft turned and looked at Mike. A cloud of smoke hovered above his head. "He let His own Son be tortured and murdered, Michael. If He wouldn't spare His own Son, how shall He spare us from the acts of evil men?" He came and sat again across from Mike. "I won't place the blame for what happened that morning. There were victims and murderers on both sides. And incompetence, my friend, kills as dead as does treachery."

"Makes us humans out to be a bad sort, eh?"

Craft shrugged at this remark. "Men do what they think they can get away with. I've seen the worst sort of so-called civilized Christians, killing and cheating these folk out of their land, their food, their very way of life."

Mike looked away, resisting any implication for himself in what the priest described.

"They do it because they know there's no one who'll stop them," Craft concluded. "Of course, the Lakota have done just as bad to other tribes."

"I'm minded of what the Brits have done to me own people back in Ireland. Sure, they took the land, destroyed our ways, starved us out!"

"It takes a righteous man to pass by what he can seize and to defend those he can crush. Are you a such a righteous man, Michael?"

Mike felt as though he'd been slapped. He sat back in his chair, unable to respond. The priest quashed his cigarette in the empty tin beside him. "Forgive me, that's an unfair question. . . . It's just that a man's conscience can be a powerful adversary. Can even cause nightmares."

It took Mike a few moments to settle himself. "God's truth, Father, me conscience ain't entirely clear. Nothin' nasty mind you. But I'll not be callin' meself a righteous man, as you say. Do you figure that a good confession will drive me visions away?"

" Maybe . . . but Jesus once said, 'First be reconciled to thy brother, and then come and offer thy gift.' Can you do that?"

Mike stood, anxious to leave. These searching questions annoyed him. He looked down on the priest and said in a hushed voice, "I don't know who. . . . there's no one person."

Craft rose from his chair and placed a hand on Mike's shoulder. The smell of tobacco was strong on him. "When a Lakota offends, he goes for the purification. It is the *Inipi*, the ceremony of the sweat lodge."

"Arrah," Mike dismissed. "Father, that's pagan stuff you're talkin'."

"It's your own free choice, friend. Remember, you're the one with the nightmares. But I've seen much that is good in what you call 'pagan stuff'."

Mike was totally flummoxed by what he was hearing. He fingered his hat brim from hand to hand. After a polite inquiry into the priest's recovery from his wound, he thanked the cleric and headed for the door.

Chapter Twenty-Two

Strikes the Ree

☩

For months, Mike resisted the advice of the missionary. He wasn't keen on the idea of the *Inipi* ceremony at all. But the vision in his nightmare would not retreat, wouldn't listen to reason or excuses. Every night, after an hour or so of sleep, the horrific scenes played and replayed.

There was also another excuse to resist. The bloody end of the Messiah movement had left the Lakota reservations in a state of dread and despair. Rumors flew—that the soldiers would come for them all eventually, that the Wounded Knee massacre had been deliberate policy of the *washichu* all along. And one didn't have to have an active imagination to find evidence that might point to such a conclusion. In these circumstances, a white man approaching the Lakota for purification might have been just enough to trigger more mayhem in return.

By early summer, Mike's powers of resistance were exhausted. His health was in decline. There was no escape, no respite from the nocturnal vision. It was sufficiently corrosive to his spirits to cause him to cast ominous glances toward his Winchester during his worst moments of desperation.

One overcast morning, he rose early at the Smithville road ranche where he often stayed when working the herd. He saddled Francie, the sorrel mare, and tied on his warbag. He was bound for Fort Pierre, or more specifically for Scotty Philip's ranche west of there. If anyone could get a hearing from the Lakota in these troubled times, it was Scotty.

As he passed through the valley of the Bad River, Mike repeatedly stopped to check the watering holes serving the open range cattle. He rode slowly through the mixed herd, picking out those with his Easy SJ brand. By noon the next day, he encountered some of the bison that Philip maintained, nearly a thousand beasts in all. Mike smiled at the sight of these remnants of the Great Northern herd. Arrah, these critters used to cover the prairie. . . . used to flow like a dark ocean.

At the ranche house, one of Philip's cowhands directed him to where Scotty was working. Mike found his friend knee-deep in mud, attempting to free a heifer immobilized by Dakota gumbo at a watering hole. A rope extended from the body of the frightened, bawling critter to the horn of his saddle. His horse was strategically placed off in thick grass. Scotty pushed at the heifer's rump while shouting commands for his horse to pull back on the rope. It wasn't working very well.

"Hold on, Scotty! I'll lead your horse away," Mike said as he dismounted. "Do you think you need another rope from me mare?"

"Hiya, Mike. One'll do it, I figure."

Relieved that he hadn't been asked to join Scotty in the mud, Mike took hold of the bridle and backed Scotty's horse through the grass. With a grunt from Scotty, the heifer pitched forward and slid through the mud to terra firma. Getting Scotty out wasn't a whole lot easier, but he was eventually roped out to dry land.

"Don't you be goin' by the land agent, Scotty. He'll make you file a claim on your britches."

Philip chuckled, but the thick coat of muck that covered him from boot to bandanna limited his amusement. "Let's get over to my place so I can shed these duds. I'm afraid once I'm dry I won't be able to move at all."

The two men went up to the house where dinner was being kept warm on the back of Sarah's cast-iron stove. She was a quiet woman, young and handsome like her husband. She was blessed with an attractive mixture of her Cheyenne mother's golden complexion and shiny black hair, and the fine, chiseled features of her French-Canadian father.

After Scotty had washed up and dressed in clean clothes, they ate and talked. Sarah busied herself with serving and, though she smiled readily, she spoke hardly at all. After they finished their dinner, she brought them more coffee.

"Can I spark that with a wee dram?" Scotty offered as he pulled a bottle from a cupboard. He poured a dollop into each cup. "You're pretty far east of your herd, Mike. Where you off to?"

"I'm after seein' you, Scotty. I need your help."

Philip looked surprised and stared at Mike for a moment. "You ain't lookin' too good, Mike. Are you sick? Shall we fetch the doctor from Pierre?"

Mike shook his head sadly. "No, no, that ain't the kind of help I'm needin'."

It took a while for Mike to lay out his story. He started from the day that he and Rico happened onto the frozen battlefield on Wounded Knee Creek, and ended with the visit he'd made to the black robe at Pine Ridge. Scotty fell back in his chair, stunned at what he heard. He ran his fingers through his short brown hair.

"You ain't had a proper night's rest for six months! No wonder you look like hell. Er, sorry for puttin' it like that, Mike."

Mike raised his empty cup. "Just the whiskey this time, Scotty." They sipped at the Scotch whiskey for a moment in silence. Then Mike asked, "Do you know what a *wichasha wakan* is?"

"Aye, it's a holy man of the Lakota. You want to find such for the *Inipi*, right? That's what this priest told you?"

"I'd be in your debt if you can help arrange it, friend. I know it's a right strange thing to ask, but I've got to try."

Scotty wrinkled his nose and then rose from his chair. "Wait right here. I need to powwow with Sarah a bit."

From where he was sitting, Mike could hear their voices, though they weren't intelligible. Sarah's voice was excited and rapid. Scotty's was soothing and slow. Mike was embarrassed. He stood to go, then sat down again. He waited some more, then stood to leave again. He was headed to the door when Scotty returned. "Look Scotty, maybe this ain't gonna work. I was fixin' to get on me way."

Scotty laughed derisively. "You can't go nowhere! Tomorrow, you and me have a ride to make down to *O-ona-gazhee*, in the Badlands. We're going to look up a fella named Strikes the Ree. Sarah says he's the only holy man who'll likely talk to whites now."

"Strikes the Ree, eh? Funny name for a holy man. Ree means Arikara don't it?"

"Aye, the Lakota and the Arikara have been bitter enemies forever. He, or his father, must have made his name in a tussle with the Arikara."

Next morning, Sarah put up some food wrapped in an oilcloth. After she handed it to Scotty, she turned and spoke to Mike for the first time since he had arrived. "You tell the *wichasha wakan* that the sister of Crazy Horse's wife sent you to him. Tell him I said to make a good *Inipi* for you."

Mike touched the brim of his Stetson and smiled appreciatively. "You are most kind, Mrs. Philip. I'll be tellin' him like you said."

The two men turned their mounts and headed southwest. To avoid having to cross the Badlands, they would need several days to get to their destination. *O-ona-gazhee* was the tableland where the ghost dancers had holed up last winter. It was the place the whites called the Stronghold. It had to be approached from the south, so they traveled through the valley of the White River for much of the way.

Though they had known each other only casually when both were freighting on the Fort Pierre-Deadwood Trail, Mike enjoyed the company of young Philip. Scotty was a 'doer', not a talker, and Mike liked that about him. With dark hair and a brush of a moustache, his youthful appearance belied the esteem in which he was held by all the stock growers. Along the way, they talked of their respective journeys across the Atlantic, both coming through Liverpool, ten years apart.

Late afternoon of the third day out, they approached the southwest corner of the Badlands. This ancient land formation encompassed over three hundred and seventy square miles of dramatic canyons and arroyos worn by millennia of wind and water. The effect was to expose layers of geological history in a rainbow of colorful strata. The lowering sun illuminated the soft purples of oxidized manganese, the orange and rust of iron oxide. Grays and tans of silt and clay lay above white volcanic ash. The beauty of the region was accompanied by a harsh topology, with steep hills, sheer cliffs, and deep ravines. It seemed devoid of

The Badlands of South Dakota (Courtesy of the South Dakota State Historical Society)

life—animal, plant or human. Scotty and Mike decided to wait until morning before searching out the narrow inlet to the mesa that formed *O-ona-gazhee*.

That night, Mike was wracked by another of his visions. Scotty heard him mumble and thrash about in his soogan, but he chose not to intervene, as he had no idea what was to be done other than what he was already doing. Strikes the Ree, if he was willing, would be better equipped to deal with these demons.

The next day as they entered the Stronghold, they rode past nearly five hundred holes, which had been dug by Lakota women the previous winter. From these, their men could have safely deployed their rifles against the *akicita tatanka* or Negro "buffalo soldiers," so-called for their black faces and buffalo robe winter coats. Mercifully for all, that battle was never fought, and the Stronghold was peacefully evacuated that January.

When they entered his camp, Strikes was seated in front of his tipi, in apparent meditation. When he heard their approach, he leapt to the front flap of the tipi and withdrew an old but serviceable Springfield rifle. Three matronly Lakota women retreated quickly from their campsite tasks and took cover behind the tipi. Beyond the campsite, two skinny ponies grazed on the mesa's new grass, prompted by a rainy spring.

"*How, Kola,*" Scotty shouted as he raised his empty hands. Mike followed his example. They sat their horses about fifty yards out of the camp. Scotty began to give assurances that they had come alone and without malice. He invoked his wife's Lakota credentials. Despite her Cheyenne-French Canadian parentage, the Lakota had raised her from an early age.

Strikes was gradually mollified. He lowered his rifle and allowed them to approach. He was a handsome man in his early sixties, bare-chested and dressed in buckskin leggings and breechclout. A string of bear claws adorned his neck and a single eagle feather stood above his two long braids of steel-gray hair. His skin was the color of tanned leather and, with its many wrinkles, resembled as much. The reluctant host demanded tobacco as soon as Mike and Scotty dismounted. Mike had a few cigars, but no loose tobacco. He gave one of these to Strikes who quickly minced it to pieces with his hunting knife. He then packed a few pinches into his red catlinite pipe, reserving the rest in a rawhide pouch.

Once they were properly seated before the near dead fire, Scotty queried the holy man as to why he had taken up residency in this dubious locale. By gestures and his rudimentary English, the older man explained, "Black Robes at Pine Ridge very angry. Strikes the Ree have three wives. Must have one wife only, to be Christian. Cannot choose which wife to keep. Red Feather cook good, no like to lie with Strikes the Ree at night. Water Singing warms my robe but burns everything she cook. Cloud Before the Wind works all day and is good with horses. She cannot cook and is not pleasing to me in the night. We come to camp of ghost dancing. Strikes the Ree keep three wives and hide from Black Robes."

After traditional pleasantries, Scotty explained the purpose of their visit. "My friend has a bad spirit, visions of the great killing in the moon of the popping trees. He asks for you to cleanse him of the evil that comes each night. He thinks that the medicine of *Inipi* is strong for this."

Strikes nodded his assent and grunted with authority, "*Hetch etu yelo!*" (It is so indeed!)

While the holy man gave instructions to his wives, Mike and Scotty conferred. They stood outside the camp, where their horses were hobbled. "I'm leavin' you to do this by yourself, Mike. Strikes don't have enough food for all of us, and you might be here a few days. I'll leave that parcel that Sarah put up. It will cover you and them while you're here."

Mike untied his warbag and accepted the food. "I understand, Scotty. You've been a real friend to come so far and place me request with Strikes. He seems friendly enough. So maybe I'll be comin' back with me hair."

A wide grin peeked out from under Scotty's moustache. "Glad to see you've kept your sense of humor. You may need it over the next few days. I just hope you come back free of what ails you. Send a wire to Fort Pierre when you get out of here. If there's more to be done, you know I'm happy to help."

Scotty went to take his leave of Strikes, and Mike looked around as they spoke. The women had been dispatched by Strikes to some tasks unknown to him. After Scotty rode out, Mike unsaddled Francie and turned her out with Strikes's two ponies.

"Come, *washichu*," Strikes demanded abruptly. "We gather *inyan* (stones) today for *Inipi*." Wondering what inyan might be, Mike followed Strikes into a nearby arroyo. The holy man moved about, selecting large stones that he threw into a pile. Mike quickly got the idea and added his own contributions. Soon they had collected fifteen to twenty good-sized stones.

Strikes suggested they sit and await the arrival of Cloud Before the Wind who would be bringing a pony and travois. He pulled a blanket over his shoulders and sat cross-legged on the ground. "*Washichu*, you tell Strikes the Ree the dream that steals sleep. Tell me of *Cankpe Opi Wakpala* (Wounded Knee)."

Mike welcomed the opportunity, not only to tell his story but also to make a better acquaintance with Strikes. The old man made no comment upon the dream. He only grunted and nodded his head gravely.

Cloud Before the Wind arrived at the edge of the mesa and the three of them transferred about half the load onto the travois. The woman then led the pony back to camp while the men resumed their resting place.

Anxious to show polite interest in his host, Mike asked, "How do you become a *wichasha wakan?*"

"*Wakan Tanka* (The Great Spirit, Great Mystery) choose holy man. No one can decide to be *wichasha wakan*. Ten winters before first vision come to Strikes the Ree. I grow to hunt and fish with my friends, and more visions come. At first, I tell no one. One day my father speak to me, but I no hear his voice. He come to me and shake me, but I no answer him. After the vision left me, father asks what sickness is upon me."

Strikes seemed to drop into a reverie. He looked out across the Badlands landscape as if seeing the memory he had conjured. Before he could continue, Cloud Before the Wind returned for the remainder of the stones. Once these were loaded, they walked back to camp behind the travois.

The other two wives had been busy. They had dug a pit on the east edge of the camp. Surrounding this pit was a lattice of pine saplings, bent and lashed into ribs and rows to create a hut about eight by twelve feet. They continued with this task while Cloud Before the Wind went to gather firewood with the travois.

That evening, Mike presented the parcel of food that Sarah had put up. His gift was well received, as they had meager provisions of their own and all had worked up a good appetite. Red Feather took charge of the dried beef and cornmeal and added these to her cook pot. When dusk fell, they gathered around the fire and ate, first the men, then the women. Water Singing made some comment that sent all three ladies into peals of laughter. Somehow Mike suspected that he was the butt of their humor. He smiled awkwardly and concentrated upon the watery concoction that served as dinner. Red Feather's reputation for culinary prowess was overdrawn, he decided. When the giggling continued, Strikes angrily ordered the women back to work.

The stones that had been gathered that day were now rolled into the campfire and additional fuel was added. The women would feed the fire continually through the night, so as to surround the stones with hot coals till morning.

While this process was underway, Mike carried a gunnysack of grain out to Francie. The evening was turning cool and a breeze was kicking up. The starry sky formed a canopy of jewels reaching from horizon to horizon. As the moon was new, it would not dominate these lesser lights tonight. He took his soogan and spread it upon the ground a short distance beyond Strikes's campsite. A case of nerves kept him awake for an hour or so, but then he dropped off. Inexplicably, he suffered no nightmare that night, sleeping right through to the predawn.

Strikes nudged him with his foot. "Dreams of Boy! Come, eat now. Soon *Inipi* will be ready." Ever since Mike described his dream the previous afternoon, Strikes began to call him "Dreams of Boy." Mike figured it was slightly more respectable than *washichu*. He looked up to see Strikes dressed only in breechclout and moccasins. The old man's body was lean and muscular.

Mike arose and pulled on his boots. A splash of water in the face sufficed for a cleanup. With his bed rolled up, he walked over to the campsite.

Red Feather presented him a bowl of who-knows-what for breakfast. It was mealy and nearly tasteless, but he figured it would keep him alive. He watched as Strikes carefully used forked deer antlers to carry glowing hot stones from the campfire to the pit in the center of the sweat lodge. The lodge was covered with layers of buckskin and blankets so as to keep in the heat and steam.

Mike had barely finished eating when Water Singing approached. She handed him a breechclout and pointed to Strikes's tipi. The cattleman was nonplussed. He hadn't previously considered how ill-suited his apparel would be once inside the sweat lodge. Reluctantly, he took the skimpy cover and turned to obey. Giggles from Red Feather and Water Singing skittered about the campsite. Mike rolled his eyes toward heaven and disappeared into the tipi.

When he emerged, Strikes was already inside the sweat lodge. Cloud Before the Wind had his little pouch of cigar tobacco from the previous day. She sprinkled particles of tobacco around the campfire and up to the entrance of the lodge. Two large skins of water sat beside the entry. Strikes came out and beckoned Mike to come forward.

The morning air raised goose bumps on Mike's exposed skin. Not having spent much time barefoot, his tender soles found every pebble and burr that littered the ground over which he passed. His skin was snowy white up to his neck, where it became brown and weathered. Strikes ushered him into the darkened lodge.

Mike's eyes gradually adjusted to the red-orange glow being thrown off by the superheated stones in the center pit. Strikes directed him to be seated upon a horse blanket placed on the left side of the fire, while he took a position opposite Mike. They were now face to face across the radiant heap between them. Strikes ordered Cloud Before the Wind to close the entrance flap; then he lit his pipe. He did not offer to share it with Mike. A period of silence ensued during which time the heat from the stones continued to warm the interior of the lodge.

Facing west, Strikes began to speak words of Lakota that Mike perceived as prayers to *Wankan Tanka*. After some minutes of this, Strikes poured a gourd of water over the stones, sending billows of steam up and over the two men. The heat went from pleasantly comfortable for a man wearing nearly nothing to a powerful intensity. More prayers and three more applications of water followed. Strikes was careful to produce more steam without squelching the heat of the stones. Sometimes his prayers were sung in an undulating voice. Mike relaxed his tense body and tried to enjoy the steam. Sweat beaded up on his skin. It was, he thought, a curious feeling of cleansing.

Strikes then turned and faced north, repeating the periods of silence, the prayers, and the water applications. After some time, he arose and left the lodge, leaving the flap open. Carefully, he re-entered with the antlers, which were holding another hot stone from the campfire outside. He repeated this several times, adding them to the pile. When he was finished, he closed the flap, walked around the pit, and assumed a position facing east.

The rhythm of the holy man's voice lulled Mike away from the details of the ceremony. Instead, he began to consider the glowing presence of each red-hot stone in front of him. With the steam and dim surroundings, each stone was no longer an object, as such, but took on a transcendental appearance. It was like looking out of a frosted windowpane, the outside scene obscured and abstracted, yet faintly recognizable. The more Mike stared at these radiant orbs, the less aware he was of Strikes's ministrations.

Jaysus! 'Tis the face. The boy! Mike looked over at Strikes as if to seek his confirmation that there was indeed a face vaguely discernible on one of the glowing stones. Never before had Mike's vision occurred in the day, while he was fully awake. But Strikes was now facing toward the south, his back to Mike. He was deeply engrossed in his incantations.

Mike returned his gaze to the vision, the dead boy staring from the heap of bodies in the snow-dusted pit. It was exactly as it had been in his dreams these many months. But the more intently he looked into the steam-shrouded pile of stones, the more the figure before him changed. The boy was soon gone, replaced with a new vision. Again, Mike looked to the holy man to get his attention, but to no avail. He resumed his focus upon a scene that he did not recognize.

There were a number of people in the emerging image. A woman was crying and leaned upon one of the men for physical support. Another man was pushing something. What's this? A cart? A wheelbarrow! Mother of God, I must be goin' daft! Mike crawled over to the water skin and poured it over his head and sweaty face. He rubbed his eyes and tried to recover his usual sensibilities. He resumed his seat and looked again into the effulgence.

The new vision was still present. But unlike the static images of his original nightmare, this was an animated scene. The group slowly progressed before him. Visible in the barrow was a bundle, a mound of gray-white shroud. Then the barrow was tipped up, and its cargo spilled out, tumbling into a large, deep pit, coming to rest upon an agglomeration of similar figures. At this, the grieving woman sank to her knees in emotional collapse. The others rushed to give her comfort.

Strikes was up again, pouring more water upon the stones. In the ensuing release of steam, the diorama faded away. Who were these people? What was this sad ritual? The holy man returned to his prayerful contemplation, assuming his original position facing Mike. Beads of liquid dripped from the extremities of Mike's goatee. His whole body was drenched in a gleaming layer of water and sweat. The heat was intense but not so intimidating as when the new stones had been added.

Mike returned his attention to the glowing stones. For several minutes, nothing was visible but the steady luminescence of the superheated mass. Gradually the image of a boy emerged; however, it was not the Miniconjou boy of the Wounded Knee burial. It was a face wholly new, yet somehow faintly familiar, as when one passes a person who is patently a stranger on a crowded city street, and yet there is a vague sense of recognition. Instead of the black shoulder-length plaits of the Indian boy, this new phantom wore a mop of shaggy, brown hair. The face! This was the strange part. The face was oddly reminiscent of Mike's brother, John. But it clearly was not John. The chin was different, more like that of his mother. 'Tis a Quinn, but none that I've ever met.

The boy appeared to be speaking, but Mike heard nothing but the chanting of the prayer song as Strikes's ceremony reached its climax. Then the old man stopped, stood, and opened the flap of hide over the entrance. Shafts of daylight dazzled Mike's eyes. He strained to focus upon this latest vision, but it was washed away in the brightness.

Clearly, they had been at the *Inipi* for hours, as the sun was high overhead. Mike felt physically drained, yet his mind raced with excitement. He needed time to think through what he had seen. He looked about the camp. The women were not there, but they had left a fresh supply of water beside the lodge. Strikes stripped naked and began to wash his body. Mike joined him in a refreshing, if rather chilling, bath. Once they were clean, they quickly dressed in their regular clothing.

"Dreams of Boy, you have more cigar? Give to Strikes the Ree. Now you are clean, we smoke pipe together." Mike retrieved another cigar from his warbag. Returning to the campsite, he offered the slightly dilapidated stogie to Strikes. The holy man immediately subjected it to his hunting knife until a pile of loose tobacco was produced. This he used to replenish the rawhide pouch. They went to the campfire. Strikes again addressed himself to the east. He sprinkled some fragments of tobacco on the ground and placed some into the bowl of his pipe.

"We give thanks to *Wakan Tanka* for the day which comes from the eastern sky." Mike stood at Strikes's side and faced east in polite reverence. Then Strikes turned in sequence to the south, the west, and the north. Each time a prayer accompanied the sprinkling and loading of tobacco. When this was complete, he touched the bowl of his pipe to the ground. "Mother Earth is source of our life and food. We give honor to her."

Pointing his pipestem to the sky, Strikes offered homage to Father Sky. After sprinkling more tobacco and placing more into the pipe, Strikes lifted his pipe straight above his head. "*Wakan Tanka*, Creator of us all, Creator of the four directions, Creator of Mother Earth and Father Sky, and of all things, we offer this pipe to You."

He retrieved a brand from the waning campfire and, sitting, lit his pipe. He took several slow draws, then passed the pipe to Mike. He showed him how to hold the pipe by placing the bowl in the palm of his hand. Mike took a few puffs and returned the pipe to Strikes. They sat beside the fire in silence for several minutes and shared the pipe.

Then Strikes spoke. "Dreams of Boy, I think bad spirit within you is gone. Now you will sleep without vision. Your heart is purified."

Mike bowed his head in acknowledgement of this verdict and smiled a little smile of gratitude. "*Inipi* is powerful medicine, as you say. Strikes the Ree makes many prayers in lodge. I'm thankin' you for that. I will trust what you say about the bad spirit."

The old Lakota leaned back and rested upon an elbow. He looked into the dying fire. "Dreams of Boy, as Strikes the Ree looks south for the Fourth Endurance, you see a vision in stones? Again, you see boy of *Cankpe Opi Wakpala*?"

Mike leaned forward, eager to share his visions and receive some interpretation from the holy man. "Aye, that I did. But he did not stay. Two new visions came. Another boy tried to speak to me, right before the *Inipi* ended." Mike related to Strikes the two new visions from the sweat lodge. Strikes shook his head, unable to offer any guidance as to the meaning of these new spirits.

"The new boy looked like he was from my family, but I did not know him. . . . Wait! Jaysus, I've got the brains of a jackass. That boy I saw must be me own brother. 'Twas me brother James what died in the workhouse back in Ireland. Sure, I was only a baby at the time." Though Mike had no personal memory of James, he could recall his father telling him of the eldest brother who was lost in the famine days. He related this now to Strikes in hopes that some meaning might be discerned.

"Brother of Dreams of Boy, he buried with many twolegged ones, like Miniconjou of *Si Tanka* (Big Foot)?"

Mike nodded excitedly. "That's it. Strikes the Ree tells the truth. In them days, the sickness was very powerful. Many people died. They must have buried them together, just like at Wounded Knee."

Strikes sat up and knocked the ash from the bowl of his pipe. He thought for a moment and then said, "Miniconjou boy call to you at night. Many times he call, but cannot speak to you. Now he find brother of Dreams of Boy to speak for him."

Mike furrowed his brow and shook his head. "You mean, in the spirit world that Injun boy and me brother are tryin' to speak to me? But, they lived far apart, in different times. They are from different tribes, Irish and Lakota."

"Dreams of Boy, you not know all twolegged ones from one tribe?"

Mike clenched his fists in frustration. "What message might it be?" he pleaded. "I ain't hearin' any of what they is sayin'."

"You must listen to brother and Miniconjou. They call to you from spirit world. This must be strong medicine."

"The Miniconjou boy, he might be foosterin' about me runnin' cattle on the reservation. Sure, I was happy to see the government take the Injun land for grazin'. That little one has rightful claim against me. But divil if I can figure what me brother James has to do with such as that."

"Dreams of Boy, you must listen. Someday, you hear brother's words." With that, Strikes rose to his feet and looked about for his wives. "We eat now. Spirit world make Strikes the Ree hungry."

After a final meal together, Mike thanked Strikes for his hospitality and for his purification. He even presented to him the last cigar from his cache. As he threw his saddle onto Francie, the ladies turned out to see him off. They giggled and waved as he left the Stronghold. With luck, he'd get to Red Shirt by nightfall, and then on to Rapid late the next day. There was a great deal to ponder along the way.

Chapter Twenty-Three

Frontier No More

✝

Mike was tired and covered in trail dust when he returned from the Badlands. His fatigue was emotional though, not physical. The experience of the *Inipi* and his visit with Strikes the Ree had been powerful and draining. To his satisfaction, Mike found that his sleep was uninterrupted by visions or nightmares. Indeed, he had slept like a dead man that night at Red Shirt. Now he was hot, thirsty, and anxious to share his good fortune with Pete Duhamel.

There were numerous saloons in Rapid City that the cattlemen favored. Among these were the bar at the Harney Hotel, Pete Sweeney's on Main Street, and the International at Main and Sixth. When Mike and his friends were looking for company, they often resorted to Patrick McCarthy's International. A native of Ireland, Pat had been an engineer for the Union Pacific. Later, he had been lured away from this career by the gold rush in the Black Hills. He did well for himself there and was smart enough to invest his earnings in diverse businesses in Rapid City, including hay and feed, wholesale liquor, land, and cattle. He had been prominent in the Black Hills

Livestock Association while it was the principal vehicle for cattle interests in the region. He didn't own the International Hotel, but acted as its manager and chief dispenser of blarney.

Mike arrived at the International as evening descended and the electric lights were coming on. These were becoming more common in town, courtesy of the Rapid City Electric Light Company. Pat McCarthy sat on the porch of the two-story hotel, enjoying his cigar and the cool of the evening.

"Hiya, Mike. Don't you look the picture of thirst? Come on in and we'll pull you a nice cold beer."

Mike stepped up to the porch and rubbed his thighs to get the blood flowing after the long ride. "I could use one—and a decent meal besides. Any of the boys about?"

McCarthy stood to go in, quashing his cigar butt in a tin of sand. "'Tis a bit early for the married lads, you know. Corb Morse is inside."

Mike only knew Corbin Morse casually, but he was impressed that Morse had been in the cattle business since he was a child, working for his father who wholesaled beeves in New York City. At sixteen, Corb left home for the cattle country of the West, where he worked as a cowpuncher for a series of Bad River outfits. Ten years Mike's junior, he was becoming a significant operator in his own right. His motto, "Corb Morse Buys and Sells Cattle," was widely recognized in the west river country, along with the gentle smile beneath his handlebar moustache. He was always ready to deal, whether for the one steer offered by a rancher in need of quick cash or for the hundreds of head moved by larger outfits. And Mike admired self-made, successful businessmen, counting himself in that category.

McCarthy escorted Mike into the bar and approached the table where Morse was awaiting his supper. "Can you stand a bit of company, Corb? I got a hungry cow chaser here."

Morse stood and reached for Mike's hand. "Why, sure I can. Looks like you've been doin' just that, chasin' cattle."

"Evening, Corb." Mike threw his hat into an empty chair. "No, I was down in the Badlands for a few days."

McCarthy sat down with the two cattlemen and beckoned the bartender. "Bring Mr. Quinn a beer and for me, a whiskey. Corb, you ready for another?"

Morse took a last swallow, pushed his empty schooner forward and nodded. "What's up with you, boys?" he asked.

Pat took the bit before Mike could reply. "You both missed a screamer last night! Tom Sweeney was in here with Charlie Buell. The counselor sure knows how to place a burr under Sweeney's saddle. First, he's joshin' him about chargin' extortionate prices over at the store. Then he opined that Tom couldn't be God-fearin' as he was gougin' folks so bad. Well, Tom jumps up and declares that ain't so."

McCarthy stood and re-enacted much of the scene. Mike chuckled at the thought of the melee between the two well-regarded friends/antagonists.

"Sweeney says, 'I got as much religion as you do, Charlie Buell!' Then Charlie says, 'I bet you don't even know the Lord's Prayer, Sweeney.'"

The bartender brought the drinks and stood by to hear the end of the yarn.

"Then Tom replies, 'I sure as hell do!' 'Well,' says Charlie, 'let's hear you recite it then.'"

McCarthy sat again, affecting a pensive posture. "Sweeney thinks for a minute and then he begins, 'Now, I lay me down to sleep—'"

At that, McCarthy's audience erupted in peals of laughter. Mike nearly choked in midgulp of his beer. The bartender shook his head and laughed as he walked back to the bar. When the suppers arrived, Pat excused himself to greet other patrons. Mike watched the door closely as he and Corb tucked into their meal, talking of cattle, the upcoming roundup, and who was buying and who was selling.

Close to an hour later, Mike saw Pete Duhamel enter the bar with several others. Mike excused himself and bid Morse a pleasant evening. In a moment, he and Pete were in a private tête-à-tête. "So, you did it, eh? You took the priest's advice after all," Pete said.

"That I did, and don't it seem to be doin' the trick? I ain't had a bad night's sleep since I met the holy man." Mike related his expedition with Scotty Philip to the Badlands. And he described the sweat lodge ceremony performed by Strikes the Ree.

But he wasn't about to tell all. He did not relate the new visions experienced during the *Inipi*, partly because he was a deeply private person, and partly because he wasn't sure what they meant. He had a pretty good idea that the message of the Miniconjou boy was a challenge to his treatment of his Oglala neighbors. Father Craft had intimated as much. But what could be the import of his long-dead eldest brother? It was something he needed time to consider. Until he figured it out, it was not for sharing, even with such a good friend.

"*Bien* for you, my friend. Katherine and me, we was sure worried."

Pete paused as the bartender delivered his beer and a coffee for Mike. When he left, Pete resumed on a different subject. "I saw you was talkin' with that Morse fella when I came in. How do you size him up? He sure is goin' like a house afire with all the stock he's been buyin'."

"I don't know him all that well. But, you know, I've got a good feelin' about him. I'm thinkin' he's a smart fella to have in our association. They say his word is like money in the bank."

Later that year, Fred Holcomb's brother, Bud, was thrown from his horse and killed. His widow, Sarah, tried to run the business for a while thereafter, but ultimately sold the 6L outfit to Corbin Morse. Together with his previous acquisitions of the Diamond 15, the GHL, and John Hart's outfit, this purchase made Morse one of the largest, non-corporate operators in the territory. He ran his herd on the open range between the Cheyenne and White Rivers. In time, Corb and Mike's shared interests in cattle and poker, and their common state of bachelorhood, cemented a real friendship between them.

In the spring of 1894, the postmaster of Rapid City received a letter addressed to Michael Quinn, care of the postmaster in Cheyenne. When Mike next came into town from Smithville, a message was waiting for him to drop by and pick it up. He made his way to the post office and collected the now rumpled envelope. "Seems the sender didn't have much idea where you could be found," the postmaster volunteered. "This looks like it's been on the road a good while."

Mike nodded and gasped as he looked at the postmark. It was from Lawrence, Massachusetts. Oh sweet Jaysus, what could this be about? He walked outside, his palms sweaty and his heart racing. This letter was surely from the family he had abandoned twenty-eight years ago. It could only be bad news, he figured. He sat on the rough wooden bench in front of the post office, absorbing the warmth of the sunlight. It felt good in the still-cool

March weather. He pushed back his John B and looked at the envelope for a few moments. From the handwriting, he guessed it was from Roderick. He ran a finger under the flap and pulled out the pencil-inscribed pages.

Dear Michael,

I pray that this letter reaches you and finds you in good health. It has been so long, we've wondered sometimes if you are dead. As you may surmise, this letter is written in sorrow. Our dear brother John has passed away. His long years at the mill had left him without his breath. Now he is with our beloved mother and father and little Elizabeth, in the arms of Lord. John left Catherine; three sons George, John, and Frank; and two daughters, Margaret and Theresa. I imagine this long period of silence is your punishment for Jane and me. You may be surprised to learn that our life together has been a hard time, despite our great affection. God gave us twelve children, but took back seven of these in early childhood. Such losses have been a heavy burden, especially for Jane. The doctor says I have the same cotton lung what killed our brother. I can't work no more. Our son James cares for us and is a great blessing.

It is our great hope that you will put away the hurt of past years. Your family misses you and still awaits your return.

Your brother,

Roderick

Mike turned his shattered face away from a passerby. Tears coursed down his ruddy cheeks and became lost in his graying beard. He recalled his last night with John and the gift of funds he had provided. It seemed an age ago. Crushing the pages in his hand, he stood and walked briskly toward the Harney Hotel.

Open-range cattle ranching became increasingly difficult in the mid-to-late 1890s. The newly formed Western South Dakota Stock Growers Association (WSDSGA) had replaced the old Black Hills Association, and its members were being squeezed by low beef prices. Many blamed the administration of Grover Cleveland and its low tariff policy. But one also had to look at the steady stream of homesteaders carving up the public lands into fenced parcels, deterring the free roaming of large mixed herds. Increasingly, cattlemen were filing claims or buying acreage and stringing it with barbed wire, as "the nesters" did. Others were not so patient.

One night at the Harney Hotel, Mike Quinn, Pete Duhamel, C. K. Howard, Fred Holcomb, and Corbin Morse were gathered for one of their frequent games of penny ante poker. Mike could tell something was up with Pete, because the old "Frenchie," now in his early sixties, wasn't his usual talkative self.

Howard was complaining about the increasing cost of dipping cattle for ticks and scabbies, and Mike noted how pervasive the mosquitoes were after recent rains. Then Pete put his cards down and took a drink. "Well, my friends, sometimes I think my herd, she's too much trouble for a fella my age." Howard, five years his senior, glared at Pete. "Oh, I ain't sayin' we're too old, C. K. I'm of a mind to let some fella take the whole shootin' match off my hands."

Corbin Morse shuffled the cards and said nothing. But Mike was not so calm at what he'd heard. He turned in his chair to meet Pete eye to eye. "Why, Pete? You've got young Alex to handle most of the business. Sure, he's quite the cattleman himself!"

"Yes, Alex, he's a fine boy and plenty of help to me. But he can't put the open range back in place, eh? No, we have talked and pretty much agreed to sell out. Might put a herd up in eastern Montana. You know, get away from all these homesteaders and their petite farms."

Fred Holcomb leaned foward and stared at Pete in disbelief. "You thinkin' on movin' the family up there to Montana?"

Pete laughed and shook his head. "*Mon Dieu*, no! My Katherine, she would kill me. We place a herd and hire some cowpunchers to tend it. We stay here in Rapid."

The friends, somewhat relieved, went silent for a minute as they studied the hand that Morse had dealt. Then Mike spoke up. "Well, since you are makin' a big announcement, Pete, I may as well be tellin' me own news."

Holcomb became visibly disturbed. His voice raised an octave as he protested, "Shit, Mike, don't tell me you're gonna quit the stock business too!"

Mike laughed and threw his hand over his friend's shoulder. "Arrah, don't you be worryin' over me. No, I just thought you fellas might be interested about me filin' papers at the courthouse." He paused momentarily, teasing their interest. "I'm after becomin' a real citizen of these United States!"

C. K. raised his glass in celebration. "It's about time, you old bull nurse! What? Did you find out that you still had to pay taxes?"

"I was thinkin' that after livin' here for thirty-odd years, maybe I should be gettin' me vote and such. After all, 'tis the new age, ain't it?"

Morse threw his cards into the center. "Hell, you had me goin' there for a minute, Mike. Your deal, C. K."

Several weeks later the *Rapid City Daily Journal* carried the headline, "Huge Deal for Cattle and Land." It disclosed what some might have guessed. Morse had made the winning offer to "set Peter Duhamel afoot." The cattle, horses and acreage netted Pete $185,000 in cash. Morse then wasted no time in buying out Alex Duhamel's shares and those of Pete's son-in-law, Max Babue. The total value of these deals was over a quarter of a million dollars. Morse claimed he never knew how many head of cattle passed hands, as the book accounts were the basis of the deal. But in successive years, he never shipped less than 10,000 head. In one year, he shipped or bought 36,000 animals.

But Morse's demeanor never changed, and his willingness to be his brother's keeper never dimmed. Corb was now the biggest independent operator in the region. He moved in exalted social circles, and his expansive ranch house became a place of hospitality and refuge to such luminaries as Theodore Roosevelt, Diamond Jim Brady, railroad presidents, actors, and opera divas. He collected rare Indian relics, paintings by Remington and Russell, and precious and semiprecious gems. His new fortune did not mean changing out his old friends, however. Whenever in town, he still looked forward to the penny ante poker games at the Harney Hotel.

One such evening occurred in May 1905. Mike, Corb, Pete and Fred were riding out a nasty late-season blizzard. For days, the snow had drifted, banking up against the side of the building. The windows were thickly frosted in a translucent white crust. The hotel staff was gradually reduced to a minimum as the storm worsened and those with families left for home. It was nearly midnight, and the card players helped themselves to whiskey and a pot of coffee.

"Damn that wind! Like to blow this old box clear to Pierre," Fred complained. He got up and peered through a window. "Can't see a damn thing. You know, poor Gene is up on the Belle Fourche tonight."

Pete looked up from four fours, repressing a smile. "Seems awful late to be gettin' such a blow. Why, the new grass, she is well up already and here comes another snow! I'm glad I ain't tryin' to hold a herd tonight."

Mike laughed. "Don't be rubbin' it in," he said. "Besides, what are you goin' to do with all the capital you're sittin' on since you quit that herd up in Montana?"

Duhamel rubbed his now clean-shaven chin and looked at his cards again. "I ain't decided yet. Might go into bankin'. There's a business that don't mind the nesters boom. Can't say as I'm done with cattle entirely, though."

Holcomb got up and poured himself more coffee. "I hear there's good range land goin' cheap down in Cuba. Once Corb's friend, Teddy, kicked the Spanish out, they put out the welcome mat for American investors. Ain't that right, Corb?"

Morse voiced his agreement absently as he studied his cards. "That's what I hear. But with cattle goin' for over thirty dollars a hundredweight in Chicago, I ain't sure you have to go to Cuba to make money ranchin'."

The card game came and went as the old friends talked into the night. About twelve-thirty the coffee was cold and the bottle on the table was nearly empty.

Bam! The front door out in the lobby blew open and everybody at the table jumped at the noise. "Jaysus, that wind! I'll get it." No sooner had Mike started out than a snow-covered figure appeared at the parlor entrance. The bedraggled stranger dropped icy gloves to the floor and reached to untie the scarf that held his fur hat in place.

"Bill!" Morse jumped to his feet and approached his younger brother. The men helped Bill peel away his ice-encrusted coat. "Get him a drink, Mike," Fred said as he headed off to the kitchen. "I'll see if there's any more coffee."

They sat Bill down at the vacated chair. His face was nearly blue except where icy whiskers covered. "Corb, I . . ."

"Now, Bill, you just take a minute to thaw out," Corb cautioned. "Where's that drink?" Mike handed over a glass of whiskey.

Bill sipped at first, then drained the glass. His hands were red and trembling. Drops of water clung to his eyebrows as the snow melted. "Corb, I . . . I come up from Rapid Valley. There's bad news."

Every face at the table was dead serious, every eye on the shivering young man before them. "Someone hurt?" Corb asked nervously.

"No, the . . . the herd. It's gone, drifted with the storm. The line crew says a bunch of 'em went over the wall!"

The wall was an abrupt gash in the prairie on the edge the Badlands. In places, the ground dropped off over a hundred feet. A fall would mean certain death, to man or beast.

"Jaysus, my beeves share the same range. God save 'em," Mike prayed.

Bill accepted coffee from Holcomb and cradled the cup in his frozen hands. He looked at his older brother, waiting for a reaction, or perhaps an explosion. "We had eleven thousand head on that range as of last roundup. The boys figure more'n half is gone."

Corb sat back in his chair, his head bowed. No one said a word. This was clearly a devastating, financial loss. Then Morse raised his eyes and looked around the table and smiled wanly. "Well, easy come, easy go."

In subsequent days, it was discovered that Mike Quinn and C. K. Howard also had significant losses, though nothing on the scale of Morse's loss of 7,000 head.

The Buell building, a two-story Italianate structure with a Moorish dome at one corner, was the most distinctive building in town. Mike, Pete and Fred were enjoying a most pleasant afternoon in late June while waiting outside for the attorney whose name adorned the landmark.

"I'm still thinkin' on runnin' cattle down in Cuba. The land is cheap, with good grazin' too," Fred Holcomb reminded his friends.

"You wouldn't have the risk of a blizzard killin' half your herd," Mike observed.

Pete tapped his walking stick impatiently. "Hold your horses! What do you boys know about Cuba anyhow? Seems you might trade problems you know for them you don't."

Fred swatted at flies with his folded *Journal*. "We don't have to invest if it don't look good," he said. "But I, for one, aim to go down there and look the place over. It can't hurt to look, Pete. What do you say?"

Mike placed a hand on Pete's knee. "You know, you're sitting on that passel of money, just earnin' what interest the banks in Chicago offer. Sure, you could do better if that capital was invested in beef."

"*Assez! Ça suffit,*" Pete exclaimed. Fred and Mike looked at each other, unable to discern the old man's meaning, only his frustration.

"Oh, we could go without you," Fred said, "but you have all that money and bankers in Chicago who'll jump to, if you ask 'em."

Mike Quinn with his friend Pete Duhamel (Courtesy of The Journey Museum, Rapid City, S.D.)

"I make no promise!" Pete replied. "But I talk to my man at the Northern Trust. Perhaps he will have a correspondence with someone in Cuba. We see."

After roundup that year, Mike, Fred, and Pete found themselves on a train, on the first leg of their trip to Cuba. Mike hadn't been through Chicago in nearly forty years. He had heard of the city's great fire, but he wasn't prepared for the explosive growth and the grim industrial conditions that had replaced the old Chicago. As they passed through the outskirts of town, they saw several of the new horseless carriages that were proliferating in the major cities.

"Jaysus, this place makes Liverpool look like a feckin' garden," Mike said. He shook his head as they rolled past stockyards, slaughterhouses, and smoky factories.

They had little time to spend looking around. With delays along the way, they had to make a rapid connection to their train destined for the port of New Orleans. From there, a steamer would carry them to Havana.

Wherever they went in New Orleans, they and the locals traded curious glances. Three middle-aged businessmen, dressed in suits, cowboy boots and Stetsons seemed a bit incongruous to the citizens of the Crescent City. Undaunted, the travelers spent the two-day interval before their embarkation enjoying the narrow streets of the French Quarter, the gardens of Jackson Square, and the exotic cuisine at Gallatoire's. Pete especially enjoyed hearing his native tongue used with such frequency throughout the city. Still, some aspects took them aback. "I wouldn'a dreamed there's so many *Nègres* all in one place," Pete observed.

Mike pulled at his collar. "Don't bother me half as much as the wet in the air. Me shirt's stickin' to me soon as I put it on."

Their ship, the *Andalusia*, was not the fine passenger steamer they had envisioned. Rather, it was an aging freighter that had seen many years of transatlantic service between Spain and Cuba during the last decades of colonial rule. To Mike, it seemed improbable that it would survive such a voyage in its current condition. In late September, they boarded the rusting vessel in the relative cool of early morning. Their cabins were small and not well kept, but these men had lived rough for years. They consoled themselves that the voyage would not be lengthy.

After less than three days on a placid Gulf, the *Andalusia* docked in the port of Havana. The harbor quarter was a different world to men who'd spent forty or fifty years on a frontier of big sky, grassy plains, and herds of cattle. They were overwhelmed at the color, the energy and the diversity of the dilapidated Cuban capital. Black women in colorful dresses carried baskets of strange fruits and vegetables upon their heads. Youngsters dove off the docks into the filthy harbor. Donkey carts carried freight from the *embarcadero* to warehouses or directly to local markets. Longshoremen, in a spectrum of racial hues, sang their way through the loading and unloading of cargo. Mike had little knowledge of Spanish, save a few phrases he'd picked up from Texan cowhands such as Rico Sandoval.

"They said Señor Navarro would meet our ship, but I got no idea what he's gonna look like," said Pete. He stood at the head of the pier leaning upon his walking stick while the other two sat on their suitcases.

"I expect he'll have an easier time findin' us than the other way 'round," Fred answered.

In about ten minutes, a middle-aged man in a white linen suit hurried through the crowd and removed his straw boater. "Señores, welcome. I am Ernesto Navarro de Bosque. You may be Señor Duhamel and colleagues, no?" The Spaniard's demeanor was friendly but harried. "*Mucho gusto.* I regret your having to wait, but the steamer docked a bit earlier than scheduled. A *maletero* will take your bags to the hotel. Come, I have a carriage waiting across the plaza."

Glancing nervously at their abandoned luggage, the three visitors followed Señor Navarro through the crush of laborers, street vendors, animals, and beggars. The streets were littered with an array of animal, vegetable, and mineral debris, which dissipated somewhat as their carriage moved away from the docks. In minutes, they were delivered to the shady central courtyard of a venerable but clean hotel in Avenue San Isidro, about halfway between the port and the Estación Central de Ferrocarriles, the rail station.

Señor Navarro assisted them in getting registered and then excused himself. "You will be tired from your journey. Perhaps after a siesta you will do me the honor to join Señora Navarro and me for dinner. There is much to discuss. The management at Northern Trust was most explicit as to your objectives. I trust you will be pleased with the arrangements I have made."

Mike whispered into Pete's ear, "Ask him about our suitcases."

Navarro smiled. "I believe, Señor Quinn, you will find your bags have been delivered to your rooms. I will send the carriage for you promptly at nine o'clock. Till then, I wish you *buenas tardes.*"

As they walked up the stairs, Mike was also worried about the schedule. "We ain't even leavin' for supper till nine o'clock! I ain't gonna last that long. We better get a regular meal about five-thirty. Nine o'clock's damn near me bedtime!"

"I was thinkin' the same thing," Fred agreed. "Fella like to starve by then."

Pete shook his head in despair at his cowboy friends. "Now, boys, this ain't Dakota. These Spanish folk got their own ways. If you can stay awake for poker, you can stay up for Navarro's supper."

The Navarro residence was a large *vivienda* at the top of a distinguished building on a broad avenue. The business agent had come from Spain thirty years ago to represent several Spanish *empresas* in their Cuban commercial affairs. After the ill-fated revolution and the Spanish-American war, the colonials had left and business had fallen off. Now Navarro offered his services to American clients.

Upon their arrival, an attractive black-haired woman in a colorful skirt and white blouse met them at the entrance. *"Buenas noches, señores. Por aquí."*

Fred swept the grey Stetson from his head and bowed slightly. "Good evening, Mrs. Navarro."

The woman giggled and flushed with embarrassment. *"Soy la criada, señor. La señora está arriba."*

Pete dug his elbow into Holcomb's side. "Take it easy, pardner, she's the maid."

The real Señora Navarro, Josephina Theresa, was also attractive, but with a mature elegance born of her native Spain. Her dark brown hair was pulled back in a bun and her dress was a beautiful deep blue, set well off the shoulders. Over cool aperitifs, she made several comments that left them with little doubt that she'd rather be back in Spain permanently.

"You gentlemen must excuse the deplorable conditions which we have now in *Habana* under the regime of President Palma. It was much better before the war."

The muscles in the Señor's jaws visibly tightened. "I'm afraid Cuba was never a high priority for the Spanish colonial office," he explained. "As you saw today, much of *Habana* is in great disrepair. The new regime is trying to recover some order, but there is still much confusion and not a little corruption."

Señora Navarro looked away, seemingly dismissive of her husband's excuses.

"No need to apologize, Señor Navarro," Pete replied. "These things, they take time, no?"

"You are most kind, Señor Duhamel. But I must also admit that my wife misses the refinements of the mother country. As for me, I have been here so long, there is nothing left of the Spain I once knew. Still, we will never be real *Cubanos.*"

"I'm sure that our American gentlemen understand," Josephina cut in. "Surely you all have family and friends from whom you would not wish to be separated. Is that not true, *señores?*"

All three nodded in agreement. But Mike felt like he'd been punched in the stomach. Sure, Fred and Pete have wives and children to whom they will soon return. What have I got but an empty hotel room? Mike addressed his hostess.

"Señora Navarro, I understand the pain of separation what you have mentioned. You see, all me family, them that's still livin', is back in the east, in the States. I figure it must be harder yet when you have a whole ocean between here and your home."

The señora gave Mike a look of gratitude, then threw a knowing glance at her husband.

A manservant, apparently the Navarro's butler, stood in the doorway and announced the evening meal, "Señor, *todo es listo.*"

The dinner was sumptuous, if drawn out. The numerous courses and fine wines were a revelation to their guests. Afterward, Josephina excused herself and the men were presented with Cuban cigars, the like of which the Dakotans had never experienced. Navarro rolled out a map upon the dinner table.

"I have surveyed many opportunities for land suitable for the cattle ranching, Señor Duhamel. While various provinces have such grazing business, the largest and best of these is here, in Camaguey."

"How far out of Havana are we talkin', Señor Navarro?" Fred asked.

"It is a journey of two hundred and fifty miles more or less. The rail line from *Habana* is rather direct to the city of Ciego de Avila. If everyone is agreed, we can depart tomorrow. The next day, we should begin to inspect the properties I have listed here. Prices for grazing land have recovered somewhat from the days of the Spanish withdrawal, but they still compare favorably to those in the United States."

The next morning, Señor Navarro collected the bleary-eyed cattlemen from their hotel at the civilized hour of ten o'clock. From there, it was a brief ride to the Estación Central. The narrow-gauge railway was as worn and battered as the rest of Havana, but the train left promptly at 10:45 and soon they were moving through the countryside at thirty miles per hour.

To the north, low mountains hugged the coast, while in the south and east, green stands of sugar cane were under attack by an army of black laborers wielding machetes. The bare backs of the field hands glistened with rivulets of perspiration.

Mike mopped his brow. "'Tis hot enough in this railroad car, I'm thankin' the good Lord it ain't meself out there slashin' away with that big knife," He wasn't alone in his sentiments, as everyone had doffed his coat and collar for the journey.

Señor Navarro looked up from what had been a brief siesta. "The harvest has recently begun, Señor Quinn. They must bring in the cane before the rainy season is upon us."

Two hours after sunset, they pulled into the sixteenth century town of Ciego de Avila. It was a town of old colonial architecture, but its beauty went unrevealed in the darkness. Only the occasional lantern lit the streets as their carriage delivered them to a modest hotel. When they arrived, Pete suggested they take a light supper and get right to bed. The impending visit to the cattle country would begin early in the morning and everyone was fatigued.

It took several days to survey all the properties Señor Navarro had identified. One afternoon, they settled upon a parcel of 230 hectares of prime grassland, northwest of Ciego de Avila. Everyone was pleased with the selection. The land in Camaguey was richly pastured and large herds of cattle could be found in all directions. Puffy clouds scudded against a background of brilliant blue above the coastal range in the distance. "Reminds me of the edge of the Black Hills," Fred commented. "You know, rich plains with them little ole mountains off aways."

Pete glanced again at the sheet of figures that he and Navarro had calculated. "She's a good parcel all right, especially at $5.00 an acre."

"Do not forget *Señores*, the railway has a line north to Moron. Shipping cattle to market will not require driving them to Ciego de Avila."

Mike looked up from his perusal of Pete's calculations. "Perhaps, Señor Navarro, you will help us find a bossman for the operation before we return to Havana?"

"Yes, of course, Señor Quinn. I will make inquiries when we get back to Ciego. I'm confident there are many good *vaqueros* in the area. After all, this has been cattle country for over three hundred years."

Chapter Twenty-Four

Facing Changes

✝

The return voyage took them from Cuba to Galveston. From there, they journeyed by rail via Ft. Worth, cutting across West Texas, and proceeding up to Denver. Fred stared out the window as they passed through the desolate landscape of scrub brush, rocks, and naked soil. "They say our west river country looks empty. But, boy, we ain't got nothin' on West Texas."

The "luxury" compartment they shared was cramped and hot. Pete looked up from the magazine in his lap and surveyed the scene out their window. "You got that right. She's a poor country, Texas. I sure'll be glad to get back to Dakota—clear, cool mornings, the first dusting of snow on the prairie."

Mike made no comment. Instead, he pulled down the brim of his Stetson and tried to sleep, but the conversation made it difficult. He shared Pete's anticipation for home, though his dialogue with Señora Navarro had left him acutely aware of the solitary life he would take up again upon their return. Traveling with his two good friends for weeks on end had reminded him of the virtues of family life.

The trip was slow and uncomfortable. By the time they reached Denver, they were dead tired of riding the rails. Pete suggested a two-day layover and the others readily agreed. It had been almost forty years since Mike had first visited Denver as a greenhorn bullwhacker, and longer still since Duhamel first took up the cattle business just east of there. In the old days, Denver had been little more than the jumping off point for the Colorado mining camps. Now the city overwhelmed them with its size and economic diversity.

"I don't believe I could ever find me way to Elephant Corral nowadays." Mike looked up and down the paved streets of the city center. "That was the main place for a bullwhacker's holiday back in '66."

"It ain't likely to be anymore," Fred replied. "Them days died with the bull trains."

In fact, the old Elephant Corral, or what was left of it, was only about a dozen city blocks from where they were staying. The splendid Brown Palace was Denver's flagship hotel. Its lobby was dominated by an impressive eight-story atrium, where the columns and wainscoting were constructed of a pale golden Mexican onyx. At the top of the atrium was a beautiful, stained-glass ceiling. Mike was uncomfortable with the tariffs at the place, but Pete had insisted on a proper stay for prosperous businessmen.

Over dinner at the hotel, they discussed how they would stock their new Cuban ranch once the paperwork closed on the purchase. Señor Navarro had suggested that he could procure stock for them locally, but they had declined the offer. "I wasn't real impressed with the looks of them Cuban steers," Fred complained. He pushed aside his plate after vanquishing a huge porterhouse steak. He was a big man, and it was easy to see how he got that way. "Looked a shadow of a healthy white-face out of Dakota."

"Aye," Mike agreed. "But our northern beeves won't fare so well in that heat. Maybe Texas beef would do well. Don't you think so, Pete? 'Tis hot enough in Texas, maybe hotter than in Cuba."

"That's good thinkin', but we need to figure in the cost of shipment," Pete replied. "By the time we transport a herd of cattle to Cuba, our profits may well disappear."

Pete pulled a pencil and a scrap of paper from his coat pocket and began to do the sums. When he finished, he took a sip of wine and paused in contemplation. "I say we begin with a small number of Texas cattle and grow the herd from there. She will take a few years before we start shippin' beef, but our quality will be the best on the Havana market."

Mike wasn't entirely comfortable with the longer period before they began to achieve any return. But, he admitted, it had the advantage of limiting the capital employed. By evening's end, all agreed to adopt Pete's proposal.

The men left Denver as the cold of winter was arriving on the plains. The final leg of the journey, from Cheyenne to Rapid City, brought back further memories for Mike, as they traversed the East Wyoming country where he had once freighted with Billy Mayhew. One more unwelcome reminder of times past, and friendships lost, he didn't need.

The open range was all but gone for history. Mike had filed for homesteads in eastern Pennington County back in 1900 and 1901, and was now grazing his cattle on these claims. He had built a modest ranch house and ensured that it would be consistently inhabited for the requisite five years for the claims to prove and make the land his outright. But Mike preferred living in Rapid City to be among his friends. An Elks Lodge was established in town, and this became the principal venue for their poker games.

Mike's foreman, Seymore Dillon, an Iowa-born cowboy with Irish roots, lived on the place full time. Dillon and another employee, a Texan ranch hand named Cilton Lucket, had daily responsibility for the herd. No longer were many cowboys and a big roundup required to sort out a mixed herd on an open range. Increasingly, barbed wire kept each herd of cattle segregated. When the season for shipping came, a number of extra cowboys would be hired on for the drive to Brennan.

Mike's selection of the two hundred and eighty acres for his ranch demonstrated his considerable foresight. In 1907, the new rail route of the Chicago & Northwestern from Pierre to Rapid City would pass within a few miles, raising the value of his land considerably. He admitted to his friends, that it was no great feat on his part. "If you made as many trips from Pierre to the Hills as I did make in me freightin' days, you wouldn't find it difficult to choose a good route for the railroad."

On the 20th of June, Mike's waiting period ended, and he was sworn in as a citizen of the United States, forty-two years after his arrival at Castle Garden in New York Harbor.

Along with his closest friends, Pete, Fred, and Corb, there was Joe Horgan, a dandy in white gloves who carried a gold-headed cane, and John Kammerer, a cattleman friend who shared the Meade County range when Mike operated from Smithville. Also present were Frank McMahon and Ike Humphrey, former freighters and now fellow cattlemen. And, of course, there was C. K. Howard, the senior member of the group at seventy-two. These aging pioneers, ex-freighters, and cattlemen were, for Mike, a proxy for the family he had missed for so many years.

When the oath of allegiance was recited, Mike couldn't repress a smirk when the clerk of the court asked, ". . . and you hereby do forswear and renounce any allegiance to King Edward VII of Great Britain?"

Mike looked at Pete Duhamel and winked. How am I to renounce what I never did have? Still, I'm happy to do, been waitin' a long time.

When the ceremony was completed, everyone stepped out onto the steps of the Pennington County Court House and offered their congratulations. The weather betokened the spirit of the occasion as the green of spring lay upon the prairie and the bright sunshine still lacked the intense heat of the approaching summer. Someone called for remarks by the guest of honor, and Mike was happy to comply, if briefly.

"'Tis a fine day for to become an official citizen and have so many of me friends come to see. Sure, this citizenship is hard work and raises a powerful thirst. If you gentlemen would care to join me at the International, I'm standin' for drinks."

Horgan raised his gloved hand, "This certainly is a special day, as my good friend here don't stand for drinks just every whipstitch."

Laughter rolled through the group till Pete Duhamel tapped his walking stick upon the stonework steps and called for quiet. "There's more to celebrate," he said. "Right here at this courthouse, a few weeks ago, a filing was made to establish a new town. It's about sixty-five miles east of here, right near Mike's Easy SJ. Now, I have it on good authority that this here town, she's gonna be named Quinn, South Dakota! The perfect way to honor our newest citizen!"

A cheer of huzzahs went up and Mike blinked away emergent tears. He was genuinely moved by the fact of becoming a real citizen, and by the recognition by his friends.

As they walked the few blocks to the International, C. K. Howard took Mike's arm. "Mike, when this hooray settles down, I got some business to jaw on with you."

"Of course, C. K. I'd be pleased to. Shall I come around in the mornin'?"

It was another fine day as Mike rode up the dirt track to the Howard ranche house near Smithville. Wild flowers of blue flax, pink prairie violets, and white starlilies carpeted his approach that morning.

C. K. was sitting on the porch, waiting for him. "I see you didn't waste no time getting out of town," he observed.

"'Tis a good day for a ride." Mike dismounted, led his horse to the shade of a bur oak, and hobbled her. After fetching her water, he climbed the steps of the porch. "How you doin' today, C. K.?"

"Aw, my leg's actin' up again." He made no effort to rise in greeting. He motioned Mike to the chair beside him. "Other'n that, I'm good. Catherine's got some lemonade, if you fancy some."

Mike dropped his Stetson on a table and wiped his brow with his bandanna. Howard's granddaughter, now in her late teens, appeared with a cold pitcher of lemonade and two glasses. After a few pleasantries, the shy young woman retired to the house.

The graying Howard wiped lemon pulp from his walrus-style moustache. "You know Henry Dawson, Mike?"

Mike paused and then shook his head. "Nothin' more than to say howdy to at the Association meetin's. I know he's got a store down at Pine Ridge. . . . and he bought the U+ from you a few years ago."

"That's right. Dawson's a good fella. He's slated to succeed me as President of the Association next time."

Mike sipped his lemonade, unsure of where all this was leading. Howard got up and paced a bit. He flexed his knee and began rubbing the thigh.

"You all right, C. K.?"

"It's tolerable, Mike. I just need to get the blood movin'. . . . Anyway, Dawson come to me awhile back and says he aims to expand the U+. He'd like some folks to throw in with him, as investors. I said I'd pass, but he asked if I'd recommend some cattlemen to talk with."

Mike drained his glass and placed it on the table. "How much capital is he lookin' for? I'm a bit tied up presently."

Howard eased himself back into his chair. "He didn't rightly say, but it could be considerable. He's hopin' to get several partners involved."

Mike glanced off at the eastern horizon where cottonwoods traced the twists and turns of the Cheyenne River. After a minute of quiet, he asked, "Who else have you mentioned to him?"

"No one. I'd like your views on that since you might end up partners. It oughta be someone easygoin'. Henry's got a temper that can sometimes be tricky."

Mike raised his eyes in contemplation. "John Hart might be a good one. . . . then, there's Ike Humphrey. He's a solid cattleman. If I was goin' in, I'd be pleased to have Ike along."

"Either one would be fine, I'm sure. I told Henry you'd drop in on him, if you was interested at all."

Mike was interested. Or more accurately, he was increasingly disinterested in the Cuba ranch partnership. It was so distant and the time to build up the herd was taking so long. *Might as well have me money in a bank. Could be the U+ deal would provide a good excuse to sell out me Cuba shares.*

A week later, Mike rode down to Pine Ridge. He hadn't been to the agency since his meeting with Father Craft fifteen years before. The days of Lakota unrest were past. Now an overwhelming spirit of helplessness and desolation pervaded the reservations. Mike could feel it as he rode past the loafers at the agency office. Some had obviously been to Rushville, a Nebraska bordertown south of the reservation. There, unscrupulous whites made an industry of selling alcohol to the Indian trade.

Mike found Dawson in his office, at the back of his store. Henry Dawson, or *Pasu Hanska* (Long Nose) as the Oglala called him, greeted Mike cordially. He was seven years younger than Mike, a big man with a ready smile. He had come to the reservation as a government clerk and within two years bought out the reservation trading post. Mike figured he had been living and working at Pine Ridge for almost twenty-five years. With his wife,

Fannie, and three surviving children, the Dawsons had become fixtures of the reservation community. Besides owning the reservation store, Henry's cattle holdings were extensive.

After a few minutes of social courtesy, Mike probed the U+ proposition, cautiously searching Dawson's eyes. He hadn't yet discovered the logic of the deal. "What I don't understand, Henry, is why you need investors at all. You have the assets to command almost any figure from the banks. What's the need for folks like me?"

Dawson spread his hands on the desk before him. A faint smile crossed his lips. "You're right, it ain't your money I need. It's land. With all the homesteaders these days, I've been driven back to a bunch of reservation leases. They just ain't big enough and they ain't all in one place. There's no efficiency in mindin' the herd or in shippin' to market. What I want is partners with land—and a bit of capital."

Dawson rose from his desk. "Let's get a stretch of the legs. It's fine outside."

Oglala women and children eyed them silently as they walked the dusty streets between the cluster of rough wooden, single-story agency buildings.

"I've got a lot of me capital tied up in this Cuba cattle ranch," Mike volunteered, "but I've been thinkin' that I might sell me shares. Are you in a big rush about the investment?"

Dawson leaned over a hitching rail and acknowledged each passerby with a wave. "Not really. Maybe when this year's sales come through. Besides, I figure I need to find me at least one more partner in this. Anyone you think I should consider?"

Mike offered his suggestion of Ike Humphrey, and Dawson promised to speak with him soon. As they made their way back to the store, they passed a wood-frame building under construction. "What's goin' up here, Henry?"

"They run out of space at the old school. This will be new classrooms for the kids here."

Mike smiled and looked at the pile of lumber stacked nearby. "Mind if we take a look?"

"No, I got plenty of time."

Mike walked up to the building site where white carpenters were framing the walls.

"What's your interest, Mike?"

"Nothin' special. It's just that it would be nice if these young'uns had a better chance than what we left their folks. Do you think they're needin' any help at all?"

Dawson pushed his hat back and smiled. "You might be gettin' a bit old to go up on a ladder and help put on the roof."

Mike dropped his eyes and said in quiet tones, "Sure, sure, but maybe there's somethin' I can do, somethin' they yet need."

"I ain't sure what, but there are lots of things they need that the government ain't goin' to provide. You might want to check at the agent's office."

After taking his leave of Dawson, Mike stopped in to see his old friend, John Brennan, who had been named the Indian Agent at Pine Ridge back in 1900. Brennan seemed surprised to receive the visit and further surprised at Mike's query.

"The Bureau is payin' for the new schoolhouse, Mike. But they didn't budget funds for books, nor supplies. Even furniture is lackin'. But that's the goverment way, ain't it. They give with one hand and take away with the other. I wrote to Washington, but got no response."

Mike shook his head sadly. He pulled a pencil from his vest pocket and touched its tip to his tongue. "Let's make a list, John, and run some figures. Could be I might give you a hand with some of what you need."

Brennan leaned back in his chair, a quizzical look upon his face. "What's it to you, Mike? You was as strong for the cessation as I was. How is it you're after worryin' over these Injun kids?"

"Am I a clawthumper now? Is that what you're askin'? Now John, do you want me money or don't you?"

The agent raised his hands in surrender and laughed. "Right! Right! We'll be makin' a list."

One evening in mid-July, Mike was playing poker with Pete and Fred at the Elks Club. Gingerly, he raised the issue of the Cuba investment, explaining his concerns and describing Dawson's offer. "You boys know I ain't no quitter. If you ain't interested in me shares, I'll stick with you and tell Dawson he'll have to be findin' another partner."

Pete placed his cards in a neat pile, face down and laughed softly. "I'm kind of glad you brought it up. You see, I got my own opportunity. I've been thinkin' about cashin' out, if you and Fred was able to buy my share."

Fred looked at Mike and Pete with a furrowed brow and eyes wide. "What opportunity are you lookin' at?" he asked.

Pete fell back in his chair and stroked his moustache. "Alex, Joe, and me, we're thinkin' we might buy Condon's Hardware. The way I figure the return, we'll do better here than in Cuba cattle."

Fred took a swig at his beer and wiped his mouth with the back of his hand. "Well, I guess that leaves me on the spot, don't it? If both you fellas want to sell, I sure ain't in a position to be carryin' the ranche by myself."

Mike could tell that Fred was hurt. Fred was the one who had suggested they invest in Cuba, and Mike thought his friend might feel that his judgment was being questioned. "It was a group decision to go in and it should be a group decision to sell. None of us wants to squeeze a pardner in the deal."

After a minute, Fred grumbled, "Well, I guess I can go along. Besides, it'll be interestin' to see what profit we can get for Cuban land."

So it was agreed. Pete had the folks at Northern Trust contact Señor Navarro. The Spaniard was more than puzzled by the abrupt decision to exit the business in Cuba, but he assisted them in selling the ranche and the small herd. To their pleasant surprise, the partners ended up making a combined gain of $46,000.

Mike and Ike Humphrey went forward with their investments in the U+ deal, placing portions of the herd on their own homestead lands. It was fortuitous timing as cattle prices were rising and, in the next few years, would reach over $52 per hundredweight. Still, the heyday of the Dakota cattle industry was drawing to a close. In 1910, nature and government combined to deal devastating blows to the Dakota stockmen.

For years, cattlemen had been offered leases on reservation land for the fee of $1.25 per head. Since reservation land was safe from encroachment from homesteaders, this was the closest thing to open range conditions yet available. But in 1910, Washington revised the policy. The new lease price was three cents per acre, and all leased acreage was required to be fenced in, at the cost of about $100.00 per mile. These cost increases were beyond what most operators were able or willing to pay.

1910 was also the first year of a sustained drought. The lack of ground water forced reductions in the herds and, eventually, their dissolution. By Thanksgiving of that year, the U+ partners shipped 16,000 head, virtually the entire herd. Henry Dawson left South Dakota and returned to his boyhood home in Maryland. Between 1909 and 1911, membership in the WSDSGA dropped from 554 to 300. Mike Quinn held on until 1912, when approaching the age of sixty-six, he made the decision to sell the Easy SJ and live in Rapid City full time. Though he retained considerable capital, he wished to find a new occupation, his third since coming west.

Chapter Twenty-Five

The Close Call

✝

After Mike left the cattle business, he employed much of his considerable capital buying property in Rapid City. He would buy a lot, build a house, and find a buyer or tenants. Often he would hold the mortgage himself, rather than have a bank do so. He also retained a bit of land near the town of Quinn and in Meade County. Despite his numerous real estate investments, he had too much time on his hands. Pete offered him a position as accountant at the Duhamel Company.

"It ain't full time, mind you," Pete needled him. "But it will keep you away from the poker table at Elk's a few days a week. The wages might even cover your losses when you do play."

Mike was pleased to accept. After all, he had been one of the original stockholders in the new Duhamel business, the largest hardware store west of the Mississippi. A new building was constructed in 1909 at Sixth and St. Joseph Streets. The store offered everything from housewares to hardware to furniture. In-house leatherworks produced custom saddles and harnesses, which were fast becoming famous throughout the west.

Employees of the Duhamel Company posed in front of the Duhamel store. Pete Duhamel kneeling at center with walking stick, Mike Quinn is third from the right. (Courtesy of the Duhamel Family)

Despite his wealth, Mike lived simply. Unlike Corbin Morse who had filled his ranch house with art and artifacts, he had few personal possessions. He kept a silver watch, a penknife, his clothing, a suitcase left over from his trip to Cuba, and an iron-frame bed.

"Andy, has Mr. Quinn been in for breakfast yet?"

The bartender looked up from his desultory effort mopping the barroom floor. "Haven't seen hide nor hair, Mr. McCarthy."

It was nearly ten o'clock on a pale April morning. Patrick McCarthy walked back into his office at the International Hotel. He was excited and frustrated. As soon as he sat in the cracked leather chair behind his overflowing desk, he was up again, pacing around the office, a copy of the *Daily Journal* clutched in his hand. Mike's as regular as a watch. Could be he skipped breakfast.

Pat picked up the receiver of his telephone and placed his request with the operator from the Nebraska Telephone Co. Nearly every business in town had a telephone in 1916. "No, Mr. McCarthy," said the secretary at the Duhamel store. "Mr. Quinn hasn't come in yet. May I have him call when he arrives?"

McCarthy grabbed his newspaper and headed out the door. The two-block walk to Mike's residence would be invigorating on this brisk spring morning. Besides, he was about to burst with his good news. In no time, he found himself in front of the Windsor Block at Seventh and St. Joe where Mike had been living for several years.

Pat climbed the wooden staircase two steps at a time. In the darkened second floor hallway, he listened for activity at the door to Room # 31. Hearing none, he knocked. "Mike, you in there?" There was no response. He knocked again. After almost a minute's wait, a shuffling sound approached the door. The key turned in the lock and the door opened slowly.

"Pat? I . . ."

"God, Mike, you look like you're ready for the knackers. Here, let's get you back in bed."

Pat put his arm around the ghostly figure in long johns and assisted him across the floor. Mike fell back against his pillow, and Pat pulled the covers up under his chin.

"Pat, I . . . I don't feel so good, ain't got the strength to blink an eye. Fever . . . since last night."

"Don't you fear, Mike. I'll be gettin' Doc Gilbert over here directly. Good job I come lookin' for you. . . . Mike!" He waved the folded newspaper in Mike's face. "'Tis all in today's Journal. The IRA struck the Brits in Dublin last Sunday morning. A revolution is begun—and on a fine Easter mornin'! What could be more fittin'?"

Mike gave his friend a wan smile and closed his eyes. "That's grand, Pat. Go get the doctor now . . . but not Gilbert. I want Bob Jackson."

McCarthy left Mike and hurried off to collect young Dr. Robert Jackson, a relative newcomer to Rapid City. Pat was crestfallen to find Mike so reduced that he could barely acknowledge the blow struck for Irish liberty. He would have to search out another compatriot with whom to celebrate the Easter Rebellion.

It was early afternoon when Mike sensed the presence of someone at his bedside. It was Dr. Jackson, a young Canadian and fellow Elk for whom the aging Irishman had developed an affection. Jackson examined Mike thoroughly. "I can't say what's wrong, Mike. Fever, sore throat, and your respiration sounds congested. All I can suggest is bed rest, plenty of liquids, and no unnecessary visitors." He snapped his black leather valise shut. "Whatever it is, it may be catching. Who's caring for you?"

The examination had so drained what little energy Mike had that he could barely shake his head. Jackson pulled a mechanical pencil from his vest and a notepad from his coat pocket.

"Right, I'll arrange a nurse to come tend you. . . . I don't want to alarm you, but this could get serious. I want you to let me contact your next of kin, just in case."

"I ain't certain who me next of kin might be," Mike croaked with difficulty. "Me brother John is gone, a sister too. . . ." A spate of coughing struck him, and it took a minute for Mike to catch his breath. "I heard some years ago . . . me brother Roderick was failin', bad lungs. I don't suppose he could've survived till now."

"Where was your family living at the time?"

Mike covered his mouth and coughed again. Jackson gave him a sip of water from a glass on the bedside table. "They was all in Lawrence, Massachusetts. I . . . I did have two other sisters, Mary Ann and Catherine. Must have married names now. That's all I know. . . . except . . . there was a nephew, James, son of me brother Roderick. He may still be there."

Mike closed his eyes. He was exhausted by the effort at conversation.

"All right, Mike. That's enough for now," he heard Jackson say. "I'll get the nurse in here directly. Try to get some sleep."

Pete Duhamel was in his office when he received an unexpected visit. A secretary ushered Dr. Jackson in, and Pete welcomed him warmly. He pulled a chair close to his own. "How's old Mike doin', Bob?"

"It's been a week and there's no sign of improvement. Whatever he's got, Pete, it's gone to pneumonia. That's a risk I'd hoped to avoid."

Pete started at the news. "*Mère de Dieu*! Mike, he ain't dyin', is he?"

"I can't say. Frankly, I'm amazed he's lasted this long. All those years livin' out on the prairie, I suppose. But, a crisis could carry him away anytime."

Pete rose and paced behind his desk, visibly shaken at such grave news. He stopped and looked out the second-story window, unable to focus upon anything below.

"I'm goin' to ask Father Fitzgerald to get over there pretty quick. Mike ain't been one for much church goin', but I reckon he'll want to make his peace just the same."

Jackson nodded and pulled out his notepad. " Pete, what do you know of Mike's family? He's not clear as to who we might notify. Might be a sister or two, he's not sure."

"He never speaks of family, even to me. Some bad blood there, I think."

Jackson glanced again at his notations. "He mentioned a nephew, James Quinn. Said they were all living in Lawrence, Massachusetts, at one time."

Pete pressed a button on the side of his desk to summon his secretary. "I'll look into the next of kin issue, Doctor. My bankers have contacts back east. They'll turn something up."

Within days, the bankers reported that a James Quinn, son of Roderick, had been located in Lawrence. Pete dispatched a telegram informing the forty-three-year-old nephew of his uncle's critical illness. Weeks passed without a response.

By the first of May, the crisis had passed, and Mike was slowly regaining his strength. Though visitors were frowned upon, Pete, Corbin Morse, Fred Holcomb, John Horgan, John Kammerer, and George Schneider all made individual visits to see their old friend. By early June, Mike was out of bed and feeling better, though he did not return to work at Duhamel's for several more weeks.

One afternoon in late June, Mike was back at his desk, amid piles of invoices and ledgers. He had his desk in a large room above the store that he shared with other administrative employees. Deeply absorbed in the backlog of entries, he didn't know what made him look up from his work, but a feeling of apprehension overcame him at the sight of the stranger in the doorway. It was a young fellow dressed in a suit and carrying a bowler. Mike had never seen him before, he was certain.

"Mr. Quinn . . . Michael Quinn?"

Mike put down his pencil and pushed his rolling chair back from the desk. "Aye, that's me. What can I do for you?"

The visitor stepped closer, somewhat timidly. "I am your nephew, sir, John Quinn."

"Me nephew?" Mike stood up, steadying himself with one hand on the desk. His face, still somewhat ashen from his illness, took on another shade of pallor.

"Yes, sir. My father was Roderick Quinn."

Mike stepped around the desk and approached the young man, looking for the characteristics of family resemblance. "I didn't know. . . . I heard of a nephew, James, but . . . I'm pleased to meet you."

They shook hands with stiff formality. John fidgeted with the bowler, a habit Mike noticed and recognized as one of his own. His nephew was a big man; in his early thirties, Mike supposed; with a high, wide forehead, and dark hair slicked down tight against his scalp. His mouth bore a thin line of serious demeanor. Mike decided he looked more like his namesake uncle than his father.

"Is there somewhere we can talk?" John asked. By now, several employees at the far end of the room were eyeing the two of them.

"Sure, there is. I can leave these numbers till mornin'. Have you eaten at all?"

"Yes, sir. I had my dinner, such as it was, on the train."

"Well, I could use a drink. Let's go over to the Elks'. 'Tis quiet there of an afternoon." Feeling flustered, Mike led his nephew to the door, only to discover his coat and hat were still hanging on the tree beside his desk. He rushed over and grabbed them, embarrassed at his oversight.

An awkward silence prevailed as they walked the few city blocks to the Elks' Club. Mike wasn't sure what to say to the first blood relative to inhabit his gaze in half a century. And how was it that John, who he never knew existed, came instead of the older boy, James?

Mike had accurately characterized the Elks' on a weekday afternoon. It was as lively as a funeral parlor between clients, and Mike even had to go looking for the bartender. As he carried a couple of beers to the table, he noticed nervous apprehension on his nephew's face. John accepted his drink gratefully and took a sip. "It's a great relief to find you have recovered from your recent illness. We didn't know. . . ."

"If I'd be of the quick or the dead?" Mike filled the gap somewhat sharply, even suspiciously. "Sure, I'm nearly the man I was."

"I'm pleased to find it so." A pause ensued as they both tried to conjure a way forward in this conversation. They tended their beers to buy time.

"How is it that you come all this way?" Mike finally asked. "A telegram was sent to your brother, James. We never—"

"Yes, he made no reply. We urged him to do, but he refused."

Mike cackled at the thought. "Refused, eh? Sounds like James has little time for his uncle."

John looked into his beer. "You will know, Uncle, that there has been some resentment." A nervousness was present in his voice. "James would say you've had little time for any of us. We all knew the hurt our mother and father carried to their graves."

Mike looked back toward the bar. His hands played along the edge of the table before him. "Hurt, eh?" His dander rose at the thought. He struggled to remain calm. "Ah, well. Sure, that's all in the past. Is it long that your folks have passed away?"

"It's been fifteen years. My mother followed but a few months after Da."

"Poor Jane," Mike whispered. He smiled a smile of remembrance and went off into a reverie. In a moment, Mike's attention returned and he called for another round.

"How is it that your brother, James, wouldn't return a telegram, and yet, you . . . you came near across the whole of the States to see an old uncle you never met. How is that?"

John uncrossed his legs and sat stiffly.

"May I speak plainly, Uncle?"

"Would you come two thousand miles and not do?"

John's gaze went to the red checkered tablecloth, unwillingly to look his uncle in the face. "Well, sir, James told us all that you should go to hell, dying or no.'"

Mike's head jerked up, his eyes flashed and his lips pursed. But he made no response.

"My sister Catherine, and my younger brother, Frank, agreed with me. No matter what happened years ago, family is family. Someone should come, if for nothing else than to say a rosary over your grave."

"So, you took no thought that me fortune was at stake?"

John stood abruptly. His face was flushed a shade off the red of the tablecloth. "If that's what you're thinking, Uncle, my brother was right. You can go to hell!"

Mike raised his palms in the air. He knew he'd gone too far by half. "Please, John, sit. I'm sorry. 'Twas not called for, I'm sure."

John threw his hat back down on the table and it skittered to the floor. He took a deep breath and, slowly, he resumed his chair. His face could have served as a railroad signal.

"You spent your own good money and came all this way," Mike said. "You figured I was a goner, I suppose."

"Mr. Duhamel's telegram was quite clear. Your illness was grave and you might not survive.

"Ah, the dear old French fart. He's given to panic on occasion. Still, I'm grateful for your concern and your trouble."

The tension eased somewhat and John sipped again at his beer. "I'd have come sooner, save my cousin George, Uncle John's eldest. He passed away suddenly last month."

"I see." Mike shook his head. Another nephew he'd never known and never would.

As talk of family continued, the two became used to each other and the once-tense minutes stretched into several more comfortable hours. "You have a family of your own?" Mike asked.

"I'm married ten years now. My wife, Rose, she's from Maine."

"No children?"

John paused, then softly answered, "Two girls, died in infancy. Must run in the family."

Mike's eyes closed in sorrow. "Sorry for your trouble. I knew your mother lost many children too. 'Tis a hard thing."

"Yes, and hard, too, to have none at all, I suppose."

Mike looked away and made no comment. *I might have had sons, like this young man . . . strong, honest, ready to fight his patch out of loyalty.* He looked at his nephew with a sense of newfound kinship. "Let's get you a room at the International, and we'll take some supper together."

The following day Mike had to work, so John explored Rapid City on his own. On the Saturday, they rented a buggy, and Mike took John out to the rangeland where his ranch had been and where he still retained some acreage.

John was impressed with what he saw—the rolling prairie, the clusters of trees near the creekbeds, and the small but busy village of Quinn. "This is grand country you have out here. The air is so clear, you can see for miles. It seems a prosperous country too."

Mike nodded and smiled with the pride of a proprietor. "Good grass!"

"Sir?"

"Folks like to say that 'twas gold that made this country rich. Not at all! 'Twas the grass! Richest country I know for raisin' cattle."

As they drove back into town, the Black Hills loomed in the distance, outlined in the gold of the setting sun. With some prodding, Mike gave John a brief summary of his life since he'd left home as a young Fenian rebel.

"You will have heard of the failed rebellion in Ireland?" John asked.

"I have read what's been in the papers," Mike answered in a matter-of-fact tone.

"You don't seem much bothered for it, Uncle."

Mike sighed, then managed an unconvincing smile. "I'll not be despairin' yet, boy. It ain't over. It will never be over while there are those who'll rise for Irish liberty. One day, God willin', they'll succeed. Then our people will have their country back."

Mike flicked his whip above the head of his horse as he urged him on toward town. "The bleedin' Brits!"

"Maybe if the Germans win the Great War in Europe, the British will have to give way," John said.

Mike spat into the encroaching twilight. "Ach, the Brits are always havin' a war with one country or another. We'll see."

At every turn, John expressed interest and pleasure in the Black Hills country, its history and its future. It seemed to Mike that his nephew was nearly reluctant to begin the long journey home on the Sunday when he escorted him to the rail station. "I'll give your regards to Aunts Mary Ann and Catherine when next I see them, Uncle Mike."

Mike nodded and said, "Grand! Yes, tell 'em I send me love. Jaysus, it's been so long. They was but young girls when we parted. Now they'll be old ladies, I suppose."

When the train arrived, Mike stuck out his hand to bid his nephew goodbye. John ignored the hand and threw his arms about the old man in an embrace that shocked Mike and embarrassed both of them. "Goodbye, Uncle Mike."

"Goodbye, lad. God bless." Mike walked slowly from the station, back to the Windsor Block. He was glad not to encounter anyone on the quiet Sunday streets, his eyes welling up with unaccustomed tears.

Chapter Twenty-Six

James's Message

✠

The Duhamel Company wasn't the only business in which Mike and Pete collaborated. Pete had left the day-to-day management of the store to his son, Alex, and had diversified his business interests, assuming the vice-presidency of the First National Bank of Rapid City. Later, he moved to the Pennington County Bank, where he became a major stockholder and also served as vice-president.

When Pete was elected president of the bank, Corbin Morse replaced him as vice-president. Mike and Gene Holcomb, Fred's older brother, became members of the bank's board of directors. The former freighters and cattlemen now adopted the dress and the interests of financial entrepreneurs. As post-war years of prosperity arrrived, their assets grew apace. They called themselves "capitalists." Mike finally achieved the goal that had driven him west so many years before—his precious fortune.

Another goal dear to Mike's heart was advanced during the 1920s— that of Irish freedom. He followed the Anglo-Irish War carefully in the newspapers. He believed firmly that the Irish people would finally unite them-

Bookkeeper George Moore (far left) and Directors of the Pennington County Bank, left to right—Bill Blair, Eugene Holcomb, George Schneider, Mike Quinn, and Peter Duhamel (Courtesy of the Duhamel family)

selves around the idea of a Republic, free from British oppression. But these hopes grew thin and bitter after the Treaty of 1922. The politicians had accepted a "Free State" under British dominion and retained an oath of allegiance to the crown. In the Irish civil war, Mike threw his sympathies to Liam Lynch and the forces of Sinn Fein. He would sometimes wear out the interest of his fellow Elks as he railed against events in Ireland.

"What's the feckin' good of having the Brits gone, when these Free Staters let 'em take Ulster with 'em as they go?"

The years brought other sorrows as one by one his comrades of the pioneer days reached the end of their trail. Even Pete, now in his late eighties, spent his time in bed or in a wheelchair. Without Pete's involvement in the business, Mike lost interest in his duties at the Duhamel Company. In 1925, he resigned from the accountant's position and directed his efforts back to real estate. He was approaching seventy-nine.

It was a cold December morning in 1927. There was a light snow blowing in the near dark morning as Mike walked from his rooms to breakfast. He made a habit of stopping each day to observe the construction of the new Alex Johnson Hotel on the corner of Sixth and St. Joe's. The eight-story grand hotel was well past its structural phase though, so there wasn't much to see anymore from the street. The hotel management had asked Mike and a number of longtime cattlemen in the area for the use of their old branding irons. A roughhewn wooden mantle, situated above the large fireplace in the lobby, was to be decorated with the imprints of their historic brands. Mike was looking forward to the grand opening next summer.

It was the Wednesday before Christmas, the height of the shopping season, yet as Mike walked past the Duhamel Store, he sensed there was something wrong. Despite the Christmas decorations in the windows, the lights were not lit and the doors were locked. Mike walked around the corner to the employees' entrance, which he had used for so many years. Jake Schreiner, a senior harnessmaker was emerging.

"What's happening, Jake? How come the store's shut?"

The longtime colleague looked up, his eyes red rimmed. "Oh, Mr. Quinn. You must not have heard yet. Mr. Pete's done gone. They found him this morning. Must have died in his sleep."

"Dear God!" Mike reached out with his gloved hand for the side of the building, anything to steady himself. He closed his eyes, gasping for breath. Given Pete's eighty-nine years, it should not have been a great shock. Still, this taste of reality was deeply disturbing.

"You okay, sir? I know you two was best of friends. I'm sorry, sir. He was a grand gentleman."

"Aye, that he was." Mike blinked back tears and turned to go. Schreiner stood and watched as the old man walked away. Mike's steps were slow and unsteady as he retraced the way to Windsor Block.

Mike Quinn in later years

The funeral Mass was held at St. Mary's on Saturday, Christmas Eve. Given Pete's prominence in the community and the esteem in which he was held, the little brick church was filled to overflowing. Mike and Corb Morse walked together in a procession with other honorary pallbearers. The service seemed long, at least to Mike. The chapel, closed tightly against the winter weather, was exceedingly warm from the many candles and the great crowd that filled the space.

During the homily, Mike's attention wandered. He found himself focused upon a young altar boy seated inside the sanctuary. He was a fine-looking lad, handsome in his black cassock and white surplice. He seemed to be intently listening to Father Boyd's words of praise for the deceased. As Mike gazed steadily at the boy, the lad's appearance seemed to change.

Jaysus, don't he look like—'Tis me brother what I saw at the *Inipi* with Strikes the Ree! I must be gettin' light-headed, 'tis so bloomin' hot in here.

With that, Father Bill Boyd's words filled Mike's ears. ". . . and it would have made Pete proud to see his large fine family here today. With all his prosperity and his many accomplishments, I know Pete felt his greatest riches were the loved ones who filled his life with joy."

Mike shut his eyes. Arrah, James! 'Tis you, after all. The message is delivered, just as Strikes the Ree promised.

When Mike opened his eyes again, the vision was gone. The resemblence of the altar boy to his long dead brother had dissipated. Mike took his handkerchief and mopped his brow.

Corb turned and looked at him with a face full of concern.

"You okay, Mike?

"Aye, 'tis only the heat. I'll be all right now."

Chapter Twenty-Seven

The Letter

✠

Rapid City
October 15, 1932

Mr. John J. Quinn
Lawrence, Massachusetts

Dear John,

You will find it odd, I'm sure, to receive this letter after sixteen years. I have not forgotten your kindness in the days after my illness. I trust that you and Rose enjoy sound health and that you have been spared the worst of the financial crisis in the States.

I write to you, as there is no one left of my immediate family. Only you know me, however slightly. I am turned eighty-six now and can't but think that I'm nearing the end of the trail. It is time I put my house in order. The hard times have reduced the value of my hold-

ings, but there is still a fair fortune. I intend this for my nieces and nephews. If you would send me a list of all such surviving, I would be most grateful. It would also be a great favor if you would act as executor of my estate when the time comes. My attorney, Mr. Walter Miser, will assist you in this regard.

In these long days, I have had the opportunity to consider how my life has turned out. The world I knew as a lad in the mills and on the frontier is fully gone and near forgotten by all. Folks dash about the country in auto cars and in aeroplanes, where I did once march beside a bull train. Some of these changes I do not welcome. Others, I embrace warmly. The Lord has blessed me with good health and good friends. For these, I am grateful.

My losses, I'm afraid, are of my own doing. When your mother and father married, I was hurt bad. I see now that I came to love my hurt more than I loved my own family. My hurt and my fortune became my family. This, I deeply regret, but it is too late to make amends to those I once did love. Perhaps you and Rose wouldn't mind being my family for the time that remains. I'd like to think it so. God bless.

Your uncle,

Michael Quinn

On the 25th of August 1934, Mike Quinn was felled by a stroke. At the height of the Great Depression, he left an estate of half a million dollars to his nieces and nephews.

John and Rose Quinn moved to Rapid City and lived there the rest of their lives. They are buried beside Michael Quinn.

Glossary

Ach – Interjection with a hint of sadness (Hiberno-English)

Akicita Tatanka – "Buffalo soldiers," Negro cavalrymen of the U.S. Army

Airtights – Nineteenth-century term for tin cans used for food items

Arrah – Interjection meaning "now, but, really" (Hiberno-English)

Assez! Ça suffit – "Enough! This is sufficient" (French)

Biretta – A hard, square hat with three or four projections and a pompom or tassel on top, worn by Roman Catholic clergy

Bobbin – A wooden spool or reel for thread or yarn, used in spinning, weaving, etc.

Boreen – A country lane, a little-used road (Hiberno-English)

Brules – One of the seven tribes of the Lakota Sioux

Cadging – Begging, sponging

Catlinite – Red pipestone, red semi-hard clay quarried in Minnesota

Cess – Luck, possibly a contraction of "success" (Hiberno-English)

Charlock – A weed of the crucifer family, with yellow flowers

Cheroot – A cigar with both ends cut square

Clachan – A nucleated group of farmhouses (Hiberno-English)

Clawthumper – An Irish term for a breast-beater, a soft-hearted person

Clevis – A u-shaped metal fitting with holes in the ends through which a pin or bolt is passed in order to attach one thing to another

Conacre – The practice of tenants letting small patches of their land for short periods for a single crop (e.g., potatoes). (Hiberno-English)

Cottier – A peasant renting a small piece of land, awarded to the highest bidder

Craythur – Intoxicating liquor, especially whiskey

Cuchullain – A hero of ancient Irish mythology, leader of a famous cattle raid

Demesne – The land or estate belonging to a lord and not rented or let, the land around a mansion

Empresa – Spanish word for enterprise, company, or firm

Erin Go Bragh – Irish motto meaning "Ireland Forever"

Feis – A festival, often featuring musical competition

Galluses – Suspenders, braces

Gandydancer – A worker on a railroad section gang, probably so named for movements while using tools from the Gandy Manufacturing Company of Chicago

Hackamore – A rope or rawhide halter, a bitless headstall used to tie or lead a horse

Hackney – A carriage for hire

Hogback – A ridge with a sharp crest and abruptly sloping sides

Hogger – Railroad slang for engineer

IRB – Irish Revolutionary Brotherhood, also known as the Fenian movement, nineteenth-century organization aimed at Irish independence

Inyan – Lakota word for stone

John B – After John B. Stetson (1830–1906), a hat worn especially by Westerners, usually of felt, with a broad brim and a high soft crown

Knackered – Tired, played out, in poor condition (see Knackers below)

Knackers – A British slang term for those who slaughter played-out horses

Kinnikinick – A mixture, as of tobacco and dried leaves, bark etc., formerly smoked by certain American Indians and pioneers

Lakota – The westernmost branch of the Dakotas (Sioux). Consists of seven tribes: Oglala, Brules, Miniconjous, Hunkpapas, Sihasapas (Blackfeet), Oohenonpas (Two-Kettles), Itazipchodans (Sans Arcs)

Left-footer – A Protestant; folklore of Northern Ireland had Catholics using the right foot for digging with a spade and the Protestants using the left foot

Maletero – Spanish for porter, luggage handler

Mire – Spanish for "Look!"

Molly Maguire(s) – Member or members of a secret society raised in Ireland in 1843 to terrorize landlords' agents in order to prevent evictions of tenant farmers

Moon of Falling Leaves – November

Moon of Popping Trees – December, after sound made by trees contracting in cold weather

Navvies – Unskilled laborers, especially on canals, roads, etc. (British)

Osnaburg – A type of coarse heavy cloth, originally of linen, later of cotton. Used for making sacks, work clothes, etc.

P – Short for pence (pennies) in the British currency

'Paulin – Nineteenth-century western slang for tarpaulin, canvas coated with a waterproofing compound

Picket Iron – A metal stake driven into the ground, used to tether an animal, especially a horse

Placer Gold – Gold that is found on or near the earth's surface, susceptible to recovering without sinking mine shafts under ground

Poignard – A dagger

Praties – Irish slang for potatoes

Ranche – Old spelling of ranch

Ribbonman – Irish term for a member of a Ribbon society, a person opposing the excesses of landlordism

Strawberry Roan – A horse of solid color (in this case a reddish gray) with a thick sprinkling of white hairs

Soogan – A cowboy's bedroll

Squaw Man – A white man, married to an Indian woman and thereby entitled to live on the reservation

Stirabout – A porridge of oatmeal and water

Tangleleg – (Also tanglefoot) Western slang for cheap whiskey

Travois – A crude sledge of North American Plains Indians, consists of a net or platform dragged along on the ground on two poles that support it and serve as shafts for the animal pulling it

Uncle Whiskers – Uncle Sam, the United States government

Van Diemen's Land – Former name for Tasmania, once used as a British penal colony

Vaquero – Spanish word for cowboy

Vivienda – Spanish word for apartment, flat, housing

Warbag – Name given to the carryall used by bullwhackers and cowboys

Wakan Tanka – Lakota for Great Spirit, Great Mystery, God

Washichu – Lakota for white man

Wichasha wakan – Lakota holy man, ceremonial leader who performs healings

Bibliography

Allen, Charles W. *From Fort Laramie to Wounded Knee: In the West That Was.* Lincoln: University of Nebraska Press, 1997.

Bateman, Robert J. (Editor?). *Captain Timothy Deasy, Patriot – Irish American.* Commemorative Pamphlet "On the Occasion of the Unveiling of a Memorial" at Lawrence, Massachusetts, November 22, 1992. Massachusetts State Board, Ancient Order of Hibernians.

Beirne, Francis. (Editor). *The Diocese of Elphin: People, Places, and Pilgrimage.* Dublin: The Columba Press, 2000.

Beirne, Rev. Francis M. *Co. Roscommon Remembers An Gorta Mór.* Co. Roscommon Famine Commemoration Committee, Roscommon, Ireland 1999.

Bennett, Estelline. *Old Deadwood Days: The Real Wild West of My Childhood.* Santa Barbara, California: The Narrative Press, 2001.

Berg, Francie M. *South Dakota – Land of Shining Gold.* Hettinger, North Dakota: Flying Diamond Books, 1982.

Blanchette, Joseph P. *The View from Shanty Pond: An Irish Immigrant's Look at Life in a New England Mill Town 1875–1938.* Charlotte, Vermont: Shanty Pond Press, 1999.

Blasingame, Ike. *Dakota Cowboy: My Life in the Old Days.* Lincoln: University of Nebraska Press, 1958.

Blewett, Mary H. *The Last Generation: Work and Life in the Textile Mills of Lowell, Massachusetts, 1910–1960.* Amherst: The University of Massachusetts Press, 1990.

Bresee, Floyd E. *Overland Freighting in the Platte Valley 1850–1870.* MA Thesis, Lincoln: University of Nebraska, 1937.

Briggs, Harold E. *Early Freight & Stage Lines in Dakota. Vol. III* pp. 229–261. North Dakota Historical Quarterly, July/1929.

Brown, Jesse. *The Freighter in Early Days.* Vol. XIX pp. 112–116. Annals of Wyoming, July/1947.

Brown, Jesse & Willard, A. M. *The Black Hills Trails.* Rapid City, South Dakota: Rapid City Journal Co, 1924.

Brown, Mark & Felton, W. R. *Before Barbed Wire*. New York: Henry Holt & Co., 1956.

Brown & Felton. *The Frontier Years*. New York: Henry Holt & Co., 1955.

Burke. *The Dormant, Abeyant, Forfeited, and Extinct Peerages*. Baltimore: 1978.

Carthy, P. *Landholding and Settlement in Co. Roscommon*. MA Thesis (unpublished), Dublin: University College, 1970.

Clarke, H. T. *Freighting – Denver and Black Hills*. Vol. V pp. 299–312. Lincoln: Nebraska State Historical Society, 1902.

Cole, Donald B. *Immigrant City – Lawrence, Massachusetts*. Chapel Hill: University of North Carolina Press, 1963.

Coleman, Anne. *Riotous Roscommon: Social Unrest in the 1840s*. Dublin: Irish Academic Press, 1999.

Cowan, Dora. *St. Joseph, Missouri as Starting Point for Western Emigration, Freight, and Mail*. MA Thesis. University of Missouri, 1939.

Crawford, E. Margaret (Editor). *The Hungry Stream, Essays on Emigration and Famine*. Belfast: The Institute of Irish Studies, The Queen's University, 1997.

D'Arcy, William. *The Fenian Movement in the United States*. A Dissertation, Washington, D.C.: Catholic University Press, 1947.

Dengler, Eartha, & Khalife, Katherine, & Skulski, Ken. (Editors). *Lawrence, Massachusetts*. Dover, New Hampshire: Arcadia Publishing, 1995.

Dolan, Terence Patrick. (Editor). *A Dictionary of Hiberno-English*. Dublin: Gill & Macmillan, 1998.

Dorgan, Maurice B. *History of Lawrence, Massachusetts*. 1924.

Ellis, Peter Beresford. *The Rising of the Moon: A Novel of the Fenian Invasion of Canada*. Methuen London Ltd., 1987.

Ellis, Peter Beresford. *Erin's Blood Royal: The Gaelic Noble Dynasties of Ireland*. London: Constable and Co. Ltd., 1999.

Foley, Thomas W. *Father Francis M. Craft: Missionary to the Sioux*. Lincoln: University of Nebraska Press, 2002.

Foster-Harris. *The Look of the Old West*. New York: The Viking Press, 1955.

Frazier, Ian. *Great Plains*. New York: Penguin, 1989.

Gacquin, William. *Roscommon Before the Famine: The Parishes of Kiltoom and Cam.* Dublin: Irish Academic Press, 1996.

Hachey, Thomas E. & Hernon, Joseph M., Jr., & McCaffrey, Lawrence J. *The Irish Experience.* Englewood Cliffs, New Jersey: Prentice Hall, 1989.

Hall, Bert L. *Roundup Years: Old Muddy to Black Hills.* Pierre, South Dakota: State Publishing Co., 1954.

Hamilton, W. H. *Dakota: An Autobiography of a Cowman.* Pierre, South Dakota: South Dakota State Historical Society Press, 1998.

Hayden, Tom. *Irish Hunger: Personal Reflections on the Legacy of the Famine.* Boulder, Colorado: Roberts Rinehart Publishers, 1997, 1998.

Haynes, Ian. *Cotton in Ashton.* Ashton-under-Lyne, United Kingdom: Libraries and Arts Committee, Tameside Metropolitan Borough, 1987.

Hill, William E. *The Oregon Trail: Yesterday and Today.* Caldwell, Idaho: The Caxton Printers, Ltd., 1994.

Hogg, Gary. *The Building of the First Transcontinental Railroad.* New York: Walker & Co., 1967.

Hooker, William Francis. *The Bullwhacker: Adventures of a Frontier Freighter.* Chicago: World Book Company, 1924.

Hughes, Richard B. *Pioneer Years in the Black Hills.* Arthur H. Clark Co. 1957.

Huidekoper, A. C. *My Experiences and Investment in the Badlands of Dakota and Some of the Men I Met There.* Baltimore: Wirth Brothers, 1947.

Hyde, George E. *Red Cloud's Folk: A History of the Oglala Sioux Indians.* Norman: University of Oklahoma Press, 1937.

Jackson, William H. *The Most Important Nebraska Highway: Nebraska City to Fort Kearny and Denver.* Vol. XIII pp. 137–159. Nebraska History, July–September, 1932.

Jensen, Richard & Paul, R. Eli & Carter, John E. *Eyewitness at Wounded Knee.* Lincoln: University of Nebraska Press, 1991.

Johnson, James R. & Larson, Gary E. *Grassland Plants of South Dakota and the Northern Great Plains.* Brookings, South Dakota: South Dakota State University, 1999.

Kemp, David. *The Irish in Dakota.* Sioux Falls, South Dakota: Rushmore House Publishing, 1992.

Kingsbury, George W. *History of the Dakota Territory,* 1915.

Klein, Maury. *Union Pacific: Birth of a Railroad 1862–1893.* New York: Doubleday, 1987.

Lass, William E. *From Missouri to the Great Salt Lake: An Account of Overland Freighting.* Vol. XXVI. Lincoln: Nebraska State Historical Society, 1972.

Lawrence Directory (1866,1868), Lawrence, Massachusetts.

Lee, Bob & Williams, Dick. *Last Grass Frontier: The South Dakota Stock Grower Heritage.* Sturgis, South Dakota: Black Hills Publishers, Inc., 1964.

Lewis, Dale. *Duhamel: From Ox Cart to Television.* Rapid City, South Dakota: Francis A. Duhamel, 1993.

Lewis, Samuel. *Topographical Dictionary of Ireland.* London, 1837.

Lindmier, Tom. *Drybone: A History of Fort Fetterman, Wyoming.* Glendo, Wyoming: High Plains Press, 2002.

Lock, Alice. (Editor). *Ashton-under-Lyne and Mossley.* Stroud, Gloucestershire, UK.: The Chalford Publishing Company, 1995.

Lowe, W. J. *The Irish in Mid-Victorian Lancashire: The Shaping of a Working Class Community.* New York: Peter Lang Publishing, Inc., 1989.

MacDonald. John A. Capt. *Troublous Times in Canada: A History of the Fenian Raids of 1866/1870.* Toronto: W. S. Johnson & Co., 1910.

MacManus, Seumas. *The Story of the Irish Race.* Old Greenwich, Connecticut: The Devin-Adair Company, 1921.

MacRaild, Donald M. *Irish Migrants in Modern Britain 1750–1922.* New York: St. Martin's Press, Inc., 1999.

Marcy, Randolph B. Capt., U.S. Army. *A Handbook for Overland Expeditions.* New York: Harper & Bros., 1859.

Mattimoe, Cyril. *North Roscommon: Its People and Past.* Boyle, Co. Roscommon, Ireland: Roscommon Herald, 1992.

McClintock, John S. *Pioneer Days in the Black Hills: By One of the Early Day Pioneers.* Norman: University of Oklahoma Press, 1939.

McDonnell-Garvey, Máire. *Mid-Connacht: The Ancient Territory of Sliabh Lugha.* Nure, Manorhamilton, Co. Leitrim, Ireland: Drumlin Publications, 1995.

McGaa, Ed., Eagle Man *Mother Earth Spirituality: Native American Paths to Healing Ourselves and Our World*. New York: HarperCollins Publishers, 1989, 1990.

McGillycuddy, Julia B. *Blood on the Moon: Valentine McGillycuddy and the Sioux*. Lincoln: University of Nebraska Press, 1990.

Moulton, Candy. *The Writer's Guide to Everyday Life in the Wild West From 1840–1900*. Cincinnati, Ohio: Writer's Digest Books, 1999.

Nadeau, Remi. *Fort Laramie and the Sioux*. Santa Barbara, California: Crest Publishers, 1997.

Nauman, Dean S. (Editor). *The Vanishing Trails Expedition – 16 Years*. Wall, South Dakota: The Vanishing Trails Committee, 1976.

Neidhardt, W. S. *Fenianism in North America*. State College: Penn State University Press, 1975.

Nichols, James D. *Bullwhacker*. New York: Leisure Books, 1981.

O'Broin, Leon. *Fenian Fever: An Anglo-American Dilemma*. New York: New York University Press, 1971.

O'Flaherty, Liam. *Famine*. Dublin: Wolfhound Press, 1937.

Owen, David. *The Year of the Fenians*. Buffalo, N.Y.: The Western New York Heritage Institute, 1990.

Peattie, Roderick. (Editor). *The Black Hills*. New York: Vanguard Press, 1952.

Peers, P. M. *The Cotton Famine in Ashton-under-Lyne 1861–1865*. Manchester, U.K.: Manchester College of Education, 1970.

Póirtéir, Cathal. (Editor). *The Great Irish Famine*. Dublin: RTE/Mercier Press, 1995.

Potter, Edgar R. *Cowboy Slang, Colorful Cowboy Sayings*. Phoenix, Arizona: Golden West Publishers, 2000.

Rental of the Estates of George Lord Baron Mount Sandford for One Year Ending 25th day of March, 1835. Dublin, Ireland: National Library of Ireland, 1835.

Robinson, Charles M. III *A Good Year to Die: The Story of the Great Sioux War*. New York: Random House, 1995.

Robinson, Doane. *History of South Dakota*. Vols. I, II. 1904.

Rollins, Philip Ashton. *The Cowboy: An Unconventional History of Civilization on the Old-Time Cattle Range*. Norman: University of Oklahoma Press, 1997.

Room, Adrian. *A Dictionary of Irish Place-Names.* Belfast: The Appletree Press, Ltd., 1994.

Rutherford, John. *The Secret History of the Fenian Conspiracy,* Vols. I, II. London, 1877.

Scally, Robert James. *The End of Hidden Ireland.* New York: Oxford University Press, 1995.

Schlissel, Lillian. (Editor). *Women's Diaries of the Westward Journey.* New York: Schocken Books, 1982.

Senior, Hereward. *The Fenians and Canada.* Toronto, 1978.

Severance, Frank. *The Fenian Raid.* Vol. 25. Buffalo, New York: Buffalo Historical Society.

Simington, R. C. *Book of Survey & Distribution 1636–1703.* Vol. I Dublin: Stationery Office, 1949.

Simington, R. C. *Transplantation to Connacht 1654–58.*

Slater's Lancashire Directory – 1855

Swift, Roger & Gilley, Sheridan (Editors). *The Irish in Victorian Britain: The Local Dimension.* Dublin: Four Courts Press, 1999.

Swiggum, S. & Kohli, M. *The Ships List.* www.theshipslist.com, 2003.

Swords, Liam. *In Their Own Words: The Famine in North Connacht 1845–1849.* Dublin: Columba Press, 1999.

Sutley, Zack T. *The Last Frontier.* New York: The Macmillan Company, 1930.

Toponce, Alexander. *Reminiscences of Alexander Toponce: Written by Himself.* Norman: University of Oklahoma Press, 1923, 1971.

Valuation of Parish of Kilkeevan, Field Book

Van Bruggen, Theodore. *Wildflowers, Grasses, and Other Plants of the Northern Plains and Black Hills.* Interior, South Dakota: Badlands Natural History Association, 1992.

Walker, Henry. *The Wagonmasters: High Plains Freighting from the Earliest Days of the Santa Fe Trail to 1880.* Norman: University of Oklahoma Press, 1966.

Walker, Mable G. *The Fenian Movement.* Colorado Springs: Ralph Myles Publisher, Inc., 1969.

Walter, John. *The Guns That Won The West: Firearms on the American*

Frontier, 1848–1898. London: Greenhill Books, 1999.

Winstanley, Michael. (Editor). *Working Children in Nineteenth-Century Lancashire.* Preston: Lancashire County Books, 1995.

Winther, Oscar. *The Transportation Frontier – Trans-Mississippi West 1865–1890.* New York: Holt, Rinehart, Winston, 1964.

Wyman, Walker D. *Nothing but Prairie and Sky: Life on the Dakota Range in the Early Days.* Norman: University of Oklahoma Press, 1954.

Yost, Nellie Snyder. (Editor) *Boss Cowman: The Recollections of Ed Lemmon 1857–1946.* Lincoln: University of Nebraska Press, 1969.

Zabel, Charley. *Freighting in to Deadwood.* Vol. XXXVII   pp. 52–54. Frontier Times June–July, 1963.

Printed in the United States
36692LVS00004B/283-375

9 781420 880922